Writer's Choice

Teacher's Annotated Edition

GRAMMAR WORKBOOK

8

McGraw-Hill

New York, New York   Columbus, Ohio   Woodland Hills, California   Peoria, Illinois

Glencoe/McGraw-Hill
A Division of The McGraw·Hill Companies

Copyright © 1996 by The McGraw-Hill Companies, Inc. All rights reserved. Permission is granted to reproduce the material contained herein on the condition that such material be reproduced only for classroom use; be provided to students, teachers, and families without charge; and be used solely in conjunction with WRITER'S CHOICE. Any other reproduction, for use or sale, is prohibited without the prior written permission of the publisher.

Printed in the United States of America.

Send all inquiries to:
Glencoe/McGraw-Hill
936 Eastwind Drive
Westerville, Ohio 43081

ISBN 0-02-635151-X (Teacher Edition)
Writer's Choice Grammar Workbook 8

5 6 7 8 9 10   024   02 01 00 99

Contents

Handbook of Definitions and Rules 1
Troubleshooter 23

Part 1 Grammar 45
Unit 1 Subjects, Predicates, and Sentences
1.1   Kinds of Sentences: Declarative and Interrogative 47
1.2   Kinds of Sentences: Exclamatory and Imperative 49
1.3   Sentence Fragments 51
1.4   Subjects and Predicates: Simple and Complete 53
1.5   Subjects and Predicates: Compound 55
1.6   Simple and Compound Sentences 57
Unit 1 Review 59
Cumulative Review 60

Unit 2 Nouns
2.7   Nouns: Proper and Common 61
2.8   Nouns: Concrete and Abstract 63
2.9   Nouns: Compounds, Plurals, and Possessives 65
2.10   Nouns: Collective 67
2.11   Distinguishing Plurals, Possessives, and Contractions 69
2.12   Appositives 71
Unit 2 Review 73
Cumulative Review: Units 1-2 74

Unit 3 Verbs
3.13   Action Verbs 75
3.14   Verbs: Transitive and Intransitive 77
3.15   Verbs with Indirect Objects 79
3.16   Linking Verbs and Predicate Words 81
3.17   Present and Past Tenses 85
3.18   Main Verbs and Helping Verbs..................89
3.19   Verb Forms: Present Progressive and Past Progressive 91
3.20   Perfect Tenses: Present and Past 93
3.21   Expressing Future Time 95
3.22   Active and Passive Voices 97
3.23   Irregular Verbs I 99
3.24   Irregular Verbs II 101
Unit 3 Review 105
Cumulative Review: Units 1-3 106

Unit 4 Pronouns
4.25   Pronouns: Personal 107
4.26   Pronouns and Antecedents 109
4.27   Using Pronouns Correctly 111
4.28   Pronouns: Possessive and Indefinite 113
4.29   Pronouns: Reflexive and Intensive 115
4.30   Pronouns: Interrogative and Demonstrative 117
Unit 4 Review 119
Cumulative Review: Units 1-4 120

Unit 5 Adjectives and Adverbs
5.31   Adjectives 121
5.32   Articles and Proper Adjectives 123
5.33   Comparative and Superlative Adjectives 125
5.34   Demonstratives 127
5.35   Adverbs...129
5.36   Comparative and Superlative Adverbs 131
5.37   Using Adverbs and Adjectives 133
5.38   Avoiding Double Negatives 135
Unit 5 Review 137
Cumulative Review: Units 1-5 138

Unit 6 Prepositions, Conjunctions, and Interjections
6.39   Prepositions and Prepositional Phrases 141
6.40   Pronouns as Objects of Prepositions 143
6.41   Prepositional Phrases as Adjectives and Adverbs 145
6.42   Conjunctions: Coordinating and Correlative 147
6.43   Conjunctive Adverbs and Interjections....149
Unit 6 Review 151
Cumulative Review: Units 1-6 152

Unit 7 Clauses and Complex Sentences
7.44   Sentences and Main Clauses 155
7.45   Complex Sentences and Subordinate Clauses................................157
7.46   Adjective Clauses...................................159
7.47   Essential and Nonessential Clauses 161
7.48   Adverb Clauses.......................................163
7.49   Noun Clauses..165
Unit 7 Review 167
Cumulative Review: Units 1-7 168

Unit 8 Verbals
8.50   Participles and Participial Phrases...........171
8.51   Gerunds and Gerund Phrases 175
8.52   Infinitives and Infinitive Phrases 179
Unit 8 Review 183
Cumulative Review: Units 1-8 184

Unit 9 Subject-Verb Agreement
9.53   Making Subjects and Verbs Agree 187
9.54   Locating the Subject 189
9.55   Collective Nouns and Other Special Subjects 191
9.56   Indefinite Pronouns as Subjects 193
9.57   Agreement with Compound Subjects.......195
Unit 9 Review 197
Cumulative Review: Units 1-9 198

Unit 10 Diagraming Sentences
10.58   Diagraming Simple Subjects and Predicates 201

Table of Contents   **iii**

10.59	Diagraming Direct and Indirect Objects and Predicate Words	203
10.60	Diagraming Adjectives and Adverbs	205
10.61	Diagraming Prepositional Phrases	207
10.62	Diagraming Compound Sentence Parts	209
10.63	Diagraming Compound Sentences	211
10.64	Diagraming Complex Sentences with Adjective or Adverb Clauses	213
10.65	Diagraming Noun Clauses	215
10.66	Diagraming Verbals	217
10.67	Diagraming Infinitives	219
Unit 10 Review		221
Cumulative Review: Units 1–10		222

Part 2 Usage Glossary 225
Unit 11 Usage Glossary

11.68	Usage: *accept* to *a lot*	227
11.69	Usage: *beside* to *less*	229
11.70	Usage: *formally* to *teach*	231
11.71	Usage: *leave* to *sit*	233
11.72	Usage: *than* to *you're*	235
Unit 11 Review		237
Cumulative Review: Units 1–11		238

Part 3 Mechanics 241
Unit 12 Capitalization

12.73	Capitalization of Sentences, Quotations, and Salutations	243
12.74	Capitalization of Names and Titles of Persons	245
12.75	Capitalization of Names of Places	247
12.76	Capitalization of Other Proper Nouns and Adjectives	249
Unit 12 Review		251
Cumulative Review: Units 1–12		252

Unit 13 Punctuation

13.77	Using the Period and Other End Marks	255
13.78	Using Commas to Signal Pause or Separation	257
13.79	Using Commas with Clauses	259
13.80	Using Commas with Titles, Addresses, and Dates	261
13.81	Using Commas with Direct Quotes, in Letters, and for Clarity	263
13.82	Using Semicolons and Colons	265
13.83	Using Quotation Marks and Italics	267
13.84	Using the Apostrophe	269
13.85	Using the Hyphen, Dash, and Parentheses	271
13.86	Using Abbreviations	273
13.87	Writing Numbers	275
Unit 13 Review		277
Cumulative Review: Units 1–13		278

Part 4 Vocabulary and Spelling 281
Unit 14 Vocabulary and Spelling

14.88	Building Vocabulary: Learning from Context	283
14.89	Building Vocabulary: Word Roots	285
14.90	Building Vocabulary: Prefixes and Suffixes	287
14.91	Building Vocabulary: Synonyms and Antonyms	289
14.92	Building Vocabulary: Homographs and Homophones	291
14.93	Basic Spelling Rules I	293
14.94	Basic Spelling Rules II	295
Review: Building Vocabulary		297
Review: Basic Spelling Rules		299

Part 5 Composition 301
Unit 15 Composition

15.95	The Writing Process: Prewriting	303
15.96	The Writing Process: Drafting	307
15.97	The Writing Process: Revising	311
15.98	The Writing Process: Editing	315
15.99	The Writing Process: Presenting	319
15.100	The Writing Process: Outlining	321
15.101	Writing Effective Sentences	323
15.102	Building Paragraphs	327
15.103	Paragraph Ordering	331
15.104	Personal Letters: Formal	335
15.105	Personal Letters: Informal	337
15.106	Business Letters: Letters of Request or of Complaint	339
15.107	Business Letters: Stating Your Opinion	341

Index 343

TAE Tests

Unit 1:	Subjects, Predicates, and Sentences	349
Unit 2:	Nouns	351
Unit 3:	Verbs	353
Unit 4:	Pronouns	357
Unit 5:	Adjectives and Adverbs	359
Unit 6:	Prepositions, Conjunctions, and Interjections	361
Unit 7:	Clauses and Complex Sentences	365
Unit 8:	Verbals	369
Unit 9:	Subject-Verb Agreement	371
Unit 10:	Diagraming Sentences	373
Unit 11:	Usage	375
Unit 12:	Capitalization	377
Unit 13:	Punctuation	379
Unit 14:	Vocabulary and Spelling	381
Unit 15:	Composition	383

Answer Key 387
Correlation Chart 393

Handbook of Definitions and Rules

SUBJECTS AND PREDICATES

1. The **simple subject** is the key noun or pronoun that tells what the sentence is about. A **compound subject** is made up of two or more simple subjects that are joined by a conjunction and have the same verb.
   The **lantern** glows.   **Moths** and **bugs** fly nearby.

2. The **simple predicate** is the verb or verb phrase that expresses the essential thought about the subject of the sentence. A **compound predicate** is made up of two or more verbs or verb phrases that are joined by a conjunction and have the same subject.
   Rachel **jogged** down the hill.
   Pete **stretched** and **exercised** for an hour.

3. The **complete subject** consists of the simple subject and all the words that modify it.
   Golden curly hair framed the child's face.
   The soft glow of sunset made her happy.

4. The **complete predicate** consists of the simple predicate and all the words that modify it or complete its meaning.
   Lindy **ate a delicious muffin for breakfast**.
   The apple muffin **also contained raisins**.

5. Usually the subject comes before the predicate in a sentence. In inverted sentences, all or part of the predicate precedes the subject.
   (You) Wait for me at the corner. (request)
   Through the toys **raced** the **children**. (inverted)
   Is the **teacher** feeling better? (question)
   There **are seats** in the first row.

PARTS OF SPEECH

Nouns

1. A **singular noun** is a word that names one person, place, thing, or idea.
   aunt   meadow   pencil   friendship

   A **plural noun** names more than one person, place, thing, or idea.
   aunts   meadows   pencils   friendships

2. To help you determine whether a word in a sentence is a noun, try adding it to the following sentences. Nouns will fit in at least one of these sentences:
   He said something about _____.   I know something about a(n) _____.
   He said something about **aunts**.   I know something about a **meadow**.

3. A **common noun** names a general class of people, places, things, or ideas.
   sailor   city   holiday   music

   A **proper noun** names a particular person, place, thing, event, or idea. Proper nouns are always capitalized.
   Captain Ahab   Rome   Memorial Day   *Treasure Island*

4. A **concrete noun** names an object that occupies space or that can be recognized by any of the senses.
   leaf   melody   desk   aroma

   An **abstract noun** names an idea, a quality, or a characteristic.
   peace   health   strength   contentment

5. A **collective noun** names a group. When the collective noun refers to the group as a whole, it is singular. When it refers to the individual group members, the collective noun is plural.
   The **family** eats dinner together every night. (singular)
   The **council** vote as they wish on the pay increase. (plural)

6. A **possessive noun** shows possession, ownership, or the relationship between two nouns.
   Monica's book   the **rabbit's** ears   the **hamster's** cage

Verbs

1. A **verb** is a word that expresses action or a state of being and is necessary to make a statement. A verb will fit one or more of these sentences:
   He _____.   We _____.   She _____ it.
   He **knows**.   We **walk**.   She **sees** it.

2. An **action verb** tells what someone or something does. The two types of action verbs are transitive and intransitive. A **transitive verb** is followed by a word or words—called the direct object—that answer the question *what?* or *whom?* An **intransitive verb** is not followed by a word that answers *what?* or *whom?*
   Transitive: The tourists **saw** the ruins.   The janitor **washed** the window.
   Intransitive: Owls **hooted** during the night.   The children **played** noisily.

3. An indirect object receives what the direct object names.
   Marcy sent **her brother** a present.

4. A **linking verb** links, or joins, the subject of a sentence with an adjective or nominative.
   The trucks **were** red. (adjective)
   She **became** an excellent swimmer. (nominative)

5. A **verb phrase** consists of a main verb and all its auxiliary, or helping, verbs.
   We **had been told** of his arrival.
   They **are listening** to a symphony.

6. Verbs have four **principal parts** or forms: base, past, present participle, and past participle.
   Base: I **talk**.   Present Participle: I am **talking**.
   Past: I **talked**.   Past Participle: I have **talked**.

   Regular verbs

7. **Irregular verbs** form their past form and past participle without adding *-ed* to the base form.

PRINCIPAL PARTS OF IRREGULAR VERBS

Base Form	Past Form	Past Participle	Base Form	Past Form	Past Participle
be	was, were	been	lead	led	led
beat	beat	beaten	lend	lent	lent
become	became	become	lie	lay	lain
begin	began	begun	lose	lost	lost
bite	bit	bitten *or* bit	put	put	put
blow	blew	blown	ride	rode	ridden
break	broke	broken	ring	rang	rung
bring	brought	brought	rise	rose	risen
catch	caught	caught	run	ran	run
choose	chose	chosen	say	said	said
come	came	come	see	saw	seen
do	did	done	set	set	set
draw	drew	drawn	shrink	shrank *or* shrunk	shrunk *or* shrunken
drink	drank	drunk			
drive	drove	driven	sing	sang	sung
eat	ate	eaten	sit	sat	sat
fall	fell	fallen	speak	spoke	spoken
feel	felt	felt	spring	sprang *or* sprung	sprung
find	found	found			
fly	flew	flown	steal	stole	stolen
freeze	froze	frozen	swim	swam	swum
get	got	got *or* gotten	take	took	taken
give	gave	given	tear	tore	torn
go	went	gone	tell	told	told
grow	grew	grown	think	thought	thought
hang	hung *or* hanged	hung *or* hanged	throw	threw	thrown
			wear	wore	worn
have	had	had	win	won	won
know	knew	known	write	wrote	written
lay	laid	laid			

8. The principle parts are used to form six verb tenses. The **tense** of a verb expresses time.

Simple Tenses

Present Tense: She **speaks**. (present or habitual action)
Past Tense: She **spoke**. (action completed in the past)
Future Tense: She **will speak**. (action to be done in the future)

Perfect Tenses

Present Perfect Tense: She **has spoken**. (action just done or still in effect)
Past Perfect Tense: She **had spoken**. (action completed before some other past action)
Future Perfect Tense: She **will have spoken**. (action to be completed before some future time)

9. **Progressive forms** of verbs are made up of a form of *be* and a present participle and express a continuing action. **Emphatic forms** are made up of a form of *do* and a base form and add emphasis or ask questions.
   Progressive: Marla **is babysitting**.   The toddlers **have been napping** for an hour.
   Emphatic: They **do prefer** beef to pork.
                We **did ask** for a quiet table.

10. The **voice** of a verb shows whether the subject performs the action or receives the action of the verb. A sentence is in the **active voice** when the subject performs the action. A sentence is in the **passive voice** when the subject receives the action of the verb.
    The robin **ate** the worm. (active)
    The worm **was eaten** by the robin. (passive)

Pronouns

1. A **pronoun** takes the place of a noun, a group of words acting as a noun, or another pronoun.

2. A **personal pronoun** refers to a specific person or thing. **First-person** personal pronouns refer to the speaker, **second-person** pronouns refer to the one spoken to, and **third-person** pronouns refer to the one spoken about.

	Singular	Plural
First Person	I, me, my, mine	we, us, our, ours
Second Person	you, your, yours	you, your, yours
Third Person	he, she, it, him, her, his, hers, its	they, them, their, theirs

3. A **reflexive pronoun** refers to the subject of the sentence. An **intensive pronoun** adds emphasis to a noun or another pronoun. A **demonstrative pronoun** points out specific persons, places, things, or ideas.
   Reflexive: **Nikki** prepares **himself** for the day-long hike.
   Intensive: **Nikki himself** prepares for the day-long hike.
   Demonstrative: **That** was a good movie! **These** are the files you wanted.

4. An **interrogative pronoun** is used to form questions. A **relative pronoun** is used to introduce a subordinate clause. An **indefinite pronoun** refers to persons, places, or things in a more general way than a personal pronoun does.
   Interrogative: **Whose** are these?   **Which** did you prefer?
   Relative: The bread **that** we tasted was whole wheat.
   Indefinite: **Someone** has already told them. **Everyone** agrees on the answer.

5. Use the subject form of a personal pronoun when it is used as a subject or when it follows a linking verb.
   He writes stories.   Are **they** ready?   It is **I**. (after linking verb)

6. Use the object form of a personal pronoun when it is an object.
   Mrs. Cleary called **us**. (direct object)   Stephen offered **us** a ride. (indirect object)
   Sara will go with **us**. (object of preposition)

7. Use a **possessive pronoun** to replace a possessive noun. Never use an apostrophe in a possessive personal pronoun.
   Their science experiment is just like **ours**.

8. When a pronoun is followed by an appositive, use the subject pronoun if the appositive is the subject. Use the object pronoun if the appositive is an object. To test whether the pronoun is correct, read the sentence without the appositive.
   We eighth-graders would like to thank you.
   The success of **us** geometry students is due to Ms. Marcia.

9. In incomplete comparisons, choose the pronoun that you would use if the missing words were fully expressed.
   Harris can play scales faster than **I** (can).
   It is worth more to you than (it is to) **me**.

10. In questions use *who* for subjects and *whom* for objects.
    Who wants another story?
    Whom will the class choose as treasurer?

    In subordinate clauses use *who* and *whoever* as subjects and after linking verbs, and use *whom* and *whomever* as objects.
    These souvenirs are for **whoever** wants to pay the price.
    The manager will train **whomever** the president hires.

11. An **antecedent** is the word or group of words to which a pronoun refers or that a pronoun replaces. All pronouns must agree with their antecedents in number, gender, and person.
    Marco's **sister** spent **her** vacation in San Diego.
    The huge old **trees** held **their** own against the storm.

12. Make sure that the antecedent of a pronoun is clearly stated.
    UNCLEAR: Mrs. Cardonal baked cookies with her daughters, hoping to sell **them** at the bake sale.
    CLEAR: Mrs. Cardonal baked cookies with her daughters, hoping to sell **the cookies** at the bake sale.
    UNCLEAR: If you don't tie the balloon to the stroller, **it** will blow away.
    CLEAR: If you don't tie the balloon to the stroller, **the balloon** will blow away.

Adjectives

1. An **adjective** modifies, or describes, a noun or pronoun by providing more information or giving a specific detail.
   The **smooth** surface of the lake gleamed.
   Frosty trees glistened in the sun.

2. Most adjectives will fit this sentence:
   The _____ one seems very _____.
   The **handmade** one seems very **colorful**.

3. **Articles** are the adjectives *a*, *an*, and *the*. Articles do not meet the preceding test for adjectives.

4. A **proper adjective** is formed from a proper noun and begins with a capital letter.
   Tricia admired the **Scottish** sweaters.
   Our **Mexican** vacation was memorable.

5. The comparative form of an adjective compares two things or people. The superlative form compares more than two things or people. Form the comparative by adding *-er* or combining with *more* or *less*. Form the superlative by adding *-est* or combining with *most* or *least*.

POSITIVE	COMPARATIVE	SUPERLATIVE
slow	slower	slowest
charming	more charming	most charming

6. Some adjectives have irregular comparative forms.

POSITIVE:	good, well	bad	far	many, much	little
COMPARATIVE:	better	worse	farther	more	less
SUPERLATIVE:	best	worst	farthest	most	least

Adverbs

1. An **adverb** modifies a verb, an adjective, or another adverb. Adverbs tell *how, where, when,* or *to what extent*.
   The cat walked **quietly**. (how)
   She **seldom** misses a deadline. (when)
   The player moved **forward**. (where)
   The band was **almost** late. (to what extent)

2. Many adverbs fit these sentences:
   She thinks _____.   She thinks _____ fast.   She _____ thinks fast.
   She thinks **quickly**.   She thinks **unusually** fast. She **seldom** thinks fast.

3. The comparative form of an adverb compares two actions. The superlative form compares more than two actions. For shorter adverbs add *-er* or *-est* to form the comparative or superlative. For most adverbs, add *more* or *most* or *less* or *least* to form the comparative or superlative.
   We walked **faster** than before.
   They listened **most carefully** to the final speaker.

4. Avoid **double negatives,** which are two negative words in the same clause.
   INCORRECT: I have not seen no stray cats.
   CORRECT: I have not seen any stray cats.

Prepositions, Conjunctions, and Interjections

1. A **preposition** shows the relationship of a noun or a pronoun to some other word. A **compound preposition** is made up of more than one word.
   The trees **near** our house provide plenty **of** shade.
   The schools were closed **because of** snow.

2. Common prepositions include these: about, above, according to, across, after, against, along, among, around, as, at, because of, before, behind, below, beneath, beside, besides, between, beyond, but, by, concerning, down, during, except, for, from, in, inside, in spite of, into, like, near, of, off, on, out, outside, over, past, round, since, through, till, to, toward, under, underneath, until, up, upon, with, within, without.

3. A **conjunction** is a word that joins single words or groups of words. A **coordinating conjunction** joins words or groups of words that have equal grammatical weight. **Correlative conjunctions** work in pairs to join words and groups of words of equal weight. A **subordinating conjunction** joins two clauses in such a way as to make one grammatically dependent on the other.
   I want to visit the art gallery **and** the museum. (coordinating)
   Both left **and** right turns were impossible in the traffic. (correlative)
   We go to the park **whenever** Mom lets us. (subordinating)

COMMON CONJUCTIONS

Coordinating:	and	but	for	nor	or	so	yet
Correlative:	both...and		neither...nor		whether...or		
	either...or		not only...but also				

Subordinating:	after	as though	since	when
	although	because	so that	whenever
	as	before	than	where
	as if	even though	though	wherever
	as long as	if	unless	whether
	as soon as	in order that	until	while

4. A **conjunctive adverb** clarifies a relationship.
   Frank loved the old maple tree; **nevertheless,** he disliked raking its leaves.

5. An **interjection** is an unrelated word or phrase that expresses emotion or strong feeling.
   Look, there are two cardinals at the feeder.   **Good grief!** Are you kidding?

CLAUSES AND COMPLEX SENTENCES

1. A **clause** is a group of words that has a subject and a predicate and is used as a sentence or a part of a sentence. There are two types of clauses: main and subordinate. A **main clause** has a subject and a predicate and can stand alone as a sentence. A **subordinate clause** has a subject and a predicate, but it cannot stand alone as a sentence.
           main   sub.
   She became a veterinarian because she loves animals.

2. There are three types of subordinate clauses: adjective, adverb, and noun.

   a. An **adjective clause** is a subordinate clause that modifies a noun or pronoun.
      The wrens **that built a nest in the backyard** are now raising their young.

   b. An **adverb clause** is a subordinate clause that often modifies the verb in the main clause of the sentence. It tells *when, where, how, why,* or *under what conditions.*
      Before they got out, the goats broke the fence in several places.

   c. A **noun clause** is a subordinate clause used as a noun.
      Whatever we do will have to please everyone. (subject)
      The prize goes to **whoever can keep the squirrels away from the feeder.** (object of preposition)

3. Main and subordinate clauses can form several types of sentences. A **simple sentence** has only one main clause and no subordinate clauses. A **compound sentence** has two or more main clauses. A **complex sentence** has at least one main clause and one or more subordinate clauses.

                               main
Simple: The apples fell off the tree.

                         main   main
Compound: The dancers bowed, and the audience clapped.

                           sub.   main
Complex: Because they turn to face the sun, these flowers are called sunflowers.

4. A sentence that makes a statement is classified as a **declarative sentence.**
My dad's favorite horses are buckskins.

An **imperative sentence** gives a command or makes a request.
Please close the door on your way out.

An **interrogative sentence** asks a question.
When will the mail carrier arrive?

An **exclamatory sentence** expresses strong emotion.
Watch out!
What a view that is!

Phrases

1. A **phrase** is a group of words that acts in a sentence as a single part of speech.

2. A **prepositional phrase** is a group of words that begins with a preposition and ends with a noun or pronoun, which is called the **object of the preposition**. A prepositional phrase can act as an adjective or an adverb.
The house **on the hill** is white. (modifies the noun *house*)
Everyone **in the house** heard the storm. (modifies the pronoun *everyone*)
The geese flew **toward warmer weather.** (modifies the verb *flew*)

3. An **appositive** is a noun or pronoun that is placed next to another noun or pronoun to identify it or give more information about it. An **appositive phrase** is an appositive plus its modifiers.
Our sister **Myra** is home from college. Her college, **Purdue University**, is in Indiana.

4. A **verbal** is a verb form that functions in a sentence as a noun, an adjective, or an adverb. A **verbal phrase** is a verbal and other words that complete its meaning.

   a. A **participle** is a verbal that functions as an adjective. Present participles end in *-ing.* Past participles usually end in *-ed.*
     The **squeaking** floor board gave me away.   The **twisted** tree was ancient.

   b. A **participial phrase** contains a participle and other words that complete its meaning.
     Moving quickly across the room, the baby crawled toward her mother.

c. A **gerund** is a verbal that ends in *-ing*. It is used in the same way a noun is used.
Sailing is a traditional vacation activity for the Andersons.

d. A **gerund phrase** is a gerund plus any complements or modifiers.
Walking to school is common for many school children.

e. An **infinitive** is a verbal formed from the word *to* and the base form of a verb. It is often used as a noun. Because an infinitive acts as a noun, it may be the subject of a sentence or the direct object of an action verb.
To sing can be uplifting. (infinitive as subject)
Babies first learn **to babble**. (infinitive as direct object)

f. An **infinitive phrase** contains an infinitive plus any complements or modifiers.
The flight attendants prepared **to feed the hungry passengers**.

SUBJECT-VERB AGREEMENT

1. A verb must agree with its subject in person and number.
   The kangaroo **jumps**. (singular)   The kangaroos **jump**. (plural)
   She **is leaping**. (singular)   They **are leaping**. (plural)

2. In **inverted sentences** the subject follows the verb. The sentence may begin with a prepositional phrase, the word *there* or *here*, or a form of *do*.
   Into the pond **dove** the *children*.
   Does a *bird* **have** a sense of smell?
   There **is** a *squeak* in that third stair.

3. Do not mistake a word in a prepositional phrase for the subject.
   The **glass** in the window **is** streaked. (The singular verb *is* agrees with the subject, *glass*.)

4. A title is always singular, even if nouns in the title are plural.
   ***Instant World Facts* is** a helpful reference book.

5. Subjects combined with *and* or *both* need a plural verb unless the parts are of a whole unit. When compound subjects are joined with *or* or *nor,* the verb agrees with the subject listed last.
   Canterbury and Coventry have famous cathedrals.
   A **bagel and cream cheese is** a filling snack.
   Either two short **stories** or a **novel is** acceptable for your book report.

6. A verb must agree in number with an indefinite pronoun subject. Indefinite pronouns that are always singular: *anybody, anyone, anything, each, either, everybody, everyone, everything, neither, nobody, no one, nothing, one, somebody, someone,* and *something*
   Always plural: *both, few, many, others,* and *several*
   Either singular or plural: *all, any, most, none,* and *some*

   Most of the snow **has** melted.   **All** of the children **have** eaten.

Handbook **11**

USAGE GLOSSARY

a lot, alot Always write this expression, meaning "very much" or "a large amount," as two words.
 The neighbors pitched in, and the job went **a lot** faster.

accept, except *Accept*, a verb, means "to receive" or "to agree to." *Except* may be a preposition or a verb. As a preposition it means "other than." As a verb it means "to leave out, to make an exception."
 I **accept** your plan.   We ate everything **except** the crust.

all ready, already *All ready* means "completely prepared." *Already* means "before" or "by this time."
 They were **all ready** to leave, but the bus had **already** departed.

all together, altogether The two words *all together* mean "in a group." The single word *altogether* is an adverb meaning "completely" or "on the whole."
 The teachers met **all together** after school.
 They were **altogether** prepared for a heated discussion.

beside, besides *Beside* means "next to." *Besides* means "in addition to."
 The sink is **beside** the refrigerator.
 Besides the kitchen, the den is my favorite room.

between, among Use *between* to refer to or to compare two separate nouns. Use *among* to show a relationship in a group.
 The joke was **between** Hilary and Megan.
 The conversation **among** the teacher, the principal, and the janitor was friendly.

bring, take Use *bring* to show movement from a distant place to a closer one. Use *take* to show movement from a nearby place to a more distant one.
 You may **bring** your model here.
 Please **take** a brochure with you when you go.

can, may *Can* indicates the ability to do something. *May* indicates permission to do something.
 Constance **can** walk to school.
 She **may** ride the bus if she wishes.

choose, chose *Choose* means "to select." *Chose* is the past participle form, meaning "selected."
 I **choose** the blue folder.
 Celia **chose** the purple folder.

fewer, less Use *fewer* with nouns that can be counted. Use *less* with nouns that cannot be counted.
 There were **fewer** sunny days this year.
 I see **less** fog today than I expected.

formally, formerly *Formally* is the adverb form of formal. *Formerly* is an adverb meaning "in times past."
They **formally** agreed to the exchange.
Lydia **formerly** lived in Spain, but now she lives in New York City.

in, into Use *in* to mean "inside" or "within" and *into* to indicate movement or direction from outside to a point within.
The birds nest **in** the trees.
A bird flew **into** our window yesterday.

its, it's *Its* is the possessive form of the pronoun *it*. Possessive pronouns never have apostrophes. *It's* is the contraction of *it is*.
The dog lives in **its** own house.   Who is to say whether **it's** happy or not.

lay, lie *Lay* means "to put" or "to place," and it takes a direct object. *Lie* means "to recline" or "to be positioned," and it never takes an object.
We **lay** the uniforms on the shelves each day.
The players **lie** on the floor to do their sit-ups.

learn, teach *Learn* means "to receive knowledge." *Teach* means "to give knowledge."
Children can **learn** foreign languages at an early age.
Mr. Minton will **teach** French to us next year.

leave, let *Leave* means "to go away." *Let* means "to allow" or "to permit."
I will **leave** after fourth period.
Dad will **let** me go swimming today.

loose, lose Use *loose* to mean "not firmly attached" and *lose* to mean "to misplace" or "to fail to win."
The bike chain was very **loose**.
I did not want to **lose** my balance.

many, much Use *many* with nouns that can be counted. Use *much* with nouns that cannot be counted.
Many ants were crawling near the anthill.
There was **much** discussion about what to do.

precede, proceed *Precede* means "to go or come before." *Proceed* means "to continue."
Lunch will **precede** the afternoon session.
Marly can **proceed** with her travel plans.

quiet, quite *Quiet* means "calm" or "motionless." *Quite* means "completely" or "entirely."
The sleeping kitten was **quiet**.
The other kittens were **quite** playful.

raise, rise *Raise* means "to cause to move upward," and it always takes an object. *Rise* means "to get up"; it is intransitive and never takes an object.
Please **raise** your hand if you would like to help.
I left the bread in a warm spot to **rise**.

sit, set *Sit* means "to place oneself in a sitting position." It rarely takes an object. *Set* means "to place" or "to put" and usually takes an object. *Set* can also be used to describe the sun going down.
Please **sit** in your assigned seats.   **Set** those dishes down.
The sun **set** at 6:14.

than, then *Than* is a conjunction that is used to introduce the second element in a comparison; it also shows exception. *Then* is an adverb meaning "at that time."
Wisconsin produces more milk **than** any other state.
First get comfortable, **then** look the pitcher right in the eye.

their, they're *Their* is the possessive form of the personal pronoun *they*. *They're* is the contraction of *they are*.
The Westons returned to **their** favorite vacation spot.
They're determined to go next year as well.

theirs, there's *Theirs* means "that or those belonging to them." *There's* is the contraction of *there is*.
Theirs is one of the latest models.
There's another pitcher of lemonade in the refrigerator.

to, too, two *To* is a preposition meaning "in the direction of." *Too* means "also" or "excessively." *Two* is the number that falls between one and three.
You may go **to** the library.
It is **too** cold for skating.
There are only **two** days of vacation left.

where at Do not use *at* in a sentence after *where*.
Where were you yesterday afternoon? (*not* Where were you at yesterday afternoon?)

who's, whose *Who's* is the contraction of *who is*. *Whose* is the possessive form of *who*.
Who's willing to help me clean up?
Do you know **whose** books these are?

your, you're *Your* is the possessive form of *you*. *You're* is the contraction of *you are*.
Please arrange **your** schedule so that you can be on time.
If **you're** late, you may miss something important.

CAPITALIZATION

1. Capitalize the first word of every sentence, including direct quotations and sentences in parentheses unless they are contained within another sentence.
   In *Poor Richard's Almanack,* Benjamin Franklin advises, "**W**ish not so much to live long as to live well." (This appeared in the almanac published in 1738.)

2. Capitalize the first word in the salutation and closing of a letter. Capitalize the title and name of the person addressed.
   Dear **P**rofessor **N**ichols:
   Sincerely yours,

3. Always capitalize the pronoun *I* no matter where it appears in the sentence.
   Since **I** knew you were coming, **I** baked a cake.

4. Capitalize the following proper nouns:
   a. Names of individuals, the initials that stand for their names, and titles preceding a name or used instead of a name
      Governor **C**ordoba   **A**. **C**. **S**hen
      Aunt **M**argaret   **D**r. **H**. **C**. **H**arada
      General **D**iaz

   b. Names and abbreviations of academic degrees, and *Jr.* and *Sr.*
      Richard Boe, **Ph**.**D**.
      Sammy Davis **Jr**.

   c. Names of cities, countries, states, continents, bodies of water, sections of the United States, and compass points when they refer to a specific section of the United States
      Boston   **D**ade **C**ounty   **N**orth **C**arolina   **A**ustralia
      Amazon **R**iver   the **S**outh

   d. Names of streets, highways, organizations, institutions, firms, monuments, bridges, buildings, other structures, and celestial bodies
      Route 51   **C**ircle **K** **S**ociety   **T**omb of the **U**nknown **S**oldier
      Golden **G**ate **B**ridge   **C**oventry **C**athedral   **N**orth **S**tar

   e. Trade names and names of documents, awards, and laws
      No-**S**neez tissues   the **F**ourteenth **A**mendment
      Golden **G**lobe **A**ward   the **M**onroe **D**octrine

   f. Names of most historical events, eras, holidays, days of the week, and months
      Boston **T**ea **P**arty   **B**ronze **A**ge   **L**abor **D**ay   **F**riday   **J**uly

   g. First, last, and all important words in titles of literary works, works of art, and musical compositions
      "**I** **A**sk **M**y **M**other to **S**ing" (poem)   *Giants in the Earth* (book)
      Venus de **M**ilo (statue)   "**A**merica, the **B**eautiful" (composition)

   h. Names of ethnic groups, national groups, political parties and their members, and languages
      Hispanics   **C**hinese   **I**rish   **I**talian   **R**epublican party

5. Capitalize proper adjectives (adjectives formed from proper nouns).
   English saddle horse   **T**hai restaurant   **M**idwestern plains

PUNCTUATION, ABBREVIATIONS, AND NUMBERS

1. Use a period at the end of a declarative sentence and at the end of a polite command.
   Mrs. Miranda plays tennis every Tuesday.
   Write your name in the space provided.

2. Use a question mark at the end of an interrogative sentence.
   When will the new books arrive?

3. Use an exclamation point to show strong feeling and indicate a forceful command.
   Oh, no!   It was a terrific concert!   Don't go outside without your gloves on!

4. Use a comma in the following situations:
   a. To separate three or more words, phrases, or clauses in a series
      A tent, sleeping bag, and sturdy shoes are essential wilderness camping equipment.
   b. To set off two or more prepositional phrases
      After the sound of the bell, we realized it was a false alarm.
   c. After an introductory participle and an introductory participial phrase
      Marveling at the sight, we waited to see another shooting star.
   d. After conjunctive adverbs
      Snow is falling; however, it is turning to sleet.
   e. To set off an appositive if it is not essential to the meaning of the sentence
      Mr. Yoshino, the head of the department, resigned yesterday.
   f. To set off words or phrases of direct address
      Micha, have you called your brother yet?
      It's good to see you, Mrs. Han.
   g. Between the main clauses of compound sentences
      Whiskers liked to watch the goldfish, and she sometimes dipped her paw in the bowl.
   h. After an introductory adverb clause and to set off a nonessential adjective clause
      Whenever we get careless, we always make mistakes.
      Spelling errors, which are common, can now be corrected by computer.
   i. To separate parts of an address or a date
      1601 Burma Drive, Waterbury, Connecticut
      She was born on February 2, 1985, and she now lives in Bangor, Maine.
   j. After the salutation and close of a friendly letter and after the close of a business letter
      Dear Dad,   Cordially,   Yours,

5. Use a semicolon in the following situations:
   a. To join main clauses not joined by a coordinating conjunction
      The house looks dark; perhaps we should have called first.
   b. To separate two main clauses joined by a coordinating conjunction when such clauses already contain several commas
      After a week of rain, the farmers around Ames, Iowa, waited hopefully; but the rain, unfortunately, had come too late.
   c. To separate main clauses joined by a conjunctive adverb or by *for example* or *that is*
      Jen was determined to win the race; nonetheless, she knew that it took more than determination to succeed.

6. Use a colon to introduce a list of items that ends a sentence.
   Bring the following tools: hammer, speed square, and drill.

7. Use a colon to separate the hour and the minute in time measurements and after business letter salutations.
   12:42 A.M.   Dear Sir: Dear Ms. O'Connor:

8. Use quotation marks to enclose a direct quotation. When a quotation is interrupted, use two sets of quotation marks. Use single quotation marks for a quotation within a quotation.
   "Are you sure," asked my mother, "that you had your keys when you left home?"
   "Chief Seattle's speech begins, 'My words are like the stars that never change,'" stated the history teacher.

9. Always place commas and periods inside closing quotations marks. Place colons and semicolons outside closing quotation marks. Place question marks and exclamation points inside closing quotation marks only when those marks are part of the quotation.
   "Giraffes," said Ms. Wharton, "spend long hours each day foraging."
   You must read "The Story of an Hour"; it is a wonderful short story.
   He called out, "Is anyone home?"
   Are you sure she said, "Go home without me"?

10. Use quotation marks to indicate titles of short stories, poems, essays, songs, and magazine or newspaper articles.
    "The Thrill of the Grass" (short story)
    "My Country 'Tis of Thee" (song)

11. Italicize (underline) titles of books, plays, films, television series, paintings and sculptures, and names of newspapers and magazines.
    Up from Slavery (book)
    Free Willy (film)
    The Spirit of '76 (painting)
    Chicago Tribune (newspaper)
    Weekend Woodworker (magazine)

12. Add an apostrophe and -s to form the possessive of singular indefinite pronouns, singular nouns, and plural nouns not ending in -s. Add only an apostrophe to plural nouns ending in -s to make them possessive.
    everyone's best friend
    the rabbit's ears
    the children's toys
    the farmers' fields

13. Use an apostrophe in place of omitted letters or numerals. Use an apostrophe and -s to form the plural of letters, numerals, and symbols.
    is + not = isn't
    will + not = won't
    1776 is '76
    Cross your *t*'s and dot your *i*'s.

14. Use a hyphen to divide words at the end of a line.
    esti-mate   mone-tary   experi-mentation

15. Use a hyphen in a compound adjective that precedes a noun. Use a hyphen in compound numbers and fractions used as adjectives.
    a blue-green parrot
    a salt-and-pepper beard
    twenty-nine
    one-third cup of flour

16. Use a hyphen after any prefix joined to a proper noun or a proper adjective. Use a hyphen after the prefixes *all-*, *ex-*, and *self-* joined to a noun or adjective, the prefix *anti-* joined to a word beginning with *i-*, and the prefix *vice-* except in the case of *vice president.*
    all-knowing   ex-spouse   self-confidence
    anti-inflammatory   vice-principal

17. Use dashes to signal a break or change in thought.
    I received a letter from Aunt Carla—you have never met her—saying she is coming to visit.

18. Use parentheses to set off supplemental material. Punctuate within the parentheses only if the punctuation is part of the parenthetical expression.
    Place one gallon (3.8 liters) of water in a plastic container.

19. Abbreviate a person's title and professional or academic degrees.
    Ms. K. Soga, **Ph.D.**
    Dr. Quentin

20. Use the abbreviations *A.M.* and *P.M.* and *B.C.* and *A.D.*
    9:45 A.M.   1000 B.C.   A.D. 1455

21. Abbreviate numerical measurements in scientific writing but not in ordinary prose.
    The newborn snakes measured 3.4 **in.** long.
    Pour 45 **ml** warm water into the beaker.

22. Spell out cardinal and ordinal numbers that can be written in one or two words or that appear at the beginning of a sentence.
    Two hundred twenty runners crossed the finish line.
    Observers counted **forty-nine** sandhill cranes.

23. Express all related numbers in a sentence as numerals if any one should be expressed as a numeral.
    There were **127** volunteers, but only **9** showed up because of the bad weather.

24. Spell out ordinal numbers.
    Nina won **third** place in the spelling bee.

25. Use words for decades, for amounts of money that can be written in one or two words, and for the approximate time of day or when A.M. or P.M. is not used.
    the **nineties**   **ten** dollars   **sixty** cents   half past **five**

26. Use numerals for dates; for decimals; for house, apartment, and room numbers; for street or avenue numbers; for telephone numbers; for page numbers; for percentages; for sums of money involving both dollars and cents; and to emphasize the exact time of day or when A.M. or P.M. is used.
    June **5, 1971**   Apartment **4**G   **$207.89**
    0.0045   **1520 14**th Street   **8:20** A.M.

VOCABULARY AND SPELLING

1. Clues to the meaning of an unfamiliar word can be found in its context. Context clues include definitions, the meaning stated; example, the meaning explained through one familiar case; comparison, similarity to a familiar word; contrast, opposite of a familiar word; and cause and effect, a reason and its results.

2. The meaning of a word can be obtained from its base word, its prefix, or its suffix.
   telegram **tele** = distant   dentate **dent** = tooth
   subarctic **sub** = below   marvelous **-ous** = full of

3. The *i* comes before the *e*, except when both letters follow a *c* or when both letters are pronounced together as an *ā* sound. However, many exceptions exist to this rule.
   y**ie**ld (*i* before *e*)   rec**ei**ve (*ei* after *c*)   w**ei**gh (*ā* sound)   h**ei**ght (exception)

4. An unstressed vowel is a vowel sound that is not emphasized when the word is pronounced. Determine how to spell this sound by comparing it to a known word.
   inform**a**nt (compare to *information*)   hospit**a**l (compare to *hospitality*)

5. When joining a prefix that ends in the same letter as the word, keep both consonants.
   illegible   **diss**ervice

6. When adding a suffix to a word ending in a consonant + *y*, change the *y* to *i* unless the prefix begins with an *i*. If the word ends in a vowel + *y*, keep the *y*.
   tr**ied**   pla**yed**   spra**ying**

7. Double the final consonant before adding a suffix that begins with a vowel to a word that ends in a single consonant preceded by a single vowel if the accent is on the root's last syllable.
   pop**ping**   transfer**red**   unforget**table**

8. When adding a suffix that begins with a consonant to a word that ends in silent *e*, generally keep the *e*. If the suffix begins with a vowel or *y*, generally drop the *e*. If the suffix begins with *a* or *o* and the word ends in *ce* or *ge*, keep the *e*. If the suffix begins with a vowel and the word ends in *ee* or *oe*, keep the *e*.
   state**ly**   nois**y**   courage**ous**   agree**able**

9. When adding -*ly* to a word that ends in a single *l*, keep the *l*. If it ends in a double *l*, drop one *l*. If it ends in a consonant + *le*, drop the *le*.
   meal, meal**ly**   full, ful**ly**   incredible, incredi**bly**

10. When forming compound words, maintain the spelling of both words.
    backpack   honeybee

11. Most nouns form their plurals by adding -*s*. However, nouns that end in -*ch*, -*s*, -*sh*, -*x*, or -*z* form plurals by adding -*es*. If the noun ends in a consonant + *y*, change *y* to *i* and add -*es*. If the noun ends in -*lf*, change *f* to *v* and add -*es*. If the noun ends in -*fe*, change *f* to *v* and add -*s*.
    mark**s**   leach**es**   rash**es**   fox**es**
    fl**ies**   el**ves**   li**ves**

12. To form the plural of proper names and one-word compound nouns, follow the general rules for plurals. To form the plural of hyphenated compound nouns or compound nouns of more than one word, make the most important word plural.
    Wilson**s**   Diaz**es**   housekeeper**s**
    sister**s**-in-law   editor**s**-in-chief

13. Some nouns have the same singular and plural forms.
    deer   moose

Composition

Writing Themes and Paragraphs

1. Use **prewriting** to find ideas to write about. One form of prewriting, **freewriting**, starts with a subject or topic and branches off into related ideas. Another way to find a topic is to ask and answer questions about your starting subject, helping you to gain a deeper understanding of your chosen topic. Also part of the prewriting stage is determining who your readers or **audience** will be and deciding your **purpose** for writing. Your purpose—writing to persuade, to explain, to describe something, or to narrate—is partially shaped by who your audience will be.

2. To complete your first **draft**, organize your prewriting into an introduction, body, and conclusion. Concentrate on unity and coherence of the overall piece. Experiment with different paragraph orders: **chronological order** places events in the order in which they happened; **spatial order** places objects in the order in which they appear; and **compare/contrast order** shows similarities and differences in objects or events.

3. **Revise** your composition if necessary. Read through your draft, looking for places to improve content and structure. Remember that varying your sentence patterns and lengths will make your writing easier and more enjoyable to read.

4. In the **editing** stage, check your grammar, spelling, and punctuation. Focus on expressing your ideas clearly and concisely.

5. Finally, prepare your writing for **presentation**. Sharing your composition, or ideas, with others may take many forms: printed, oral, or graphic.

Outlining

1. The two common forms of outlines are **sentence outlines** and **topic outlines**. Choose one type of outline and keep it uniform throughout.

2. A period follows the number or letter of each division. Each point in a sentence outline ends with a period; the points in a topic outline do not.

3. Each point begins with a capital letter.

4. A point may have no fewer than two subpoints.

```
SENTENCE OUTLINE                          TOPIC OUTLINE
  I. This is the main point.                I. Main point
     A. This is a subpoint of I.               A. Subpoint of I
        1. This is a detail of A.                 1. Detail of A
           a. This is a detail of 1.                 a. Detail of 1
           b. This is a detail of 1.                 b. Detail of 1
        2. This is a detail of A.                 2. Detail of A
     B. This is a subpoint of I.               B. Subpoint of I
 II. This is another main point.           II. Main point
```

Writing Letters

1. **Personal letters** are usually handwritten in indented form (first line of paragraphs, each line of the heading and inside address, and the signature are indented). **Business letters** are usually typewritten in block or semiblock form. Block form contains no indents; semiblock form indents only the first line of each paragraph.

2. The five parts of a personal letter are the heading (the writer's address and the date), salutation (greeting), body (message), complimentary close (such as "Yours truly,"), and signature (the writer's name). Business letters have the same parts and also include an inside address (the recipient's address).

PERSONAL LETTER

Heading

Salutation

Body

Complimentary Close
Signature

BUSINESS LETTER

Heading

Inside Address

Salutation

Body

Complimentary Close
Signature

3. Reveal your personality and imagination in colorful personal letters. Keep business letters brief, clear, and courteous.

4. **Personal letters** include letters to friends and family members. **Thank-you notes** and **invitations** are personal letters that may be either formal or informal in style.

5. Use a **letter of request**, a type of business letter, to ask for information or to place an order. Be concise, yet give all the details necessary for your request to be fulfilled. Keep the tone of your letter courteous, and be generous in allotting time for a response.

6. Use an **opinion letter** to take a firm stand on an issue. Make the letter clear, firm, rational, and purposeful. Be aware of your audience, their attitude, how informed they are, and their possible reactions to your opinion. Support your statements of opinion with facts.

Troubleshooter

frag	Sentence Fragments	24
run-on	Run-on Sentences	26
agr	Lack of Subject-Verb Agreement	28
tense	Incorrect Verb Tense or Form	32
pro	Incorrect Use of Pronouns	34
adj	Incorrect Use of Adjectives	36
com	Incorrect Use of Commas	38
apos	Incorrect Use of Apostrophes	41
cap	Incorrect Capitalization	44

Sentence Fragments

PROBLEM 1

Fragment that lacks a subject

frag	Martha asked about dinner. ⟨Hoped it was lasagna.⟩
frag	I jogged around the park twice. ⟨Was hot and tired afterward.⟩
frag	Li Cheng raced to the bus stop. ⟨Arrived just in the nick of time.⟩

SOLUTION

Martha asked about dinner. She hoped it was lasagna.
I jogged around the park twice. I was hot and tired afterward.
Li Cheng raced to the bus stop. He arrived just in the nick of time.

Make a complete sentence by adding a subject to the fragment.

PROBLEM 2

Fragment that lacks a predicate

frag	The carpenter worked hard all morning. ⟨His assistant after lunch.⟩
frag	Ant farms are fascinating. ⟨The ants around in constant motion.⟩
frag	Our class went on a field trip. ⟨Mammoth Cave.⟩

SOLUTION

The carpenter worked hard all morning. His assistant helped after lunch.
Ant farms are fascinating. The ants crawl around in constant motion.
Our class went on a field trip. Mammoth Cave was our destination.

Make a complete sentence by adding a predicate.

PROBLEM 3

Fragment that lacks both a subject and a predicate

frag	I heard the laughter of the children. (In the nursery.)
frag	(After the spring rain.) The whole house smelled fresh and clean.
frag	The noisy chatter of the squirrels awakened us early. (In the morning.)

SOLUTION

I heard the laughter of the children in the nursery.
After the spring rain, the whole house smelled fresh and clean.
The noisy chatter of the squirrels awakened us early in the morning.

Combine the fragment with another sentence.

More help in avoiding sentence fragments is available in Lesson 3.

Run-on Sentences

Problem 1

Two main clauses separated only by a comma

run-on Extra crackers are available, they are next to the salad bar.

run-on Hurdles are Sam's specialty, he likes them best.

Solution A

Extra crackers are available. They are next to the salad bar.

Make two sentences by separating the first clause from the second with end punctuation, such as a period or a question mark, and starting the second sentence with a capital letter.

Solution B

Hurdles are Sam's specialty; he likes them best.

Place a semicolon between the main clauses of the sentence.

Problem 2

Two main clauses with no punctuation between them

run-on The law student studied hard she passed her exam.

run-on Kamil looked for the leash he found it in the closet.

SOLUTION A

The law student studied hard. She passed her exam.

Make two sentences out of the run-on sentence.

SOLUTION B

Kamil looked for the leash, and he found it in the closet.

Add a comma and a coordinating conjunction between the main clauses.

PROBLEM 3

Two main clauses without a comma before the coordinating conjunction

run-on You can rollerskate like a pro but you cannot ice skate.

run-on Julian gazed at the moon and he marveled at its brightness.

SOLUTION

You can rollerskate like a pro, but you cannot ice skate.
Julian gazed at the moon, and he marveled at its brightness.

Add a comma before the coordinating conjunction.

More help in avoiding run-on sentences is available in Lesson 6.

Lack of Subject-Verb Agreement

PROBLEM 1

A subject separated from the verb by an intervening prepositional phrase

agr	The stories in the newspaper (was) well written.
agr	The house in the suburbs (were) just what she wanted.

SOLUTION

The stories in the newspaper were well written.
The house in the suburbs was just what she wanted.

Make sure that the verb agrees with the subject of the sentence, not with the object of a preposition. The object of a preposition is never the subject.

PROBLEM 2

A sentence that begins with **here** or **there**

agr	Here (go) the duck with her ducklings.
agr	There (is) the pencils you were looking for.
agr	Here (is) the snapshots from our vacation to the Grand Canyon.

> **SOLUTION**
>
> **Here goes the duck with her ducklings.**
> **There are the pencils you were looking for.**
> **Here are the snapshots from our vacation to the Grand Canyon.**
>
> In sentences that begin with *here* or *there,* look for the subject after the verb. Make sure that the verb agrees with the subject.

PROBLEM 3

An indefinite pronoun as the subject

> *agr*   Each of the animals (have) a unique way of walking.
>
> *agr*   Many of the movies (was) black and white.
>
> *agr*   Most of the leaves (is) turning colors.

> **SOLUTION**
>
> **Each of the animals has a unique way of walking.**
> **Many of the movies were black and white.**
> **Most of the leaves are turning colors.**
>
> Some indefinite pronouns are singular, some are plural, and some can be either singular or plural. Determine whether the indefinite pronoun is singular or plural, and make the verb agree.

Troubleshooter

PROBLEM 4

A compound subject that is joined by and

agr   The students and the teacher **adores** the classroom hamster.

agr   The expert and best source of information **are** Dr. Marlin.

SOLUTION A

The students and the teacher adore the classroom hamster.

Use a plural verb if the parts of the compound subject do not belong to one unit or if they refer to different people or things.

SOLUTION B

The expert and best source of information is Dr. Marlin.

Use a singular verb if the parts of the compound subject belong to one unit or if they refer to the same person or thing.

PROBLEM 5

A compound subject that is joined by or *or* nor

agr   Either Hester or Sue **are** supposed to pick us up.

agr   Neither pepper nor spices **improves** the flavor of this sauce.

agr   Either Caroline or Robin **volunteer** at the local food pantry.

agr   Neither the coach nor the screaming fans **agrees** with the referee's call.

---

30   *Writer's Choice Grammar Workbook 8*, Troubleshooter

SOLUTION

Either Hester or Sue is supposed to pick us up.

Neither pepper nor spices improve the flavor of this sauce.

Either Caroline or Robin volunteers at the local food pantry.

Neither the coach nor the screaming fans agree with the referee's call.

Make the verb agree with the subject that is closer to it.

More help with subject-verb agreement is available in Lessons 53–57.

Incorrect Verb Tense or Form

PROBLEM 1

An incorrect or missing verb ending

tense	We *talk* yesterday for more than an hour.
tense	They *sail* last month for Barbados.
tense	Sally and James *land* at the airport yesterday.

SOLUTION

We talked yesterday for more than an hour.
They sailed last month for Barbados.
Sally and James landed at the airport yesterday.

To form the past tense and the past participle, add *-ed* to a regular verb.

PROBLEM 2

An improperly formed irregular verb

tense	Our hair *clinged* to us in the humid weather.
tense	Trent *drinked* all the orange juice.
tense	The evening breeze *blowed* the clouds away.

SOLUTION

Our hair clung to us in the humid weather.
Trent drank all the orange juice.
The evening breeze blew the clouds away.

Irregular verbs vary in their past and past participle forms. Look up the ones you are not sure of. Consider memorizing them if you feel it is necessary.

PROBLEM 3

Confusion between a verb's past form and its past participle

tense Helen has took first place in the marathon.

SOLUTION

Helen has taken first place in the marathon.

Use the past participle form of an irregular verb, and not its past form, when you use the auxiliary verb *have*.

 **More help with correct verb forms is available in Lessons 18–24.**

Incorrect Use of Pronouns

Troubleshooter

PROBLEM 1

A pronoun that refers to more than one antecedent

pro	The wind and the rain came suddenly, but (it) did not last.
pro	Henry ran with Philip, but (he) was faster.
pro	When Sarah visits Corinne, (she) is glad for the company.

SOLUTION

The wind and the rain came suddenly, but the rain did not last.
Henry ran with Philip, but Philip was faster.
When Sarah visits Corinne, Corinne is glad for the company.

Substitute a noun for the pronoun to make your sentence clearer.

PROBLEM 2

Personal pronouns as subjects

pro	(Him) and Mary unfurled the tall, white sail.
pro	Nina and (them) bought theater tickets yesterday.
pro	Karen and (me) heard the good news on the television.

34 Writer's Choice Grammar Workbook 8, Troubleshooter

SOLUTION

He and Mary unfurled the tall, white sail.
Nina and they bought theater tickets yesterday.
Karen and I heard the good news on the television.

Use a subject pronoun as the subject part of a sentence.

PROBLEM 3

Personal pronouns as objects

pro	The horse galloped across the field to Anne and ⓘ.
pro	The new signs confused Clark and ⓣⓗⓔⓨ.
pro	Grant wrote ⓢⓗⓔ a letter of apology.

SOLUTION

The horse galloped across the field to Anne and me.
The new signs confused Clark and them.
Grant wrote her a letter of apology.

An object pronoun is the object of a verb or preposition.

More help with correct use of pronouns is available in Lessons 25–30.

Incorrect Use of Adjectives

PROBLEM 1

Incorrect use of good, better, best

adj	Is a horse ⟨more good⟩ than a pony?
adj	Literature is my ⟨most good⟩ subject.

SOLUTION

Is a horse better than a pony?
Literature is my best subject.

The words *better* and *best* are the comparative and superlative forms of the word *good*. Do not use the words *more* or *most* before the irregular forms of comparative and superlative adjectives.

PROBLEM 2

Incorrect use of bad, worse, worst

adj	That game was the ⟨baddest⟩ game our team ever played.

SOLUTION

That game was the worst game our team ever played.

Do not use the words *more* or *most* before the irregular forms of comparative and superlative adjectives.

PROBLEM 3

Incorrect use of comparative adjectives

adj   This bike is (more faster) than my old bike.

SOLUTION

This bike is faster than my old bike.

Do not use *-er* and *more* together.

PROBLEM 4

Incorrect use of superlative adjectives

adj   Kara said it was the (most biggest) lawn she ever had to mow.

SOLUTION

Kara said it was the biggest lawn she ever had to mow.

Do not use *-est* and *most* together.

 **More help with the correct use of adjectives is available in Lessons 31–34.**

Incorrect Use of Commas

Problem 1

Missing commas in a series of three or more items

com   We saw ducks geese and seagulls at the park.

com   Jake ate dinner watched a movie and visited friends.

Solution

We saw ducks, geese, and seagulls at the park.

Jake ate dinner, watched a movie, and visited friends.

If there are three or more items in a series, use a comma after each item except the last one.

Problem 2

Missing commas with direct quotations

com   "The party" said José "starts at seven o'clock."

com   "My new book" Roger exclaimed "is still on the bus!"

Solution

"The party," said José, "starts at seven o'clock."

"My new book," Roger exclaimed, "is still on the bus!"

If a quotation is interrupted, the first part ends with a comma followed by quotation marks. The interrupting words are also followed by a comma.

Problem 3

Missing commas with nonessential appositives

com   Maria our new friend is from Chicago.

com   The old lane a tree-lined gravel path is a great place to walk on a hot afternoon.

Solution

Maria, our new friend, is from Chicago.

The old lane, a tree-lined gravel path, is a great place to walk on a hot afternoon.

Decide whether the appositive is truly essential to the meaning of the sentence. If it is not essential, set it off with commas.

Troubleshooter 39

PROBLEM 4

Missing commas with nonessential adjective clauses

com   Karen who started early finished with her work before noon.

SOLUTION

Karen, who started early, finished with her work before noon.

Decide whether the clause is truly essential to the meaning of the sentence. If it is not essential, then set it off with commas.

PROBLEM 5

Missing commas with introductory adverb clauses

com   When the wind rises too high the boats lower their sails.

SOLUTION

When the wind rises too high, the boats lower their sails.

Place a comma after an introductory adverbial clause.

More help with commas is available in Lessons 78–81.

40   Writer's Choice Grammar Workbook 8, Troubleshooter

Incorrect Use of Apostrophes

PROBLEM 1

Singular possessive nouns

apos	Pablos new bicycle is in Charles yard.
apos	Bills video collection is really great.
apos	That horses saddle has real silver on it.

SOLUTION

Pablo's new bicycle is in Charles's yard.

Bill's video collection is really great.

That horse's saddle has real silver on it.

Place an apostrophe before a final -s to form the possessive of a singular noun, even one that ends in -s.

PROBLEM 2

Plural possessive nouns that end in -s

apos	The girls team won the tournament.
apos	The boats sails are very colorful against the blue sky.
apos	The model cars boxes are in my room.

> **SOLUTION**
>
> **The girls' team won the tournament.**
> **The boats' sails are very colorful against the blue sky.**
> **The model cars' boxes are in my room.**
>
> Use an apostrophe by itself to form the possessive of a plural noun that ends in -s.

PROBLEM 3

Plural possessive nouns that do not end in -s

> **apos** The ⟨deers⟩ best habitat is a deep, unpopulated woodland.
>
> **apos** The ⟨childrens⟩ clothes are on the third floor.

> **SOLUTION**
>
> **The deer's best habitat is a deep, unpopulated woodland.**
> **The children's clothes are on the third floor.**
>
> When a plural noun does not end in -s, use an apostrophe and an -s to form the possessive of the noun.

PROBLEM 4

Possessive personal pronouns

> **apos** The poster is ⟨her's⟩ but the magazine is ⟨their's⟩.

SOLUTION

The poster is hers, but the magazine is theirs.

Do not use apostrophes with possessive personal pronouns.

PROBLEM 5

Confusion between its *and* it's

apos	The old tree was the last to lose (it's) leaves.
apos	(Its) the best CD I have ever heard them put out.

SOLUTION

The old tree was the last to lose its leaves.
It's the best CD I have ever heard them put out.

Use an apostrophe to form the contraction of *it is*. The possessive of the personal pronoun *it* does not take an apostrophe.

More help with apostrophes and possessives is available in Lesson 84.

Troubleshooter 43

Incorrect Capitalization

PROBLEM 1

Words that refer to ethnic groups, nationalities, and languages

cap   Many irish citizens speak both english and gaelic.

SOLUTION

Many Irish citizens speak both English and Gaelic.

Capitalize proper nouns and adjectives referring to ethnic groups, nationalities, and languages.

PROBLEM 2

The first word of a direct quotation

cap   Yuri said, "the rain off the bay always blows this way."

SOLUTION

Yuri said, "The rain off the bay always blows this way."

Capitalize the first word of a direct quotation if it is a complete sentence. A direct quotation is the speaker's exact words.

More help with capitalization is available in Lessons 73–76.

44 Writer's Choice Grammar Workbook 8, Troubleshooter

Grammar

Name _____ Class _____ Date _____

Unit 1: Subjects, Predicates, and Sentences

Lesson 1
Kinds of Sentences: Declarative and Interrogative

A group of words that expresses a complete thought is a **sentence**. All sentences begin with a capital letter. A **declarative sentence** makes a statement. It ends with a period. An **interrogative sentence** asks a question. It ends with a question mark.

Florida summers are very hot. (declarative)
Are summers in Florida very hot? (interrogative)

▶ **Exercise 1** Write in the blank *dec.* (declarative) if the sentence makes a statement or *int.* (interrogative) if the sentence asks a question.

__int.__   Can you help me with my algebra?

__dec.__ **1.** I'm going swimming today.

__int.__ **2.** Is the president addressing the nation on television tonight?

__dec.__ **3.** My grandfather was an army sergeant.

__dec.__ **4.** Mitchell plans to audition for the choir.

__dec.__ **5.** Margaret bought this dress in Mexico.

__int.__ **6.** Claire, will you help me practice my lines?

__int.__ **7.** Are you going to camp this summer?

__dec.__ **8.** You are good at solving puzzles.

__int.__ **9.** How long did it take you to read *The Red Badge of Courage?*

__dec.__ **10.** Our soccer team won the league championship.

__dec.__ **11.** The butterfly slowly unfolded its wings.

__dec.__ **12.** The wind knocked down a large tree.

__int.__ **13.** Have you met the new teacher yet?

__int.__ **14.** Which wrestlers won their matches?

__dec.__ **15.** The title of the mystery novel was misleading.

__dec.__ 16. Kyle pulled the burrs out of Queenie's matted hair.

__int.__ 17. What is the weather forecast for tomorrow?

__int.__ 18. Has anyone seen my blue folder?

__int.__ 19. Are snowflakes all the same shape?

__int.__ 20. Do you and your friends appreciate the same kinds of music?

▶ **Exercise 2** Punctuate each of the following sentences with a period or question mark.

The new car is midnight blue.

1. Have you met Danielle yet?
2. Who is hungry?
3. This computer doesn't work.
4. The fire engines roared past us.
5. Suzanne wandered home from school.
6. Did Clyde get the part he wanted in the musical comedy?
7. The desk was cluttered with all kinds of papers.
8. Janice and Shawna went to the movies last night.
9. Will you put up a new bulletin board?
10. Will Pablo know what to do?
11. Paula opened the door carefully.
12. Can you hear the music from the auditorium?
13. Does anyone here know Italian?
14. Akira does not like to read mysteries.
15. Did you read the entire book last night?
16. Could everyone stay seated until we're finished?
17. How much would this famous painting be worth?
18. The clouds gave way to sunshine.
19. What made the dog bark?
20. The window blinds are closed.

Name _____ Class _____ Date _____

Lesson 2
Kinds of Sentences: Exclamatory and Imperative

A sentence may do more than express a statement or ask a question. An **exclamatory sentence** expresses a strong emotion. It ends with an exclamation point. An **imperative sentence** gives a command or makes a request. It ends with a period.

Look out! (strong emotion)
Don't forget the party Saturday. (command)
Please mail these letters on your way to Janet's house. (request)

▶ **Exercise 1** Write in the blank *exc.* (exclamatory) if the sentence expresses a strong feeling. Write *imp.* (imperative) if the sentence gives a command or makes a request. Add a period or an exclamation point as needed.

imp.   Remember to keep your eyes on the ball at all times**.**

imp.   1. Don't stay up too late**.**

exc.   2. What a terrific day we had at the zoo**!**

exc. *or* **imp.**   3. Watch out for that low branch**! or .**

imp.   4. Tell me more about your fishing trip**.**

exc. *or* **imp.**   5. Don't run in the halls**! or .**

imp.   6. Buy more glue when you go to the store**.**

imp.   7. Clean up your desk, please**.**

imp.   8. Let's go watch the parade**.**

exc.   9. That muddy dog just stole my hamburger**!**

imp.   10. Try to solve the puzzle before the contestant does**.**

imp.   11. Let the baby sleep**.**

exc.   12. Oh, you just sat in some wet paint**!**

imp.   13. Feed the dog at the same time every day**.**

imp.   14. Turn in your book report next week**.**

exc.   15. I can't wait until Grandma gets here**!**

Name _____ Class _____ Date _____

___imp.___ 16. Go to sleep.

___imp.___ 17. Walk through the flower bed carefully.

___exc. *or* imp.___ 18. Speak louder! or .

___exc.___ 19. I have never felt so frightened!

___imp.___ 20. Play that song again.

___imp.___ 21. Be home by ten o'clock.

___imp.___ 22. Wait for me at the corner.

___imp.___ 23. Put more paint on the other side.

___imp.___ 24. Don't cross the street against the light.

___imp.___ 25. Wait for an hour before you go swimming.

___exc.___ 26. That's my favorite song!

___imp.___ 27. Put on some mosquito repellant.

___imp.___ 28. Walk quickly to the nearest exit.

___exc.___ 29. This movie is funny!

___exc.___ 30. I never even saw the ball!

___imp.___ 31. Answer the phone politely.

___exc.___ 32. I aced the test!

___imp.___ 33. Please come to our party.

___exc.___ 34. You did a great job!

___exc.___ 35. I lost my keys!

___imp.___ 36. Be sure to remember your umbrella.

___imp.___ 37. Be careful going down the stairs.

___imp.___ 38. Bring a Number 2 pencil to class.

___imp.___ 39. Watch how I do this.

___exc.___ 40. This food is delicious!

Name _____ Class _____ Date _____

Lesson 3
Sentence Fragments

Every sentence must have a subject and a predicate to express a complete thought. The **subject** part of a sentence names who or what the sentence is about. The **predicate** part tells what the subject does or has. It can also describe what the subject is or is like.

SUBJECT   PREDICATE
My friend Joel   will play in the volleyball tournament.

A **sentence fragment** is a group of words that lacks a subject, a predicate, or both. A fragment does not express a complete thought.

Will play in the volleyball tournament. (lacks a subject)
My friend Joel. (lacks a predicate)
Without a doubt. (lacks both a subject and a predicate)
Without a doubt, my friend Joel will play in the volleyball tournament. (expresses a complete thought)

▶ **Exercise 1** Write *sentence* in the blank before each word group that expresses a complete thought. Write *fragment* next to each word group that does not express a complete thought.

__fragment__ Wore her warmest sweater.
__sentence__ 1. The survivors of the earthquake showed great courage.
__fragment__ 2. Caused problems everywhere.
__sentence__ 3. Every Sunday their family went hiking.
__sentence__ 4. Even the rain couldn't dampen their spirits.
__fragment__ 5. Rode calmly and quietly in the backseat.
__fragment__ 6. Rose in the air like a bird.
__fragment__ 7. Of his meal untouched.
__sentence__ 8. Hundreds of firefighters fought the forest fires last summer.
__sentence__ 9. The thought escaped him.
__fragment__ 10. As fragile as glass.
__fragment__ 11. In the park for our picnic.

Unit 1, Subjects, Predicates, and Sentences

Name _____ Class _____ Date _____

__sentence__ 12. Our newspaper arrived late on Tuesday.

__fragment__ 13. Janette, who's coming at four.

__fragment__ 14. Simply everywhere.

__fragment__ 15. Postponed for the second time.

__sentence__ 16. Ted climbed to the top of the stadium.

__sentence__ 17. They played their very best.

__fragment__ 18. In every nook and cranny.

__fragment__ 19. Available at five o'clock.

__sentence__ 20. She was preparing her résumé.

▶ **Exercise 2** Write a complete sentence by adding a subject, a predicate, or both to each sentence fragment. Punctuate your sentences correctly. **Answers may vary.**

Grinned and cackled. **The ugly troll grinned and cackled.**

1. Marla and Kimberly. **Marla and Kimberly walked home.**
2. On the shelves. **Theo put the books on the shelves.**
3. Dusted the books. **Ramona dusted the books.**
4. Maple and elm trees. **Maple and elm trees lined the avenue.**
5. Greeted Eloisa. **Mr. Sanders greeted Eloisa.**
6. At the library. **Rosa's class looked at books at the library.**
7. John Kimura the dentist. **John Kimura, the dentist, opened his office.**
8. Looked at Isabel. **Everyone looked at Isabel.**
9. Flat, sandy fields. **Flat, sandy fields surround the town.**
10. The mystery of space. **The mystery of space still amazes us.**
11. In the closet. **She hung her coat in the closet.**
12. Busy traffic. **Busy traffic clogged city streets.**
13. Carmen and her sister. **Carmen and her sister baked cookies.**
14. Followed the directions. **The tourists followed the directions.**
15. Saw the falling star. **Steve and Todd saw the falling star.**
16. Around the bend. **The raft floated around the bend.**

Name _____ Class _____ Date _____

Lesson 4
Subjects and Predicates: Simple and Complete

Both a subject and a predicate may consist of more than one word. The **complete subject** includes all of the words in the subject part of a sentence. The **complete predicate** includes all of the words in the predicate part of a sentence.

COMPLETE SUBJECT | COMPLETE PREDICATE
My younger brother | likes alphabet soup for lunch.

The **simple subject** is the main word or group of words in the complete subject. The **simple predicate** is the main word or group of words in the complete predicate. The simple predicate is always a **verb**, a word or words that express an action or a state of being.

SIMPLE SUBJECT | SIMPLE PREDICATE
My younger **brother** | **likes** alphabet soup for lunch.

▶ **Exercise 1** Draw a vertical line between the complete subject and the complete predicate.

People | call Australia the continent "down under."

1. Australia | is one of the most spectacular countries in the world.
2. The country | is both the smallest continent and the largest island.
3. This small continent | lies in the Southern Hemisphere.
4. The coastline of Australia | is irregular.
5. It | measures 12,210 miles.
6. The island state of Tasmania | once formed the southeastern corner of the mainland.
7. The Great Barrier Reef | continues along the eastern coast for 1,250 miles.
8. Four species of coral reef | compose the chain of reefs and islands.
9. Australia's western regions | form a great plateau.
10. The climate | ranges from temperate to tropical.
11. Forty percent of Australia | has only two seasons: hot and wet or warm and dry.
12. The average rainfall | ranges from five to fifteen inches.
13. Australia's natural lakes | fill with water only after heavy rains.

Unit 1, Subjects, Predicates, and Sentences 53

Name _____ Class _____ Date _____

14. The country's major lakes are salt water.

15. Most of the land is desert.

16. Australia's four deserts include the Simpson, the Gibson, the Great Sandy, and the Great Victoria.

17. Few rivers exist in the western part of this country.

18. Aqueducts and tunnels channel water from the Snowy Mountains for irrigation and hydroelectric power in the southeast.

19. The Australian Alps rise to 7,310 feet in the Eastern Highlands.

20. Ayers Rock in central Australia is a tourist attraction.

▶ **Exercise 2** Draw one line under the simple subject and two lines under the simple predicate.

<u>Australia</u> <u><u>has</u></u> many unique plants and animals.

1. <u>Forests</u> <u><u>cover</u></u> the east coast of Tasmania.
2. The <u>forests</u> <u><u>consist</u></u> mainly of pine trees.
3. The <u>dingo</u> <u><u>is</u></u> a doglike animal.
4. <u>It</u> <u><u>hunts</u></u> sheep.
5. <u>Dingoes</u> <u><u>prey</u></u> on kangaroos as well.
6. Many <u>people</u> <u><u>find</u></u> wallabies interesting.
7. <u>They</u> <u><u>are</u></u> small members of the kangaroo family.
8. <u>Wallabies</u> <u><u>belong</u></u> to the marsupial order.
9. Female <u>wallabies</u> <u><u>carry</u></u> their young in a pouch.
10. Two <u>species</u> of crocodiles <u><u>dwell</u></u> in Australia.
11. The Queensland <u>lungfish</u> <u><u>has</u></u> no gills.
12. A <u>lungfish</u> <u><u>breathes</u></u> with a single lung.
13. Six hundred fifty <u>species</u> of birds <u><u>live</u></u> in Australia.
14. One hundred <u>species</u> of venomous snakes <u><u>lurk</u></u> on the ground.
15. The <u>ocean</u> <u><u>offers</u></u> seventy species of sharks.
16. <u>Sharks</u> <u><u>pose</u></u> no threat to people in most cases.

Name _____ Class _____ Date _____

Lesson 5
Subjects and Predicates: Compound

A sentence may have more than one simple subject or simple predicate.

A **compound subject** is two or more simple subjects that have the same predicate. The subjects are joined by *and, or, either...or, neither...nor,* or *but.*

Oregon and **Washington** lie in the Pacific Northwest. (compound subject)

A **compound predicate** is two or more simple predicates, or verbs, that have the same subject. The verbs are connected by *and, or, either...or, neither...nor,* or *but.*

Many people neither **enjoy** nor **appreciate** modern art. (compound predicate)

▶ **Exercise 1** Each of these sentences has either a compound subject, a compound predicate, or both. Draw one line under the simple subjects in each compound subject. Draw two lines under the simple predicates in each compound predicate.

Water <u>streamed</u> across the street and <u>ran</u> into the gutter.

1. <u>Apples</u> and <u>pears</u> grow on trees.
2. Workers <u>pick</u> apples and <u>package</u> them for sale.
3. <u>Joi</u> and her <u>sisters</u> sang for the congregation.
4. <u>Wes</u> or <u>Raquel</u> showed the office to the guests.
5. We <u>ate</u> and <u>slept</u> on the bus.
6. The <u>ceiling</u> and the <u>walls</u> are the same color.
7. Both <u>Arizona</u> and <u>New Mexico</u> have hot deserts.
8. Thoughtful <u>neighbors</u> and <u>friends</u> of the family sent sympathy cards.
9. Either <u>red</u> or <u>blue</u> clashes with this color.
10. <u>Copper</u> and <u>iron</u> have many uses.
11. In 1947, French president <u>Charles de Gaulle</u> and his <u>party</u> strengthened the central government of France.
12. Many Europeans both <u>understand</u> and <u>use</u> the English language.
13. <u>Crocodiles</u> and <u>alligators</u> <u>swim</u> in the water but <u>hunt</u> on land.

Name _____ Class _____ Date _____

14. Boll weevils seek the scent of cotton and destroy the plants.
15. A city council or other government body discusses the proposed law and votes on it.
16. Both tennis and badminton require rackets.
17. Puppies and kittens play and sleep most of the day.
18. Scientists perform research with care and conduct experiments with even more care.
19. Crabs and lobsters crawl along the ocean floor.
20. Farmers grow crops in the summer and harvest them in the fall.
21. Marie and Pierre Curie won the 1903 Nobel Prize in physics.
22. Exercise and diet are the keys to good health.
23. Fred Astaire and Ginger Rogers danced, acted, and sang in many movies.
24. Dams hold back water and prevent flooding.
25. The papers, books, and pencils lie in a neat pile on the desk.
26. Students study in the classroom and exercise in the gymnasium.
27. A calculator or computer adds, subtracts, multiplies, and divides rapidly.
28. One large box or several small cartons hold many books.
29. Trains and trucks carry large amounts of food and goods.
30. Tomas and his family swam and hiked last weekend.
31. Water freezes at 32°F and boils at 212°F.
32. The soccer team ran and kicked its way to victory.
33. Hurricanes or other strong winds uproot trees.
34. The carpenters measured and cut the wood for our new barn.
35. Cars and trucks burn diesel fuel.
36. The president and her cabinet posed for photographs.
37. The freshman class raised money and donated presents to charity.
38. Lorraine read the book and wrote her report in one week.
39. Prisms and other glass objects separate light into its component colors.
40. The Congo River begins in Zaire, flows 2,718 miles, and empties into the Atlantic Ocean.

Lesson 6
Simple and Compound Sentences

A **simple sentence** has one subject and one predicate. The subject and the predicate in a simple sentence may be simple or compound.

SUBJECT	PREDICATE
Oscar	fed the dog.
Oscar and Cathy	fed and groomed the dog.

A **compound sentence** contains two or more simple sentences joined by a comma and a coordinating conjunction (*or, nor, and, either...or, neither...nor, but*) or by a semicolon.

Oscar fed the dog, **and** he groomed him.
Oscar's dog likes to run; Cathy's dog prefers to sleep.

Two or more simple sentences joined incorrectly result in a **run-on sentence**. Correct a run-on sentence by writing separate sentences, by adding a comma and a conjunction, or by adding a semicolon.

Patti practiced every day for the recital she played flawlessly. (run-on)

Patti practiced every day for the recital. She played flawlessly. (separated)

Patti practiced every day for the recital, and she played flawlessly. (joined by a comma and a conjunction)

Patti practiced every day for the recital; she played flawlessly. (joined by a semicolon)

▶ **Exercise 1** Write *S* in the blank before each simple sentence, *C* before each compound sentence, and *R* before each run-on sentence.

__C__ The trumpets blared, and the king entered the room.

__S__ 1. Ketchup makes french fries taste better.

__S__ 2. I walked and walked for days.

__C__ 3. Hydrogen has weight, but you can't weigh it on an ordinary scale.

__R__ 4. Air is taken into the lungs oxygen is absorbed into the bloodstream.

__C__ 5. You can buy your ticket in advance, or you can buy it at the door.

__S__ 6. Radar detects objects in darkness and bad weather.

__C__ 7. Humans can't see well in the dark, nor can they hear sounds more than about one kilometer away.

Name _____ Class _____ Date _____

__C___ 8. I read it, but I didn't understand it.

__S___ 9. Korean foods and Thai foods can be very spicy.

__C___ 10. You can ask questions, but you may not find the answers.

__S___ 11. The choir sang and clapped for the audience.

__S___ 12. Neither fog nor hail stops the letter carrier.

__R___ 13. Max found the light bulb he couldn't find a ladder.

__C___ 14. The first modern computer was built in 1946; it processed 5,000 calculations per minute.

__S___ 15. The South American condor is smaller and heavier than the California condor.

▶ **Exercise 2** Draw one line under each simple subject and two lines under each simple predicate. Circle each coordinating conjunction.

Stuart dialed the phone, (and) he waited for someone to answer.

1. The athletes ran for a long time, (and) they breathed hard.
2. I went there last year, (but) I cancelled my reservation this year.
3. She called me, (but) she wrote more often.
4. I studied hard, (and) I passed the test.
5. Did you find it, (or) do you need my help?
6. The skies were cloudy, (but) I saw no rain.
7. He just sat there; nobody talked to him.
8. Most plants require plenty of sunlight, (but) some plants thrive in low light.
9. Colorado is a beautiful state, (and) it has nice weather.
10. The game was close, (but) we won it in the last minute.
11. I can ride a bike, (and) I can also fix it.
12. Chimpanzees live in the rain forests of Africa; they eat berries, fruit, and some meat.
13. Pluto is the smallest planet in the solar system, (and) it is farthest from the sun.
14. Rice tastes good, (but) I prefer potatoes.
15. Tanya saw the birds, (and) she heard their calls.

58   Writer's Choice Grammar Workbook 8, Unit 1

Name _____ Class _____ Date _____

# Unit 1 **Review**

▶ **Exercise 1** Draw a vertical line between each complete subject and complete predicate. If a sentence is compound, circle the coordinating conjunction.

Evelyn | heard the birds, (but) she | couldn't see them.

1. An American, Theodore Maiman, | developed the laser in 1960.
2. The Canadian flag | bears a red maple leaf.
3. The flags of Italy and Hungary | share the same colors, (but) the stripes | differ.
4. Scott Joplin | received a special Pulitzer citation in 1976.
5. Amphibians and reptiles | are cold-blooded animals.
6. Chicago and Atlanta | have big, busy airports, (but) Chicago's airport | is busier.
7. Babe Zaharias | won three U.S. Women's Open golf titles, (and) Betsy Rawls | claimed the title four times.
8. Vostok, Antarctica, | holds the record for the lowest temperature on the earth's surface.
9. A galaxy | is a system of stars, dust, and gas.
10. Sharon | walked out the door, (and) everyone | waved good-bye.
11. The Senate | has 100 members, (and) the House of Representatives | consists of 435 members.
12. Islam | is the major religion of northern Africa and the Middle East.
13. Both Presidents Harrison and Tyler | began their terms in 1841.
14. The respiratory system | provides the body with oxygen and rids it of carbon dioxide.
15. The plate tectonic theory | explains certain changes in the earth's crust.
16. Nina | wore a blue shirt, (and) both she and Robin | wore blue jeans.
17. The carpenters | painted and wallpapered the bedroom and the hallway.
18. Billie Jean King | holds four U.S. tennis championship titles and won at Wimbledon six times.
19. Umberto Nobile, an Italian, | flew over the North Pole in an airship in 1926.
20. Warm air | expands and rises, (and) cool air | descends.

Unit 1, Subjects, Predicates, and Sentences **59**

Name _____ Class _____ Date _____

Cumulative Review: Unit 1

▶ **Exercise 1** Write *declarative, interrogative, exclamatory,* or *imperative* in the blank to identify the kind of sentence. Add the correct punctuation mark. Write *fragment* if the word group is not a complete thought.

imperative	Bring me a glass of water, please.
declarative	1. On Tuesday morning the choir leaves for its European tour.
declarative	2. Our area of the state has received twelve inches of snow.
interrogative	3. Which person concealed the evidence?
exclamatory	4. What a mess that puppy made!
fragment	5. On a day everyone could be there
imperative	6. Sit over here away from the door.
declarative	7. Brianna was promoted to editor of the school newspaper.
interrogative	8. Have you ever tried fly-fishing?
exclamatory	9. This ride is making me dizzy!
imperative	10. Meet us outside the restaurant at 11:30 A.M.

▶ **Exercise 2** Write *S* in the blank before each simple sentence and *C* before each compound sentence. Draw one line under each simple subject and two lines under each simple predicate.

S	The nail had punctured the right front tire.
S	1. The tallow was used in candles and soap.
C	2. Are these blueprints all right, or will you need others?
C	3. Pikes Peak is in Colorado; it is 14,110 feet above sea level.
S	4. Outdoor sports are great, but only in the summer.
S	5. Cardinals nest in our yard every spring.
C	6. Ballet interests Emily; she is seeing *The Nutcracker* this weekend.
S	7. People lease cars from Uncle Ferdinand.
C	8. We decided on the Italian food, and Margo ordered Mexican food.

60 Writer's Choice Grammar Workbook 8, Unit 1

Name _____ Class _____ Date _____

Unit 2: Nouns

Lesson 7
Nouns: Proper and Common

A **noun** names a person, place, thing, or idea. When a word names a specific person, place, thing, or idea, it is a **proper noun**. The first word and all other important words in proper nouns are capitalized. When a word names any person, place, thing, or idea, it is a **common noun**. Common nouns are not capitalized.

	PERSON	PLACE	THING	IDEA
Proper Noun:	Sinia Yakov	Canada	Bill of Rights	Islam
Common Noun:	man	country	document	religion

▶ **Exercise 1** Underline each common noun and circle each proper noun. Draw three lines under each proper noun that should be capitalized.

Dr. martin luther king Jr. was the highly respected african american who led the civil rights movement during the 1950s and 1960s.

1. A baby named martin luther king jr. was born in atlanta, Georgia.

2. His family lived in a two-story house on Auburn avenue.

3. His father, martin Luther King sr., was a minister and the son of a sharecropper.

4. His mother, Alberta williams king, was a teacher.

5. King skipped two grades at booker T. Washington high school.

6. Still a teenager, king graduated from morehouse College.

7. King first thought of becoming a doctor or a lawyer but finally decided to go into the ministry.

8. While still at morehouse, king was ordained in the church of his father.

9. King was elected co-pastor at the church upon his graduation from college.

Unit 2, Nouns 61

10. The hardworking young man went on to graduate school at crozer theological Seminary in chester, Pennsylvania.

11. King was very intelligent and an avid reader.

12. King studied the ideas of people such as martin luther, mohandas Gandhi, jesus of nazareth, aristotle, plato, and adam smith.

13. King earned the degree of bachelor of divinity at crozer.

14. King won a fellowship to go to the university of his choice for his doctorate.

15. King chose to go to boston university.

16. King also took courses in philosophy at Harvard.

17. While at boston university, king met an intelligent and beautiful woman named coretta scott.

18. Coretta scott was a soprano, studying voice at the new england conservatory of music.

19. King and scott married a few years after their first encounter.

20. Coretta and Martin Luther King jr. had four children: yolanda denise, Martin luther III, dexter, and Bernice albertine.

21. While still working on his doctoral degree, king received a letter from a church in montgomery, Alabama.

22. The letter stated that the church would be happy to have king preach.

23. The church was located on dexter avenue and was called the dexter avenue baptist church.

24. The church was close to the impressive alabama state capitol, where the legislature meets.

25. Ironically, Jefferson davis had been sworn in as the new president of the Confederacy on the steps of that same building.

62 Writer's Choice Grammar Workbook 8, Unit 2

Name _____ Class _____ Date _____

Lesson 8
Nouns: Concrete and Abstract

Concrete nouns name things that can be experienced with any of the five senses—touch, sight, hearing, smell, and taste. **Abstract nouns** name ideas, qualities, or feelings that cannot be experienced with any of the five senses.

Abstract Nouns:	sadness	truth	freedom	intelligence	justice
Concrete Nouns:	frown	book	rain	library	music

▶ **Exercise 1** Underline each concrete noun once and each abstract noun twice.

My <u>dad</u> tells me <u><u>cleanliness</u></u> is important.

1. A commercial <u>pilot</u> must have a lot of flying <u><u>experience</u></u>.
2. My <u>uncle</u>, <u>aunt</u>, and <u>cousin</u> live in a large <u>trailer</u>.
3. The <u>judge</u> reminded the <u>witness</u> to tell the <u><u>truth</u></u>.
4. The <u>inventor</u> had an <u><u>idea</u></u> that would help the auto <u>industry</u> improve <u><u>safety</u></u>.
5. The playful <u>beagle</u> liked to chase its <u>tail</u>.
6. The hardworking <u>farmer</u> was disappointed with the <u>weather</u>.
7. The <u>walls</u> and <u>ceiling</u> of the <u>room</u> were black with <u><u>age</u></u> and <u>dirt</u>.
8. <u>Clouds</u> covered the <u>sun</u> and <u>sky</u>.
9. Many <u>people</u> voted in the <u><u>elections</u></u> last <u><u>fall</u></u>.
10. The <u>veterinarian</u> spent <u><u>time</u></u> and <u><u>energy</u></u> examining <u>horses</u>.
11. My <u>cat</u> gets great <u><u>pleasure</u></u> on the <u>windowsill</u> on a sunny <u><u>day</u></u>. **(or day)**
12. During the holiday <u>season</u>, the <u>malls</u> are bursting with <u>people</u>.
13. The <u>museum</u> held <u>paintings</u> and <u>sculptures</u> of great <u><u>beauty</u></u>.
14. The girl's <u><u>bravery</u></u> during the <u>disaster</u> did not go unnoticed. **or disaster**
15. As huge <u>waves</u> crashed onto the <u>shore</u>, the <u>beachcombers</u> fled in <u><u>fear</u></u>.
16. The college <u>students</u> lived in a quiet <u>dormitory</u>.
17. The <u>florist</u> made a <u>bouquet</u> of <u>roses</u> for their <u><u>anniversary</u></u>.
18. The <u>teacher</u> at the <u>preschool</u> showed much <u><u>patience</u></u>.

Name _____ Class _____ Date _____

19. Small children like to play with blocks.
20. The tennis player hit the ball with accuracy and determination.
21. At the traffic light, the driver pressed the brake.
22. The long-legged spider spun a web under the stairs in the basement.
23. The newspaper had a big article about the economy.
24. The black crow sat on the fence and stared at the scarecrow.
25. Using coupons is a good way for shoppers to cut costs.
26. The triathlete collapsed with exhaustion after reaching the finish line.
27. While taking the test, the student frowned in concentration.
28. Tourists watched in fascination as the volcano oozed lava.
29. The leek is a type of onion that blooms in the spring.
30. The bird in the tree held the interest of the cat.
31. The painter looked at the canvas in satisfaction.
32. After listening to the patient, the psychologist fell deep into thought.
33. Late into the evening, the chemist worked in the laboratory.
34. The children took great care to be gentle when holding the hamster.
35. The bodybuilder lifted the heavy barbell with ease.
36. Unable to find the toy, the baby cried in frustration.
37. The athlete possessed raw talent and ability.
38. A conference to deal with hunger and starvation was held in a hotel.
39. A well-balanced diet helps to maintain good health.
40. Scientists have found that many industrial processes are not good for the environment.

▶ **Writing Link** Write a paragraph that describes your city or town and what you like or dislike about it. Use both concrete and abstract nouns.

_____
_____
_____

64 Writer's Choice Grammar Workbook 8, Unit 2

Name _____ Class _____ Date _____

Lesson 9
Nouns: Compounds, Plurals, and Possessives

Compound nouns are nouns that are made up of two or more words. Compound nouns can be one word, like the word *football,* or more than one word, like *rocking chair.* Other compound nouns have two or more words that are joined by hyphens, such as *hand-me-down.*

To form the plural of most compound nouns written as one word, add *-s* or *-es.* To form the plural of compound nouns that are hyphenated or written as more than one word, make the most important part of the noun plural.

ONE WORD
snowmobile**s**, baseball**s**, grandfather**s**

HYPHENATED
father**s**-in-law   baby-sitter**s**   runner**s**-up

MORE THAN ONE WORD
home run**s**   music box**es**   quarter horse**s**   surgeon**s** general

A **possessive noun** names who or what has something. Possessive nouns can be common or proper nouns, singular or plural, compound or not. To form the possessive of all singular nouns and of plural nouns not ending in *-s,* add an apostrophe and *-s.* To form the possessive of plural nouns already ending in *-s,* add only an apostrophe.

boy**'s**   boss**'s**   Luis**'s**   women**'s**   puppies**'**

▶ **Exercise 1** Write in the blank the plural form of each compound noun.

jelly bean **jelly beans**

1. fund-raiser **fund-raisers**
2. attorney-at-law **attorneys-at-law**
3. sister-in-law **sisters-in-law**
4. nutcracker **nutcrackers**
5. stomachache **stomachaches**
6. funny bone **funny bones**
7. sweatshirt **sweatshirts**
8. motor home **motor homes**
9. sergeant at arms **sergeants at arms**
10. beehive **beehives**
11. color guard **color guards**
12. steam iron **steam irons**
13. farmhand **farmhands**
14. workshop **workshops**

Unit 2, Nouns   65

Name _____ Class _____ Date _____

15. stepfather __**stepfathers**__ 18. minute hand __**minute hands**__
16. mailbox __**mailboxes**__ 19. drawstring __**drawstrings**__
17. bill of health __**bills of health**__ 20. field trip __**field trips**__

▶ **Exercise 2** Complete each sentence by writing the correct possessive form of the noun in parentheses.

__**Marietta's**__ hands felt cold and clammy. (Marietta)

1. The young sailor sounded the __**ship's**__ horn. (ship)
2. The __**players'**__ performance during the big game was not good enough to win. (players)
3. __**Dennis's**__ test scores improved dramatically. (Dennis)
4. The __**bobcat's**__ teeth were sharp as razors. (bobcat)
5. The __**Ramoses'**__ vacation was relaxing and fun. (Ramoses)
6. I can do a lot of my homework on my __**parents'**__ computer. (parents)
7. The __**birds'**__ loud and persistent chirping caused Cole to wake up. (birds)
8. The teacher enjoyed the sound of the __**children's**__ laughter. (children)
9. During autumn, the __**leaves'**__ colors change. (leaves)
10. The __**Liberty Bell's**__ weight is more than one ton. (Liberty Bell)
11. The __**women's**__ movement began to gain momentum. (women)
12. After the touchdown, the __**fans'**__ cheering was deafening. (fans)
13. The hook caught in the __**fish's**__ mouth. (fish)
14. In the sunlight, the __**plant's**__ leaves grew wildly. (plant)
15. The __**cook's**__ soup was piping hot and delicious. (cook)
16. __**Illinois's**__ largest city is Chicago. (Illinois)
17. The __**bus's**__ route never changed. (bus)
18. __**Queen Victoria's**__ reign was one of the longest in Great Britain's history. (Queen Victoria)

Name _____ Class _____ Date _____

Lesson 10
Nouns: Collective

A **collective noun** names a group that is made up of individuals.

The **family** struggled through the **crowd** to see the **band**.

COLLECTIVE NOUNS

| class | family | herd | audience | orchestra | panel |
| staff | team | swarm | jury | flock | |

Collective nouns can have either a singular or a plural meaning. When referring to the group as a unit, the noun has a singular meaning and takes a singular verb. When referring to the individual members of the group, the noun has a plural meaning and takes a plural verb.

The **team works** on its defensive plays.
The **team go** to their individual lockers.

▶ **Exercise 1** Underline the verb form in parentheses that best completes each sentence.

The audience (leaves, <u>leave</u>) their seats.

1. The book club (discusses, <u>discuss</u>) their personal opinions of the plot.
2. The class (<u>is</u>, are) going on a bus to the art museum.
3. The choir from East High School (<u>sings</u>, sing) the loudest.
4. The elephant herd (<u>makes</u>, make) a thundering noise during a stampede.
5. The baseball team (<u>boasts</u>, boast) an excellent batting average.
6. The budget committee (<u>reaches</u>, reach) a final decision.
7. The entire class (<u>takes</u>, take) a trip to Washington, D.C.
8. The theater troupe (comes, <u>come</u>) out separately at the end of the play.
9. The bee swarm (<u>buzzes</u>, buzz) around the hive.
10. The jury (argues, <u>argue</u>) among themselves over the verdict.
11. The debating team (<u>wins</u>, win) almost every time.
12. The band (puts, <u>put</u>) their instruments away after practice.
13. The barbershop quartet (knows, <u>know</u>) their individual parts.

Name _____ Class _____ Date _____

14. The audience (**gives**, give) the singer a standing ovation.

15. The class (reports, **report**) on their chosen topics.

16. The math department (decides, **decide**) which classes they will teach.

17. Boy Scout Troop 10 (**raises**, raise) money for a camping trip.

18. The Supreme Court (**rules**, rule) on many of its cases each year.

19. The wolf pack (**decreases**, decrease) in size after a hard winter.

20. City council (goes, **go**) to their respective seats before the meeting begins.

21. The flock (**flies**, fly) in a southerly direction.

22. The restaurant staff (shares, **share**) their tips with each other.

23. The army platoon (**marches**, march) on the military base.

24. The U.S. Congress (**consists**, consist) of members from all fifty states.

25. College athletics (**seems**, seem) to be a profession in some cases.

26. The crowd (**stirs**, stir) as the politician takes the platform.

27. The family (sleeps, **sleep**) soundly in their rooms.

28. The orchestra (**draws**, draw) a big crowd.

29. The track team (**runs**, run) well as a whole.

30. The subcommittee (**calls**, call) for a meeting with the entire committee.

31. The band (**appeals**, appeal) to people of all ages.

32. The school board (**presents**, present) its proposal to the superintendent.

33. The volleyball team (practices, **practice**) their serving techniques.

34. The Music Club (**listens**, listen) to operas together every Tuesday.

35. The public (**supports**, support) its mayor.

36. The herd (**roams**, roam) the countryside aimlessly.

37. The jury (**submits**, submit) its verdict to the judge.

38. The mob of protestors (**is**, are) getting out of hand.

39. The Senate (**contains**, contain) fewer members than the House of Representatives.

40. The choir (knows, **know**) their individual parts.

Name _____ Class _____ Date _____

Lesson 11
Distinguishing Plurals, Possessives, and Contractions

A **contraction** is a word made by combining two words into one and leaving out one or more letters from the two words. An apostrophe shows where the letters have been omitted.

can + not = can't   singer + is = singer's

Most plural and possessive nouns and certain contractions end with the letter *-s*. As a result, they sound alike, but their spellings and meanings are different.

Plural Noun	The **singers** wrote the song.
Plural Possessive Noun	The **singers'** song is enjoyable.
Singular Possessive Noun	We heard the **singer's** song.
Contraction	The **singer's** the songwriter.

▶ **Exercise 1** Write *pl.* above each plural noun (not including plural possessives), *poss.* above each possessive noun, and *con.* above each contraction.

            con.   **pl.**
Ernest Hemingway's one of the most influential American writers of the twentieth century.

     con.   **pl.**
1. Hemingway's won two prestigious awards—the Nobel Prize and the Pulitzer Prize.
    poss.
2. Hemingway's birthplace was Oak Park, Illinois.
                                         poss.
3. As a boy and youth, Hemingway spent many a summer's day in northern Michigan.
    poss.
4. Hemingway's family owned a cottage on Waloon Lake.
                pl.
5. Hemingway made many friends there.
    pl.   **pl.**
6. Native Americans of the region were among his group of friends.
        poss.   **pl.**   **pl.**   **pl.**
7. Some of his friends' adventures appeared in his books and short stories.
           poss.
8. The young Hemingway's writing career began in Kansas City.
               pl.   **poss.**
9. Hemingway was one of many reporters for the city's newspaper, the *Kansas City Star*.
    con.   **pl.**
10. Kansas City's one of many cities Hemingway visited.
         poss.   **pl.**
11. At age eighteen, the young man's thoughts wandered overseas.
                                                pl.
12. Hemingway traveled to Milan, Italy, on the first of his transatlantic flights.

Name _____ Class _____ Date _____

13. World War I's battles were still raging. [poss. pl.]
14. Hemingway's job was ambulance deputy with an American field service unit. [poss.]
15. The day that Hemingway arrived, a factory full of munitions blew up. [pl.]
16. After a few months' time, Hemingway was badly wounded in both legs. [poss. pl.]
17. These wartime experiences provided many of the details for Hemingway's novel about World War I, called *A Farewell to Arms*. [pl. pl. poss. pl.]
18. Several of his short stories' details can also be traced back to Hemingway's time spent in Milan. [poss. pl. poss.]
19. After the war, Hemingway took trips to many different cities and countries. [pl. pl. pl.]
20. Hemingway's known for discovering places that would later become tourist attractions. [con. pl. pl.]

▶ **Exercise 2** Underline the word in parentheses that best completes the sentence.

One of (<u>Hemingway's</u>, Hemingways') adventures was an African safari.

1. Hemingway made (preparation's, <u>preparations</u>) for the trip.
2. Some of Hemingway's finest (story's, <u>stories</u>) were written as a result of the safari.
3. The (writers', <u>writer's</u>) imagination was also captured by Spain.
4. (Hemingways, <u>Hemingway's</u>) first exposure to a bullfight overwhelmed the writer.
5. Many of his (stories, <u>stories'</u>) themes are about bullfighting.
6. Hemingway also journeyed to (<u>Switzerland's</u>, Switzerlands') cities.
7. The writer made several (<u>trips</u>, trip's) to Switzerland as a reporter for the *Toronto Star*.
8. Hemingway wrote stories about the (countries', <u>country's</u>) winter sports.
9. (<u>Readers'</u>, Readers) admiration for Hemingway's writing was strong.
10. Hemingway lived in the (United States', <u>United States</u>) for much of his adult life.
11. Hemingway put his (<u>roots</u>, root's) down in Key West, Florida, in the 1920s and 1930s.
12. Key West was a source for a great deal of Hemingway's (<u>writings</u>, writing's).
13. The themes of these stories are as diverse as the (writers, <u>writer's</u>) life.
14. (Boats', <u>Boats</u>) always appealed to Hemingway.

70 Writer's Choice Grammar Workbook 8, Unit 2

Name _____ Class _____ Date _____

Lesson 12
Appositives

An **appositive** is a noun that is placed next to, or in apposition to, another noun to identify it or add information to it.

Franklin Delano Roosevelt's wife, **Eleanor,** was a famous humanitarian.

An **appositive phrase** is a group of words that includes an appositive and other words that describe the appositive.

Roosevelt, **our thirty-second president,** was the only U.S. president to be elected to the presidency four times.

An appositive phrase that is not essential to the meaning of the sentence is set off from the rest of the sentence by commas. However, if the appositive is essential to the meaning of the sentence, commas are not used.

▶ **Exercise 1** Underline each appositive or appositive phrase, and circle the noun it identifies.

(George Washington), commander of the Continental Army, led troops during the Revolutionary War.

1. Washington's picture is on a (coin), the quarter.
2. John Adams succeeded the (president) George Washington, as head of the United States.
3. Adams's (wife,) Abigail, was well read and outspoken.
4. Thomas Jefferson wrote the first draft of a historic (document,) the Declaration of Independence.
5. Jefferson designed (Monticello,) his thirty-two room house.
6. (Dolly Madison,) wife of James Madison, rescued important government documents from the White House before fire could destroy them.
7. James Monroe was said to have nursed the wounds of the famous French (soldier) the Marquis de Lafayette.
8. Monroe was president when the United States acquired (Florida,) a populous territory.
9. (John Quincy Adams,) the son of the second president, served only one term.

Unit 2, Nouns 71

10. A former governor of New York, Martin Van Buren capitalized on the popularity of his predecessor, Andrew Jackson.

11. William Henry Harrison's nickname, "Old Tippecanoe," came from his military victory at the Battle of Tippecanoe in 1811.

12. Harrison's successor, John Tyler, was the first person to become president because of the death of the current president.

13. The "dark horse" candidate, James K. Polk, was backed by the Democratic party.

14. Polk wished to acquire California, a Mexican territory.

15. Zachary Taylor, "Old Rough and Ready," achieved much popularity as a general in the Mexican War.

16. Taylor, the twelfth president, died after only a year in office.

17. Franklin Pierce's good friend Nathaniel Hawthorne helped to promote his presidential candidacy.

18. The Supreme Court case *Dred Scott* v. *Sanford* was decided during James Buchanan's presidency.

19. Buchanan was defeated by the Republican candidate, Abraham Lincoln.

20. Lincoln, one of our greatest presidents, had to lead the country during a bloody civil war.

21. Lincoln earned the nickname the "Great Emancipator."

22. The assassin John Wilkes Booth shot and killed Lincoln one month after he began his second term.

23. The vice president, Andrew Jackson, was sworn in as president after Lincoln's death.

24. The celebrated Civil War general Ulysses S. Grant became the eighteenth president of the United States in 1869.

25. Rutherford B. Hayes's wife, Lucy, was the first wife of a president to hold a college degree.

26. The United States battleship *Maine* blew up in Cuba's harbor during William McKinley's presidency.

Unit 2 Review

▶ **Exercise 1** Underline each common noun once and each proper noun twice. Write in the blank *plural*, *possessive*, *contraction*, or *appositive* to identify the word in italics.

contraction	*Neil Armstrong's* a famous astronaut.
possessive	1. The Empire State Building used to be *America's* tallest building.
contraction	2. Jon's an excellent skater, and his *brother's* a great swimmer.
contraction	3. The *buckeye's* a kind of chestnut.
plural	4. Edwin Hubble was the first to show that the universe contains other *galaxies* besides the Milky Way.
possessive	5. The boy's teacher taught him *volleyball's* finer points.
possessive	6. The crowd at Cape Kennedy cheered the *rocket's* liftoff.
possessive	7. Neal was born on his *grandfather's* farm in western Oklahoma.
plural	8. The Pointer *Sisters* sing songs with complicated harmonies.
appositive	9. Isaiah, my best *friend*, is moving to Kansas City, Missouri.
plural	10. Governor Stevenson is the best governor our state has had in several *years*.
plural	11. The campers took backpacks and *flashlights* when they camped out in the Appalachian Mountains.
contraction	12. *Hillary's* going to try out for the next musical.
appositive	13. The musical *Oklahoma!* will be presented to the Parent-Teacher Association.
possessive	14. The contestants had to memorize one of *Robert Frost's* poems.
plural	15. The *tourists* attended the rodeo celebrating Annie Oakley.
contraction	16. *Maureen's* the most talented flutist in the Johnson Middle School Orchestra.
appositive	17. Mrs. Phillips, the children's *teacher*, has a keen sense of fashion.
possessive	18. The *fullback's* helmet fell off when he was tackled.

Unit 2, Nouns

Name _____ Class _____ Date _____

Cumulative Review: Units 1–2

▶ **Exercise 1** Draw a vertical line between the subject and the predicate. Underline the noun in parentheses that best completes each sentence.

The (<u>bicycle's</u>, bicycles) tire | rolled down the street.

1. My dad's scrambled (<u>eggs</u>, eggs') | were too runny to eat.
2. The identical (twins, <u>twins'</u>) clothes | always matched.
3. Madame Dupont | taught her (student's, <u>students</u>) how to make Croque Monsieurs.
4. I | love to read the Brontë (sisters, <u>sisters'</u>) books.
5. Carlos, Isaac, and Hasan | sold popcorn at (Saturdays', <u>Saturday's</u>) soccer match.
6. Edgar Allan (<u>Poe's</u>, Poes') story *The Black Cat* | is very scary.
7. Shirley and her (friend's, <u>friends</u>) | went to the mall after cheerleading practice.
8. John (Hancocks, <u>Hancock's</u>) signature | was the first signature on the Declaration of Independence.
9. Many tourists | are attracted to (Hawaiis', <u>Hawaii's</u>) beaches.
10. My parents' favorite singing group | was the (Beatle's, <u>Beatles</u>).
11. The collie | chewed up the (childrens', <u>children's</u>) toys.
12. My mother's (brother-in-laws, <u>brothers-in-law</u>) from Detroit | go to the Pistons' games.
13. The five (maid of honors, <u>maids of honor</u>) at my sister's wedding | wore pink.
14. The (newspapers, <u>newspapers'</u>) headlines | were about the earthquake in Japan.
15. The chicken pox | attacked both (<u>preschools'</u>, preschools) children.
16. Eugene and Jennifer | were (runner-ups, <u>runners-up</u>) in the poetry contest.
17. Paul Cézanne | painted many still-life (paintings', <u>paintings</u>).
18. The drama club | invited all the (actor's, <u>actors'</u>) families to the play's dress rehearsal.
19. My (friends', <u>friends</u>) and I | had ice cream after dinner and before the concert.
20. Susie and Maria | enjoy trying (<u>Grandmother's</u>, Grandmothers) recipes.

74 Writer's Choice Grammar Workbook 8, Unit 2

Name _____ Class _____ Date _____

Unit 3: Verbs

Lesson 13
Action Verbs

The main word in a complete predicate of a sentence is the verb. An **action verb** is a word that names an action. Action verbs can express either physical or mental actions.

The white cloud **floated** lazily across the sky. (physical action)
Mary **thought** about the painting. (mental action)

Have, has, and *had* are also action verbs when they name what the subject owns or holds.

Jim **has** an entire set of Mark Twain books. (owns)
Jim **has** experience as a character actor. (holds)

▶ **Exercise 1** Draw two lines under the action verb in each sentence. Write *physical* or *mental* in the blank to indicate if the verb expresses physical action or mental action.

__physical__ Horses help humans in many ways.

__physical__ 1. Long ago, medieval knights fought battles atop powerful horses.

__physical__ 2. Lighter horses carried lords and ladies on fox hunts.

__physical__ 3. Travelers sometimes rode horses on long journeys.

__physical__ 4. Later, the wealthy traveled in horse-drawn carriages.

__mental__ 5. Farmers also relied on horses in the past.

__physical__ 6. American farms had more than 20 million horses and mules in 1900.

__physical__ 7. Today, many persons keep horses.

__mental__ 8. Children especially love shaggy, bright-eyed ponies.

__mental__ 9. Gentle Shetland ponies delight young children.

__physical__ 10. Shetlands stand only four hands (21 inches) high!

__physical__ 11. Sturdy and energetic, ponies perform many tasks.

__physical__ 12. The Chincoteague ponies run wild on an island off the Virginia coast.

__physical__ 13. According to legend, they swam ashore from a Spanish ship.

Unit 3, Verbs 75

Name _____ Class _____ Date _____

___physical___ 14. The Spanish also <u>brought</u> horses to the Native Americans.

___physical___ 15. Some Native Americans <u>became</u> skillful horsemen.

___physical___ 16. They <u>used</u> horses in bison hunts.

___mental___ 17. The Native Americans <u>preferred</u> the colorful Pinto and Appaloosa breeds.

___physical___ 18. Bands of wild horses—Mustangs—<u>roamed</u> wild and free in the American West.

___physical___ 19. Other types of horses never <u>left</u> the city.

___physical___ 20. Shire horses <u>pull</u> wagons and carts through the narrow streets of London.

___physical___ 21. Circus horses <u>perform</u> before appreciative audiences around the world.

___physical___ 22. Police officers <u>ride</u> horses through busy city streets.

___physical___ 23. Inside or outside the city, people <u>train</u> horses for many kinds of tasks.

___mental___ 24. Horses <u>learn</u> signals through constant repetition.

___physical___ 25. Eventually they <u>respond</u> to even the slightest signal from the rider.

___physical___ 26. A good rider <u>commands</u> his or her mount effortlessly.

___physical___ 27. The horse <u>follows</u> the rider's hand, leg, and body signals.

___mental___ 28. Horses <u>appreciate</u> a familiar set of rules.

___physical___ 29. For example, the rider always <u>mounts</u> a horse from its left side.

___mental___ 30. Unfamiliar situations <u>frighten</u> some horses.

___physical___ 31. However, horses <u>have</u> many excellent qualities.

___mental___ 32. A horse <u>remembers</u> pleasant and unpleasant events from years before.

___mental___ 33. Horses <u>enjoy</u> a thorough grooming each day.

___physical___ 34. Horses <u>eat</u> grass, hay, and grain.

___physical___ 35. Their stomachs <u>hold</u> eighteen quarts of food.

___physical___ 36. A horse <u>requires</u> ten to twelve gallons of fresh water daily.

▶ **Writing Link** Imagine that you can have any horse you want. Use action verbs to describe the horse you would choose.

_____

_____

Name _____ Class _____ Date _____

Lesson 14
Verbs: Transitive and Intransitive

Depending on its use in a particular sentence, an action verb can be either transitive or intransitive. A **transitive verb** is followed by a word or words—called the direct object—that answer the question *what?* or *whom?* An **intransitive verb** is an action verb that does not have a direct object.

Transitive: The pilot **landed** the antique **airplane**. (*Airplane* is the direct object that answers the question *landed what?* after the verb *landed*.)

Intransitive: The pilot **landed** carefully. (There is no direct object answering the question *landed what?* or *whom?*)

▶ **Exercise 1** Draw two lines under each action verb. Circle each direct object. Write *T* in the blank if the verb is transitive or *I* if the verb is intransitive.

__T__ The pilot started the (airplane).

__T__ 1. Wilbur and Orville Wright built the first successful (airplane).

__T__ 2. They built their (machine) in Ohio.

__T__ 3. They took (it) to Kitty Hawk, North Carolina, for its first flight.

__T__ 4. Orville Wright flew the first (airplane) on December 17, 1903.

__I__ 5. The winds at Kitty Hawk blew steadily that day.

__I__ 6. The twelve-horsepower engine sputtered.

__T__ 7. Soon it lifted the 750-pound (plane) into the air for a flight of 120 feet.

__I__ 8. Orville's brother, Wilbur, ran alongside.

__T__ 9. This first flight lasted only twelve seconds.

__T__ 10. The Wright brothers made three more (flights) that day.

__T__ 11. The longest one lasted fifty-nine seconds.

__T__ 12. Few newspapers carried (news) about the first flight.

__T__ 13. The brothers made (improvements) on their airplane and their flight techniques.

__I__ 14. Other designers worked hard.

__I__ 15. More successful airplanes appeared.

Unit 3, Verbs 77

Name _____ Class _____ Date _____

__T__ 16. Of course, the first pilots <u>had</u> no flight (instructors).

__I__ 17. Louis Blériot <u>flew</u> across the English Channel in 1909.

__T__ 18. In 1910, Glenn H. Curtiss <u>piloted</u> his (craft) from Albany to New York City.

__I__ 19. Airplane technology <u>grew</u> quickly.

__T__ 20. At first, persons <u>used</u> open (fields) as airports.

__T__ 21. Some airports today <u>retain</u> the (word) *field* in their names.

__I__ 22. Air fields <u>operated</u> as early as 1909.

__T__ 23. Workers <u>built</u> twenty (airports) in three years.

__I__ 24. In 1914, the First World War <u>began</u>.

__T__ 25. Both sides in the war <u>found</u> new (uses) for airplanes.

__I__ 26. The number of air fields <u>expanded</u> because of the new airplane technologies.

__T__ 27. After the war, even the U.S. Postal Service <u>realized</u> its (need) for airplanes.

__T__ 28. In the 1930s, passengers <u>used</u> (planes) as an important means of transportation.

__T__ 29. The government <u>counted</u> 1,036 (airports) in the United States in 1927.

__I__ 30. Today more than eleven thousand airports <u>exist</u> in the United States.

__T__ 31. Fewer than one thousand of them <u>serve</u> large (planes).

__T__ 32. Planners <u>established</u> (airports) close to cities for convenience.

__T__ 33. They <u>chose</u> the (sites) carefully.

__T__ 34. Nonetheless, airports <u>created</u> (problems) for some persons.

__T__ 35. Jet engines <u>generate</u> more (noise) than propeller engines.

__I__ 36. Nearby residents <u>complain</u> sometimes about the noise problem.

▶ **Writing Link** Would you like to become a pilot someday? Write a paragraph explaining why or why not. Use transitive and intransitive verbs.

_____
_____
_____
_____

Name _____ Class _____ Date _____

Lesson 15
Verbs with Indirect Objects

Both a direct object and an indirect object may follow an action verb in a sentence. An **indirect object** tells *to whom* or *for whom* the verb's action is done.

Kara sold **Matt** the bicycle. (*Matt* tells *to whom* Kara sold the bicycle. *Bicycle* is the direct object.)

Indirect objects follow certain rules. First, indirect objects are found only in sentences that have direct objects. Second, an indirect object always comes before a direct object. Finally, the prepositions *to* or *for* can be inserted before the indirect object; its position in the sentence can be changed, and the sentence will still make sense.

Levi threw **Jake** the football. (*Jake* is the indirect object before the direct object, *football*.)

Levi threw the football **to Jake**. (The meaning of the sentence is unchanged. *Jake* was an indirect object in the first example.)

▶ **Exercise 1** Write *DO* above each direct object and *IO* above each indirect object. Not every sentence has an indirect object.

              IO   DO
    Wrenn left Josh his video.

1. Yuri threw Karen the ball. [IO DO]
2. The jeweler sold the couple two lovely rings. [IO DO]
3. Roberto refunded Rayna the cost of the unused ticket. [IO DO]
4. Mr. Kenja gave Miki and Vance permission for their project. [IO IO DO]
5. The student council assigned our class the clean-up project. [IO DO]
6. Pablo paid the clerk two dollars for the birthday card. [IO DO]
7. Ted's mom sent our family the photograph. [IO DO]
8. Jean-Luc speaks French fluently. [DO]
9. Sarah guaranteed Ali full payment for his work at her print shop. [IO DO]
10. Alicia lent Steve her history book. [IO DO]
11. Mona showed Emilio her new tennis racket. [IO DO]
12. Mr. Hayes presented the team the first-place trophy. [IO DO]

Unit 3, Verbs 79

                        Name _____ Class _____ Date _____

13. Joanna handed the mail **IO** carrier her **DO** letter.
14. Boris gave **IO** Anita the **DO** ruler.
15. Seth taught our **IO** class sign **DO** language last year.
16. Will made his **IO** dog a **DO** house.
17. During the game, Salahi passed **IO** Harry the **DO** ball for three lay-ups.
18. Carl approached the **DO** intersection cautiously.
19. Sheila asked her **IO** teacher the new **DO** student's name.
20. We chose Tammi **DO** as our team captain.
21. James offered his **IO** classmate a **DO** ride to the science fair.
22. They refunded **IO** Dad the **DO** overcharge.
23. Sally owed **IO** Tanya a **DO** CD.
24. Akira sold a children's **IO** magazine his **DO** story.
25. Drew told the **IO** children a **DO** story at the library last Saturday.
26. Alex bought **IO** Jean a **DO** ticket to the movie.
27. Isabel lent **IO** me her portable **DO** radio for the picnic.
28. Debra walked her **DO** dog after dinner.
29. The carpenter built the **IO** Rileys some beautiful kitchen **DO** cabinets.
30. The captain showed his **IO** troops the **DO** plan.
31. She assigned the **IO** class a **DO** paper that would be due in one week.
32. Ahmed left the rare **IO** bird some **DO** food on his way to school.
33. The principal often offers **IO** students and **IO** teachers his **DO** advice.
34. Charlie taught the **IO** vocalist the new **DO** aria.
35. Terry assured the **DO** client of his support in the matter.
36. The deer leapt the **DO** creek with ease.
37. Philip conceded **IO** Kamil the **DO** argument.
38. Mrs. Jones brought **IO** Henry his **DO** homework.

Name _____ Class _____ Date _____

Lesson 16
Linking Verbs and Predicate Words

A **linking verb** joins the subject of a sentence with a noun or adjective in the predicate that identifies or describes the subject. *Be* in all its forms *(am, is, are, was, were)* is the most common linking verb. Other linking verbs include *appear, become, feel, grow, look, seem, smell, sound, taste,* and *turn.*

Corinne **was** captain. (The linking verb *was* links *captain* to the subject, *Corrine*.)

▶ **Exercise 1** Draw two lines under each verb. Place a check in the blank next to each sentence that contains a linking verb.

✔ The bird <u>is</u> red.

✔ 1. The grass <u>became</u> brown and dry during the drought.

✔ 2. The delicious dessert <u>was</u> cherry cobbler.

____ 3. Karen <u>asked</u> for that book for her birthday.

____ 4. His answer <u>annoyed</u> me.

✔ 5. The exterior of the new auditorium <u>appears</u> stately.

✔ 6. Cally <u>looks</u> hot and weary after mowing the grass.

✔ 7. The wonderful train ride <u>became</u> an impressive memory.

____ 8. My younger sister <u>played</u> Tiny Tim in the play.

✔ 9. The auctioneer of the old property <u>was</u> Alice's father.

✔ 10. The annual school choral production <u>was</u> a success.

____ 11. The smell of burning leaves <u>brought</u> memories of the past.

____ 12. The country church bells <u>sounded</u> across the meadow.

✔ 13. Our old barn <u>is</u> a warm shelter for the cattle in winter.

____ 14. Colette <u>ran</u> the marathon in record time.

✔ 15. Jamal's new bicycle <u>seemed</u> too large for him.

✔ 16. The long line of school buses <u>became</u> a caravan for the team.

✔ 17. Today the summer skies <u>seem</u> extremely blue.

Unit 3, Verbs **81**

Name _____ Class _____ Date _____

✔ 18. The old candy bar tasted stale.

✔ 19. The novel soon turned dull.

____ 20. The movie ended too quickly.

The words that follow a linking verb and identify or describe the subject are called **subject complements**. The two kinds of subject complements are predicate nouns and predicate adjectives. A **predicate noun** follows a linking verb and renames the subject. A **predicate adjective** follows a linking verb and describes the subject. Predicate nouns and predicate adjectives may be compound.

Corinne was a **team captain** and a **friend**. (compound predicate noun)
She sounded **tired** but **hopeful**. (compound predicate adjective)

▶ **Exercise 2** Write *PN* above each predicate noun and *PA* above each predicate adjective.

The Grand Canyon is **[PA]** spectacular at any time of the year.

1. Those mountains become a **[PN]** source of water for our city.
2. The toddler sounded **[PA]** fussy and **[PA]** sleepy.
3. Their opinions on the matter turned **[PA]** sour.
4. Manufacturing was the major **[PN]** industry.
5. The new foreign exchange student seems **[PA]** homesick.
6. The young actor's face appeared **[PA]** old and **[PA]** unhappy with the makeup.
7. Ellie looked **[PA]** joyful over her first-place award.
8. The storm grew **[PA]** intense during the early morning hours.
9. The secretary automatically becomes the **[PN]** president the following year.
10. The old trapper's cabin smelled **[PA]** damp and **[PA]** musty.
11. Jamil felt **[PA]** anxious about his driver's test.
12. The proposed program sounds **[PA]** innovative.
13. Professor Kohler became an **[PN]** authority on the Mesozoic era.
14. The tin soldier looked **[PA]** serious and **[PA]** strong in his place on the shelf.
15. The first buds of spring soon became beautiful **[PN]** flowers.

Name _____ Class _____ Date _____

16. Robyn grew nervous before exams. **PA**
17. The green apples tasted bitter to everyone. **PA**
18. Sonja became the class expert on astronomy. **PN**
19. The weather turned sunny during our camping trip. **PA**
20. Every other Saturday Mel was the substitute mail carrier. **PN**
21. The handblown glass ornament looked fragile. **PA**
22. The twin boys sounded excited about their new baby sister. **PA**
23. These frogs were tadpoles not too long ago. **PN**
24. The authors felt honored by the recognition. **PA**
25. The highway was once an old wagon train route. **PN**

▶ **Exercise 3** Draw two lines under each verb. Write *PN* above each predicate noun and *PA* above each predicate adjective. Some sentences do not have a predicate noun or a predicate adjective.

My birthday cake looks beautiful. **PA**

1. The car appeared old and rusty. **PA PA**
2. Those tulips look fantastic in the spring sunshine. **PA**
3. The old stairway in Kelly's house seems long. **PA**
4. Jafar convinced Jennifer of his sincerity.
5. The November weather turned cold and miserable. **PA PA**
6. Steve sickened at the thought of missing his plane.
7. The new team member is Laurie's cousin. **PN**
8. Last winter began too soon.
9. The shadows were dark and silent. **PA PA**
10. The roads appeared glassy after the ice storm. **PA**
11. My little brother begged for the video.

Unit 3, Verbs **83**

12. The stately bare tree <u>looked</u> eerie against the sky at twilight. **PA**

13. In the middle of the street <u>sat</u> a yellow cat.

14. Mr. Smith <u>grew</u> angry at himself. **PA**

15. That farm truck <u>is</u> full of golden corn. **PA**

16. Teri <u>became</u> the fastest runner on the track team. **PN**

17. Mrs. Vaughn <u>sounded</u> confident about the new computer program. **PA**

18. Pecan pie <u>tastes</u> rich and sweet. **PA PA**

19. The snow <u>lies</u> heavily on the rooftops.

20. Marcie's father <u>is</u> a firefighter. **PN**

21. Vacation time <u>grew</u> short toward the end of August. **PA**

22. Buffalo, New York, <u>was</u> their destination. **PN**

23. The salty sea air <u>smelled</u> fresh and welcoming to Kirsten. **PA PA**

24. The dinosaurs in the movie <u>appeared</u> lifelike. **PA**

25. The small acorn <u>became</u> a giant oak. **PN**

▶ **Writing Link** Write a paragraph describing what you might see on a winter walk in the woods. Use linking verbs and predicate words.

_____
_____
_____
_____
_____
_____
_____
_____

84 *Writer's Choice Grammar Workbook 8,* Unit 3

Lesson 17
Present and Past Tenses

Tense refers to the form of the verb that shows the time of the action.

The **present tense** refers to an action that is happening now, to an action that happens regularly, or to a situation that is generally true. The present tense and the base form of a verb are the same when used with all subjects except singular nouns or *he, she,* or *it*. In these cases *-s* or *-es* is added to the verb.

I **smell** the fresh bread. (happening now)
The coach **calls** practice daily. (happens regularly, generally true)

The **past tense** refers to an action that has already occurred. The past tense of many verbs is formed by adding *-ed* to the base form of the verb.

I **smelled** the bread earlier.
Isabel **called** the coach.

▶ **Exercise 1** Draw two lines under each verb. Write its tense, *present* or *past,* in the blank.

present		Archaeologists study the past.
past	1.	Herodotus lived centuries ago in Asia Minor.
present	2.	No one knows the exact dates of his birth and death.
past	3.	According to historians, he lived between 484 B.C. and 420 B.C.
past	4.	The Roman orator Cicero once called Herodotus "the Father of History."
present	5.	Today historians study his books about the Persian Empire.
past	6.	Herodotus considered his own work an "inquiry."
present	7.	Many individuals enjoy his lively style of writing.
past	8.	The historian gained knowledge for his books during his journeys.
past	9.	He traveled widely through Greece, the Middle East, and North Africa.
present	10.	His books show his gift as a storyteller of history.
past	11.	Other historians of this period encountered difficulties with some of Herodotus's accounts.

Unit 3, Verbs

Name _____ Class _____ Date _____

___present___ 12. Herodotus <u>remains</u> the main source of original information on Greek history between 550 B.C. and 479 B.C.

___past___ 13. Through his travels he <u>learned</u> about the customs and history of other peoples.

___present___ 14. His books <u>show</u> his boundless curiosity about peoples and their customs.

___past___ 15. Herodotus <u>described</u> his accounts of their customs.

___present___ 16. His first four books <u>describe</u> the history and divisions of the Persian empire.

___past___ 17. Ancient rulers <u>accumulated</u> large archives of documents and records about their achievements.

___present___ 18. Archaeologists <u>study</u> records and remains.

___past___ 19. Even Herodotus <u>showed</u> interest in fossils as a link to the past.

___present___ 20. The works of Herodotus <u>preserve</u> the past for all humankind.

▶ **Exercise 2** Draw two lines under each verb. Correct each sentence by writing in the blank the past tense form of the verb.

___conducted___ Archaeologists <u>conduct</u> that excavation in 1936.

___uncovered___ 1. Two travelers first <u>uncover</u> Native American cities in 1839.

___discovered___ 2. John Lloyd Stephens and Frederick Catherwood <u>discover</u> the lost city of Copan.

___persisted___ 3. Stephens and Catherwood <u>persist</u> in their search.

___noticed___ 4. They <u>notice</u> great stone stairs in the Honduran jungle.

___hacked___ 5. They <u>hack</u> the jungle undergrowth.

___gripped___ 6. Amazement <u>grips</u> them at the top of the stairs.

___perceived___ 7. The two <u>perceive</u> a vast temple below them.

___traced___ 8. Catherwood <u>traces</u> outlines on ruled paper.

___produced___ 9. He <u>produces</u> drawings and paintings of Copan's monuments.

___contracted___ 10. Unfortunately, Catherwood <u>contracts</u> malaria.

___published___ 11. Stephens <u>publishes</u> a book about their discoveries.

Name _____ Class _____ Date _____

described	12.	He describes the ancestors of the region's Mayan peoples.
thrived	13.	The Mayan civilization thrives from the fourth to the sixteenth centuries.
lived	14.	More than 1,000 years ago, 100,000 persons live in the ancient city of Tikal.
lasted	15.	Classic Mayan civilization lasts until the tenth century.
possessed	16.	City centers possess great numbers of pyramids and palaces.
weakened	17.	Civil war weakens the cities, however.
abandoned	18.	Eventually, the common citizens abandon their mighty rulers.
improved	19.	Their greatest contribution improves the lives of everyone.
developed	20.	They develop foods different from any other foods in the world.

▶ **Exercise 3** Draw two lines under each verb. Correct each sentence by writing in the blank the present tense of the verb.

wonder		People constantly wondered about life on Earth many years ago.
excite	1.	Discoveries about prehistoric times on Earth excited even young children.
provide	2.	Archaeologists, geologists, and paleontologists provided us with these discoveries and their revelations about the past.
study	3.	Geologists studied the history of Earth and its life through rocks.
collect	4.	Scientists who collected fossils are paleontologists.
examine	5.	Archaeologists examined material remains such as fossils, artifacts, and relics of past human life and activities.
contain	6.	Rocks contained such fossils and remains of the past.
reveal	7.	Fossils revealed to us the history of life on Earth.
form	8.	They formed over long periods of time.
show	9.	Fossils such as pieces of bone, a tooth, or an impression in a rock showed us examples of past life.
calculate	10.	Geologists calculated the ages of the layers of rock.

Unit 3, Verbs   **87**

Name _____ Class _____ Date _____

determine	11. From this, they <u>determined</u> the time of existence of the formerly live material.
locate	12. Geologists <u>located</u> the simplest forms of life in the oldest layers of rock.
present	13. Rocks <u>presented</u> an incomplete history of the earth for various reasons.
destroy	14. Weather and erosion <u>destroyed</u> rocks and their geological records.
cause	15. Also, heat and pressure deep in the earth's crust <u>caused</u> changes in the rocks.
consists	16. The history of Earth <u>consisted</u> of five periods of time called eras.
include	17. These eras <u>included</u> the Archeozoic, the earliest of the five periods.
outlines	18. A chart, or geological time scale, <u>outlined</u> the history of Earth according to these five eras.
appears	19. On such a chart, Earth's earliest history <u>appeared</u> at the bottom and the most recent at the top.
remains	20. Unfortunately, the complete history of Earth <u>remained</u> a secret.

▶ **Writing Link** Write a paragraph describing what you might see as a traveler in the ancient Mayan world. Use the past tense of verbs to describe your journey.

_____
_____
_____
_____
_____
_____
_____
_____
_____
_____

Name _____ Class _____ Date _____

Lesson 18
Main Verbs and Helping Verbs

All verbs have four principal parts that are used to form the tenses.

PRINCIPAL PARTS OF THE VERB *TALK*

BASE FORM	PRESENT PARTICIPLE	PAST	PAST PARTICIPLE
talk	talking	talked	talked

Other tenses are formed by combining the present participle and the past participle with helping verbs. A **helping verb** helps the **main verb** tell about an action or make a statement. One or more helping verbs followed by a main verb is called a **verb phrase**.

They **are talking** to Sheila about the game. (*Are* is the helping verb, and *talking* is the main verb. Together they form a verb phrase.)

Be, *have*, and *do* are the most common helping verbs. Forms of the helping verb *be* are *am*, *is*, and *are* in the present and *was* and *were* in the past. These forms combine with the present participle of the main verb. The helping verb that combines with the past participle of a verb is *have*. Its forms include *have* and *has* in the present and *had* in the past.

▶ **Exercise 1** Draw two lines under the correct helping verb in parentheses and two lines under the participle. Write *pres. part.* or *past part.* in the blank to indicate whether the participle is present or past.

pres. part.		Alonso (**is**, has) <u>winning</u> the race.
pres. part.	1.	Ricardo and Craig (**are**, have) <u>arriving</u> tomorrow.
past part.	2.	Our team (was, **had**) <u>worked</u> hard to win the pennant.
pres. part.	3.	Sally (**is**, has) <u>joining</u> our debate team.
pres. part.	4.	My dog Rusty (**is**, has) always <u>barking</u> at something.
pres. part.	5.	The class (**is**, has) <u>going</u> to the museum.
past part.	6.	The buses (were, **had**) <u>arrived</u> late at the auditorium.
past part.	7.	The workers (**had**, were) <u>painted</u> the bleachers for the first time.
pres. part.	8.	My bike (**is**, has) <u>working</u> fine since it was in the shop.
past part.	9.	Mason's sisters (are, **have**) <u>played</u> many women's sports.
past part.	10.	Dad (was, **had**) <u>looked</u> everywhere for his keys.

Unit 3, Verbs

Name _____ Class _____ Date _____

pres. part. 11. Georgia's friends (have, **are**) receiving the awards.

past part. 12. Trent (were, **had**) printed the poster.

pres. part. 13. The new student (**is**, has) registering at school.

pres. part. 14. My friends (have, **are**) watching the video this afternoon.

pres. part. 15. The Sanchez family (**is**, has) moving in next door.

pres. part. 16. Mr. Chen (**is**, had) reserving the tickets.

past part. 17. Isabel (are, **was**) awarded a prize.

past part. 18. Someone (is, **has**) marked up my new book.

pres. part. 19. The horses (**are**, have) running across the park.

past part. 20. The sailboats (**were**, had) tossed by the storm.

pres. part. 21. Anne (**is**, had) walking to the store.

pres. part. 22. Don and Karen (have, **are**) joining us for the trip.

past part. 23. Jodi and Hasan (are, **have**) experimented with a glider.

pres. part. 24. The teachers (**were**, had) evaluating the students.

pres. part. 25. The clouds (**are**, have) gathering to produce a shower.

past part. 26. The jet planes (is, **had**) soared over the town.

past part. 27. The airplane (is, **has**) replaced the train for rapid travel.

past part. 28. Our pen pals (are, **have**) enjoyed the video of our school.

pres. part. 29. Artists (have, **are**) coming to give us a presentation.

past part. 30. Music (are, **has**) ranked among my favorite subjects.

pres. part. 31. The sleek cat (**is**, had) crouching as if ready to pounce.

past part. 32. The birthday gifts (**were**, had) covered in shiny paper.

past part. 33. We (**were**, have) exposed to excellent sound quality at the concert.

past part. 34. Tina (is, **had**) succeeded in every sport she tried last year.

pres. part. 35. Languages (**are**, has) fascinating to me.

past part. 36. I (were, **had**) suspected that it would rain.

past part. 37. The garden (is, **has**) remained my parents' pride and joy.

past part. 38. The owners (are, **have**) placed the sheep in their pens.

Lesson 19
Verb Forms: Present Progressive and Past Progressive

The present tense of a verb describes an action that occurs repeatedly. The **present progressive form** of a verb refers to an action that is continuing in the present. The present participle of the main verb and the helping verb *am*, *are*, or *is* combine to make up the present progressive form.

PRESENT PROGRESSIVE FORM

SINGULAR
I **am painting**.
You **are painting**.
He, she *or* it **is painting**.

PLURAL
We **are painting**.
You **are painting**.
They **are painting**.

The **past progressive form** of a verb refers to an action that was continuing at some point in the past. The present participle of the main verb and the helping verb *was* or *were* combine to make up the past progressive form.

PAST PROGRESSIVE FORM

SINGULAR
I **was painting**.
You **were painting**.
He, she, *or* it **was painting**.

PLURAL
We **were painting**.
You **were painting**.
They **were painting**.

▶ **Exercise 1** If the verb in italics is in the present tense, write its present progressive form in the blank. If it is in the past tense, write its past progressive form.

was looking	Brett *looked* at the history book.
was hindering	1. The rain *hindered* our plans yesterday.
is greeting	2. I see Carl's father *greets* visitors at the door today.
is pacing	3. Sally *paces* her sports training wisely.
was placing	4. Ted *placed* first in the finals this year when he won the meet.
was missing	5. Duwane *missed* the announcement.
are moving	6. If you *move* tomorrow, let me know.
is surviving	7. Apparently, our grass *survives* the long dry spell.
is regulating	8. Carrie *regulates* her study time.
is heating	9. The summer sun *heats* up the morning.

Name _____ Class _____ Date _____

are laboring	10.	The ants in Margo's ant farm *labor* ceaselessly.
is registering	11.	Chet *registers* before the game begins.
am recommending	12.	I *recommend* you see that movie before its run is over.
is singing	13.	My parakeet *sings* while I study.
is measuring	14.	The play-off game *measures* up with the one last year.
are tying	15.	You *tie* the package securely.
is touching	16.	Harry *touches* on the main point of the idea.
were scolding	17.	The birds *scolded* me for disturbing their nest.
were settling	18.	The exchange students *settled* down in their new homes.
am treating	19.	I *treat* my bike better than my brother treats his car.
was thanking	20.	Susan *thanked* us before she left.
is walking	21.	Naomi *walks* to school every day this term.
is washing	22.	Ali *washes* his uniform after every competition.
is wavering	23.	Linda *wavers* between majoring in chemistry and majoring in biology.
are wrestling	24.	The neighbors *wrestle* with the move.
are urging	25.	They *urge* us to see the play.
am returning	26.	I *return* your book to the library.
was watching	27.	Elizabeth *watched* that program after the news.
are utilizing	28.	When you *utilize* your best speed on the turn, be careful.
is shaping	29.	Ophelia *shapes* the clay into the beautiful figurine.
was smiling	30.	The sun *smiled* warm and bright on the afternoon.
are sparkling	31.	The stars *sparkle* on a cloudless night.
is occurring	32.	It *occurs* every evening before sunset.
were meriting	33.	Our efforts *merited* a break in our work schedule.
am oiling	34.	I *oil* the machine more often now.
was guessing	35.	She *guessed* about the time.
was humming	36.	Sonia *hummed* that tune during art class.

Name _____ Class _____ Date _____

Lesson 20
Perfect Tenses: Present and Past

The **present perfect tense** of a verb names an action that happened at some time in the past. It also names an action that happened in the past and is still occurring. The past participle of the main verb and the helping verb *have* or *has* make up the present perfect tense.

PRESENT PERFECT TENSE

SINGULAR	PLURAL
I **have studied**.	We **have studied**.
You **have studied**.	You **have studied**.
He, she, *or* it **has studied**.	They **have studied**.

The **past perfect tense** of a verb names an action that was completed before another action or event in the past. The past participle of the main verb and the helping verb *had* make up the past perfect tense.

PAST PERFECT TENSE

SINGULAR	PLURAL
I **had studied**.	We **had studied**.
You **had studied**.	You **had studied**.
He, she, *or* it **had studied**.	They **had studied**.

▶ **Exercise 1** Draw two lines under each verb. Write its present perfect tense in the blank.

have offered   I offered my services for their anniversary celebration.

have remembered   1. They remember the gifts for the guest speakers.

has referred   2. Kenji refers to the book on the top shelf.

has performed   3. Kara performs the dance already.

has navigated   4. The old sailing ship navigates the difficult shallows.

have followed   5. I follow Marty's suggestions.

has growled   6. The neighbor's dog growls at me each morning.

has napped   7. That cat naps every chance he gets!

has influenced   8. That old movie influences many people.

has loved   9. James loves that book.

Unit 3, Verbs   93

__have demolished__ 10. They demolish our team every year!

__have attended__ 11. We attend Mr. Kumba's class regularly.

__have confined__ 12. You confine your campfire to this small area.

__have attracted__ 13. Connie's track victories attract press attention.

__have amazed__ 14. At sunset the clouds amaze me with their beautiful colors.

__has wandered__ 15. In the story, Gilgamesh wanders forever.

__has united__ 16. The plot of the play unites the friends in the end.

__has turned__ 17. The tree turns a brilliant red.

__have demonstrated__ 18. These pictures demonstrate Sunee's artistic style.

__has ruled__ 19. Logic rules our scientific thought.

__have served__ 20. Jay and Dave serve the class project well.

▶ **Exercise 2** Fill in the blank using the verb and tense given in parentheses. *Past perf.* indicates past perfect tense, and *pres. perf.* indicates present perfect tense.

Jake and Luis __have rafted__ down the river in Colorado. (*raft,* pres. perf.)

1. She __had telephoned__ him before school started. (*telephone,* past perf.)
2. The dog __has slipped__ out of its collar. (*slip,* pres. perf.)
3. The waters of the lake __have sparkled__ in the sunlight. (*sparkle,* pres. perf.)
4. The tulips __had sprouted__ before the frost. (*sprout,* past perf.)
5. Native Americans __have played__ a basketball-like game for many years. (*play,* pres. perf.)
6. If you __had moved__, you would have had a better view. (*move,* past perf.)
7. If I __had noticed__ it before, I wouldn't have to hunt for it now. (*notice,* past perf.)
8. When you __have obtained__ the package, will you open it? (*obtain,* pres. perf.)
9. Simon __had leaned__ toward running the race. (*lean,* past perf.)
10. The dog __has harmed__ the cat once before. (*harm,* pres. perf.)
11. The wind __had grabbed__ my hat before I could react. (*grab,* past perf.)
12. When you __had cleaned__ it, did the model shine? (*clean,* past perf.)

Name _____ Class _____ Date _____

Lesson 21
Expressing Future Time

The **future tense** of a verb is formed by adding the helping verb *will* before the main verb. When the subject is *I* or *we*, the helping verb *shall* is sometimes used.

Our big tournament **will begin** next week.

Time words such as *tomorrow, next year,* and *later* are used to refer specifically to future time to show that an action has yet to occur. They are used with the present tense of the verb.

Our big tournament **starts next week**.

The present progressive form can also be used with time words to express future actions.

Our big tournament **is starting next week**.

The **future perfect tense** of a verb refers to an action that will be completed before another future action begins. The future perfect tense is formed by inserting *will have* or *shall have* before the past participle of the verb.

By that time, our big tournament **will have started**.

▶ **Exercise 1** Draw two lines under each verb or verb phrase. In the blank write the tense of the verb: *present, pres. prog.* (present progressive), *future,* or *fut. perf.* (future perfect).

fut. perf.	Trent <u>will have received</u> the award by eight o'clock.
future	1. I <u>will unhook</u> the chain.
fut. perf.	2. Gina <u>will have walked</u> home by now.
pres. prog.	3. Ted <u>is advising</u> us about our leaky roof tomorrow.
future	4. They <u>will watch</u> a video on that classic story.
pres. prog.	5. The school's chess match <u>is beginning</u> tomorrow afternoon.
fut. perf.	6. By then, I <u>shall have tired</u> of it.
future	7. Camilla <u>will smooth</u> over the problem.
pres. prog.	8. The dancers <u>are settling</u> on a program next week.
future	9. I <u>will perform</u> up to my instructor's expectations.

fut. perf.	10.	Juan will have persisted until the end of the match.
present	11.	Chen practices his violin every day.
future	12.	We shall respect his achievements.
future	13.	Tomorrow they will mutter about the team's loss.
future	14.	Karen will organize the class project.
pres. prog.	15.	They are responding to our suggestion soon.
future	16.	Our relatives will stop at our house on their vacation.
fut. perf.	17.	They will have measured the right amount in chemistry class.
fut. perf.	18.	He will have impressed everyone with his vocal talents.
fut. perf.	19.	The store will have inscribed the ring before delivery.
fut. perf.	20.	I shall have earned the coach's respect.
present	21.	Kyle distinguishes one of that group's songs from another.
pres. prog.	22.	Jeanne is gathering her books together.
fut. perf.	23.	The station will have fulfilled its promise by Tuesday.
present	24.	Next season we debate the other teams in our conference.
future	25.	I will describe the plot in my oral book report on Friday.
fut. perf.	26.	Your efforts will have contributed to the environment.
present	27.	Sheila advises everyone on financial matters.
future	28.	Saturday I will clean my room.
present	29.	The marathon runners compete next fall.
future	30.	Farm horses will astonish you with their size.
fut. perf.	31.	Before evening, I will have looked everywhere.
future	32.	Our team will turn around yet.
fut. perf.	33.	We shall have suggested several options by then.
future	34.	Your science project will stimulate great interest.
fut. perf.	35.	Maybe then he will have perceived the solution.
present	36.	Darla opposes a picnic in that park every year.

Name _____ Class _____ Date _____

Lesson 22
Active and Passive Voices

A sentence is in the **active voice** when the subject performs the action of the verb.

Neil Armstrong **landed** the *Apollo* lunar module on the moon in 1969.

A sentence is in the **passive voice** when the subject receives the action of the verb. The verb in a passive-voice sentence consists of a form of *be* and the past participle. Often a phrase beginning with *by* follows a verb in a passive-voice sentence.

The *Apollo* lunar module **was landed** on the moon in 1969 **by** Neil Armstrong. (*was* and the past participle of *land* followed by a phrase beginning with *by*)

The active voice is stronger and emphasizes the performer. Use the passive voice when you want to emphasize the receiver of the action or de-emphasize the performer. Also, use the passive voice if you do not know who the performer is.

The moon **was reached** in 1969. (focuses on the event)
The spacecraft **was landed**. (You do not want to state who landed it.)

▶ **Exercise 1** Write in the blank whether the sentence is in the *active* or *passive* voice. Draw a line under the receiver of the action.

__passive__ The heavens were studied by ancient astronomers.

__passive__ 1. A solar eclipse was predicted by Thales of Miletus in 585 B.C.

__active__ 2. Hipparchus established an observatory in the third century B.C.

__passive__ 3. A supernova, or exploding star, was recorded by Chinese astronomers in 1054.

__active__ 4. According to the Greek astronomer Ptolemy, the sun and the planets circled Earth once a day.

__passive__ 5. In 1543, a new theory was suggested by a Polish astronomer, Copernicus.

__active__ 6. In this theory, Earth and other planets orbited the sun.

__passive__ 7. The use of Copernicus's theory was forbidden by religious leaders until 1757.

Unit 3, Verbs **97**

Name _____ Class _____ Date _____

__passive__ 8. However, persons were convinced about Copernicus's theory by the discoveries of other astronomers.

__passive__ 9. The law of universal gravitation was discovered by Sir Isaac Newton.

__active__ 10. The Copernican theory gained support after this discovery.

__passive__ 11. Uranus was found by Sir William Herschel in 1781.

__passive__ 12. Pluto was discovered by Clyde William Tombaugh in 1930.

__active__ 13. The closest planet to the sun, Mercury, orbits the sun in eighty-eight Earth days.

__passive__ 14. Venus is called "the Morning Star" by many persons.

__active__ 15. An American space probe, *Mariner II,* reached Venus in 1962.

__active__ 16. It sent back data about conditions on and near Venus.

__passive__ 17. The surface of Venus has been mapped by succeeding American space probes.

__active__ 18. We call Mars "the Red Planet."

__passive__ 19. This planet was named by ancient Romans after the red god of war in Roman mythology.

__active__ 20. Limonite, a brick-colored mineral, gives Mars its red color.

__active__ 21. Mars orbits the sun in about 687 Earth days.

__passive__ 22. Mars was observed by the U.S. spacecraft *Mariner IV* in 1965.

__active__ 23. In 1976, the United States landed *Viking I* near the planet's equator.

__passive__ 24. Photographs of the surface of Mars were sent back to Earth by both *Viking I* and *Viking II.*

__active__ 25. They showed the canyons, deep gorges, and "dry river beds" on the surface of Mars.

__passive__ 26. The first space shuttle, *Columbia,* was launched by the United States in 1981.

__active__ 27. Two big booster rockets launch the space shuttle into orbit.

__active__ 28. It uses its wings to land like a glider.

Name _____ Class _____ Date _____

Lesson 23
Irregular Verbs I

These irregular verbs are grouped according to the way they form their past and past participles.

IRREGULAR VERBS

PATTERN	BASE FORM	PAST	PAST PARTICIPLE
One vowel changes to form the past and the past participle.	begin	began	begun
	drink	drank	drunk
	ring	rang	rung
	sing	sang	sung
	spring	sprang *or* sprung	sprung
	swim	swam	swum
The past form and past participle are the same.	bring	brought	brought
	buy	bought	bought
	catch	caught	caught
	creep	crept	crept
	feel	felt	felt
	get	got	got *or* gotten
	keep	kept	kept
	lay	laid	laid
	leave	left	left
	lend	lent	lent
	lose	lost	lost
	make	made	made
	pay	paid	paid
	say	said	said
	seek	sought	sought
	sit	sat	sat
	sleep	slept	slept
	teach	taught	taught
	think	thought	thought
	win	won	won

▶ **Exercise 1** Complete each sentence with the past tense or past participle of the irregular verb in parentheses.

Wendy had __**sat**__ down before the music began. (sit)

1. Ethan had __**slept**__ late that morning. (sleep)

2. Ria __**got**__ her new book yesterday. (get)

Unit 3, Verbs **99**

Name _____ Class _____ Date _____

3. Harry ____kept____ me waiting for an hour. (keep)
4. Mai-Lin had ____thought____ about her topic before she wrote the report. (think)
5. My cat just ____sat____ there while the mouse escaped. (sit)
6. I had ____paid____ too much for the CD at the mall. (pay)
7. Akira ____won____ the art prize last year. (win)
8. Jessica ____brought____ success to our track team last season. (bring)
9. I ____caught____ this cold last week. (catch)
10. Mary had ____begun____ the homework before I arrived. (begin)
11. The horse never ____lost____ a race until yesterday. (lose)
12. Duwana had ____sung____ in the choir before. (sing)
13. We had ____left____ before the buses arrived. (leave)
14. Mr. Hasan ____taught____ that class last year. (teach)
15. My front tire had ____sprung____ a leak. (spring)
16. Cal ____felt____ bad about the test. (feel)
17. Susan's dog ____sought____ a sunny nook in which to sleep. (seek)
18. They have always ____got *or* gotten____ new books for their birthdays. (get)
19. The cat ____crept____ up on me before he pounced playfully. (creep)
20. They ____said____ they thought the snow was too good to be true. (say)
21. My little brother had ____drunk____ all the orange juice. (drink)
22. The door bell ____rang____ sharply against the quiet. (ring)
23. Sheila ____swam____ across the lake last year. (swim)
24. Shawn had ____bought____ one last week. (buy)
25. I ____laid____ the book down somewhere and lost it completely. (lay)
26. Yesterday Tama ____began____ her science project. (begin)
27. Two of the art students have ____made____ the set for this play. (make)
28. He had ____lent____ his jacket to another member of the team. (lend)

Name _____ Class _____ Date _____

Lesson 24
Irregular Verbs II

The following irregular verbs are grouped according to the way their past form and past participle are formed.

IRREGULAR VERBS

PATTERN	BASE FORM	PAST FORM	PAST PARTICIPLE
The base form and the past participle are the same.	become come run	became came ran	become come run
The past form ends in *-ew* and the past participle ends in *-wn.*	blow draw fly grow know throw	blew drew flew grew knew threw	blown drawn flown grown known thrown
The past participle ends in *-en.*	bite break choose drive eat fall give ride rise see speak steal take write	bit broke chose drove ate fell gave rode rose saw spoke stole took wrote	bitten *or* bit broken chosen driven eaten fallen given ridden risen seen spoken stolen taken written
The past form and the past participle do not follow any pattern.	am, are, is do go tear wear	was, were did went tore wore	been done gone torn worn
The base form, past form, and past participle are all the same.	cut let	cut let	cut let

Unit 3, Verbs

Name _____ Class _____ Date _____

▶ **Exercise 1** Complete each sentence with the past tense or past participle of the irregular verb in parentheses.

    I had ____**chosen**____ the gift before you called. (choose)

1. We ____**drew**____ names to select a winner. (draw)
2. My friends had ____**eaten**____ all the pizza by the time I arrived. (eat)
3. I ____**took**____ the pictures to class yesterday. (take)
4. They had ____**seen**____ the horses before riding them. (see)
5. Rick ____**wrote**____ to Mr. Tanabe last week. (write)
6. You could have ____**risen**____ if you had tried. (rise)
7. I had ____**been**____ happy to hear from her. (be)
8. Carlos ____**went**____ to the grocery store yesterday. (go)
9. Sandra had ____**cut**____ her finger on the paper. (cut)
10. The wind ____**blew**____ until the trees looked like green banners. (blow)
11. Davina has ____**drawn**____ her picture many times. (draw)
12. The yard ____**became**____ a dreamland of shapes due to the snow drifts. (become)
13. Had you ever ____**grown**____ a bonsai tree before? (grow)
14. I should never have ____**let**____ them use the car. (let)
15. We ____**drove**____ to Yellowstone Park for our vacation last year. (drive)
16. The temperature had ____**fallen**____ drastically during the night. (fall)
17. The butterfly ____**flew**____ lazily to another bright flower. (fly)
18. Last summer, I had been ____**bitten**____ all over by mosquitoes. (bite)
19. The old tree ____**grew**____ bare as winter approached. (grow)
20. Had you ____**spoken**____ at a seminar before? (speak)
21. The moon had ____**risen**____ before the sky grew black. (rise)
22. Have you ever ____**ridden**____ a roller coaster? (ride)
23. Seth had ____**known**____ the answers to all the questions. (know)
24. Judi ____**threw**____ a huge party for her daughter's sixteenth birthday. (throw)
25. Mom and Dad ____**stole**____ away for a quiet weekend at the beach. (steal)

Name _____ Class _____ Date _____

26. We _____saw_____ the brilliant winter sunrise this morning. (see)

27. Kate _____broke_____ the school's free throw shooting record. (break)

28. We had never _____done_____ anything like this safari before. (do)

29. Cheryl had _____given_____ every ounce of energy to the successful performance. (give)

30. The morning has _____gone_____ by too quickly for us to enjoy it. (go)

31. My aunt had _____worn_____ her new dress to the theater. (wear)

32. Chen _____drew_____ upon his memories to write that story. (draw)

33. Jennifer had _____run_____ her best in the hurdles event. (run)

34. Seth _____tore_____ the picture out of the magazine. (tear)

35. Have you ever _____flown_____ a model airplane like that one before? (fly)

36. We _____ran_____ cross-country instead of trying out for baseball. (run)

37. Who _____did_____ the crossword puzzle? (do)

38. Jodi has _____become_____ a famous singer. (become)

39. Unfortunately, I _____chose_____ to throw out my old comic book collection years ago. (choose)

40. The snow had _____come_____ in the night, silently, unexpectedly. (come)

▶ **Exercise 2** Underline the word in parentheses that best completes each sentence.

Ms. Joyce has (wrote, <u>written</u>) several successful novels.

1. If I had (knew, <u>known</u>) you were coming, I would have cleaned my room.

2. Cynthia (<u>gave</u>, given) her sister a fabulous birthday present.

3. George and Mike have often (spoke, <u>spoken</u>) of their trip to Japan.

4. The rainbow (<u>grew</u>, grown) more brilliant as the sky cleared.

5. Unfortunately, Julia (<u>tore</u>, torn) her favorite blouse.

6. The entire family (<u>ate</u>, eaten) some of Aunt Vivian's peach cake.

7. Louis had (became, <u>become</u>) bored with his hobby.

8. Simone had (took, <u>taken</u>) some flowers to her cousin in the hospital.

9. Jeff (ran, run) the last four blocks, but he was still late for school.

10. Marcia (threw, thrown) the football back to Peter.

11. The desk had (was, been) Grandfather's favorite place to write.

12. The bridesmaids (wore, worn) pink organza dresses.

13. Fans had (came, come) from many cities to see the historic concert.

14. The birds (flew, flown) north when the weather turned mild.

15. Everyone watching the parade (rose, risen) when they saw the American flag.

16. Linda had (did, done) all the work for the surprise party herself.

17. The breeze had (blew, blown) rose petals across the sidewalk.

18. Alan (stole, stolen) second base when the pitcher wasn't looking.

19. You have (saw, seen) that movie twice already.

20. Celia (chose, chosen) chicken, and Pam ordered fish.

▶ **Writing Link** Use the forms of irregular verbs to write a paragraph about your first day in kindergarten or in junior high.

✓ Unit 3 Review

▶ **Exercise 1** Write *T* (transitive), *I* (intransitive), or *LV* (linking verb) above each verb. Write *PN* above each predicate noun and *PA* above each predicate adjective.

                LV   PA
    The dog becomes nervous during each thunderclap.

          T
1. They brought the presents for the party.
        LV   PA
2. Sean became content.
        I
3. Charles rode easily and gracefully.
        T
4. Isabel rang the bell.
            LV PA   PA
5. That old white cat is fat and lazy.
          T
6. Mr. Tanaka assigned our group the project.
            T
7. The softball team leaves a great record.
          LV   PN
8. The ladybug seems a gentle, harmless creature.
        I
9. Carol paints beautifully.
         T
10. Crystal saw the dead cactus.
        T
11. The trees shaded the park.
        T
12. Camilla sold her cards to Irene.
            LV   PA
13. Sally's track record is impressive.
        T
14. Marie taught me a few Breton words.
           T
15. The archery team won first place.
        T
16. Emily makes expressive, moving portraits.
    LV PA
17. We are ready with these clothes.
         T
18. They guaranteed Sandra a place on the team.
           I
19. The airplane taxied before take-off.
       LV PN
20. That rock is quartz.

Name _____ Class _____ Date _____

Cumulative Review: Units 1–3

▶ **Exercise 1** Draw two lines under each verb. Write in the blank the tense of the verb: *present, past, present progressive, past progressive, present perfect, past perfect, future,* or *future perfect.*

__past perfect__ An enthusiastic group <u>had given</u> the performance.

__past progressive__ 1. Experts <u>were examining</u> the book.

__future__ 2. Lennie <u>will call</u> before Tuesday.

__past perfect__ 3. Their team <u>had lost</u> the game during the first quarter.

__present perfect__ 4. The sun <u>has hidden</u> behind the clouds all day.

__past__ 5. Critics <u>praised</u> that animated movie.

__future perfect__ 6. He <u>will have torn</u> some of his clothing on the hike.

__present__ 7. Ayita <u>pulls</u> weeds in her garden all summer long.

__present progressive__ 8. The crowds <u>are flooding</u> the malls every weekend.

__past perfect__ 9. Alice <u>had talked</u> about the shop for some time.

__past progressive__ 10. We <u>were leaving</u> on a jet plane.

▶ **Exercise 2** Identify each kind of sentence. Write *dec.* (declarative), *int.* (interrogative), *exc.* (exclamatory), or *imp.* (imperative) in the blank. Then write *com.* above each common noun and *prop.* above each proper noun.

__int.__ Where will you go after **com.** school, **prop.** Tina?

__int.__ 1. Had **prop.** Dara seen the **com.** video before the other **com.** students?

__dec.__ 2. **prop.** Belinda, our new **com.** president, will have talked to you about our **com.** plan.

__imp., exc.__ 3. Hurry! Our **com.** dog is barking wildly!

__int.__ 4. When will you paint the old **com.** barn, **prop.** Winona?

__dec.__ 5. "You will ride your **com.** horse in the **com.** parade," **prop.** Father stated firmly.

__dec.__ 6. That famous **com.** piece of **com.** art was painted by **prop.** Picasso, who was born in **prop.** Spain.

__dec.__ 7. **prop.** Kurt had received a **com.** call from the **com.** state of **prop.** New York on **prop.** Friday.

__int.__ 8. Was the **com.** museum well attended last **com.** year?

106 Writer's Choice Grammar Workbook 8, Unit 3

Name _____ Class _____ Date _____

Unit 4: Pronouns

Lesson 25
Pronouns: Personal

A **pronoun** is a word that takes the place of one or more nouns and the words that describe those nouns. A **personal pronoun** refers to a specific person or thing. When a personal pronoun is the subject of a sentence, it is a **subject pronoun**. When a personal pronoun is the object of a verb or preposition, it is an **object pronoun**

Tito is a sports fan. **He** especially likes football. (subject)

Tito coaches younger players. Tito coaches **them**. (direct object of a verb)

The head coach gave Tito some responsibility. The coach gave **him** responsibility. (indirect object of a verb)

For Tito, football is enjoyable. For **him,** football is enjoyable. (object of a preposition)

SUBJECT PRONOUNS		OBJECT PRONOUNS	
SINGULAR	PLURAL	SINGULAR	PLURAL
I	we	me	us
you	you	you	you
he, she, it	they	him, her, it	them

▶ **Exercise 1** Write *S* above each subject pronoun and *O* above each object pronoun.

   S   O
He gave her a bouquet.

   S
1. They have a black and white cat named Max.

               O
2. The Rangers beat us four to nothing.

   S
3. You might see David and Jeremy at the carnival.

     S
4. Is he the main character in the book?

                   O
5. Did Mr. Rodriguez send you the brochure?

                      O
6. Dana stood in line in front of her.

   S
7. We gave the first report.

               O
8. The teacher gave them a *B* plus.

     S
9. Are you going to the volleyball game?

Name _____ Class _____ Date _____

10. When training a dog, always speak gently but firmly to it. [O above "it"]
11. She thought the geology museum was fascinating. [S above "She"]
12. I can't remember meeting Sarah's aunt. [S above "I"]
13. Just give us a chance! [O above "us"]
14. Darren saw him at the youth group meeting. [O above "him"]
15. Raquel has the flu and is taking medication for it. [O above "it"]
16. Does it include batteries or should Mom buy some? [S above "it"]
17. We went to Aunt Martha's house for Thanksgiving. [S above "We"]
18. Were they interested in buying a magazine subscription? [S above "they"]
19. Angela is coming to the dance with me. [O above "me"]
20. It slowly stalked the rabbit out in the field. [S above "It"]
21. The Lions Club donated it to our school. [O above "it"]
22. It became clear that Robby had missed the bus. [S above "It"]
23. Jasmine came with me to the park. [O above "me"]
24. When Dad and Mom went canoeing, they had a great time. [S above "they"]
25. When the mouse ran out of the hole in the stump, the eagle saw it. [O above "it"]
26. Did Jan send you the box of chocolates? [O above "you"]
27. The police officer said calmly to the man, "Give me the briefcase, please." [O above "me"]
28. Could you repeat those instructions, please? [S above "you"]
29. Nicole and Sharon were at the party, which is where Paul saw them. [O above "them"]
30. Did the counselor ask to have the application mailed to you? [O above "you"]
31. I felt as if Caruso were singing the song just for me. [S above "I"] [O above "me"]
32. The first speaker said, "You will enjoy four years at Franklin Middle School." [S above "You"]
33. Walk right up to the woman at the window and hand her the ticket stub. [O above "her"]
34. The Tigers are talented; in fact, they won the state tournament two years in a row. [S above "they"]
35. The actors presented scenes from *Our Town* for us. [O above "us"]
36. If Judy tells Dad about the broken glass, he will understand. [S above "he"]

108 Writer's Choice Grammar Workbook 8, Unit 4

Name _____ Class _____ Date _____

Lesson 26
Pronouns and Antecedents

The noun or group of words that a pronoun refers to is called its **antecedent**. Be sure every pronoun agrees with its antecedent in number (singular or plural) and gender. The gender of a noun or pronoun may be masculine, feminine, or neuter (referring to things).

Puccini and Verdi wrote many great operas. **They** wrote **them** in Italian. (The plural pronoun *they* refers to *Puccini* and *Verdi*. The plural pronoun *them* refers to *operas*.)

Mary sent a letter to Aunt Fran. Mary sent **it** to **her**. (The singular pronoun *it* refers to *letter*. The singular pronoun *her* refers to *Aunt Fran*.)

▶ **Exercise 1** Draw an arrow from each italicized pronoun in the second sentence to its antecedent in the first sentence.

Norway has many mountains and fiords. *It* has little farmland.

1. Norway is a small country in northern Europe. *It* hosted the 1994 Winter Olympics.

2. Many people knew little about Norway before the Olympics. *They* learned more about *it* by watching the Olympics on television.

3. Much of Norway is covered by mountains. *They* make transportation difficult.

4. The Norwegians invented the sport of skiing. *They* often ski daily during the long winter.

5. Thousands of skiers participate in the annual Birkebeiner ski race. Many people consider *it* the world's toughest ski race.

6. Unlike the United States, Norway is a kingdom. *It* also has a prime minister.

7. Queen Sonja and King Haakon reign in Norway. *They* have little power but serve as symbols of the country.

8. Sonja Henie is a famous Norwegian figure skater. *She* won three Olympic gold medals.

Unit 4, Pronouns **109**

Name _____ Class _____ Date _____

9. Sonja Henie won the world figure skating championship ten years in a row. *She* practically made *it* her private property!

10. Sonja Henie won the title from 1927 to 1936. Many other skaters tried to beat *her* but were unsuccessful.

11. After an Olympic career, Sonja Henie made many movies. *They* were popular around the world.

12. Trygve Lie is another famous Norwegian. *He* was the first secretary general of the United Nations.

13. Trygve Lie was elected to the top post at the UN in 1946. *He* led *it* for seven years.

14. Sigrid Undset, a Norwegian author, wrote many novels. *They* often describe life in the Middle Ages.

15. In 1928 Undset won the Nobel Prize for literature. *It* is one of the world's most prestigious awards.

16. In northern Norway live the people known as Sami, or Lapp. *They* have raised reindeer for hundreds of years.

17. The ancestors of today's Norwegians were called Vikings. *They* lived from about A.D. 700 to A.D. 1200.

18. Vikings sailed the seas in sailboats with dragon heads for decorations. *They* were carved on the prow, or front, of the boats.

19. A famous Viking is Leif Ericsson. Many historians believe *him* to be the first European to land in North America.

20. Vikings left traces in Newfoundland and Canada. *They* called this area Vinland.

Lesson 27
Using Pronouns Correctly

Subject pronouns are used in compound subjects, and object pronouns are used in compound objects.

Deon and Lisa played chess. **He** and **she** played chess. (*He* and *she* form the compound subject.)

The game of chess interests Deon and Lisa. The game interests **him** and **her**. (*Him* and *her* form the compound object.)

Whenever the subject pronoun *I* or the object pronoun *me* is part of the compound subject or object, it should come last.

Deon and **I** went to a chess tournament. (not *I* and *Deon*)

Sometimes a noun and pronoun are used together for emphasis. The form of the pronoun depends on the function of the noun in the sentence.

We chess players study chess intently. (*Players* is the subject, so the subject pronoun *we* is used.)

That book is the most interesting to **us** chess players. (*Chess players* is the object of the preposition *to,* so the object pronoun *us* is used.)

Some sentences make incomplete comparisons. The forms of the pronoun can affect the meaning of such sentences. In any incomplete comparison, use the pronoun that would be correct if the comparison were complete.

Deon was more interested in chess than **she** (was).
Deon was more interested in chess than (he was interested in) **her**.

In formal writing, use a subject pronoun after a linking verb.

Deon's best friend is **he**.

▶ **Exercise 1** Underline the pronoun in parentheses that best completes each sentence.

(<u>We</u>, Us) athletes need your enthusiastic support.

1. Jan and (<u>she</u>, her) are our class representatives.
2. Are you going to come with Rudy and (I, <u>me</u>)?
3. The tallest player on the team is (<u>he</u>, him).
4. My sister always says (<u>we</u>, us) Kozlowskis stick together!
5. What did (<u>they</u>, them) do for their history project?

Unit 4, Pronouns **111**

Name _____ Class _____ Date _____

6. The award was given to Dale and (she, **her**).

7. If you ask (I, **me**), there's too much emphasis on winning.

8. Please give (she, **her**) the letter.

9. The president asked (we, **us**) citizens to make some sacrifices.

10. If you have any questions, talk to Ms. Ramirez or (I, **me**).

11. Stefan and Neil saw Aubra and (they, **them**) at the music store.

12. Were you and (**she**, her) interested in signing up for the Drama Club?

13. Let's divide the assignment between you and (we, **us**).

14. The winners of the science competition were Dorreen and (**she**, her).

15. We make a pretty good team, you and (**I**, me).

▶ **Exercise 2** Complete each sentence by writing in the blank a pronoun of the type indicated. There may be more than one correct answer for each item. **Accept any personal pronoun if its form is correct. Sample answers are given.**

The coach will give the players and **them** the details later. (object)

1. Dad bought **us** kids a camera. (object)

2. **We** members of the park committee are very proud of our work. (subject)

3. Did you and **she** see the soccer game? (subject)

4. I don't understand why no one will help you or **me**. (object)

5. Why didn't Nicole and **she** try out for the musical? (subject)

6. You are much more patient than **I**. (subject)

7. The last ones to finish were **she** and **I**. (subject)

8. **It** is not a really difficult course. (subject)

9. We returned our applications to **him** and **her**. (object)

10. Do my parents and **I** need to sign the form in two places? (subject)

11. When I approached the squirrel, **it** scampered away. (subject)

12. The conductor will need an assistant, either **him** or **me**. (object)

13. The woman was standing right behind Don and **me** in the line. (object)

14. **They** and **we** are going to meet in the semifinal. (subject)

15. You can sit with **us** freshmen if you want. (object)

112 Writer's Choice Grammar Workbook 8, Unit 4

Name _____ Class _____ Date _____

Lesson 28
Pronouns: Possessive and Indefinite

A **possessive pronoun** shows who or what has something. Possessive pronouns replace possessive nouns. They may come before a noun or they may stand alone.

His bike was stolen. The bike was **his**.

	USED BEFORE NOUNS	USED ALONE
Singular:	my, your, his, her, its	mine, yours, his, hers, its
Plural:	our, your, their	ours, yours, theirs

An **indefinite pronoun** does not refer to a particular person, place, or thing. The indefinite pronouns *all, any, most, none,* and *some* can be singular or plural depending on the phrase that follows. When an indefinite pronoun is used as the subject of a sentence, the verb must agree with it in number.

Everyone attends the weekly assemblies. (singular)
Several look forward to them very much. (plural)
Most of the assembly **is** interesting to the students. (singular)
Most of the assemblies **are** in the afternoon. (plural)

COMMON INDEFINITE PRONOUNS

Singular:	another	anything	everybody	much	no one	somebody
	anybody	each	everyone	neither	nothing	someone
	anyone	either	everything	nobody	one	something
Plural:	both	few	many	others	several	

▶ **Exercise 1** Underline the correct pronoun in parentheses. In the blank identify the pronoun as *poss.* (possessive) or *ind.* (indefinite).

__ind.__ (Most, <u>One</u>) of the greatest Chinese explorers was Chang Ch'ien.

__poss.__ 1. Chang Ch'ien lived during the second century B.C. in China and was an officer in (<u>its</u>, others) army.

__poss.__ 2. (Yours, <u>His</u>) explorations helped the Han dynasty to flourish.

__poss.__ 3. (<u>Its</u>, Some) emperor at the time, Wu-Ti, sent him on many missions.

__poss.__ 4. During (<u>his</u>, my) lifetime, China was invaded by the Huns, a fierce warrior people.

__ind.__ 5. Finally, the Chinese emperor, Wu-ti, decided that (<u>something</u>, several) had to be done about the marauding Huns.

__poss.__ 6. Wu-ti knew that China needed an ally in (<u>its</u>, either) fight against the Huns.

Unit 4, Pronouns 113

Name _____ Class _____ Date _____

__poss.__ 7. (My, <u>His</u>) choice was a people called the Yueh-chih from central Asia.

__ind.__ 8. (<u>Few</u>, Either) knew the exact location of the Yueh-chih.

__ind.__ 9. To find them, (<u>somebody</u>, their) would have to undertake a dangerous search through unknown country.

__poss.__ 10. China was a large kingdom, but (<u>its</u>, much) western border had not been completely explored.

__poss.__ 11. To protect (neither, <u>his</u>) kingdom, an earlier emperor, Shih Huang-ti, had built the Great Wall, four thousand miles long.

__ind.__ 12. Although the Great Wall was able to slow down the invading Hun army, (<u>nothing</u>, either) could keep them out completely.

__ind.__ 13. Emperor Wu-ti chose Chang Chien, (<u>one</u>, others) of his best and bravest officers, to lead the dangerous mission.

__poss.__ 14. Along with one hundred soldiers and precious gifts for the Yueh-chih king, Chang Ch'ien and his party began (her, <u>their</u>) journey.

__ind.__ 15. However, as soon as they passed the Great Wall on their way west, they were attacked by Huns and almost (<u>everybody</u>, nothing) was killed.

__poss.__ 16. Chang himself spent ten years as a prisoner but learned much about (its, <u>his</u>) captors while planning his escape.

__ind.__ 17. When Chang finally escaped, he traveled west, where (several, <u>few</u>) had ever gone before.

__poss.__ 18. He crossed the vast and deadly Gobi, with (<u>its</u>, their) broiling heat and bitter cold, and traveled almost ten thousand miles!

__ind.__ 19. He explored areas of present-day Afghanistan and Tibet, heard of faraway civilizations in Persia, India, and even Rome, and learned (everybody, <u>much</u>) that would prove valuable to Emperor Wu-ti.

__poss.__ 20. At last in 126 B.C., twelve long years after (their, <u>his</u>) departure, Chang returned to the emperor's court, where he was welcomed as a great hero and given the title of the Great Traveler.

114 Writer's Choice Grammar Workbook 8, Unit 4

Name _____ Class _____ Date _____

Lesson 29
Pronouns: Reflexive and Intensive

A **reflexive pronoun** refers to a noun or another pronoun and indicates that the same person or thing is involved. Reflexive pronouns are formed by adding *-self* or *-selves* to certain personal and possessive pronouns.

The cat saw **itself** in the mirror.   We helped **ourselves** to apples.

REFLEXIVE PRONOUNS
Singular: myself   yourself   himself, herself, itself
Plural: ourselves yourselves   themselves

An **intensive pronoun** emphasizes a noun or pronoun already named.

The president **herself** couldn't be prouder.   We **ourselves** have not yet decided.

▶ **Exercise 1** Place a check (✔) next to the sentence in each pair that correctly uses a reflexive or intensive pronoun.

_____ Myself made this quilt.

__✔__ I made this quilt myself.

1. __✔__ They didn't give themselves enough time to do the job.

   _____ They didn't give theirselves enough time to do the job.

2. _____ The fouled-out player pointed to hisself and asked, "Who, me?"

   __✔__ The fouled-out player pointed to himself and asked, "Who, me?"

3. _____ She found himself in the middle of a dark forest.

   __✔__ She found herself in the middle of a dark forest.

4. __✔__ The governor herself presented the citation.

   _____ The governor she presented the citation.

5. __✔__ Thomas's cat injured itself when it fell off the roof.

   _____ Thomas's cat injured it when it fell off the roof.

6. _____ The hungry soldiers helped theirselves to the farmer's apples.

   __✔__ The hungry soldiers helped themselves to the farmer's apples.

7. _____ Mr. Banks offered to make the reservations hisself.

Unit 4, Pronouns   **115**

Name _____ Class _____ Date _____

___✔___ Mr. Banks offered to make the reservations himself.

8. _____ Yourselves agree with the decision, don't you?

___✔___ You yourselves agree with the decision, don't you?

9. ___✔___ The story itself seemed like a fairy tale come true!

_____ The story it seemed like a fairy tale come true!

10. _____ The soccer players improved them through hard work.

___✔___ The soccer players improved themselves through hard work.

11. ___✔___ The Russians themselves have become our allies.

_____ The Russians and themselves have become allies.

12. _____ Myself was completely confused by the question.

___✔___ I myself was completely confused by the question.

13. _____ My best friend herselves was accepted in the honors program.

___✔___ My best friend herself was accepted in the honors program.

14. ___✔___ We ought to be proud of ourselves for doing the right thing.

_____ We ought to be proud of ourself for doing the right thing.

15. ___✔___ My brother is a good tennis player himself.

_____ My brother is a good tennis player herself.

▶ **Exercise 2** Complete each sentence by filling in a reflexive or intensive pronoun. In the blank write *R* if the pronoun you wrote is reflexive. Write *I* if it is intensive.

__I__ The movie ___itself___ was unbelievably good!

__I__ 1. We built the whole model ___ourselves___.

__R__ 2. I knew the dog had fleas because it was always scratching ___itself___.

__I__ 3. She ___herself___ is the owner of the gas station.

__R__ 4. You boys will have to ask ___yourselves___ that question.

__I__ 5. They ___themselves___ gave us the good news.

__I__ 6. We ___ourselves___ found homes for the abandoned kittens.

__I__ 7. I decided to try to score the winning goal ___myself___.

__I__ 8. Without oxygen, life ___itself___ would not be possible.

Lesson 30
Pronouns: Interrogative and Demonstrative

An **interrogative pronoun** is used to introduce an interrogative sentence. The interrogative pronouns are *who, whose, whom, which,* and *what. Who* is used when the interrogative pronoun is the subject of the sentence. *Whom* is used when the interrogative pronoun is the object of a verb or preposition.

Who saw the accident? (subject)   **Whom** did the driver hit? (direct object)
To **whom** did the police officer give a ticket? (object of a preposition)
That's a beautiful dog. **Whose** is it? (shows possession)
What bothers you? **Which** of those cassettes is it?

A **demonstrative pronoun** is one that points out something. The demonstrative pronouns are *this, that, these,* and *those.*

This is a lovely painting. (singular, refers to something nearby)
These are lovely paintings. (plural, nearby)
That is a tall building. (singular, refers to something at a distance)
Those are tall buildings. (plural, at a distance)

▶ **Exercise 1** Underline each interrogative pronoun. Circle each demonstrative pronoun.

<u>Who</u> will volunteer for (this)?

1. <u>Whom</u> did you see behind the curtain?
2. I think (this) looks best on her.
3. <u>Which</u> is the Grand Champion ewe?
4. <u>Who</u> ate the last piece of cake?
5. (That) isn't my backpack!
6. <u>What</u> are Jeff and Kevin talking about?
7. (Those) are really cool shoes.
8. <u>Whose</u> is the yellow house on Vine Street?
9. I think I'll take four of (these).
10. <u>Which</u> of you would like to go bowling?
11. (This) will do nicely, I think.
12. <u>What</u> is your answer for the last question?

Name _____ Class _____ Date _____

13. **That** is a plan I fear will never work!
14. Whose is **this**?
15. I'd love to have a pair of **those**.
16. Who is at the front door?
17. I'm sorry, **these** are not for sale.
18. Which is the tape you want to buy?
19. From whom did you get **that**?
20. What is happening here?

▶ **Exercise 2** Complete each sentence by writing a pronoun of the type indicated.

___**What**___ is your favorite after-school snack? (interrogative)

1. ___**This or That**___ is the best pizza I've ever eaten! (demonstrative)
2. ___**Who**___ is the architect of that building? (interrogative)
3. To ___**whom**___ did you lend your raincoat? (interrogative)
4. ___**Whose**___ is that green mountain bike? (interrogative)
5. I don't think ___**this or that**___ is a good idea! (demonstrative)
6. Whose boots are ___**these or those**___? (demonstrative)
7. ___**Who**___ was elected club treasurer? (interrogative)
8. Give ___**these or those**___ to David because he was looking for them. (demonstrative)
9. ___**Whom**___ are you going to meet on Saturday? (interrogative)
10. ___**Whose**___ are those computer printouts? (interrogative)
11. ___**Which**___ of the candidates do you support? (interrogative)
12. ___**Who**___ will be at the party tonight? (interrogative)
13. ___**What**___ does she mean by that? (interrogative)
14. ___**Those**___ are my parents standing over there. (demonstrative)
15. ___**Which**___ should I choose? (interrogative)
16. ___**This or That**___ is probably my favorite color. (demonstrative)
17. ___**Whose**___ is that set of tools on the bench? (interrogative)
18. By ___**whom**___ is that symphony? (interrogative)

Name _____ Class _____ Date _____

Unit 4 Review

▶ **Exercise 1** Underline each pronoun. Above each pronoun write *per.* (personal), *poss.* (possessive), *ind.* (indefinite), *ref.* (reflexive), *int.* (intensive), *inter.* (interrogative), or *dem.* (demonstrative).

     inter. per.   poss.
What do I smell coming from your kitchen?

                       per.   ref.
1. Dana laughed hysterically when she saw herself in the fun-house mirror.

  poss.   poss.
2. My uncle owns his own engine repair shop.

   ind.   dem.
3. Many of those were stale.

  ind.
4. Each of the items on the menu sounds delicious.

  per. int.   dem.
5. I myself will finish this tomorrow.

  dem.   ind.
6. That will be something to see!

  per.   ref.   per.
7. They consider themselves better than we are.

  inter.   poss.
8. Who is coming to your graduation party?

  per. int.   ind.
9. You yourself won't be able to decide anything.

  per.   ind.   poss.
10. We can't do anything about his refusal to help.

  per.   ind.   per.
11. I heard several of them scurrying under a rock.

  dem. poss. per.   per.
12. That is theirs, so you had better not touch it.

         dem.   per.
13. Please send these to the McDaniels when you have time.

  inter.   dem.
14. Whose are those?

  per.   per. dem.
15. I will tell you this.

  per.   int.   ind.   per.
16. We ourselves must keep a secret and tell no one about it.

  ind.   per.
17. If anyone moves, she will be really angry.

 per.   per. per.   per.
18. I am telling you I saw them in Smuggler's Cove around midnight!

Unit 4, Pronouns **119**

Name _____ Class _____ Date _____

Cumulative Review: Units 1–4

▶ **Exercise 1** Write *S* in the blank for each group of words that is a sentence, and write *F* for each fragment. For each sentence, draw one line under the complete subject and two lines under the complete predicate.

__S__ <u>My neighbor, Trisha,</u> <u><u>plays the piano and the flute.</u></u>

__F__ 1. The delivery truck up the street.

__S__ 2. <u>The large parking lot across the street</u> <u><u>was filled.</u></u>

__S__ 3. <u>The Great Wall of China, nearly four thousand miles long,</u> <u><u>was built entirely by hand.</u></u>

__S__ 4. <u>One of the visiting students</u> <u><u>told of his experiences in Thailand.</u></u>

__F__ 5. Hastened quickly up the maple tree in our backyard.

__S__ 6. <u>The office building</u> <u><u>was once a schoolhouse.</u></u>

__S__ 7. <u>My favorite celebrity, Oprah Winfrey,</u> <u><u>is an inspiration to many.</u></u>

__F__ 8. The rustic lodge at the foot of the scenic mountain.

__F__ 9. Designed by several architects.

__S__ 10. <u>The first Texas Rangers</u> <u><u>were hired by settlers to protect them against attacks.</u></u>

▶ **Exercise 2** Underline each pronoun. Above each pronoun write *per.* (personal), *poss.* (possessive), *ind.* (indefinite), *ref.* (reflexive), *int.* (intensive), *inter.* (interrogative), or *dem.* (demonstrative).

   per.   **poss.**
<u>She</u> opened <u>their</u> gift last night.

  poss.   **ind.**   **poss.**
1. <u>My</u> aunt knows <u>everyone</u> in <u>her</u> neighborhood.

  per.   **per.**   **poss.**
2. <u>He</u> helped <u>us</u> rehearse <u>our</u> lines for the school play.

     inter.   **per.**   **dem.**
3. With <u>whom</u> did <u>you</u> get in touch about <u>that</u>?

  per. **int.**
4. <u>You</u> <u>yourself</u> should enter the contest.

                 ref.
5. The skunk defends <u>itself</u> by spraying a foul-smelling liquid.

  dem.   **ind.**
6. <u>This</u> seems riper than the <u>others</u>.

Name _____ Class _____ Date _____

Unit 5: Adjectives and Adverbs

Lesson 31
Adjectives

An **adjective** modifies, or describes, a noun or a pronoun. An adjective provides information about the size, shape, color, texture, feeling, sound, smell, number, or condition of a noun or a pronoun.

Brown wrens sometimes build nests above **front** doors.

Most adjectives come before the words they modify. A **predicate adjective** follows a linking verb and modifies the noun or pronoun that is the subject of the sentence.

The clerks in this store are **polite** and **friendly**.

The present participle and past participle forms of verbs may be used as adjectives and predicate adjectives.

A **barking** dog kept me awake all night. (present participle)
The crowd was **excited**. (past participle)

▶ **Exercise 1** Underline each adjective. Draw an arrow to the noun or pronoun it modifies.

Common ants are fascinating insects.

1. Ants are social insects that live in organized colonies.
2. Female ants are either queen ants or worker ants.
3. Male ants mate with young queens and live very short lives.
4. Queens live several years and lay numerous broods of eggs.
5. Ants are also extremely strong and energetic.
6. They are industrious and build structured nests.
7. To do this, they use two sets of powerful jaws that allow them to chew, to dig, and to carry large objects.

Unit 5, Adjectives and Adverbs   121

Name _____ Class _____ Date _____

8. Ant nests often have several rooms with connecting tunnels.

9. Communication is essential in such complex societies.

10. Ants have interesting ways to share information.

11. Elbowed antennae are extremely active and sensitive; they serve as sense organs for touch and smell.

12. When two ants meet, they rely on antennae to determine if they are nestmates or enemies.

13. If they discover they are true nestmates, they touch mouths and pass on stored chemicals and stored food.

14. Various chemicals give ants full "reports" on colony conditions.

15. Received information then directs behaviors of individual ants.

▶ **Exercise 2** Complete each sentence by writing an adjective in the blank. You may use a present or past participle form of a verb in some sentences. **Answers will vary.**

An **excited** swarm of bees buzzed around the **lumbering** bear.

1. In the spring we see many **interesting** insects in our yards.
2. The honey bee is a very **useful** insect.
3. In springtime honey bees visit the **fragrant** blossoms of plants.
4. They make **delicious** honey from the flowers' nectar.
5. Butterflies, like honey bees, help pollinate **spring** flowers.
6. Some butterflies, such as the monarch, migrate **long** distances from the northern United States or Canada to California, Florida, or Mexico.
7. A butterfly's **colorful** wings delight people of all ages.
8. Another **appealing** insect with pretty wings is the ladybug.
9. Ladybugs are **cute** because of their bright color and spots.
10. Ladybugs are useful to farmers because they control **harmful** pests.

Lesson 32
Articles and Proper Adjectives

The words *a, an,* and *the* make up a special group of adjectives called **articles**. *A* and *an* are called **indefinite articles** because they refer to one of a general group of people, places, things, or ideas. Use *a* before words beginning with a consonant sound, and use *an* before words beginning with a vowel sound.

a film **a** bicycle **a** union **an** omelet **an** honor

The is called a **definite article** because it identifies specific people, places, things, or ideas.

The river had flooded **the** nearby fields.

▶ **Exercise 1** Write in the blank the indefinite article that comes before each word or words.

__an__ invigorating hike

__an__ 1. arch
__a__ 2. scientific experiment
__an__ 3. infection
__a__ 4. world atlas
__an__ 5. art exhibit
__an__ 6. underground passage
__an__ 7. inside pitch
__a__ 8. ball of yarn
__an__ 9. avid fan
__a__ 10. clever invention

__a__ 11. vast empire
__an__ 12. honest mistake
__an__ 13. emotional response
__a__ 14. herd of goats
__an__ 15. individual
__an__ 16. hour-long film
__an__ 17. X ray
__an__ 18. application form
__an__ 19. egg yolk
__a__ 20. university

Unit 5, Adjectives and Adverbs 123

Name _____ Class _____ Date _____

A **proper adjective** is formed from a proper noun and always begins with a capital letter. In some cases a proper noun keeps the same form when used as a proper adjective.

April is my favorite month.   I enjoy **April** showers.

In other cases, as with names of places, the proper adjective often adds one of the endings listed below. For those not listed, you may need to consult a dictionary.

ENDING	PROPER ADJECTIVE
-an	American, Texan, German, Tibetan, Mexican, Ohioan, Guatemalan, Moroccan, Alaskan, African, Minnesotan
-ese	Chinese, Japanese, Sudanese, Taiwanese, Portuguese, Lebanese
-ian	Canadian, Italian, Brazilian, Californian, Russian, Asian, Australian, Nigerian, Arabian, Egyptian, Austrian, Indian, Bolivian, Floridian
-ish	Spanish, Irish, Turkish, English, Polish

▶ **Exercise 2** Rewrite each group of words by changing the proper noun to a proper adjective. Change the article if necessary.

a suit from Italy   **an Italian suit**

1. a skier from Austria   **an Austrian skier**
2. a heat wave in August   **an August heat wave**
3. the flag of Lebanon   **the Lebanese flag**
4. a tour of Alaska   **an Alaskan tour**
5. a river in Asia   **an Asian river**
6. the ambassador from Turkey   **the Turkish ambassador**
7. a poem from Japan   **a Japanese poem**
8. a birthday in November   **a November birthday**
9. a writer from Mexico   **a Mexican writer**
10. a rug from Egypt   **an Egyptian rug**
11. a painting from China   **a Chinese painting**
12. the visitor from Morocco   **the Moroccan visitor**
13. a meeting on Monday   **a Monday meeting**
14. a monk from Tibet   **a Tibetan monk**
15. a student from Taiwan   **a Taiwanese student**

Name _____ Class _____ Date _____

Lesson 33
Comparative and Superlative Adjectives

The **comparative** form of an adjective compares two things or people. The **superlative** form of an adjective compares more than two things or people. For most adjectives of one syllable and some of two syllables, *-er* and *-est* are added to form the comparative and superlative.

Comparative: Brazil is **bigger** than Venezuela.
Superlative: Brazil is the **biggest** country in South America.

For most adjectives of two or more syllables, the comparative or superlative is formed by adding *more* or *most* before the adjective. Never use *more* or *most* with adjectives that already end with *-er* or *-est*.

Comparative: Marco is **more adventurous** than Kuan.
Superlative: Pete is the **most adventurous** of all.

Some adjectives have irregular comparative forms.

ADJECTIVE	COMPARATIVE	SUPERLATIVE
good, well	better	best
bad	worse	worst
many, much	more	most
little (amount)	less	least
little (size)	littler	littlest

▶ **Exercise 1** Write *C* in the blank if the sentence is correct and *I* if the sentence is incorrect.

__I__   The bestest vacation Sandra ever took was a trip to Wyoming.

__I__ 1. She visited Yellowstone National Park, the most old national park in the world.

__C__ 2. It is also the largest park in the United States.

__C__ 3. Of all the U.S. parks, Yellowstone has the most extensive wildlife preserve.

__I__ 4. The park has much natural wonders that are amazing to behold.

__I__ 5. Among the park's better attractions are huge canyons, cascading waterfalls, and clear blue lakes.

__I__ 6. There are most geysers and hot springs than any other place in the world.

__C__ 7. Geysers are one of nature's most interesting phenomena.

__C__ 8. Geysers make a most spectacular display as they roar high above the ground.

Unit 5, Adjectives and Adverbs   **125**

Name _____ Class _____ Date _____

__I__ 9. While there are over two hundred geysers in Yellowstone, some shoot water more high than others.

__I__ 10. Some erupt oftener than others.

__I__ 11. Old Faithful is famouser than the other geysers in the park.

__C__ 12. It spurts a stream of hot steaming water higher than one hundred feet into the air.

__C__ 13. This most splendid geyser erupts from every half hour to every two hours.

__I__ 14. For many visitors of Yellowstone, seeing Old Faithful is their funnest memory of the park.

__I__ 15. After seeing Old Faithful, Sandra understood more well how the term *geyser* came from the Icelandic word *geysir,* which means "to rush forth."

▶ **Exercise 2** Complete each sentence by writing in the blank the correct comparative or superlative form of the adjective indicated.

Yellowstone is the _____**most beautiful**_____ park I've ever seen. (beautiful)

1. In 1872 Congress established Yellowstone National Park, the _____**oldest**_____ national park in the world. (old)

2. The United States has _____**more**_____ than fifty national parks. (many)

3. The _____**best**_____ known include Yellowstone in Wyoming, the Grand Canyon in Arizona, Yosemite in California, and Great Smoky Mountain in Tennessee and North Carolina. (well)

4. The national park system also includes many parks _____**less famous**_____ than these four. (famous)

5. The national park system protects some of this country's _____**most intriguing**_____ natural areas. (intriguing)

6. The Everglades in Florida is the _____**largest**_____ subtropical wilderness in the United States. (large)

7. Denali National Park in Alaska is the site of the nation's _____**highest**_____ mountain, Mount McKinley. (high)

8. While a few of the national parks are near cities, _____**most**_____ parks are far from big towns. (many)

9. Not surprisingly, those parks that are _____**nearest**_____ to population centers receive the _____**most**_____ visitors. (near, many)

10. Among the _____**most crowded**_____ parks are Great Smoky Mountain and Acadia. (crowded)

126 Writer's Choice Grammar Workbook 8, Unit 5

Name _____ Class _____ Date _____

Lesson 34
Demonstratives

Demonstrative adjectives point out something and describe nouns by answering the question *which one?* or *which ones?* The words *this, that, these,* and *those* are demonstrative adjectives when they describe nouns. *This* and *that* describe singular nouns. *These* and *those* describe plural nouns.

This, that, these, and *those* can also be used as **demonstrative pronouns**. They are pronouns when they take the place of nouns.

DEMONSTRATIVE ADJECTIVES	DEMONSTRATIVE PRONOUNS
This book is exciting.	**This** is an exciting book.
I enjoy **these** types of stories.	I enjoy **these**.
That plot is convincing.	**That** is a realistic setting.
She writes **those** kinds of books.	Our class liked reading **those**.

▶ **Exercise 1** Underline the word in parentheses that best completes each sentence.

Did Bella find (that, <u>those</u>) missing shoes?

1. (<u>This</u>, These) window needs to be repaired.
2. (Those, <u>That</u>) man must be over seven feet tall!
3. Did Ashley say she was bringing (this, <u>those</u>) kinds of cookies?
4. I believe (these, <u>this</u>) is what you're looking for.
5. Would you please see that Serafina gets (<u>those</u>, that) reports?
6. I think (these, <u>this</u>) plan of yours is quite practical.
7. (<u>Those</u>, These) animals over there are llamas.
8. Not just anyone can do (<u>this</u>, these) job, you know.
9. Does everyone in the class wear (that, <u>those</u>) kinds of shoes?
10. You often see (<u>this</u>, these) kind of movie during the holiday season.
11. The Computer Club adviser said that (<u>these</u>, this) keyboards were easier to use than the old ones.
12. (<u>That</u>, This) pass was way over his head!
13. How about (them, <u>those</u>) '49ers!

Name _____ Class _____ Date _____

14. The speaker said that (**this**, these) product is the wave of the future.

15. (**These**, This) types of illnesses are not common anymore.

16. I didn't really care for (**those**, them) remarks.

17. (These, **This**) rose is lighter in color than that one.

18. (**Those**, Them) rocks contain iron pyrite.

19. (These, **This**) application form is not complete.

20. (**That**, Those) hat she's wearing is a little bit unusual.

▶ **Exercise 2** Underline each demonstrative adjective. Circle each demonstrative pronoun.

(This) appears to be the lid for that box.

1. Please give them these tickets.
2. Have you been to that new CD and tape store at the mall?
3. The doctor said to take one teaspoon of (this) twice a day.
4. (These) are not the right parts.
5. Those new videotapes aren't tracking properly.
6. That speedboat is the fastest on the river.
7. (Those) are not the runners who finished near the front of the pack.
8. This old clarinet squeaks whenever I try to play it.
9. These cows give more milk than any other type.
10. Without a doubt, (this) is the best campsite we've had yet.
11. (That) is a wonderful idea!
12. My mother heard those women speaking Swahili.
13. If you eat any more of (those), you'll get a stomachache.
14. (These) were on the top shelf to the left.
15. That girl by the door has a twin sister.
16. We'll never make it to Denver in this beat-up car.
17. Those boots leak because the rubber has cracked.
18. (That) was the pony she rode during the fair.

Name _____ Class _____ Date _____

Lesson 35
Adverbs

An **adverb** modifies, or describes, a verb, an adjective, or another adverb. When modifying an adjective or another adverb, an adverb usually comes before the word. When modifying a verb, an adverb can occupy different positions in the sentence.

The woman walked **slowly**. (modifies a verb)
Extremely cold weather can be dangerous. (modifies an adjective)
It snows **very** often in November. (modifies another adverb)

An adverb may tell *when, where,* or *how* about a verb. It may also tell to *what extent* a quality exists. This kind of adverb is called an **intensifier**. *Very, too, rather, quite,* and *almost* are intensifiers.

Many adverbs are formed by adding *-ly* to adjectives. However, not all words that end in *-ly* are adverbs. The words *kindly, friendly, lively,* and *lonely* are usually adjectives. Similarly, not all adverbs end in *-ly*. Some that do not are *afterward, sometimes, later, often, soon, here, there, everywhere, fast, hard, long, slow,* and *straight.*

▶ **Exercise 1** Draw an arrow from each adverb to the word it modifies. In the blank, write *V* if the adverb modifies a verb, *adj.* if it modifies an adjective, or *adv.* if it modifies another adverb. A sentence may have more than one adverb.

V, adj.   Lena and Trent thoroughly enjoyed the truly vigorous hike.

V   1. When hiking in the American West, you must proceed carefully.

V   2. People walking in rocky areas sometimes come across rattlesnakes.

adj.   3. Some people are quite afraid of snakes.

V, adj.   4. If not provoked, rattlesnakes are not very dangerous.

adv., V   5. All rattlesnakes are poisonous, but they bite people relatively rarely.

V   6. People often find rattlesnakes in dry, rocky areas.

adj.   7. They are particularly numerous in the Southwest.

V   8. However, they also exist in the eastern part of the country.

For item 4 *not* **may be construed as modifying** *very*, **an adverb.**

Unit 5, Adjectives and Adverbs   **129**

Name _____ Class _____ Date _____

__V___ 9. Surprisingly, the largest rattler is native to the East.

__V___ 10. The eastern diamondback rattlesnake lives there.

__adj.__ 11. Practically all eastern diamondbacks live on the southeast coast, from North Carolina to Florida.

__adj.__ 12. This largest of rattlers can grow to almost eight feet!

__V___ 13. Rattlesnakes have adapted well to their environment.

__V___ 14. A snake's body temperature depends entirely on the temperature of the air around it.

__V___ 15. If the temperature drops quickly, a rattlesnake can die.

__V___ 16. Snakes will often lie in the sun to get warm.

▶ **Exercise 2** Complete each sentence by writing an adverb in the blank. **Answers will vary.**

Emilio and Zina will meet us at the zoo _____**later**_____.

1. Rattlers, like all snakes, are _____**greatly**_____ misunderstood.
2. Snakes are often killed because _____**so**_____ many people have a fear of them.
3. Some people _____**wrongly**_____ assume that snakes are evil.
4. _____**Actually**_____, all snakes, including poisonous ones, are frightened of people.
5. When hiking in rattlesnake country, _____**simply**_____ follow a few safety rules.
6. Look _____**carefully**_____ before you step into bushes or behind rocks.
7. Before you put your hand on a ledge, look _____**carefully**_____ .
8. _____**Always**_____ wear leather boots when you are hiking in rattlesnake country.
9. Rattlers are unable to bite _____**hard**_____ enough to penetrate boot leather.
10. _____**Never**_____ try to chase or pick up a snake.
11. If you see a rattlesnake, walk _____**away**_____ from it.
12. _____**Finally**_____, carry a first-aid kit.

130 Writer's Choice Grammar Workbook 8, Unit 5

Lesson 36
Comparative and Superlative Adverbs

The **comparative** form of an adverb compares two actions. The **superlative** form of an adverb compares more than two actions. Long adverbs and adverbs ending in *-ly* require the use of *more* or *most*. Shorter adverbs need *-er* or *-est* as an ending.

Comparative: She records the experiment **more accurately** than he does.
Alicia studied **harder** than Rex did.
Superlative: She recorded the experiment **most accurately** of all the students.
Alicia studied **hardest** of all.

Some important adverbs have irregular comparative and superlative forms.

ADVERB	COMPARATIVE	SUPERLATIVE
well	better	best
badly	worse	worst
little (amount)	less	least

The words *less* and *least* are used before both short and long adverbs to form the negative comparative and negative superlative.

Jarrett sings **less well**. Amie sings **least rhythmically** of all.

▶ **Exercise 1** Fill in each blank with the correct form of the adverb.

ADVERB	COMPARATIVE	SUPERLATIVE
swiftly	more swiftly	most swiftly
1. easily	more easily	most easily
2. rapidly	more rapidly	most rapidly
3. far	farther	farthest
4. well	better	best
5. dangerously	more dangerously	most dangerously
6. fast	faster	fastest
7. neatly	more neatly	most neatly
8. happily	more happily	most happily

Name _____ Class _____ Date _____

9. badly	worse	worst
10. straight	straighter	straightest
11. recklessly	more recklessly	most recklessly
12. **truly**	more truly	most truly
13. **incredibly**	more incredibly	most incredibly
14. often	more often	most often
15. **little**	less	least
16. **proudly**	more proudly	most proudly
17. **closely**	more closely	most closely
18. **fully**	more fully	most fully
19. soon	sooner	soonest
20. **quickly**	more quickly	most quickly

▶ **Exercise 2** Complete each sentence by writing in the blank the correct form, comparative or superlative, of the adverb in parentheses.

I sat ___**closer**___ to the window than Stuart did. (close)

1. That's the ___**fastest**___ I've ever seen our cat run! (fast)

2. Tornadoes occur ___**more often**___ in the Midwest and Plains states than in other areas of the country. (often)

3. Mandy performed ___**better**___ in the gymnastics meet than Robert did. (well)

4. The soprano section sings ___**most strongly**___ of all. (strongly)

5. Talk ___**more loudly**___ so we can hear you! (loudly)

6. I'm sure she did ___**worse**___ on the math test than I did. (badly)

7. The DeAngelos had to walk ___**farthest**___ of all to school. (far)

8. Spot approached the food dish ___**less enthusiastically**___ than the hungry stray did. (enthusiastically)

9. No one was running around ___**more frantically**___ than Lisa! (frantically)

10. My brother plays that blues song ___**best**___ of all. (well)

Name _____ Class _____ Date _____

Lesson 37
Using Adverbs and Adjectives

Adverbs and **adjectives** are often confused, especially when they appear after verbs. A predicate adjective follows a linking verb. An adverb follows an action verb.

The teachers in our school are **enthusiastic**. (adjective describing *teachers*)
Teachers in our school must work **hard**. (adverb describing *work*)

The words *bad, badly, good,* and *well* can be confusing. *Bad* and *good* are adjectives. They are used after linking verbs. *Badly* and *well* are adverbs. They describe action verbs. When used after a linking verb to describe a person's health, *well* is an adjective.

ADJECTIVE	ADVERB
This movie is **bad**.	The actors performed **badly**.
The popcorn is **good**.	The seats recline **well**.
I don't feel very **well**.	

People also confuse *real* and *really, sure* and *surely,* and *most* and *almost. Real, sure,* and *most* are adjectives. *Really, surely,* and *almost* are adverbs.

ADJECTIVE	ADVERB
Skating is a **real** workout.	Skating is **really** fun.
A skater needs **sure** feet.	To go fast is **surely** the most fun.
Most skaters are careful.	I **almost** never fall.

▶ **Exercise 1** Underline the word in parentheses that best completes the sentence.

Jordan's (<u>sure</u>, surely) delivery guaranteed the success of his speech.

1. Josh had (most, <u>almost</u>) completed the lifesaving class at the YMCA.
2. We didn't do too (bad, <u>badly</u>), all things considered.
3. Learning bird songs and calls is a (<u>good</u>, well) way to identify them.
4. My geometry test is today, and I don't feel very (<u>well</u>, good).
5. Janelle was (real, <u>really</u>) glad to hear from them.
6. Always walk (quiet, <u>quietly</u>) in the woods in case you come upon some deer.
7. (Sure, <u>Surely</u>), he isn't serious about dropping out of the Camera Club!
8. All the staff members felt this issue of the paper turned out fairly (good, <u>well</u>).

Unit 5, Adjectives and Adverbs   133

Name _____ Class _____ Date _____

9. (Most, Almost) guitars have six strings, but some have twelve.

10. Making the yearbook staff is a (real, really) accomplishment.

11. That group of kids is so (loud, loudly) I can barely hear the film.

12. The coach said the team played just (good, well) enough to win.

13. She seemed very (sure, surely) of herself when she walked into the classroom.

14. Kari finished the quiz (most quick, most quickly) of all.

15. The baby ducklings (ready, readily) took to the water.

16. The nurse took her temperature after noticing she didn't look very (good, well).

17. Tina wanted very (bad, badly) to make the softball team.

18. Pete was (most, almost) finished with lunch when I arrived.

19. The plan is (possible, possibly) to carry out, although it will be quite risky.

20. I (sure, surely) will not go there with you!

21. The twelfth of November last year was (real, really) chilly.

22. Luis tried to look at his chances (realistic, realistically).

23. Frankly, this Chinese food doesn't taste (good, well) to me.

24. The judges felt his singing was (more beautiful, more beautifully) than Ellen's.

25. They're not (sure, surely) they'll be able to participate in the math contest.

26. The sound quality at that concert was very (bad, badly).

27. My dad looked (real, really) happy when we gave him his present.

28. Marianne was (extreme, extremely) surprised when she heard who had called her.

▶ **Writing Link** Write a short paragraph about your favorite extracurricular activity. Include several adjectives and adverbs.

_____
_____
_____
_____
_____
_____

Name _____ Class _____ Date _____

Lesson 38
Avoiding Double Negatives

The adverb *not* is a negative word. **Negative words** express the idea of "no." *Not* often appears in a shortened form as part of a contraction.

CONTRACTIONS WITH *NOT*

is not=isn't	will not=won't	do not=don't	had not=hadn't
was not=wasn't	cannot=can't	did not=didn't	would not=wouldn't
were not=weren't	could not=couldn't	have not=haven't	should not=shouldn't

Other negative words are listed below. Each negative word has several opposites. These are **affirmative words**, or words that show the idea of "yes."

NEGATIVE	AFFIRMATIVE	NEGATIVE	AFFIRMATIVE
never	ever, always	no one	everyone, someone
nobody	anybody, somebody	nothing	something, anything
none	one, all, some, any	nowhere	somewhere, anywhere

Be careful to avoid using two negative words together in the same sentence. This is called a **double negative**. Correct a double negative by removing one of the negative words or by replacing one with an affirmative word.

Incorrect: That isn't no beautiful sofa.
Correct: That isn't a beautiful sofa.   That is no beautiful sofa.

▶ **Exercise 1** Place a check next to the sentence in each pair that is correct.

_____   Soto hasn't never saved that amount of money.
__✓__   Soto hasn't ever saved that amount of money.

_____ 1. I haven't never met my great-grandfather because he lives in Korea.
__✓__   I haven't ever met my great-grandfather because he lives in Korea.

__✓__ 2. You can't go anywhere in New York City without seeing tall buildings.
_____   You can't go nowhere in New York City without seeing tall buildings.

__✓__ 3. He didn't do anything about that cut on his arm.
_____   He didn't do nothing about that cut on his arm.

_____ 4. It wasn't no big deal when we won the game.
__✓__   It was no big deal when we won the game.

Unit 5, Adjectives and Adverbs **135**

Name _____ Class _____ Date _____

_____ 5. My guinea pig wouldn't eat none of his lettuce.

✓ My guinea pig wouldn't eat any of his lettuce.

✓ 6. Mr. Jankowski could find no one to operate the VCR.

_____ Mr. Jankowski couldn't find no one to operate the VCR.

✓ 7. Don't worry, it isn't anything important.

_____ Don't worry, it isn't nothing important.

_____ 8. The detective shouted, "Don't nobody move!"

✓ The detective shouted, "Don't anybody move!"

_____ 9. The family shopping for a car said they weren't interested in nothing too expensive.

✓ The family shopping for a car said they weren't interested in anything too expensive.

✓ 10. A person shouldn't ever eat wild mushrooms without checking if they're safe.

_____ A person shouldn't never eat wild mushrooms without checking if they're safe.

▶ **Exercise 2** Complete each sentence by filling in a word that makes a correct negative sentence. **Answers may vary.**

Greg ___**couldn't**___ have known someone planned a surprise party.

1. There isn't ___**any**___ paper in the copier.
2. We couldn't find ___**anyone**___ to be the ninth player on our softball team.
3. ___**Nothing**___ can take the place of the photo I lost.
4. They divided the pizza, but I didn't get ___**any**___.
5. Our team ___**hadn't**___ ever beaten the Chargers until today.
6. I really don't want ___**anybody**___ fooling around with my stereo.
7. I ___**would**___ be nowhere without the help of my parents.
8. You're wasting your time, Xenon—I ___**will**___ tell you nothing!
9. The weather forecaster promised there ___**would**___ be no rain today.
10. The witness claimed she ___**had**___ seen nothing at all.

Name _____ Class _____ Date _____

✓ Unit 5 Review

▶ **Exercise 1** Complete each sentence by writing in the blank the type of word indicated in parentheses. Answers will vary.

The pesky pooch shuffled ____**softly**____ across the dark room. (adverb)

1. Lemurs and marmosets are among nature's most ____**fascinating**____ creatures. (adjective)

2. We decided to eat at a ____**Mexican**____ restaurant. (proper adjective)

3. Kasem and Rudy wore ____**almost**____ identical expressions of bewilderment. (adverb)

4. Hope will be ____**more careful**____ with that crystal vase than Jason was. (adjective, comparative form)

5. I suggest that you don't ____**ever**____ argue with them. (adverb)

6. The character in the book was on a TV show called *The* ____**Restless**____ *Hearts*. (adjective)

7. That float was ____**the**____ best in the entire parade. (definite article)

8. ____**Those**____ reptiles in that cage are called tuataras. (demonstrative adjective)

9. We don't ____**usually**____ eat ice cream for breakfast. (adverb)

10. That tree produces the ____**sweetest**____ cherries! (adjective, superlative form)

11. We couldn't find ____**anybody**____ to help us hang the mural. (affirmative word)

12. Siberia is a ____**vast**____ land of contrasts. (adjective)

13. I heard the sophisticated woman speaking with a ____**French**____ accent. (proper adjective)

14. Keenan learned the formulas ____**more easily**____ than Kara did. (adverb, comparative form)

Unit 5, Adjectives and Adverbs   **137**

Name _____ Class _____ Date _____

Cumulative Review: Units 1–5

▶ **Exercise 1** Draw one line under each noun and two lines under each verb.

<u>Kyle</u> and <u>Steve</u> <u><u>buried</u></u> themselves in their <u>work</u>.

1. The <u>trees</u> <u><u>swayed</u></u> majestically from <u>side</u> to <u>side</u>.
2. <u>William</u> <u><u>prefers</u></u> <u>politics</u> to <u>football</u>.
3. Each <u>guest</u> <u><u>received</u></u> a colorful <u>collection</u> of <u>cards</u>.
4. Deep red and white <u>roses</u> <u><u>decorated</u></u> the <u>hall</u>.
5. <u>Joan</u> <u><u>wrote</u></u> to her Russian <u>friend</u> twice a <u>month</u>.
6. This historic <u>staircase</u> <u><u>has been renovated</u></u> recently.
7. Aunt <u>Clara</u> <u><u>cannot decide</u></u> which <u>lamp</u> <u><u>is</u></u> best.
8. <u>Obi</u> <u><u>will dedicate</u></u> his next <u>song</u> to his <u>mother</u>.
9. The <u>Kazuos</u> <u><u>donated</u></u> three <u>sets</u> of <u>encyclopedias</u> to the local <u>library</u>.
10. The track <u>team</u> <u><u>has been practicing</u></u> for more than an <u>hour</u>.
11. Mr. <u>Stanton</u> <u><u>plays</u></u> <u>racquetball</u> at the sports <u>club</u>.
12. <u>Rodolfo</u> and <u>Nicole</u> <u><u>will meet</u></u> us in front of the <u>restaurant</u>.
13. <u>Carmen</u> <u><u>bought</u></u> her grandmother a beautiful <u>sweater</u>.
14. Many <u>stars</u> <u><u>became</u></u> visible above the <u>clouds</u>.
15. <u>Florida</u> <u><u>boasts</u></u> several tourist <u>attractions</u>.
16. <u>Rashida</u> <u><u>invited</u></u> everyone in our <u>class</u> to the <u>celebration</u>.
17. The <u>crew</u> of the <u>ship</u> <u><u>spotted</u></u> <u>land</u> this <u>morning</u>.
18. Before <u>Tuesday</u>, <u>Matsue</u> <u><u>will have completed</u></u> her <u>report</u>.
19. <u>Goldfish</u> briskly <u><u>swam</u></u> around the <u>aquarium</u>.
20. <u>Visitors</u> to the <u>museum</u> often <u><u>enjoy</u></u> the <u>planetarium</u>.
21. <u>Versailles</u> <u><u>is</u></u> the <u>name</u> of the <u>palace</u> that <u>France</u> <u><u>built</u></u> for <u>Louis XIV</u>.
22. <u>Jules Verne</u> <u><u>wrote</u></u> excellent science-fiction <u>stories</u>.
23. The school <u>choir</u> <u><u>traveled</u></u> to <u>New York</u> and <u><u>performed</u></u> at <u>Carnegie Hall</u>.
24. <u>June</u> <u><u>is</u></u> her favorite <u>month</u> of the <u>year</u>.

Name _____ Class _____ Date _____

▶ **Exercise 2** Complete each sentence by writing in the blank the tense of the verb indicated in parentheses. Circle each pronoun.

Ayita ___hoped___ (she) would arrive in time to board the plane. (past tense of *hope*)

1. The stack of papers ___will grow___ faster than Mr. Yee can read (them). (future tense of *grow*)

2. ___Wait___ until (they) finish clearing the road. (present tense of *wait*)

3. The jury ___stayed___ at the hotel near that courthouse. (past tense of *stay*)

4. Both students ___have helped___ (us) before. (present perfect tense of *help*)

5. (Her) charm ___will have reached___ the entire audience by the end of (her) performance. (future perfect tense of *reach*)

6. Dr. Wilcox (herself) ___demonstrates___ the experiment. (present tense of *demonstrate*)

7. Timothy ___had wanted___ to canoe across the river before (he) saw how choppy the water was. (past perfect tense of *want*)

8. Apple and cherry pies ___were baking___ in the oven. (past progressive form of *bake*)

9. (That) ___seems___ to be a highly unlikely excuse. (present tense of *seem*)

10. Sada ___will teach___ (anyone) to play the piano. (future tense of *teach*)

11. (Someone) said that Ryan ___had given___ (his) autographed baseball to a sick friend. (past perfect tense of *give*)

12. The most valuable players of the game ___were___ Julio and (he). (past tense of *be*)

13. The flower garden ___has contained___ more varieties than (this). (present perfect tense of *contain*)

14. (We) ___are working___ on a new method of kite-flying. (present progressive form of *work*)

15. Renata and (she) ___painted___ the picket fence. (past tense of *paint*)

Unit 5, Adjectives and Adverbs 139

Name _____ Class _____ Date _____

16. The clowns in the parade _____**were smiling**_____ as (they) greeted the children. (past progressive form of *smile*)

17. Coach Rodriguez _____**will have won**_____ more games than any coach in (our) school's history by the end of the season. (future perfect tense of *win*)

18. Ms. Kotlinski _____**allowed**_____ (herself) plenty of time to drive to Canada. (past tense of *allow*)

19. (Most) of the trees in (our) neighborhood _____**shed**_____ (their) leaves in October. (present tense of *shed*)

20. (This) _____**has appeared**_____ to be the longest winter yet. (present perfect tense of *appear*)

▶ **Exercise 3** Draw one line under each adjective. (Ignore the articles *a*, *an*, and *the*.) Draw two lines under each adverb. Draw an arrow from each adjective or adverb to the word it modifies.

A playful squirrel ran quickly to the tree.

1. Julius joyfully delivered presents to eager nieces.
2. Falling snow already has covered the landscape.
3. Church bells rang merrily.
4. The humble director graciously accepted her two awards.
5. To please the young birds, the red cardinal went in search of food.
6. That music store hardly ever has what I am looking for.
7. Purple wildflowers danced in the spring breeze.
8. Light from the sun bathed the sandy beach sooner than we expected.
9. Neighbors often bring me marvelous apples.
10. Grandmother served a delicious meal of wedding soup and manicotti.
11. The soccer team almost won a difficult game.
12. She carefully chose a new piece of jewelry.

Unit 6: Prepositions, Conjunctions, and Interjections

Lesson 39
Prepositions and Prepositional Phrases

A **preposition** is a word that relates a noun or a pronoun to another word in a sentence. Prepositions of more than one word are **compound prepositions**

The magazine **on** the table just arrived.
Darlene will perform the solo **instead of** Retta.

COMMONLY USED PREPOSITIONS

about	at	by	like	over	up
above	before	down	near	since	upon
across	behind	during	of	through	with
after	below	for	off	throughout	within
against	beneath	from	on	to	without
along	beside	in	onto	toward	
among	between	inside	out	under	
around	beyond	into	outside	until	

COMPOUND PREPOSITIONS

according to	aside from	in front of	instead of
across from	because of	in place of	on account of
along with	far from	in spite of	on top of

▶ **Exercise 1** Underline each preposition or compound preposition.

The development <u>of</u> flea markets <u>in</u> the United States is an outgrowth <u>of</u> the bazaar.

1. A bazaar is an Asian marketplace held <u>inside</u> the city.

2. Here, traders <u>in</u> small stalls or shops sell miscellaneous goods.

3. Some bazaars are located <u>along</u> a single, narrow street.

4. Others spread <u>throughout</u> a number <u>of</u> streets.

5. <u>For</u> example, there might be a street <u>of</u> coppersmiths <u>beside</u> two streets <u>of</u> booksellers.

6. One section could house a huge covered bazaar <u>with</u> four hundred shops.

7. The bazaar originated <u>in</u> early times.

8. During that period, it served for gossip and trade.

9. One city known for its colorful bazaars since ancient times is Istanbul, Turkey.

10. It is the only major city located on two continents—Asia and Europe.

11. Istanbul, called Constantinople from A.D. 330 to 1453, is Turkey's leading center of industry, trade, and culture.

12. Tourists visit the city to see its museums and palaces, along with its bazaars.

13. A lucky sightseer might find an antique beneath the many wares or trinkets at one of these unique shops.

14. Some shopkeepers might expect the tourist to bargain over the cost instead of paying a fixed price.

15. Aside from the large crowds, many one-of-a-kind items can be found throughout the bazaar-laden streets.

A **prepositional phrase** is a group of words that begins with a preposition and ends with a noun or pronoun called the **object of the preposition**.

The pitcher **in the rear** is filled **with sweetened tea**.

▶ **Exercise 2** Draw one line under each prepositional phrase. Draw a second line under each object of the preposition.

Sadie Jenkins hired Heloise and me to clean the large shed behind her house.

1. After the discovery of many antiques, we suggested that she sell the items.

2. Three porcelain dolls and a wooden chess set of Renaissance design were among our best finds.

3. Mrs. Jenkins smiled at us and said that along with our pay we could have twenty percent of the money we generated.

4. Diving into our task with new enthusiasm, we searched through every box and container inside the shed.

5. When Dad contacted two antique dealers and told them about the dozens of items, they agreed to come to the house and make an offer.

Lesson 40
Pronouns as Objects of Prepositions

When a pronoun is the object of a preposition, use an object pronoun and not a subject pronoun.

The burly man sang a lullaby to Karen. The burly man sang a lullaby to **her**.

Sometimes a preposition will have a compound object consisting of a noun and a pronoun. Remember to use an object pronoun in a compound object.

I sold tickets to Carrie and Seana. I sold tickets to Carrie and **her**.
Alberto agreed with Willie and **me**.

The subject pronoun *who* is never the object of a preposition; only the object pronoun *whom* can be an object.

The woman to **whom** I spoke is from Colombia.
Of **whom** did you ask directions?

▶ **Exercise 1** Underline the pronoun that best completes each sentence.

For (who, <u>whom</u>) are these party favors intended?

1. Community service is important to Simon and (we, <u>us</u>).
2. Did you give instructions to Waldo and (she, <u>her</u>)?
3. Is this carnation plant intended for (he, <u>him</u>)?
4. For Lee Chan and (he, <u>him</u>), did the lesson present much difficulty?
5. The decision was easy for Michael and (he, <u>him</u>).
6. The stranger to (who, <u>whom</u>) I spoke turned out to be Pietro's brother.
7. I explained the situation to Mickey, Juan, and (<u>her</u>, she).
8. With (who, <u>whom</u>) did you go to the movies?
9. For his brother and (he, <u>him</u>), sleeping late meant rising at eight.
10. The results of the poll were released by Twila, Arthur, and (she, <u>her</u>).
11. They were telling stories about (who, <u>whom</u>)?
12. According to Myron and (she, <u>her</u>), they never watered the lawn during the drought.
13. How many of (they, <u>them</u>) bought tickets for the basketball game?

Unit 6, Prepositions, Conjunctions, and Interjections

Name _____ Class _____ Date _____

14. Upon (who, <u>whom</u>) did the blocks collapse?

15. We sat near (they, <u>them</u>) at the band concert.

▶ **Exercise 2** Underline each pronoun that is an object of a preposition. Write *C* in the blank if the pronoun is correct. Write the correct pronoun if necessary.

<u>me</u>   John gave a knowing look to Frieda and <u>I</u>.

<u>C</u>   **1.** The party was a surprise to <u>me</u>.

<u>her</u>   **2.** The newcomers were neighbors of Lisa and <u>she</u>.

<u>me</u>   **3.** Treg should have called you or <u>I</u>.

<u>C</u>   **4.** Vacations are boring for <u>whom</u>?

<u>me</u>   **5.** The waitress spilled juice on <u>I</u>.

<u>C</u>   **6.** Gently rolling hills are unfamiliar to <u>us</u> in Iowa.

<u>him</u>   **7.** All of those murals were painted by <u>he</u>.

<u>them</u> **8.** Alice introduced her parents to <u>they</u>.

<u>whom</u> **9.** Shawnda is the person to <u>who</u> we report.

<u>C</u>   **10.** David raised twenty dollars for <u>us</u> to give to the needy family.

<u>me</u>   **11.** The map that she drew looked very confusing to Juan and <u>I</u>.

<u>whom</u> **12.** "To <u>who</u> are you speaking, Richard?" asked the teacher.

<u>them</u> **13.** I'll share my lunch with you and <u>they</u>.

<u>C</u>   **14.** The winner certainly wasn't with <u>me</u>!

<u>me</u>   **15.** Will you come to the dance with Bill and <u>I</u>?

▶ **Writing Link** Write a paragraph about an interesting place you have visited. Include pronouns as objects of prepositions.

Lesson 41
Prepositional Phrases as Adjectives and Adverbs

A prepositional phrase that modifies or describes a noun or pronoun is an **adjective phrase**. Notice that, unlike most adjectives, an adjective phrase usually comes after the word it modifies.

I noticed a man **with bushy eyebrows**.

A prepositional phrase that modifies a verb, an adjective, or another adverb is an **adverb phrase**. An adverb phrase tells *when, where,* or *how* an action occurs.

The hikers rested **beside a brook**. (describes a verb)
The vista was breathtaking **from this view**. (describes an adjective)
The quartet performed well **for such an early hour**. (describes an adverb)

▶ **Exercise 1** Underline each prepositional phrase. Draw an arrow to the word it modifies.

Movies began in the late 1800s. People experimented with devices to make pictures move.

1. One of these experimenters was Thomas A. Edison.

2. George Eastman, a pioneer in photographic equipment, helped Edison invent the kinetoscope.

3. Motion pictures were projected for the first time on December 28, 1895.

4. Early filmmakers photographed almost anything near the camera.

5. Language differences presented no problem because movies, at that time, were silent.

6. Titles, or printed dialogue, were inserted between scenes.

7. Soon audiences became bored, and attendance at the movies declined.

8. One development that saved movies from extinction was that they began to tell stories.

9. One such story, *The Great Train Robbery,* led to the establishment of nickelodeons.

Unit 6, Prepositions, Conjunctions, and Interjections **145**

Name _____ Class _____ Date _____

10. A nickelodeon was an early movie theater with a five-cent admission charge.

11. Around 1927, a sound system called Movietone was developed in the studios.

12. These first talkies were awkward and tense compared to the silent films.

13. Many silent film stars had voices unsuited to sound films.

14. New techniques in photography and editing were tried during this time.

15. The most successful movies of the 1930s and 1940s were musicals, gangster films, and horror shows.

▶ **Exercise 2** Draw one line under each adjective phrase. Draw two lines under each adverb phrase.

Within the last few years, the quality of home entertainment has changed dramatically.

1. With modern advancements, high-quality sound no longer requires huge speakers.

2. Some of the most advanced systems use only three-inch speakers.

3. "Home theater" sound systems place speakers behind the listeners.

4. With stunning realism, these rear speakers enhance the recordings almost to the level of a live performance.

5. It is difficult to imagine the improvement beyond stereo; you must hear it for yourself.

6. Video images with greater resolution and clarity are also reaching new heights of quality.

7. Until the last two to three years, projection televisions, with their huge screens, were inferior to sets with cathode ray tubes.

8. Manufacturers have responded to consumer demands by building television sets with greater brightness and resolution.

9. As digital recording spreads throughout the industry, one can expect virtually perfect sound reproduction even after years of use; old-style records deteriorate with every play.

10. Superb production within the confines of our homes is a reality within reach of even modest budgets.

Lesson 42
Conjunctions: Coordinating and Correlative

A **coordinating conjunction** is a word that connects parts of a sentence. *And, but, or, for,* and *nor* are coordinating conjunctions.

Allison **and** Rosita have lived in Texas.
Do you remember if Tony plays soccer **or** sings in the choir?
Geraldo chose spaghetti, **but** we ate lasagna.

To strengthen the relationship between words or groups of words, use a correlative conjunction. **Correlative conjunctions** are pairs of words that connect words or phrases in a sentence. Correlative conjunctions include *both ... and, either ... or, neither ... nor,* and *not only ... but also.*

The NFL has franchises in **both** Green Bay **and** San Diego.

When a compound subject is joined by the conjunction *and,* it takes a plural verb.

Wilma **and** Helga **are** class officers.

When a compound subject is joined by *or* or *nor,* the verb agrees with the nearest part of the subject.

Neither the boys **nor** Mr. Ferguson **is** afraid of the rapids.

▶ **Exercise 1** Circle each conjunction. Write in the blank *coord.* if it is a coordinating conjunction and *correl.* if it is a correlative conjunction.

coord.   Rugby (and) cricket are examples of English sports.

coord.   1. The soil is rich, (and) the climate is moderate.

correl.   2. The ceremony was covered by (either) radio (or) television.

coord.   3. Rags (and) Mittens are litter mates.

correl.   4. (Neither) the Johnsons (nor) the Montoyas are our next-door neighbors.

coord.   5. Jeremy had English (and) gym before lunch.

correl.   6. (Neither) rain (nor) snow is in the immediate forecast.

coord.   7. Erin had a fever, (but) Maria felt fine.

coord.   8. Before selecting a computer, Mr. Oleson collected brochures (and) flyers.

coord.   9. Hector ate corn (and) green beans with his steak.

Name _____ Class _____ Date _____

___**correl.**___ 10. (Both) her essay (and) her speech were flawless.

___**coord.**___ 11. Molly had an umbrella, (but) Alfonso was unprepared for the shower.

___**correl.**___ 12. (Both) carnations (and) chrysanthemums are popular flowers for corsages.

___**correl.**___ 13. The whole family (not only) learned snorkeling (but also) learned water skiing.

___**coord.**___ 14. Herve was an expert in the diagnosis (and) repair of diesel engines.

___**coord.**___ 15. Ford, General Motors, (and) Chrysler are the three major American auto producers.

▶ **Exercise 2** Draw two lines under the correct form of the verb in parentheses. Circle each coordinating or correlative conjunction.

(Neither) the volleyball players (nor) their coach (<u>likes</u>, like) the facility.

1. Red hots (and) candy corn (is, <u>are</u>) Erika's favorite candy.
2. (Neither) Ahmed (nor) the rest of the group (<u>is</u>, are) interested in the side trip.
3. (Both) Benny (and) Jerry (dislikes, <u>dislike</u>) winter.
4. Fruits (and) vegetables (is, <u>are</u>) part of a balanced diet.
5. (Neither) Fido (nor) the cats (was, <u>were</u>) to be seen.
6. The band (and) the soloist (performs, <u>perform</u>) this evening.
7. (Either) a deer (or) pheasants (was, <u>were</u>) eating his chicken feed.
8. Chan (and) her family (drives, <u>drive</u>) Cadillacs.
9. Marcus (or) one of his sisters (<u>makes</u>, make) these clever posters.
10. (Was, <u>Were</u>) the Jacksons (or) Kenny involved in the accident?
11. (Neither) my partner (nor) I (gives, <u>give</u>) legal advice.
12. To each family reunion, Mom, Uncle Charley, (and) my aunts (brings, <u>bring</u>) pictures from their childhood.
13. As choices for the banquet entree, steak (and) chicken (tops, <u>top</u>) the list.
14. (Neither) the parakeets (nor) the cockatiel (<u>was</u>, were) trained.
15. (Neither) Ishmael (nor) the other scouts (prefers, <u>prefer</u>) hiking to horseback riding.

Name _____ Class _____ Date _____

Lesson 43
Conjunctive Adverbs and Interjections

A **conjunctive adverb** may be used instead of a conjunction in a compound sentence. It is usually preceded by a semicolon and followed by a comma.

Many Asians use chopsticks; **however,** some use forks.

USE CONJUNCTIVE ADVERBS
To replace *and*   also, besides, furthermore, moreover
To replace *but*   however, nevertheless, still
To state a result   consequently, therefore, so, thus
To state equality   equally, likewise, similarly

▶ **Exercise 1** Write in each blank a conjunctive adverb that logically links the two simple sentences. **Answers may vary.**

There is a gazebo in her backyard; _____**also**_____, there is a garden.

1. The old museum was drafty and rundown; _____**furthermore**_____, the exhibits were boring and outdated.

2. The team uniforms faded in the wash; _____**consequently**_____, the school colors are now mint green and pale yellow.

3. Our tour bus departed an hour late; _____**thus**_____, we arrived just before the aquarium closed.

4. The Tigers are talented; _____**moreover**_____, they have won the state championship three years in a row.

5. Mika doesn't know much about opera; _____**still**_____, he would like to go.

6. Vern enjoys watching birds; _____**moreover**_____, he tries to attract them.

7. Many kinds of dogs are found at the animal shelter; _____**likewise**_____, cats are regular inhabitants.

8. Nina was unable to play tennis this season; _____**still**_____, she attended every match.

9. Margi had her braces removed; _____**however**_____, she must still wear a retainer.

Unit 6, Prepositions, Conjunctions, and Interjections   **149**

Name _____ Class _____ Date _____

10. All the holiday flights were booked; __**consequently**__, we drove to Chicago.

11. I enjoy watching old movies; __**however**__, Dan prefers the sports channel.

12. Due to the flu, Kareem had missed several days of history class; __**therefore**__, he was excused from the test.

13. Janice loves to go shopping; __**similarly**__, Mai enjoys hunting for a bargain.

14. My brother is very creative with his hands; __**so**__, most of the presents that he gives are homemade.

15. Bird watching is very educational; __**besides**__, it is great fun.

An **interjection** is a word or group of words used to express strong feeling or to attract attention. Use interjections sparingly in your writing because overuse spoils their effectiveness.

COMMON INTERJECTIONS

aha	come on	ha	oh	ouch	what	yes
alas	gee	hey	oh, no	phew	whoops	
awesome	good grief	hooray	oops	well	wow	

An interjection that expresses very strong feeling may stand alone. An interjection that expresses milder feeling remains a part of the sentence.

The exams are finally over. **Hooray!**
Oh my, I've lost my key again.

▶ **Exercise 2** Write in the blank an interjection that makes sense. **Answers may vary.**

__**Ha**__, you can't catch me!

1. Cleveland just scored a touchdown. __**Hooray**__!

2. __**Hey**__, what's going on here?

3. __**Good grief**__! Didn't you understand a word I said?

4. That was a rough test. __**Phew**__!

5. __**Ouch**__! The door pinched my finger.

6. __**Well**__, are you going to play cards or talk?

7. Marsha gasped as Eli limped off the court. "__**Oh, no**__, now we'll never win."

8. The shot went in right at the buzzer. __**Awesome**__!

Name _____ Class _____ Date _____

 Unit 6 Review

▶ **Exercise 1** Underline each prepositional phrase. Circle each conjunction and conjunctive adverb. Write in the blank *coord.* for coordinating conjunction, *correl.* for correlative conjunction, or *conj.* for conjunctive adverb.

coord. The little girl (and) her dog skipped merrily by the playground.

conj. 1. Maxwell jumped off the wagon; (likewise), Todd followed behind him.

correl. 2. (Neither) the Ferrari (nor) the Porsche is made in America.

coord. 3. The flag glistened (and) flapped in the breeze as the national anthem was played.

coord. 4. The drug store was around the corner from the pet shop (and) the candy store.

correl. 5. Alberto (not only) caught the pass in one hand (but also) gained four yards before the whistle.

coord. 6. The store in the mall has higher prices than this one, (but) I like the clothes here better.

conj. 7. The music on the radio was making me sleepy; (therefore), I did my homework without it.

conj. 8. Casey wanted a golden retriever; (thus), she never stopped hinting for one.

correl. 9. (Either) the black car (or) the car with the blue roof ran the traffic light at the corner.

coord. 10. After school Raoul went to the dentist (and) had a cleaning.

coord. 11. One of the cheerleaders (and) Myra won the spirit award.

coord. 12. Underneath the car seat, I found eighty-seven cents (and) a piece of licorice.

conj. 13. Computers cannot think; (consequently), they will never be a replacement for humans.

conj. 14. A hawk circled lazily in the evening sky; (moreover), the wolves began to howl.

correl. 15. (Not only) was the semester finished, (but) Jeremy (also) did well on his exams.

correl. 16. You must choose (either) the electronic game (or) a baseball glove made of leather.

Unit 6, Prepositions, Conjunctions, and Interjections **151**

Name _____ Class _____ Date _____

Cumulative Review: Units 1–6

▶ **Exercise 1** Write in the blank the past form or past participle of each irregular verb in parentheses. Draw one line under each simple subject.

My <u>brother</u> __**broke**__ the new vase. (break)

1. The <u>pond</u> has not __**frozen**__ over. (freeze)
2. <u>Isabel</u> __**burst**__ into tears when she heard the news. (burst)
3. <u>Chad</u> had __**lost**__ the election by only ten votes. (lose)
4. <u>Dad</u> __**taught** or **had taught**__ me how to drive defensively. (teach)
5. Have <u>you</u> __**eaten**__ all your vegetables? (eat)
6. These <u>shoes</u> __**cost**__ twice as much as my old ones. (cost)
7. <u>I</u> have __**written**__ my friend several times. (write)
8. <u>Jane</u> __**swam** or **swum**__ the length of the pool and back. (swim)
9. <u>Hakeem</u> had __**grown**__ quite a few inches in the past year. (grow)
10. My <u>grandmother</u> has __**shown**__ her quilts to many visitors over the years. (show)
11. A <u>pipe</u> in the basement __**burst** or **had burst**__ while we were on vacation. (burst)
12. <u>She</u> grabbed a tissue and __**blew**__ her nose. (blow)
13. <u>Someone</u> must have __**stolen**__ his wallet during gym. (steal)
14. Mr. <u>Tadashi</u> has __**spoken**__ to Jeff's parents about his behavior in class. (speak)
15. <u>They</u> have finally __**chosen**__ a name for their new puppy. (choose)
16. The luxury <u>liner</u> __**sank** or **had sunk**__ during the violent storm. (sink)
17. The <u>bells</u> __**rang** or **had rung**__ loudly at the stroke of midnight. (ring)
18. <u>We</u> __**drank** or **had drunk**__ a quart of water following the race. (drink)
19. <u>Manuel</u> had __**fallen**__ from the horse and broken his arm. (fall)
20. Unfortunately, <u>Carla</u> __**threw** or **had thrown**__ the lucky ticket into the trash. (throw)

Name _____ Class _____ Date _____

▶ **Exercise 2** Draw one line under each adjective (excluding articles) and two lines under each adverb.

Three old nests fell quickly from the tree.

1. The sharp pencils suddenly broke in the middle of the hard test.
2. Stormy weather severely damaged the playground at the elementary school.
3. The one mother sang awhile as she waited nervously in the lobby.
4. The enormous yacht sailed slowly out to the open sea.
5. I will not receive the best grade in the class today.
6. The lengthy description of the social event made me laugh hysterically.
7. A fragrant bouquet made me sneeze suddenly.
8. The last class listened very silently as the new teacher gave the assignment.
9. Patrick always lived in the same house.
10. The bald assistant carefully cleaned the empty cage.
11. Several friends enjoyed the party yesterday.
12. We work hard for this coach because he is the greatest!
13. We finally found the beautiful new house.
14. The weary professor put the heavy book down.
15. My grades are slowly improving now.
16. The lost dog gradually disappeared over the far horizon.
17. The four musical instruments were badly out of tune.
18. The young baby-sitter reluctantly surrendered to the sorrowful pleas.
19. The wild beasts silently stalk nocturnal prey.
20. A quite strange man drove slowly past the red house.

Unit 6, Prepositions, Conjunctions, and Interjections   153

Name _____ Class _____ Date _____

▶ **Exercise 3** Circle each prepositional phrase and draw an arrow to the word it modifies. For each italicized word, write *correl.* (correlative conjunction), *coord.* (coordinating conjunction), *conj.* (conjunctive adverb), or *int.* (interjection) in the blank provided.

coord. Do you want the large boxes *or* the small ones that are stacked (in the attic)?

coord. 1. Please take the picture (off the wall) *and* hang the new one.

correl. 2. *Neither* Jake *nor* Paul is participating (in the staff meeting).

coord. 3. I selected ice cream (in a cup), *but* Rosa chose ice cream (on a cone).

int. 4. *Ugh!* I dislike eggs (in the morning).

correl. 5. *Not only* do I disagree (with the cost) (of the antique), *but also* it didn't seem to be valuable.

int. 6. You scored much higher (on this test) than you did (on the last one). *Congratulations!*

conj. 7. Different kinds (of birds) prefer different kinds (of seeds); *therefore,* Juan buys several mixtures.

coord. 8. The new exhibit (at the art gallery) is whimsical, *but* it has a serious side.

correl. 9. Doctors say that *both* exercise *and* a good diet lead (to a healthy life).

conj. 10. Binoculars allow a closer look (at the wild animals); *similarly,* a camcorder saves their activities (for later review).

coord. 11. A water pipe broke (at the high school) *and* classes were cancelled.

int. 12. *Ouch!* I slammed my finger (in the car door).

coord. 13. Andy ran (up the stairs) *and* closed the door (to his room).

conj. 14. Collies are Karen's favorite breed (of dog); *however,* she enjoys all (of the varieties).

correl. 15. *Neither* Brett *nor* Samantha got the lead role (in the musical).

int. 16. *Aha,* look what I found (in the drawer).

coord. 17. You'll find the cows (over the hill) *and* (beside the brook).

conj. 18. Many flowers and shrubs help attract a large variety (of birds); *besides,* they beautify the yard.

Name _____ Class _____ Date _____

Unit 7: Clauses and Complex Sentences

Lesson 44
Sentences and Main Clauses

A **simple sentence** has one complete subject and one complete predicate. The subject, the predicate, or both may be compound.

SUBJECT	PREDICATE
Lightning	struck our oak.

COMPOUND SUBJECT	PREDICATE
Branches and leaves	fell.

SUBJECT	COMPOUND PREDICATE
The oak	has stood for years and will stand for many more.

A **compound sentence** contains two or more simple sentences. Each simple sentence is called a **main clause**. Main clauses may be joined by a comma followed by a conjunction or by a semicolon. A semicolon is also used before a conjunctive adverb, such as *moreover*.

Lightning struck our oak, **but** it did not fall. (two main clauses joined by a comma and a conjunction)

Lightning struck our oak; it did not fall. (two main clauses joined by a semicolon)

Lightning struck our oak; **moreover,** it fell to the ground. (two main clauses joined by a semicolon and a conjunctive adverb)

▶ **Exercise 1** Write in the blank whether the sentence is *simple* or *compound*.

compound Volcanoes can sit idle, or they can erupt frequently.

compound 1. Earth's surface seems calm, but its interior seethes with energy.

simple 2. Pressure and heat inside the earth melt rock.

compound 3. Molten rock is lighter than its surroundings; it rises to the surface.

compound 4. Molten rock inside the earth is magma; magma on the earth's surface is lava.

simple 5. A volcano is formed from magma.

compound 6. Some volcanoes erupt with great power; others are less violent.

Name _____ Class _____ Date _____

____simple____ 7. Thick magma is forced from inside the earth by great pressure.

____compound____ 8. Thin magma flows more easily; moreover, it contains less explosion-causing gas.

____simple____ 9. Kiluaea on Hawaii is an example of a peaceful volcano.

____simple____ 10. Scientists from all over the world observe its eruptions.

____compound____ 11. Mount Saint Helens is another story; the mountain in the state of Washington literally blew its top in 1980.

____simple____ 12. A chain of volcanic mountains lies across the Pacific Northwest.

____compound____ 13. It is called the Cascade Range, and it includes Mount Saint Helens.

____simple____ 14. Earth is not the only planet with volcanoes.

____simple____ 15. Photographs reveal active volcanoes on the moons of Jupiter and Neptune and extinct volcanoes on Venus and Mars.

▶ **Exercise 2** Underline each main clause. Add a comma or a semicolon as needed.

Peter has a great interest in volcanoes; he hopes to become a volcanologist.

1. Volcanologists study volcanoes.

2. They had always hunted an active eruption, and in 1980 they got their chance.

3. Mount Saint Helens is an active volcano in Washington, but it had not erupted since 1847.

4. In March of 1980, Mount Saint Helens began shaking; moreover, its top began to bulge.

5. Scientists raced to Washington from around the world.

6. They knew the mountain would erupt, but they could not tell when or how violently.

7. Officials kept people away from the mountain, but some adventurous souls went anyway.

8. Mount Saint Helens erupted early on May 18, 1980, and more than sixty people were killed.

9. The destruction to the earth and wildlife was extreme; the blast leveled 150 square miles of forest.

10. The avalanche after the blast killed millions of animals and birds.

Lesson 45
Complex Sentences and Subordinate Clauses

A **complex sentence** contains a main clause and one or more subordinate clauses. A main clause can stand alone as a sentence. A **subordinate clause** has a subject and a predicate, but it is not a complete sentence. It depends on the main clause to complete its meaning.

MAIN CLAUSE	SUBORDINATE CLAUSE
We were sailing on the lake	when the thunderstorm hit.
We didn't know	that the paint was wet.
This is the place	where I dropped my pen.

▶ **Exercise 1** Underline each main clause. Place a check in the blank next to each complex sentence.

✓   <u>The game will be postponed</u> because the rain is falling steadily.

✓   1. When it is foggy, <u>driving is very dangerous</u>.

✓   2. Before I start my workout, <u>I always do some warmup exercises</u>.

✓   3. <u>We were surprised</u> when we learned of the arrest.

_____ 4. <u>We bought our new sofa during the sale at the local furniture store</u>.

✓   5. Although it rained all day, <u>we still enjoyed our trip</u>.

✓   6. <u>I will help you with your homework</u> after you watch the baby.

✓   7. <u>Jake stared at me</u> as if he had seen a ghost.

✓   8. Whenever the wind blows the trees against the windows, <u>the dog howls</u>.

_____ 9. <u>Our choir went on a field trip to the senior citizens' center</u>.

✓   10. <u>Owen felt responsible for the missing book</u> though it was not his fault.

_____ 11. <u>The new computer and printer really make our work easier</u>.

✓   12. <u>You can order</u> whatever you want from the menu.

✓   13. <u>We will be on time</u> unless there is a traffic jam.

✓   14. If our team wins, <u>everyone will celebrate</u>.

✓   15. <u>The police did not arrive</u> until the thieves had left.

_____ 16. <u>You can leave early tomorrow and go to the game</u>.

Name _____ Class _____ Date _____

_✔_ 17. We cannot start the concert until the weather clears.
_✔_ 18. Sam can mail these packages if they have enough postage on them.
_✔_ 19. Jill had her petition filled out so that she could run for office.
_____ 20. Our class is making the community more aware of the importance of recycling.
_✔_ 21. The road is safe as long as there is no ice.
_✔_ 22. The building swayed whenever the wind blew.
_____ 23. Hasan and Mike clapped their hands to the beat.
_✔_ 24. Sandy cried because her beloved dog had run away.
_✔_ 25. When the room warms up, we can take off our sweaters.
_✔_ 26. The pool will be cleaned when spring comes.
_✔_ 27. Because Alison loves jazz, she attends every concert.
_____ 28. The rain ceased, and the stuffy air cleared.
_✔_ 29. Since I first saw you, I have wondered if we ever met before.
_✔_ 30. While we waited for the feature, we were annoyed by several ads.
_✔_ 31. Because our history class is so large, we meet in the auditorium.
_✔_ 32. The mountain climber checked her equipment before she started up the slope.
_✔_ 33. Please be quiet when you come in late.
_____ 34. I will lock the door and turn off the lights before leaving.
_✔_ 35. Stu is leaving for vacation when he completes his courses.
_✔_ 36. If Stan wants to play hockey, he will need more discipline.
_✔_ 37. I'll wear a red hat so that you can recognize me.
_✔_ 38. The mice darted underground as the owl dived at them.

▶ **Writing Link** Write at least three complex sentences about your favorite sport.

_____
_____
_____
_____

Name _____ Class _____ Date _____

Lesson 46
Adjective Clauses

When a subordinate clause modifies a noun or a pronoun, it is called an **adjective clause**. Often, an adjective clause begins with a relative pronoun. An adjective clause can also begin with *where* or *when*.

Ms. Parker, **who is from Colorado,** is coming for dinner.
She has written a book **that tells the history of the Rocky Mountains**.

RELATIVE PRONOUNS		
that	who	whose
which	whom	whomever

▶ **Exercise 1** Draw one line under each adjective clause and two lines under each word that introduces an adjective clause.

The present <u>**that** Tanya received</u> lifted her spirits.

1. Is this the place <u>**where** you had the accident</u>?
2. The woman <u>**whose** briefcase you found</u> is here to pick it up.
3. Is this the toaster <u>**that** always burns the toast</u>?
4. The phone call <u>**that** I just answered</u> was for you.
5. The people <u>**who** own that black dog</u> live around the corner.
6. The cookbooks are in the cupboard <u>**where** we keep the spices</u>.
7. The doctor <u>**who** originally saw us</u> was out today.
8. We will leave next Friday, <u>**which** is my birthday</u>.
9. The band <u>**that** I like best</u> is The Rovers.
10. Anyone <u>**who** believes that politician</u> is very gullible.
11. The basement is the last place <u>**where** I should have stored the film</u>.
12. The excuse <u>**that** he used to explain his lateness</u> was laughable.
13. The moment <u>**when** Jason arrives</u> will signal the start of the party.
14. Is this the video <u>**that** you recommended</u>?
15. Connie, <u>**who** is the winner</u>, will get the trophy.

Name _____ Class _____ Date _____

16. Lainie, who is the star of the play, is signing autographs.

17. Scientists explore rain forest canopies, where many species live.

18. Is this the location where the battle took place?

19. Harry bought a ten-speed, which is his favorite kind of bike.

20. Is the actor whom you like in the movie?

▶ **Exercise 2** Draw one line under each adjective clause. Draw an arrow to the noun or pronoun that it modifies.

The student who won the spelling bee donated her prize to the class.

1. The days when thousands of buffalo roamed the plains must have been long ago.

2. Is this the documentary that you wanted?

3. The flood happened at a time when everyone was away from home.

4. King, who smelled the smoke, woke us up by barking.

5. I have seen the movie that you are discussing.

6. My favorite class is the one that Mr. Clark teaches.

7. Simone met our new neighbor who lives down the street.

8. Anyone who disagrees with the proposal should vote no.

9. The crystal vase, which was a present from Aunt Sandra, is filled with roses.

10. Is Ralph the neighbor whom you invited to the party?

11. Boris knows the captain whose team won the tournament.

12. Have you talked to the artist who painted this picture?

13. Uncle Vincent bought the biggest refrigerator that he could find.

14. Bridalveil Falls, which is in Yosemite National Park, is lovely.

15. The person whose place I held wants to get back in line.

Name _____ Class _____ Date _____

Lesson 47
Essential and Nonessential Clauses

Adjective clauses may be either essential or nonessential. **Essential clauses** are necessary to make the meaning of a sentence clear. A clause beginning with *that* is essential. **Nonessential clauses** add interesting information but are not necessary for the meaning of a sentence. A clause beginning with *which* is usually nonessential. Use commas to set off nonessential clauses from the rest of the sentence.

The sweater **that you knitted for me** fits perfectly. (essential clause)

Dr. Adams, **whose train arrives today,** is a well-known writer. (nonessential clause)

▶ **Exercise 1** Underline each adjective clause. Write *e* (essential) or *non.* (nonessential) in the blank to identify the type of clause. Add commas as needed.

non. *Wingless Flight*, which I saw yesterday, depicted space travel.

e 1. The explorers whom I most admire are astronauts.

e 2. One man who made space travel possible was Robert Goddard.

non. 3. Goddard, who tested many rockets, helped develop liquid fuel.

non. 4. Space travel, which is very dangerous, began with uncrewed spacecraft.

non. 5. The Soviet Union was the first nation with a space satellite, which they called *Sputnik*.

non. 6. The United States, whose first satellite was called *Explorer I*, followed the Soviet Union four months later.

non. 7. Yuri Gagarin, who was the Soviet Union's first astronaut, orbited Earth once.

e 8. Alan Shepard became the American astronaut who first traveled into space.

e 9. One event that really captured Americans' attention was the space walk of Edward White.

non. 10. White, who had so much fun on the walk, was finally ordered back into the spacecraft by Mission Control.

Unit 7, Clauses and Complex Sentences **161**

___non.___ 11. The Apollo program, which we studied this year, was the American moon landing project.

___e___ 12. The astronauts who were selected for this mission had to be in superb physical condition.

___non.___ 13. *Apollo 8*, which did not land, orbited the moon and sent back pictures of the surface.

___e___ 14. *Apollo 11* developed as the mission that was to land an American on the moon.

___e___ 15. The astronauts who held Americans' interest in 1969 were Armstrong, Aldrin, and Collins.

___non.___ 16. Neil Armstrong, who was the commander of the mission, walked on the moon with Buzz Aldrin.

___e___ 17. People who care about space exploration wonder if we will ever go to the moon again.

___e___ 18. The argument that we should not continue is partly based on safety.

___e___ 19. The astronauts who died in the *Apollo 1* fire and the *Challenger* tragedy are reminders of the dangers of space travel.

___non.___ 20. Their names, which will always be remembered, are the names of heroes.

___non.___ 21. Other spacecraft, which carried no people, have also explored the solar system.

___e___ 22. The planet that has long attracted science-fiction writers was not photographed until the mid-1960s.

___non.___ 23. *Viking 1*, which photographed Mars in 1976, showed a huge volcano.

___e___ 24. The scientists who analyze photographic data could study Viking photographs of Mars for years.

___e___ 25. The spacecraft that took the most punishment were the Soviet *Venera* probes.

___non.___ 26. The *Venera* probes landed on Venus, which has a crushing atmosphere, and took pictures before being destroyed.

162   Writer's Choice Grammar Workbook 8, Unit 7

Name _____ Class _____ Date _____

Lesson 48
Adverb Clauses

An **adverb clause** is a subordinate clause that gives information about the verb in the main clause of the sentence. It tells *how, when, where, why,* or *under what conditions* the action occurs. An adverb clause can also modify an adjective or another adverb.

Because she was so exhausted, Sheila could not keep her eyes open. (The adverb clause tells *why* Sheila could not keep her eyes open.)

Ed's family lived in Atlanta **after he was born**. (The adverb clause tells *when* Ed's family lived in Atlanta.)

Notice that when an adverb clause begins a sentence, a comma is used. However, a comma is not needed before an adverb clause that completes a sentence. Adverb clauses are introduced by **subordinating conjunctions**. These conjunctions tell you that a clause is subordinate and cannot stand alone as a sentence.

COMMON SUBORDINATING CONJUNCTIONS

after	before	though	whenever
although	if	unless	where
as	since	until	whereas
because	than	when	wherever

▶ **Exercise 1** Underline each adverb clause. Circle the subordinating conjunction.

My little sister rides her bicycle more carefully (since) she fell and scraped her knee.

1. (Although) Tricia works hard, she always welcomes extra projects.

2. (Whenever) my aunt is in town, she takes me to lunch.

3. He is thinner (than) he was the last time.

4. Should we go save seats (after) you buy some popcorn?

5. Do not make a commitment (unless) you are sure.

6. (If) I remember correctly, that street goes only one way.

7. The puppy ran under a chair (when) it heard the cat hiss.

8. Our spelling team performed well (although) we did not win.

9. (Because) I had no sleeping bag, I slept in the cabin.

10. I hope we get to the party (before) they yell "Surprise!"

11. (As) I told you yesterday, my answer is no.

12. I cannot turn in my paper (until) I have completed this problem.

13. Mother sat (where) she could see the stage clearly.

14. (Since) I broke my leg, I need help getting to school.

15. My favorite team is the Knicks (whereas) Pablo likes the Suns.

▶ **Exercise 2** Draw one line under the adverb clause and two lines under the verb or verb phrase that the adverb clause modifies.

<u>Before he ordered his meal</u>, Dad <u><u>read</u></u> the menu.

1. <u>When he got off the train</u>, the streets <u><u>were deserted</u></u>.
2. I <u><u>will work</u></u> all day <u>unless I get a call from Dad</u>.
3. I hope Ken <u><u>will visit</u></u> us <u>when he is in town</u>.
4. Plenty of leftovers <u><u>remain</u></u> <u>because several people did not come to the party</u>.
5. Do not <u><u>make</u></u> any noise <u>unless you want to wake the baby</u>.
6. <u>Since my horse was ill</u>, I <u><u>stayed</u></u> all night in her stall.
7. <u>As we approached</u>, the mourning doves <u><u>fluttered</u></u> away.
8. The villagers <u><u>fled</u></u> the town <u>before the volcano erupted</u>.
9. <u>After the meeting ended</u>, the mayor <u><u>met</u></u> with the press.
10. <u>If you cannot stop fighting</u>, <u><u>study</u></u> in separate rooms.
11. <u>Because she could not choose</u>, Juliet <u><u>bought</u></u> both books.
12. Nell <u><u>will not skate</u></u> on the lake <u>until she tests the ice</u>.
13. <u><u>Move</u></u> the furniture <u>wherever it looks best</u>.
14. <u>Although the dinner was a success</u>, the cook <u><u>created</u></u> a mess!
15. I <u><u>would like</u></u> that video <u>when you have finished with it</u>.

Name _____ Class _____ Date _____

Lesson 49
Noun Clauses

Noun clauses are subordinate clauses that act as nouns.

Actors must have good memories. (noun)
Whoever acts on stage must have a good memory. (noun clause)

The clause in the second sentence above replaces the noun in the first sentence. Noun clauses can be used in the same way as nouns—as subject, direct object, object of a preposition, and predicate noun.

Whoever runs for office needs much money. (subject)
Candidates know **that the game of politics is expensive.** (direct object)
This is the candidate about **whom I wrote.** (object of a preposition)
Election day is **when the results are known.** (predicate noun)

WORDS THAT INTRODUCE NOUN CLAUSES

how	what	where	who	whomever
however	whatever	which	whom	whose
that	when	whichever	whoever	why

▶ **Exercise 1** Underline each noun clause.

<u>Why the posters are not finished</u> is the question Ms. Rivera would like answered.

1. The band will play <u>whatever song we choose</u>.
2. The shopping center is <u>where the old forest stood</u>.
3. <u>Whoever wins the most games</u> wins the trophy.
4. Vicky knows <u>how the VCR is hooked up</u>.
5. Do you know <u>where that new student comes from</u>?
6. Kim wonders <u>when the film opens here</u>.
7. I didn't know <u>where these books belonged</u>.
8. The team didn't realize <u>that their quarterback was ill</u>.
9. The starting point for the hike is <u>where the path follows the cliff</u>.
10. <u>Why you chose to bicycle in the rain</u> is a mystery to me.
11. Pass the refreshments to <u>whomever you want</u>.
12. The reporter will question <u>whatever statement the official makes</u>.

Unit 7, Clauses and Complex Sentences **165**

Name _____ Class _____ Date _____

13. Could you tell me <u>how you perform that magic trick</u>?
14. <u>How you survived the snowstorm</u> is beyond me.
15. Ken is wondering <u>what will be served for dinner</u>.
16. <u>What really annoys me</u> is loud rock music.
17. This room is <u>where the band practices its halftime program</u>.
18. I don't know <u>which knob controls the color</u>.
19. Save these papers for <u>whoever is recycling them</u>.
20. The students know <u>that they must study for the test</u>.

▶ **Exercise 2** Underline each noun clause. In the blank, indicate its use in the sentence: *subj.* (subject), *d.o.* (direct object), *o.p.* (object of a preposition), or *p.n.* (predicate noun).

subj. <u>How Constance could have bought that dog</u> continues to baffle me.

d.o. 1. Do you know <u>who is in charge of counting votes</u>?
o.p. 2. Give your ticket to <u>whoever would enjoy the concert</u>.
subj. 3. <u>Where we will go on our field trip</u> is the subject of debate.
p.n. 4. This is <u>where the fire broke out</u>.
d.o. 5. Kendra is asking <u>why you are acting that way</u>.
p.n. 6. The best choice for you is <u>whatever you think best</u>.
subj. 7. <u>How they escaped the flood</u> is something I don't understand.
d.o. 8. Sue believes <u>that her skills in soccer need help</u>.
d.o. 9. We don't understand <u>why the cat likes the rain</u>.
o.p. 10. This mail goes in <u>whichever box is marked "Smith."</u>
o.p. 11. The fish will hide under <u>whatever rock it can find</u>.
p.n. 12. My parents' surprise was <u>what we had hoped for</u>.
p.n. 13. The route for the contest became <u>whichever way they went</u>.
o.p. 14. The boys work long hours for <u>whatever they can earn</u>.
subj. 15. <u>What the team should do</u> is punt.
d.o. 16. The dogs know <u>where the cat often hides</u>.

Unit 7 Review

▶ **Exercise 1** Identify each underlined clause as *main*, *adjective*, *adverb*, or *noun*. If the underlined clause modifies a specific word or words, circle the word or words.

__adjective__ (Of Mice and Men,) which is my favorite book, made me cry.

__adverb__ 1. My dog (lounges) around the house wherever she pleases.

__adjective__ 2. The (years) when the Great Depression hit were terribly hard for many people.

__noun__ 3. Did anybody see where that snowball came from?

__adverb__ 4. If the school ever sells its old computers, I (will buy) one.

__main__ 5. I have always liked Eric Clapton's music.

__adjective__ 6. The recreation room in my basement is the (place) where I relax.

__main__ 7. Rance ran to the bus stop, but he missed his ride anyway.

__adverb__ 8. We (will go) to the new movie unless it is sold out.

__noun__ 9. Whatever restaurant you choose is okay with me.

__adverb__ 10. (Solve) the mystery before any other player does.

__noun__ 11. Whoever sells the most candy receives an award.

__noun__ 12. Science still cannot explain why some animals behave oddly before earthquakes.

__main__ 13. On our way to Texas, our plane flew over the Gulf of Mexico.

__adjective__ 14. My little (brother,) who still believes in Santa Claus, puts milk and cookies out on Christmas Eve.

__main__ 15. Because the movie was sold out, we went home.

__noun__ 16. Calid is disturbed at how his family reacted to the news.

__adjective__ 17. Please give me the (remote control,) which is sitting on the television.

__main__ 18. I bought the latest newspaper.

__adjective__ 19. (Socrates), whose writings are still studied, affected Western philosophy.

__adverb__ 20. I always (shower) after I exercise heavily.

Name _____ Class _____ Date _____

Cumulative Review: Units 1–7

▶ **Exercise 1** Underline the correct pronoun in parentheses. In the blank, write the tense of the verb that is in italics: *present, past, future, present perfect, past perfect,* or *future perfect.*

present perfect		Craig and Julio *have decided* (he, **they**) will start a recycling campaign.
present	1.	Wayne *works* for (**his**, their) father on weekends.
past	2.	Ms. Rothchild *waited* impatiently for (**her**, hers) luggage to arrive.
future perfect	3.	The band *will have begun* playing by the time (**they**, their) reach the stadium.
past perfect	4.	Kelly, Steve, and Kwasi *had finished* the entire project by the time Lorna joined (their, **them**).
past	5.	Our waiter *forgot* (**we**, us) wanted some rolls.
future	6.	Aunt Sophie *will light* the candles on (**her**, his) own birthday cake and let one of the children blow them out.
present	7.	*Does*n't (no one, **anyone**) *know* what time the bus leaves?
present perfect	8.	(That, **Those**) *have caught* Marisa's attention.
future	9.	Mr. Concepción *will demonstrate* how (she, **he**) performs this dance.
past	10.	Ms. Stanberg *promised* to help us with (**our**, her) homework.
present	11.	The painting is lovely, but (**it**, they) *seems* a little crooked.
future perfect	12.	Tessa *will have walked* five miles by the time (**she**, it) reaches the Chungs' house.
past perfect	13.	Danny and Pedro *had watched* the game for nearly an hour when (**they**, them) went to the refreshment stand for a snack.
past perfect	14.	The audience *had caught* one more glimpse of the beautiful singer before (**she**, her) left the theater.
past	15.	Rosalinda (**herself**, himself) *wrote* that haunting melody.

168 Writer's Choice Grammar Workbook 8, Unit 7

Name _____ Class _____ Date _____

___present___ 16. Gifts *bring* joy to (those, them) who receive them.

___future___ 17. I *will give* Joe the book that (she, he) left in the car.

___past___ 18. Mr. Kristofic, who *spoke* earlier, is (him, himself) a noted scientist.

___future___ 19. To (who, whom) *will* Sabrina *take* the broken watch?

___future perfect___ 20. (This, These) *will have been* the longest book I have ever read.

▶ **Exercise 2** Circle each conjunction. In the blank, write whether it is *coordinating* or *correlative*.

___coordinating___ Stephan likes to fish, (but) his brother prefers to hike.

___coordinating___ 1. Uncle Wilhelm (and) Cousin Janet are planning a surprise party.

___correlative___ 2. (Either) ravioli (or) fettucine is her favorite pasta dish.

___coordinating___ 3. Dr. Ortiz remains kind (but) firm when dealing with patients.

___coordinating___ 4. Justin will hold the camera, (and) Tonya will gather everyone together for the picture.

___correlative___ 5. (Not only) did Kristy win the contest, (but) she (also) received some expert advice.

___coordinating___ 6. Ryan is wearing a green shirt, (for) that is his favorite color.

___coordinating___ 7. The wind began to increase, (but) the storm veered south.

___correlative___ 8. (Neither) roses (nor) tulips would bloom in that garden.

___coordinating___ 9. The car will have to be covered tonight, (or) it will be covered with frost tomorrow.

___coordinating___ 10. The pastry chef will bake (and) decorate a cake.

▶ **Exercise 3** Underline each subordinate clause. In the blank, identify the clause as *adjective*, *adverb*, or *noun*.

___adverb___ Although they were tired, the basketball team continued practicing.

___adverb___ 1. Stacy will meet us at the roller-skating rink unless she has not finished her homework.

Unit 7, Clauses and Complex Sentences **169**

__adverb__ 2. After she addressed the birthday card, Aunt Rose mailed it.

__adjective__ 3. Tom's friend, who is a mechanic, showed us how to change a flat tire.

__adjective__ 4. Greg bought the book that Mr. Harkin recommended.

__adjective__ 5. That new television program, which aired last night, captured Gabrielle's imagination.

__noun__ 6. What Samdi baked was my favorite dish at the potluck.

__adverb__ 7. Though others performed better, no one worked harder than Colleen.

__adjective__ 8. Our teacher invited the scientist who made this discovery to speak to our class.

__adverb__ 9. Sue will check the luggage before Mom gets the boarding passes.

__noun__ 10. Nashoba is wondering when this city will develop a professional baseball team.

__noun__ 11. Curtis asked how we planned to travel to the festival.

__adverb__ 12. Dr. Spencer will examine Kendra's eyes before he prescribes glasses for her.

__adjective__ 13. The play that Rudy and I saw amused both of us.

__noun__ 14. Who let the dog out concerns our neighbor, Mr. Martinez.

__adverb__ 15. Whenever Maria sees a music store, she has to go inside and look around.

__adjective__ 16. The person who can answer your questions is seated by the window.

__adjective__ 17. The second floor, which has been vacant for three years, is finally being renovated.

__adjective__ 18. Give your ticket to the person who is standing at the door.

__adverb__ 19. James waited as though he had something else to say.

__adverb__ 20. Since she visited Greece, Wendy cannot stop talking about the customs there.

Unit 8: Verbals

Lesson 50
Participles and Participial Phrases

A **present participle** is formed by adding *-ing* to a verb. A **past participle** is usually formed by adding *-ed* to a verb. Sometimes a participle acts as the main verb in a verb phrase. As a verb, the present participle is used with forms of the helping verb *to be,* and the past participle is used with forms of the helping verb *to have.* A participle can also act as an adjective to describe, or modify, a noun or a pronoun.

The robin was **singing** in the tree. (present participle as a main verb)
Our cat stared at the **singing** robin. (present participle as an adjective)
Tammy has **tossed** the water balloon. (past participle as a main verb)
The **tossed** water balloon hit the sidewalk. (past participle as an adjective)

▶ **Exercise 1** Underline each participle. Write in the blank *pres.* if it is a present participle and *past* if it is a past participle.

pres.		The running guard caught the pass from Troy.
pres.	1.	The nervous bird was pecking at the girl.
past	2.	A printout of the results has been taped to the door.
pres.	3.	The freezing lady put on her sweater.
past	4.	The spilled oil spread over the floor.
past	5.	By evening, they will have finished their assignment.
past, pres.	6.	Everyone has wondered what the great detective was thinking.
past, pres.	7.	Carol has rescued the trembling cat.
past	8.	The elected chairperson must work hard.
pres.	9.	David is throwing the rings at the milk bottles.
past	10.	They found out too late that they had entered by the wrong door.
pres.	11.	I made a running leap to clear the last hurdle.
pres., past, past	12.	The engaging film star has smiled and posed for pictures.

Unit 8, Verbals

Name _____ Class _____ Date _____

__pres.__	13.	We were unable to keep warm from the <u>blistering</u> wind.
__past__	14.	Allan should have <u>looked</u> at the price tag first.
__past, past__	15.	We had <u>recycled</u> our <u>discarded</u> newspapers.
__past__	16.	The new video store had a <u>limited</u> number of foreign films.
__pres.__	17.	Do you see the antique car that is <u>passing</u> the new car?
__past__	18.	Have you ever <u>watched</u> *Rain Man*?
__past__	19.	I had <u>noticed</u> the necklace on the table.
__pres.__	20.	The bucket was rapidly <u>filling</u> with water.

▶ **Exercise 2** Write *V* above each participle that is part of a verb phrase. Write *adj.* above each participle that is used as an adjective.

       adj.   **V**
The forgiving teacher has accepted the boy's apology.

          V
1. I feel as if I've been carrying this backpack for three days!
    V   **adj.**
2. Drew has decided to order a piece of the tempting chocolate cake.
     adj.
3. The determined police officer chased the thief.
     adj.   **adj.**
4. The accomplished musician prepared for the approaching concert.
     V   **adj.**
5. We had overlooked the hiding puppy.
    V   **adj.**
6. George had worked a great deal at the amazing water park.
    V   **adj.**
7. Will you be deciding soon about the posted job?
    adj.   **adj.**
8. The flashing lightning scared the dazed children.
   adj.
9. The sitting boy believed no one could see him behind the bush.
    V   **V**
10. We were thinking about your offer and have decided to accept it.
     V   **adj.**
11. Marcus has uncovered the missing final clue.
   adj.   **V**
12. The rusted door was beginning to break.
   adj.   **V**
13. The startled horse had galloped over the fence.
   adj.   **adj.**
14. The charging defense team sacked the exhausted quarterback.
   adj.
15. The following program is my dad's favorite.
   adj.   **adj.**
16. The winning team waved to the remaining crowd.

Name _____ Class _____ Date _____

17. That dog will be **chasing** [V] bicyclists for as long as he runs loose.
18. For the **organized** [adj.] talent show, Gary will be **impersonating** [V] Mr. Highfield.
19. I felt sorry for the **beached** [adj.] baby whale.
20. What were you **thinking** [V] when you put the **melted** [adj.] caramels in the freezer?

A **participial phrase** includes a participle and all the other words that complete its meaning. It is used as an adjective and can appear before or after the word it modifies. Place the phrase as close as possible to the modified word to avoid unclear meaning. A participial phrase placed at the beginning of a sentence is set off with a comma. Other participial phrases may or may not need commas, depending on whether or not they are essential to the meaning of the sentence.

The girl **throwing the water balloon** is Tammy DiGiovanni.
Tammy, **throwing the water balloon,** aimed at the target.
Running quickly after Tammy, I threw the balloon back.
Tammy, **scared of getting wet,** hid behind a bush.

▶ **Exercise 3** Underline each participial phrase. Draw an arrow to the word the phrase modifies.

Blackie, <u>catching the stick in mid-air</u>, trotted proudly back to Steve.

1. <u>Surprised by our gift of a new winter coat</u>, Grandmother began to cry for joy.
2. The lot, <u>filled with cars</u>, was enormous.
3. The box of fruit <u>containing pears, apples, and oranges</u> arrived at the door.
4. Homeless families often stayed at a shelter <u>operated by a local church</u>.
5. <u>Carrying plenty of water</u>, we set out for the summit of the mountain.
6. Did they see the train <u>coming around the bend</u>?
7. <u>Urged on by the fans</u>, the basketball team began its comeback.
8. The tall man <u>wearing the gray suit</u> is a judge.
9. That newspaper <u>blowing all over the yard</u> is a real mess.

Unit 8, Verbals

Name _____ Class _____ Date _____

10. A banana peel <u>lying on the ground</u> caused the comedian to slip.

11. <u>Giggling like a child</u>, Marie handed the package to her brother.

12. <u>Tapping her way up Pearl Street</u>, Margie was the hit of the parade.

13. The king, <u>unrecognized by all his subjects</u>, walked around his kingdom in disguise.

14. I believe I saw the maid <u>climbing the stairs toward the forbidden room</u>.

15. <u>Confused by the identical twins</u>, Mr. Fatar threw up his hands in wonder.

16. The frog, <u>hopping from one rock to the next</u>, managed to get away from the boy.

17. <u>Beginning with the kitchen</u>, they painted every room in the apartment.

18. My mom told us about the new library <u>planned for this neighborhood</u>.

19. I ordered the special, <u>consisting of a ham sandwich and tomato soup</u>.

20. Alberto, <u>asked by the choir director</u>, agreed to sing in the talent show.

▶ **Writing Link** Write a paragraph about a sport you either like to watch or play. Use both present and past participles.

_____
_____
_____
_____
_____
_____
_____
_____
_____
_____
_____

Name _____ Class _____ Date _____

Lesson 51
Gerunds and Gerund Phrases

In addition to being used as an adjective (as in participles and participial phrases), a verb form ending in *-ing* may also serve as a noun. A **gerund** is a verb form that ends in *-ing* and is used as a noun. It can be the subject of a sentence, the direct object, or the object of a preposition.

Flying is a skill birds must learn. (subject)
Young birds practice **flying**. (direct object)
They can escape from dangers by **flying**. (object of a preposition)

A **gerund phrase** is a group of words that includes a gerund and other words that complete its meaning.

Flying in a storm takes practice. (subject)
Birds learn **flying in high winds** at a young age. (direct object)
Many birds owe their survival to **flying away from enemies**. (object of a preposition)

▶ **Exercise 1** Circle each gerund. Underline each gerund phrase.

One way people share good times is by (observing) holidays together.

1. Some people keep Valentine's Day by (sending) heart-shaped cards to friends.

2. (Sharing) valentines with others can brighten a wintry February day.

3. The custom of (celebrating) Valentine's Day stretches back a long way.

4. Many historians believe the holiday sprang from an ancient Roman custom of (honoring) two brothers by the name of Valentine.

5. (Coloring) eggs is an activity that belongs to another holiday.

6. Easter is often associated with the (blooming) of spring flowers.

7. In Christian traditions, Easter marks the (rising) of Jesus from the dead.

8. At the same time as Easter, Jews observe Passover by (preparing) a special meal, a *seder*.

9. By (eating) the special foods at the seder, Jews remember the flight of their ancestors from slavery in Egypt.

Unit 8, Verbals **175**

Name _____ Class _____ Date _____

10. *Playing* jokes on people seems a strange way to celebrate a holiday.

11. However, *exchanging* gag gifts was a custom in France that grew into our April Fool's Day.

12. A lesser-known spring holiday is dedicated to *planting* trees—Arbor Day.

13. Various states enjoy *observing* Arbor Day any time from December to May.

14. Most people would agree that *respecting* mothers is important every day of the year.

15. In 1914 Congress approved *reserving* a specific day for mothers.

16. The second Sunday in May is the day set aside for *remembering* Mom.

17. *Remembering* our patriotic dead is the purpose of another May holiday, Memorial Day.

18. By *decorating* the graves of soldiers, we honor their memories.

19. In *celebrating* Memorial Day at the end of May, we pay tribute to those who died for their country.

20. *Honoring* all members of the armed services is the purpose of Veterans Day, celebrated in November.

▶ **Exercise 2** Underline each gerund phrase. Write in the blank how it is used in the sentence: *S* for subject, *DO* for direct object, *OP* for object of a preposition, or *none* if the sentence does not contain a gerund.

__DO__ Our neighbor, Mr. Montoya, enjoys seeing his sons on Father's Day.

__S__ 1. Having a special day for fathers was the idea of a Spokane, Washington, woman.

__OP__ 2. On the third Sunday in June, Father's Day, children show their fathers how they feel about them by sending cards and giving presents.

__DO__ 3. A holiday in June features flying the American flag, a tradition that began after the Civil War.

__OP__ 4. June 14 is Flag Day, a day for remembering the first American flag.

Name _____ Class _____ Date _____

__OP__ 5. Just one year earlier, thirteen colonies went to war with England by <u>declaring their independence</u>.

__none__ 6. The colonies knew they were entering a dangerous and fateful time.

__OP__ 7. With <u>the signing of the Declaration of Independence</u>, the American Revolution began.

__OP__ 8. In <u>winning the War of Independence</u>, the colonies became a new and independent nation.

__none__ 9. Ringing out over the streets of Philadelphia on July 4, 1776, was the historic Liberty Bell.

__S__ 10. <u>Celebrating America's birth</u> is the purpose of our Independence Day.

__S__ 11. In almost every American town, <u>holding parades on the Fourth of July</u> is a tradition.

__S__ 12. <u>Watching fireworks</u> is also a big part of the Fourth.

__S__ 13. However, <u>remembering our country's early days</u> should also be a part of the celebrations.

__none__ 14. Signaling the end of summer, Labor Day comes at the start of September.

__OP__ 15. This holiday is also an occasion for <u>honoring the nation's workers</u>.

__none__ 16. Adopting the holiday in 1882, New York City was the first place to celebrate workers.

__S__ 17. For many Americans, <u>having a day off from work</u> is the best way to celebrate Labor Day!

__S__ 18. The <u>keeping of the fast of Ramadan</u> occurs during the ninth month of the Islamic calendar.

__OP__ 19. American Muslims celebrate this religious festival by <u>fasting during the day</u>.

__DO__ 20. But when the sun sets, Muslims can stop <u>their fasting</u> and celebrate their holy month.

Exercise 3 Identify the word in italics. Write *V* in the blank if the word is a verb in a verb phrase, *part.* if the word is a participle used as an adjective, or *ger.* if the word is a gerund.

ger. *Eating* special foods is one way to celebrate special days.

ger. 1. Americans have many different ways of *celebrating* holidays.

part. 2. *Bringing* customs and traditions from their homelands, immigrants add to the rich holiday mix in the United States.

part. 3. Holidays *belonging* to three major groups are celebrated.

ger. 4. *Observing* religious holidays is common throughout the United States.

ger. 5. *Commemorating* national holidays seems important to most Americans.

V 6. Certain states are *celebrating* regional holidays.

ger. 7. *Staying* up late the night before makes the first holiday of the year seem like the shortest.

ger. 8. Many people celebrate New Year's Day by *making* noise.

ger. 9. *Wearing* funny hats is also a part of New Year's festivities.

part. 10. *Singing* songs such as "Auld Lang Syne," people say good-bye to the old year and hello to the new.

ger. 11. *Making* New Year's resolutions is another tradition.

V 12. By making resolutions, many people are *hoping* to stop old habits or begin new ones.

V 13. Are you *thinking* of making any resolutions this New Year's Day?

part. 14. Some of our New Year's traditions come from the ancient Romans, who celebrated the *approaching* year.

ger. 15. In fact, the first month of the year is named after Janus, the Roman god of *beginnings* and endings.

part. 16. *Having* two faces, Janus looked forward and backward.

ger. 17. January 1—New Year's Day—is a good time for *looking* at both the past and the future.

part. 18. The early months of the year are rich in holidays *honoring* important Americans.

Name _____ Class _____ Date _____

Lesson 52
Infinitives and Infinitive Phrases

An **infinitive** is another verb form that may function as a noun. It may also function as an adjective or an adverb. An infinitive is formed from the word *to* followed by the base form of a verb. The word *to* is not a preposition when it is used immediately before a verb.

Jenny is always looking for a chance **to read**. (infinitive)
She goes **to the library** at least once a week. (not an infinitive; the word *to* is used as a preposition)

An infinitive used as a noun can be the subject of a sentence or the direct object of a verb.

To read is enjoyable. (subject) Jenny tries **to read** every day. (direct object)

An **infinitive phrase** is a group of words that includes an infinitive and other words that complete its meaning.

Jenny has decided **to read all of Sue Ellen Bridgers's books this summer.**

▶ **Exercise 1** Circle each infinitive. Underline each infinitive phrase.

My sister is teaching me (to play) chess.

1. Do you like (to eat) Chinese food?
2. It's hard (to choose) a video because the selection here is so large.
3. I'm lucky (to go) to such a good school.
4. My little brother finds it almost impossible (to wait) until his birthday.
5. (To ignore) a sore throat is not a very good idea.
6. We have (to leave) immediately (to go) to the meeting at the recreation center.
7. (To win) the last three games of the season will not be easy.
8. (To get) a *B* on the next test is her objective.
9. (To grow) a moustache in time for the play became my dad's plan.
10. Let's get together (to watch) old Laurel and Hardy movies.
11. I know how (to fix) the glitch in your computer program.
12. (To take) a cruise in the Caribbean would be wonderful.

Name _____ Class _____ Date _____

13. We love *to wander* around the old-fashioned shops at the history museum.
14. I don't want *to argue* about it now.
15. She said she'd love *to hear* from us.
16. The hospital chaplain stopped *to say* hello to Maggie after her operation.
17. Does Jordan like *to sing* in the Glee Club?
18. Did you ever want *to go* to a Broadway musical?
19. *To wait* for dinner doesn't bother me at all.
20. On her family's trip to the ocean, Megan is going *to try* scuba diving.
21. I'm trying *to break* my habit of saying *whatever* all the time.
22. I think it would be fun *to speak* a foreign language.
23. *To multiply* big numbers in her head is my sister's special talent.
24. The teacher asked William *to think* about taking algebra.
25. Martin's goal is *to play* the saxophone as well as Kenny G.
26. Doug went to Florida *to see* the Everglades.
27. Can you believe we're actually going *to make* it to the playoffs?
28. I'll bet a young kangaroo—called a *joey*—likes *to hang* on tightly when its mother jumps around!

▶ **Exercise 2** Place a check (✔) next to the sentence in each pair that contains an infinitive phrase.

✔	Everyone would like to get good grades.
_____	I gave my report card to my mother.
_____	1. She sent Chanukah cards to many different people.
✔	Christine likes to read historical novels.
✔	2. I hate to go to bed without brushing my teeth.
_____	Let me say thanks to everyone involved with the project.
✔	3. To munch on peanuts reminds me of being at the circus!
_____	The raft floated down the Ohio River to the Mississippi River.

180 Writer's Choice Grammar Workbook 8, Unit 8

Name _____ Class _____ Date _____

_____ 4. We awarded a prize to the tallest girl in the class.

✓ How are those tiny butterflies able to fly all the way to South America?

_____ 5. The letter began "To whom it may concern."

✓ It took a lot of courage to speak out about injustice the way she did.

_____ 6. It's really up to her whether we continue.

✓ It would be safer to put that money in a bank account, don't you think?

✓ 7. To think that anyone could devote so much time to a painting is beyond my comprehension!

_____ Mr. Barnard was transferred to San Diego.

✓ 8. It takes a certain kind of person to work in an emergency room.

_____ I gave the leftover tuna to Sandy's cat.

_____ 9. Please move that chair to the living room.

✓ To sail the skies in a glider would be a fantastic experience.

✓ 10. I'd like to visit Hawaii someday.

_____ In some countries kids go to school on Saturdays.

_____ 11. For Thanksgiving my family drove to my grandparents' house.

✓ She ought to pay more attention to the rules.

_____ 12. One day, I'd enjoy going to the desert.

✓ To pay for anything in cash is rather rare these days.

_____ 13. He spoke to the manager of the restaurant about a part-time job.

✓ I would like you all to notice the "Wet Paint" sign on the wall.

_____ 14. Tell Kelly if you're interested in going to Aspen, Colorado, for the ski trip.

✓ She wants to return her new shoes because they feel too big.

▶ **Exercise 3** Underline each infinitive phrase. Write *S* in the blank if it is used as a subject, *DO* if it is used as a direct object, or *none* if the sentence has no infinitive phrase.

DO My uncle Jerry loves <u>to hit golf balls</u>.

DO 1. She hadn't even learned <u>to turn on the computer</u>.

DO 2. Please don't forget <u>to water the plants</u> while I'm gone.

Unit 8, Verbals **181**

Name _____ Class _____ Date _____

__none__ 3. We all piled into the car and drove to the garden center.

__S__ 4. To say you're not interested seems unfair.

__S__ 5. To make a donation to SADD in our names was a nice gesture.

__none__ 6. This certainly means a lot to my family and me.

__DO__ 7. What do you want to do this Saturday?

__none__ 8. Going to the moon seemed impossible to our grandparents.

__S__ 9. To go swimming in frigid Lake Superior is no picnic!

__none__ 10. On the tour, they will travel to Oregon and Washington.

__DO__ 11. Would you like to lend me a pencil for fifth period?

__S__ 12. To be myself is the best advice I have been given.

__DO__ 13. Have you ever wanted to go on a whale-watching trip?

__S__ 14. To eat a crisp apple is one of the joys of autumn.

__none__ 15. Lee and I walked to DeShon's dad's house.

__DO__ 16. When her cousins arrived, Ramona decided to take them on a scavenger hunt.

__DO__ 17. Colin hopes to be a good friend to everyone.

__none__ 18. To us and them, the matter just didn't seem all that important.

__none__ 19. Does anyone feel like going to the grocery store?

__S__ 20. To build a fire in a strong wind takes skill.

__DO__ 21. Do you want to go out for a pizza after the concert?

__S__ 22. To postpone the wedding will upset everyone's plans.

__DO__ 23. People sometimes would like to change the weather, but, of course, they can't.

__none__ 24. The mayor gave a citation to the members of the rescue squad who saved the child.

__S__ 25. To succeed in gymnastics takes dedication.

__S__ 26. To point at people is not polite.

__DO__ 27. Ethan wanted to go to the theme park with his family.

__none__ 28. I wish she could have talked to me about the problem.

Name _____ Class _____ Date _____

Unit 8 Review

▶ **Exercise 1** Underline each participial, gerund, or infinitive phrase. Write in the blank what kind of phrase it is: *part.* for participial phrase, *ger.* for gerund phrase, or *inf.* for infinitive phrase. Write *none* if the sentence has none of these phrases.

ger.   Lila greatly enjoys <u>planting rose bushes</u>.

part.   1. The news showed pictures of houses <u>destroyed by the hurricane</u>.

inf.   2. Would you ever want <u>to go on a two-week trip to Colorado</u>?

ger.   3. <u>Taking it easy</u> is my brother's idea of a good vacation.

inf.   4. <u>To eat too many desserts</u> is not a very good idea.

none   5. Rod is playing the piano in the school jazz band.

part.   6. <u>Hearing my dad's voice on the phone</u>, I answered quickly.

ger.   7. She doesn't really enjoy <u>working after school</u>.

none   8. Nicole was wondering which class would be better for her major.

inf.   9. In soccer, players use their feet <u>to do almost everything</u>.

ger.   10. Thomas prefers <u>swimming in a pool rather than in the ocean</u>.

part.   11. We opened the door for the carolers <u>touring the neighborhood</u>.

none   12. We took the subway to Columbia Square.

none   13. I have talked to almost everyone about the talent show.

inf.   14. I love <u>to watch the fireworks display on the Fourth of July</u>.

part.   15. <u>Accepted by every college she applied to</u>, my sister must make a difficult decision.

ger.   16. <u>Deciding on one</u> will be hard.

none   17. Please take the laundry basket to the bedroom.

ger.   18. <u>Finishing all my homework by eight o'clock</u> won't be easy.

inf.   19. Do you want <u>to go to the early movie or the late one</u>?

part.   20. The dog <u>lapping up water so fast</u> must have been very thirsty.

Unit 8, Verbals   **183**

Cumulative Review: Units 1–8

▶ **Exercise 1** Underline the correct pronoun in parentheses. Write in the blank whether the sentence is *dec.* (declarative), *int.* (interrogative), *exc.* (exclamatory), or *imp.* (imperative).

__int.__   Where did (<u>he</u>, him) leave the instructions?

__imp.__ 1. Don't forget to send an invitation to (they, <u>them</u>).

__exc.__ 2. What an incredible jump shot (<u>she</u>, her) has!

__dec.__ 3. The bridge begins on the east side of the river, and (<u>it</u>, they) ends on the west side of the river.

__dec.__ 4. Looking through a telescope, Imena could see that constellation and (<u>its</u>, their) nearest neighbor.

__int.__ 5. Why did you give (they, <u>them</u>) directions to the secret cave?

__dec.__ 6. Reynaldo promised to give (we, <u>us</u>) students a tour of the television station.

__imp.__ 7. Place Mother's flowers on the table, and take the card to (its, <u>her</u>).

__exc.__ 8. I can't believe (<u>our</u>, us) school won the contest!

__dec.__ 9. Wendy and Jasmine are donating (her, <u>their</u>) old clothing to a local charity.

__dec.__ 10. Either Alan or Jerome will collect signatures for (<u>his</u>, theirs) petition on Tuesday.

__dec.__ 11. Young deer roam freely through this park, but Susan worries that (it, <u>they</u>) will wander onto the highway.

__int.__ 12. Who can deliver Hector's homework to (her, <u>him</u>)?

__imp.__ 13. Bring me the plant that is drooping and I will water (<u>it</u>, him).

__imp.__ 14. Please ask the Fuelas to bring pictures of (his, <u>their</u>) trip to Texas.

__exc.__ 15. Look how high Marta can throw (<u>her</u>, his) baton!

__int.__ 16. When can Ron show (we, <u>us</u>) how to use the new computer?

__dec.__ 17. (<u>Those</u>, Them) were the best doughnuts Irene had ever tasted.

__dec.__ 18. (<u>We</u>, Us) travelers sometimes forget to pack everything.

184 Writer's Choice Grammar Workbook 8, Unit 8

Name _____ Class _____ Date _____

__imp.__ 19. Take Ms. Gorman's tools to (her, his) house.

__exc.__ 20. Wow! Jerry surprised even (herself, himself)!

▶ **Exercise 2** Draw one line under each main clause and two lines under each subordinate clause. Write in the blank whether the sentence is *simple*, *compound*, or *complex*.

__complex__ Before they began the concert, the orchestra tuned their instruments.

__compound__ 1. Laura baked brownies for the party, and Chad made submarine sandwiches.

__simple__ 2. Tulips and daffodils dotted the hillside.

__compound__ 3. Ms. Devereaux may teach her class indoors today, or she may take everyone outside.

__complex__ 4. As Shirlene was entering her house, she noticed the puppy had been playing with her slippers.

__simple__ 5. Several colorful boats lined up for the race.

__complex__ 6. The cast will pose for pictures after the performance ends.

__compound__ 7. Isabel and Mai Lin waited for nearly an hour, but the bus never came.

__complex__ 8. The festival preparations were delayed because high winds blew the tents over.

__complex__ 9. When you leave, be sure to tell the leader where you are going.

__complex__ 10. Uncle Dominic insisted that we all try the new Italian restaurant.

__complex__ 11. After the Thompsons sent us a fruit basket, we made them some homemade pies.

__complex__ 12. Brigitta found her lost button while she was jogging through the neighborhood.

__compound__ 13. The trees swayed in the breeze, and the wheat danced in the sunlight.

__compound__ 14. The department store was crowded, but Natasha and her mother were able to finish their shopping without difficulty.

__complex__ 15. Lesharo finished his chores before his brother returned home.

Unit 8, Verbals   185

Name _____ Class _____ Date _____

▶ **Exercise 3** Underline each participial, gerund, or infinitive phrase. Write in the blank what kind of phrase it is: *part.* for participial phrase, *ger.* for gerund phrase, or *inf.* for infinitive phrase.

ger.   Omar is looking forward to <u>camping with John and Travis</u>.

part. 1. Jason, <u>working on a shrimp boat</u>, enjoyed his summer.

inf.   2. Sandy needs <u>to sleep at least seven hours</u>.

ger.   3. Tabitha learned <u>sewing</u> from her mother.

part. 4. <u>Approaching at a rapid pace</u>, the storm darkened the western sky.

ger.   5. <u>Closing the window</u> reminded Amos of the alarm system.

part. 6. <u>Trapped in the spider's web</u>, the locust awaited its captor.

ger.   7. <u>Mashing potatoes</u> has never been Helen's favorite task.

inf.   8. Did the Lone Ranger learn <u>to speak the Apache language</u>?

part. 9. <u>Referring to her notes</u>, Dr. Cordero spoke about the medical profession.

inf.   10. Mrs. Maxwell knew how <u>to avoid an unpleasant confrontation</u>.

ger.   11. Martin heard <u>loud knocking at the door</u>.

inf.   12. Jocelyn wanted <u>to hear the famous guitarist</u>.

ger.   13. <u>The crowing of the rooster</u> awakened everyone on the farm.

part. 14. <u>Sinking like a big red ball</u>, the sun disappeared from the western horizon.

inf.   15. The goalkeeper lunged <u>to block Jeremy's kick</u>.

ger.   16. <u>Going to school</u> consumes most of Jim's time.

part. 17. <u>Stopping for lunch</u>, Ella was late for her appointment.

ger.   18. <u>Walking to the downtown mall</u> requires about twenty minutes.

ger.   19. Carmella enjoys <u>talking to Morris</u>.

inf.   20. Jesse raised his left foot <u>to tie the shoelace on his basketball shoe</u>.

Name _____ Class _____ Date _____

Unit 9: Subject-Verb Agreement

Lesson 53
Making Subjects and Verbs Agree

If the subject of a sentence is singular, then the verb of the sentence must also be singular. If the subject is plural, then the verb must also be plural. When the subject and the verb are both singular or both plural, they are said to **agree in number**.

Mr. Lawrenz teaches art. (singular subject, singular verb)
Wade and Lee teach art. (plural subject, plural verb)
I walk to the store. (singular subject, singular verb)
She walks to the store. (singular subject, singular verb)
They walk to the store. (plural subject, plural verb)

Whether the irregular verbs *be*, *do*, and *have* are used as main verbs or helping verbs, they must agree with the subject.

The window **is** stuck. (singular subject, singular verb)
These windows **do** stick in humid weather. (plural subject, plural helping verb)
He **has** saved money. (singular subject, singular helping verb)

▶ **Exercise 1** Draw two lines under the correct form of the verb in parentheses.

Carla (bake, <u>bakes</u>) brownies once a week.

1. Cows (<u>produce</u>, produces) milk at the dairy farm.
2. This airplane (fly, <u>flies</u>) to Milwaukee.
3. A wave (<u>crashes</u>, crash) against the breakwater.
4. These mountains (<u>appear</u>, appears) taller than the clouds.
5. These lights (<u>do</u>, does) not work.
6. The rodeo (start, <u>starts</u>) next week.
7. Fred and Ginger (<u>dance</u>, dances) very well together.
8. These books (seems, <u>seem</u>) heavy.
9. She (<u>sings</u>, sing) in the school choir.
10. He (<u>was</u>, were) not home when Coach Lewis called.
11. Tony (do, <u>does</u>) not go to the movies very often.

Name _____ Class _____ Date _____

12. Forecasters (predicts, **predict**) many bad storms this year.

13. Two hundred people (was, **were**) in the audience.

14. You and I (trains, **train**) for the same position on the team.

15. Two airports (**serve**, serves) the Washington, D.C., area.

16. This container (hold, **holds**) one gallon of liquid.

17. These crates (weighs, **weigh**) twenty pounds.

18. President Smith (**leaves**, leave) at three o'clock.

19. Redwood trees (**grow**, grows) very tall.

20. May High School and Brush High School (**have**, has) been sports rivals for many years.

▶ **Exercise 2** Write in the blank the correct present-tense form of the verb in parentheses.

Richard ____**plans**____ to visit London in the spring. (plan)

1. King Alexander III of Macedonia ____**is**____ commonly known as Alexander the Great. (be)

2. Mr. Collins ____**waits**____ impatiently for the mail to arrive. (wait)

3. Saul and Keith ____**play**____ checkers after school. (play)

4. The birds ____**hunt**____ for food by the pond. (hunt)

5. These sandwiches ____**taste**____ very good. (taste)

6. There ____**is**____ only one right answer to this question. (be)

7. Kathy ____**likes**____ this music. (like)

8. Leonard ____**hopes**____ spring practice will begin soon. (hope)

9. The wall ____**has**____ two windows. (have)

10. The Mississippi River ____**flows**____ through Louisiana. (flow)

11. Light ____**shines**____ through the stained glass windows. (shine)

12. Art classes ____**help**____ Donna develop her skills. (help)

13. West Point and the Naval Academy ____**are**____ near the East Coast. (be)

14. Electric guitars ____**sell**____ extremely well in this city. (sell)

15. Dolphins ____**live**____ in water. (live)

16. Only two weeks ____**remain**____ in the semester. (remain)

Name _____ Class _____ Date _____

Lesson 54
Locating the Subject

Making a subject and verb agree is easy when the verb directly follows the subject. However, sometimes a prepositional phrase comes between the subject and its verb.

The **books** on the table **belong** to Edwina. (The plural verb, *belong*, agrees with the plural subject, *books*.)

To help determine subject-verb agreement, say the sentence without the prepositional phrase.

The **books belong** to Edwina.

Inverted sentences are those in which the subject follows the verb. Some of these sentences begin with a prepositional phrase. Other inverted sentences begin with *here* or *there*. Do not mistake the object of a preposition or *here* and *there* for the subject.

In the ocean **live animals** of many species.
There **is** the **road** into town.
Here in the storeroom **are** the **tapes** you ordered.

Some interrogative sentences may have a helping verb before the subject. The subject is found between the helping verb and the main verb.

Does this **store sell** videotapes? (*Store* is the subject, *sell* is the main verb, and *does* is the helping verb.)

▶ **Exercise 1** Draw two lines under the correct form of the verb in parentheses. Write *S* in the blank if the subject and verb are singular. Write *pl.* if the subject and verb are plural.

__pl.__   The flowers in Marta's garden (<u><u>appear</u></u>, appears) each spring.

__pl.__ 1. The lands near the South Pole (<u><u>are</u></u>, is) very cold.

__pl.__ 2. The football players, except for John, (<u><u>are</u></u>, is) warming up on the field.

__S__   3. On the wall (<u><u>hangs</u></u>, hang) a certificate of appreciation.

__pl.__ 4. From this junior high (comes, <u><u>come</u></u>) tomorrow's graduates.

__S__   5. The classroom near the north stairs (get, <u><u>gets</u></u>) very cold in the winter.

__pl.__ 6. (<u><u>Do</u></u>, Does) the freshmen understand French?

Unit 9, Subject-Verb Agreement **189**

Name _____ Class _____ Date _____

__S__ 7. Alaska, before becoming part of the United States, (was, were) called "Seward's Folly" or "Icebergia."

__S__ 8. There (lie, lies) the finest watchdog in the county!

__pl.__ 9. Do the ingredients in these cereals (includes, include) sugar?

__S__ 10. Pluto, which is the farthest planet from the sun, (orbit, orbits) the sun every 90,000 days.

__pl.__ 11. The streets in this city (contains, contain) little asphalt.

__pl.__ 12. Here (are, is) your instructions.

__S__ 13. Amber, which is used in jewelry, (come, comes) from fossilized tree sap.

__pl.__ 14. Americans in each region of the country (speak, speaks) with distinct accents.

__S__ 15. In the back of the room (sit, sits) the next speaker.

__S__ 16. There across the hall (are, is) the language lab.

__pl.__ 17. The leaves on the tree (turn, turns) color every fall.

__S__ 18. The abacus, although centuries old, (are, is) still used in many parts of the world.

__S__ 19. Does he (think, thinks) this is going to work?

__pl.__ 20. The pieces of the puzzle (fits, fit) together perfectly.

▶ **Exercise 2** Underline the simple subject of each sentence. Write in the blank the correct present-tense form of the verb in parentheses.

The players in the game ___rest___ at halftime. (rest)

1. Here in our city ___works___ a world-renowned author. (work)

2. Rivers in Ohio, except for the Ohio River, ___are___ shallow-draft waterways. (be)

3. Only one bird in our yard ___builds___ its nest in that tree. (build)

4. Do these lockers ___have___ numbers? (have)

5. The microphones in the auditorium ___are___ professional quality. (be)

6. In the desert ___live___ many plants. (live)

190 *Writer's Choice Grammar Workbook 8, Unit 9*

Name _____ Class _____ Date _____

Lesson 55
Collective Nouns and Other Special Subjects

A **collective noun** names a group. It has a singular meaning when the group acts as a unit. It has a plural meaning when showing that each member of the group acts as an individual. The meaning of the noun in the sentence determines whether the singular or plural form of the verb is needed. You can determine whether a collective noun takes a singular or plural verb by substituting the pronoun *it* or *they*.

The **team wants** to buy the coach a gift. (one group, singular)
The **team agree** to purchase their own jerseys. (individuals, plural)

Certain nouns, such as *mathematics* and *mumps*, end in *-s* but use a singular verb form. Nouns such as *jeans* and *scissors* also end in *-s* and take a plural verb, yet they are single objects.

The **news is** on the radio now. (singular)
These **jeans are** torn. (plural)

When the subject refers to an amount as a single unit, it is considered singular. When it refers to more than one unit, it is plural.

Two weeks seems like a long time to wait. (single unit, singular verb)
Two weeks have passed since you called. (several units, plural verb)

The name of a company, title of a book, movie, play, song, or work of art is a proper noun and should be treated as singular even if the subject within the title is plural.

***The Flintstones* is** a television show that was made into a movie. (single title)

▶ **Exercise 1** Underline the simple subject of each sentence. In the blank, write *S* if the subject is singular and *pl.* if the subject is plural.

__S__   Broadcast <u>news</u> continues to be a popular field of study.

__S__ 1. Ms. Tanaka's <u>class</u> is interested in journalism.

__pl.__ 2. Three <u>weeks</u> have been spent studying newscasts.

__S__ 3. Television <u>news</u> excites several of the students.

__S__ 4. Jeremy's <u>family</u> gives tours of the television station where his mother works.

__pl.__ 5. The <u>class</u> appreciate the time they each received with Mrs. Ramos, who showed them how to operate a video camera.

Name _____ Class _____ Date _____

__S___ 6. The <u>group</u> hopes to produce its own news show.

__S___ 7. Student <u>council</u> suggests ideas for a school newscast.

__S___ 8. The school <u>band</u> volunteers to record music for the show.

__S___ 9. A target <u>audience</u> is selected.

__pl.__ 10. The softball <u>team</u> grant their interviews to three student reporters.

__S___ 11. <u>Youth News</u> is the name chosen for the program.

__pl.__ 12. <u>Faculty</u> assist in obtaining permission for students to videotape background material for their news stories.

__S___ 13. The Art <u>Club</u> volunteers to draw weather maps.

__pl.__ 14. The coaching <u>staff</u> offer advice on the sports report.

__S___ 15. Current <u>events</u> fills the top slot in the newscast.

__pl.__ 16. <u>Ratings</u> are unimportant according to Ms. Tanaka.

__pl.__ 17. The <u>public</u> need to be informed about events that affect their lives.

__pl.__ 18. Ten <u>days</u> pass before all the arrangements are made.

__S___ 19. Finally, the <u>class</u> is ready to produce a newscast.

__S___ 20. "Jobs for Teens" is the first story they will run.

▶ **Exercise 2** Draw one line under the simple subject. Draw two lines under the correct form of the verb in parentheses.

Television <u>news</u> (<u>explains</u>, explain) what is happening in government.

1. <u>Media</u> (reports, <u>report</u>) on the daily activities of each branch of government.
2. A network <u>team</u> (<u>gathers</u>, gather) the news each day.
3. The press <u>corps</u> (records, <u>record</u>) what the politicians have to say to them.
4. A dedicated <u>group</u> (presents, <u>present</u>) the information they have each obtained.
5. The <u>audience</u> (watches, <u>watch</u>) to find out what their elected officials are doing.
6. <u>Politics</u> (<u>becomes</u>, become) confusing without someone to describe what the politicians are trying to do.
7. However, a citizens' <u>group</u> (<u>has</u>, have) more power than it might think.
8. A voting <u>bloc</u> (<u>determines</u>, determine) who will win an election.

192 Writer's Choice Grammar Workbook 8, Unit 9

Name _____ Class _____ Date _____

Lesson 56
Indefinite Pronouns as Subjects

An **indefinite pronoun** is a pronoun that does not refer to a specific person, place, or thing. Most indefinite pronouns are singular. Some are plural, and some can be either singular or plural. When an indefinite pronoun is the subject of a sentence, the verb must agree in number with the indefinite pronoun.

COMMON INDEFINITE PRONOUNS

Singular: another, anybody, anyone, anything, each, either, everybody, everyone, everything, much, neither, nobody, no one, nothing, one, somebody, someone, something
Plural: both, few, many, others, several
Either Singular or Plural: all, any, most, none, some

Nobody lives without air. (singular)
Many study the process of photosynthesis. (plural)

A prepositional phrase can follow the indefinite pronouns *all, any, most, none,* or *some.* The object of the preposition will determine whether the pronoun is singular or plural.

Some of the building **is** brick. (singular)
Some of the sunflowers **are** large. (plural)

▶ **Exercise 1** Draw two lines under the correct form of the verb in parentheses.

Few (expects, <u>expect</u>) to win a prize in the contest.

1. Another (<u>wants</u>, want) to look at the bike.

2. Anybody (study, <u>studies</u>) French before taking a trip to France.

3. Anyone (understand, <u>understands</u>) the importance of this issue.

4. One (tell, <u>tells</u>) us about his days in baseball.

5. Each of the members (speak, <u>speaks</u>) for three minutes.

6. Either of these books (convey, <u>conveys</u>) the mood of the 1980s.

7. Everybody (want, <u>wants</u>) a copy of that videotape.

8. Both of these schools (is, <u>are</u>) outstanding.

9. Everyone who participates (<u>receives</u>, receive) an award.

10. Everything in this room (<u>appears</u>, appear) to be an antique.

Unit 9, Subject-Verb Agreement   **193**

Name _____ Class _____ Date _____

11. Much of what is in the book (is, are) on the test.

12. Neither (becomes, become) a first-place contender.

13. Some of the students (visits, visit) their schools after they graduate.

14. Thankfully, many (returns, return) to inspire new students.

15. Nobody (like, likes) to see rain during a picnic.

16. Most of the dancers (perform, performs) the same steps.

17. No one (know, knows) how hard we worked on this project.

18. Nothing (is, are) going to change my mind.

19. One (wonders, wonder) how that computer program works.

20. Somebody (wants, want) to talk to you.

▶ **Exercise 2** Write in the blank the correct present-tense form of the verb in parentheses.

All __**ride**__ the rollercoaster first. (ride)

1. Someone __**is**__ at the door. (be)

2. Something __**does**__ not look right in this equation. (do)

3. Others __**walk**__ this path each morning. (walk)

4. Several __**describe**__ the process to us. (describe)

5. Much of this course work __**requires**__ outside study. (require)

6. Few __**play**__ the trombone. (play)

7. Many __**understand**__ the importance of clean air. (understand)

8. Much __**occurs**__ during a space shuttle launch. (occur)

9. Another __**waits**__ to ride the horse. (wait)

10. Some of the questions __**test**__ reading comprehension. (test)

11. Many __**contain**__ several items. (contain)

12. One __**needs**__ to understand the reasons for making such a rule. (need)

13. None of the stores __**carry**__ that brand. (carry)

14. Neither __**likes**__ the play as well as the movie. (like)

15. No one in this class __**studies**__ painting. (study)

Name _____ Class _____ Date _____

Lesson 57
Agreement with Compound Subjects

A **compound subject** contains two or more simple subjects that have the same verb. It requires a singular or plural verb, depending on how the parts of the subject are connected. When two or more simple subjects are joined by the coordinating conjunction *and* or by the correlative conjunction *both...and*, the verb is plural. Sometimes *and* is used to join two words that are part of a single unit or refer to a single person or thing. In this case, the subject is considered to be singular. When two or more subjects are joined by the coordinating conjunction *or* or *nor*, or the correlative conjunction *either...or* or *neither...nor*, the verb agrees with the subject that is closest to it.

Lakes, rivers, **and** streams **have** fish. (plural)
Both rivers **and** streams **carry** silt. (plural)
Our chief cook **and** bottle-washer **wants** to see you! (singular)
The printout **or** the disks **contain** the information. (plural; one singular and one plural subject; the verb agrees with the subject closest to it)
Either the disks **or** the printout **contains** the information. (singular; one plural and one singular subject; the verb agrees with the subject closest to it)

▶ **Exercise 1** Draw two lines under the correct form of the verb in parentheses. In the blank, write *S* if the verb form is singular or *pl.* if it is plural.

__pl.__ Both the Atlantic Ocean and the Indian Ocean (meets, <u>meet</u>) the African continent.

__S__ 1. The second-largest continent and the most diverse one (<u>is</u>, are) Africa.

__pl.__ 2. Both the east and west coastlines (is, <u>are</u>) smooth.

__pl.__ 3. Africa's northernmost and southernmost points (<u>extend</u>, extends) almost equal distances from the equator.

__pl.__ 4. The Northern Plateau, Central/Southern Plateau, and Eastern Highlands (is, <u>are</u>) the three major continental regions.

__pl.__ 5. Both the Senegal and Niger rivers (empties, <u>empty</u>) into the Sudan drainage basin.

__S__ 6. Africa's most famous mountain and highest peak (<u>is</u>, are) Mt. Kilimanjaro.

Name _____ Class _____ Date _____

__S__ 7. Either the desert or the tropical rain forest (<u>has</u>, have) an average temperature of 80°.

__S__ 8. Neither the Sahara nor the Kalahari (<u>is</u>, are) a cold desert.

__pl.__ 9. Desert and semidesert conditions (<u>prevail</u>, prevails) in northern Africa.

__pl.__ 10. Tall grasses and low trees (grows, <u>grow</u>) on grasslands called savannas.

__pl.__ 11. Giraffes, elephants, and zebras (lives, <u>live</u>) on these savannas.

__pl.__ 12. Both flooding and drought (<u>plague</u>, plagues) Africa.

__pl.__ 13. The forests and grasslands (serves, <u>serve</u>) as home to several species of antelope.

__S__ 14. Either the lion or the elephant (stand, <u>stands</u>) guard over his territory.

__pl.__ 15. Insects and diseases (<u>attack</u>, attacks) plants and animals.

__pl.__ 16. National parks and game reserves (protects, <u>protect</u>) Africa's endangered wildlife.

__pl.__ 17. The baobab, borassus palm, and acacia trees (survives, <u>survive</u>) through underground moisture.

__S__ 18. For many years, the only source of either radium or diamonds (were, <u>was</u>) the Congo.

__pl.__ 19. Both the Nile and Congo rivers (is, <u>are</u>) important natural resources.

__S__ 20. Either the Nile or the Zaire (<u>begins</u>, begin) at Lake Victoria.

__pl.__ 21. Lake Victoria, Owen Falls, and Kariba Gorge (<u>provide</u>, provides) water for hydroelectric generators.

__pl.__ 22. Irrigation and hydroelectric power (<u>use</u>, uses) water from the Nile.

__pl.__ 23. The treasures and sarcophagus of King Tutankhamen (was, <u>were</u>) discovered in 1922.

__pl.__ 24. South and east Africa (<u>contain</u>, contains) many fossils.

__pl.__ 25. Both the Tibesti and Ahaggar mountains (<u>have</u>, has) prehistoric rock drawings.

__pl.__ 26. Africa's traditional art and stories (<u>tell</u>, tells) about the past.

__S__ 27. Either historical realities or mythology (<u>is</u>, are) conveyed through traditional art.

__pl.__ 28. Masks and statues (is, <u>are</u>) the most common forms of African art.

Name _____ Class _____ Date _____

 Unit 9 **Review**

▶ **Exercise 1** Draw two lines under the correct form of the verb in parentheses.

Neither Tom nor Steve (remember, <u>remembers</u>) leaving his bicycle on the sidewalk.

1. Either a cup or a glass (hold, <u>holds</u>) water.
2. Arizona and New Mexico, particularly in the summer, (is, <u>are</u>) very hot.
3. In the winter (come, <u>comes</u>) frigid air from the north.
4. The budget committee (accept, <u>accepts</u>) your proposal.
5. The pliers (<u>do</u>, does) us no good if we cannot find them.
6. Here on the table (<u>lie</u>, lies) the missing keys.
7. Does this cooler (<u>contain</u>, contains) any ice?
8. Twenty-five cents (<u>was</u>, were) the cost of the phone call.
9. *Duel of Eagles* (give, <u>gives</u>) a good description of the Mexican and American fight for the Alamo.
10. My last and best song (<u>is</u>, are) "Maple Leaf Rag."
11. At the corner of Jefferson Avenue and High Street (<u>occur</u>, occurs) many accidents.
12. Their dedication to their profession (serve, <u>serves</u>) the company well.
13. Bowling, hockey, and basketball (is, <u>are</u>) popular sports.
14. The flock of sheep (graze, <u>grazes</u>) contentedly.
15. Scissors (<u>come</u>, comes) in all sizes.
16. Neither boots nor an umbrella (<u>is</u>, are) necessary in sunny weather.
17. Over the horizon (rise, <u>rises</u>) a beautiful pink sun.
18. Five months (has, <u>have</u>) passed since the last school field trip.
19. Many (<u>think</u>, thinks) this test was easy.
20. Both Joshua and Stacy (<u>dance</u>, dances) in the school ballet.

Unit 9, Subject-Verb Agreement **197**

Cumulative Review: Units 1–9

▶ **Exercise 1** Above each word in italics, label its part of speech: *N* (noun), *V* (verb), *adj.* (adjective), *adv.* (adverb), *pro.* (pronoun), or *prep.* (preposition).

           adj.   V   N   prep.
The *foggy* weather *caused problems with* the traffic.

1. *Clear* (adj.) and cold Lake Superior *holds* (V) one tenth *of* (prep.) the world's *unfrozen* (adj.) fresh water.
2. The *brilliantly* (adv.) colored butterfly *fluttered* (V) *lazily* (adv.) over the bright *flowers* (N).
3. The late-afternoon sunbeams created *long* (adj.) *shadows* (N) *across* (prep.) the city park.
4. A chameleon *uses* (V) its *ability* (N) to camouflage *itself* (pro.) to hide from danger.
5. The tour company *carefully* (adv.) planned the fabulous *European* (adj.) *excursion* (N) *for* (prep.) the students.
6. Schools are *rarely* (adv.) closed in *Thunder Bay* (N) because of the *harsh* (adj.) *winter* (adj.) weather.
7. The little boy *napped* (V) *peacefully* (adv.) on a blanket *during* (prep.) the *long* (adj.) parade.
8. *Pollution* (N) and over-fishing lead to severe *problems* (N) for the fishing *industry* (N).
9. The *night-time* (adj.) temperature *plunged* (V) *rapidly* (adv.) to *ten* (adj.) degrees below zero.
10. The huge airliner *quickly* (adv.) descended *in* (prep.) *preparation* (N) for landing.
11. *Moods* (N) and attitudes *are lifted* (V) by a *bright* (adj.) and *sunny* (adj.) day.
12. The *higher* (adj.) altitude *of* (prep.) Nairobi quickly *left* (V) us *breathless* (adj.) during our hikes.
13. The howling of the coyote *echoed* (V) *early* (adv.) *through* (prep.) the canyon.
14. *She* (pro.) depended *on* (prep.) her sophisticated camera for her *scientific* (adj.) *research* (N).
15. The old *Model T's* (N) were equipped *quite* (adv.) *differently* (adv.) from the comfortable cars of *today* (N).
16. *Our* (pro.) ancient *past* (N) is *revealed* (V) to *us* (pro.) through the *efforts* (N) of dedicated archaeologists.
17. The Vietnam *Women's* (adj.) Memorial *honors* (V) women *who* (pro.) *served* (V) during that war.
18. The Statue of Freedom on top of the U.S. Capitol *dome* (N) *was lowered* (V) and *cleaned* (V) for the *first* (adj.) time in 130 *years* (N).
19. People *everywhere* (adv.) enjoy *performances* (N) of Tchaikovsky's *famous* (adj.) ballet, The *Nutcracker* (N).
20. The northern *resort* (N) *offered* (V) fishing in the *summer* (N) and snowmobiling *in* (prep.) the *winter* (N).

198 Writer's Choice Grammar Workbook 8, Unit 9

Name _____ Class _____ Date _____

▶ **Exercise 2** Draw a line under each adjective clause, adverb clause, and noun clause. In the blank, indicate the kind of clause by writing *adj.*, *adv.*, or *noun*.

__adv.__ Whenever you write your name on these forms, please print it.

__adj.__ 1. Our state parks and reserves, which make excellent natural classrooms, hold exciting discoveries for students and families.

__adv.__ 2. Fritz saw the same car at a lower price after he had already bought his car.

__noun__ 3. Mrs. Rovtar explained that she would be taking early retirement.

__noun__ 4. Whoever joins an environmental club will learn much.

__adj.__ 5. Pearl S. Buck, who wrote *The Wave*, won the 1938 Nobel Prize for literature.

__noun__ 6. Priorities for your life are whatever you decide.

__adv.__ 7. Scott stopped his exercise routine early since he had another obligation.

__adv.__ 8. Jessica loved to read whenever she had free time.

__adv.__ 9. Wherever they are, animals love to play.

__noun__ 10. She wanted to go into whichever shop they came to first.

__adj.__ 11. The train that travels at midnight carries coal.

__adj.__ 12. Muffin, who is a finicky eater, turned up her nose at the new cat food.

__noun__ 13. The costume designer will help us with whatever costume changes are needed.

__noun__ 14. Whatever choice you make is fine with me.

__adv.__ 15. Wherever he went, the man's happy whistling could be heard.

__adv.__ 16. The ski runs were closed until the wind diminished.

__adj.__ 17. Troy's German shepherd is one dog that is truly faithful to its master.

__noun__ 18. I don't know why he stayed home.

__adj.__ 19. Shana cherished the family heirloom that she received from her grandmother.

__adv.__ 20. The fisherman wished to remain by the sea because his entire life had revolved around the water.

Name _____ Class _____ Date _____

▶ **Exercise 3** Draw two lines under the verb in parentheses that agrees in number with the subject.

Painting houses (**is**, are) their family's business.

1. Young chimps and baboons often (**become**, becomes) playmates in the wild.
2. Vacationing in the mountains (remain, **remains**) a favorite get-away for many families.
3. Each of his many songs (**is**, are) a favorite of my dad's.
4. Neither their old gramophone nor their antique chairs (**go**, goes) to the moving sale.
5. Five dollars (seem, **seems**) too much to pay for a student admission.
6. The members of the new theater group (**perform**, performs) tonight.
7. The cowboy and rodeo star (walk, **walks**) safely out of the arena after being thrown from his horse.
8. The largest piece of luggage (weigh, **weighs**) eighty pounds.
9. Does this book on foreign cities (**appeal**, appeals) to you?
10. In the wilderness (lie, **lies**) undiscovered treasures.
11. Each of the four opportunities (offer, **offers**) valuable experience.
12. Houston, New Orleans, and Atlanta (is, **are**) located in the southern part of the United States.
13. The principal or the teachers always (**arrive**, arrives) at school before the students.
14. Their family (organize, **organizes**) a reunion every five years.
15. Sometimes four weeks (**pass**, passes) before I see another movie.
16. In the corner of the flower bed (remain, **remains**) one lone blossom.
17. There (leave, **leaves**) the train on its daily journey.
18. In Grandfather's day, trousers (was, **were**) worn after a boy was too big for knickers.
19. Both old merchant vessels and old warships (**interest**, interests) our world history teacher.
20. Mathematics, as well as science and reading, (**is**, are) offered during the summer session.

Unit 10: Diagraming Sentences

Lesson 58
Diagraming Simple Subjects and Predicates

To diagram a sentence, draw a horizontal line with a vertical line going through it. Write the simple subject to the left of the vertical line and the simple predicate to the right of the line.

Diagramed below are only the simple subject and simple predicate of the four basic kinds of sentences. Regardless of the word order in the sentence, the location of the simple subject and simple predicate in a sentence diagram is always the same.

DECLARATIVE
People ride horses.

People | ride

IMPERATIVE
Ride the horse.

(you) | Ride

INTERROGATIVE
Do people ride horses?

people | Do ride

EXCLAMATORY
How those horses run!

horses | run

▶ **Exercise 1** Diagram only the simple subject and simple predicate in each sentence.

1. Cally had spoken.

    Cally | had spoken

2. The old barn collapsed.

    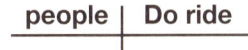

3. Buy that video.

    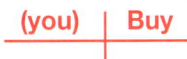

4. Did you give it to her?

    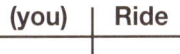

5. The dog damaged the flowers.

    dog | damaged

6. When did you wake him?

    you | did wake

Unit 10, Diagraming Sentences **201**

Name _____ Class _____ Date _____

7. I took my team jacket.

8. You are muttering.

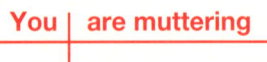

9. Hand me the book.

10. Are you motivated?

11. Duwana felt sorry.

12. Our team desires a win.

13. Earn the money for it.

(you) | Earn

14. Have you examined your notes?

15. How the ice glitters!

16. Enter the contest.

17. I have prepared for the quiz.

18. He wrecked my bike!

19. Where is my CD?

20. Quartz is beautiful.

202 Writer's Choice Grammar Workbook 8, Unit 10

Lesson 59
Diagraming Direct and Indirect Objects and Predicate Words

Place the direct object to the right of the verb and next to a vertical line that does not extend below the horizontal line. Locate indirect objects on a horizontal line below and to the right of the verb, connected to the verb by a slanted line.

Do take a free sample.   Shana gave her brother a video.

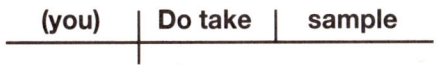   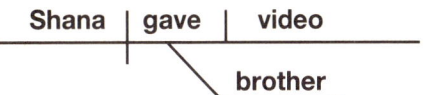

Use a slanted line to separate a predicate noun or predicate adjective from the linking verb.

Kyle was sorry.   Priscilla does seem very friendly.

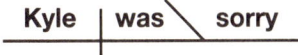   Priscilla | does seem \ friendly

▶ **Exercise 1** Diagram the subject, predicate, direct object, indirect object, and any predicate words in each sentence.

1. You look hungry.

    You | look \ hungry

2. Ruth thanked him.

    Ruth | thanked | him

3. I sent Susan the notes.

4. Henry overtook the other runners.

    Henry | overtook | runners

5. Fred brought Sarah the money.

6. Camilla seemed happy.

    Camilla | seemed \ happy

Unit 10, Diagraming Sentences **203**

Name _____ Class _____ Date _____

7. We love that movie.

8. Candrika told us the story.

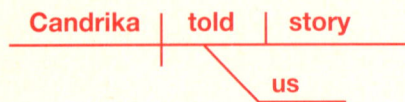

9. They remained angry.

10. Wrenn did me a favor.

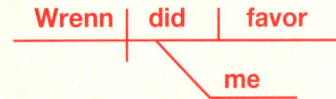

11. Jennifer threw Sam the ball.

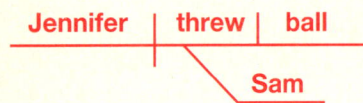

12. Mr. Hassan is nice.

13. Aaron grasped the discus.

14. Rebecca was pleasant.

15. Tiffany lent Cal the recorder.

16. Our work advanced the school's reputation.

17. My dog fetched me the stick.

18. When did you drink it?

19. Carol will be ready.

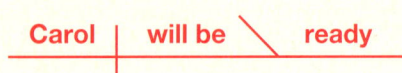

20. Boil the potatoes.

(you) | Boil | potatoes

Name _____ Class _____ Date _____

Lesson 60
Diagraming Adjectives and Adverbs

Place adjectives, including articles, and adverbs on slanted lines beneath the words they modify. Predicate adjectives remain on the horizontal line.

Social customs quickly change.   The black cats are very beautiful animals.

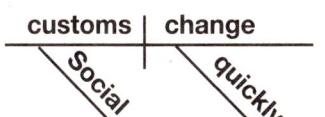 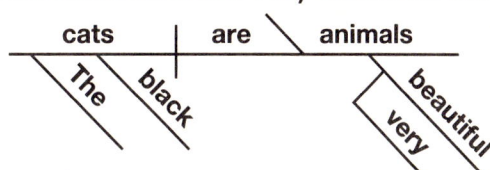

▶ **Exercise 1** Diagram each sentence.

1. Cumulus clouds are fluffy.

   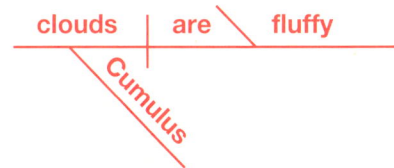

2. The parade featured historical vehicles.

3. He eagerly ate the green grapes.

   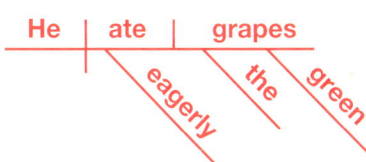

4. Bret is a fine student.

5. Sunee paints wonderful portraits.

6. Mr. Martinez runs fast.

7. Our old tree has become rotten.

8. Sailboats always look lovely.

   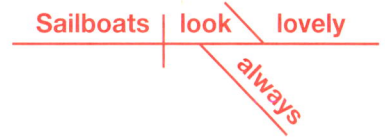

Unit 10, Diagraming Sentences **205**

9. The round balloons were absolutely huge.

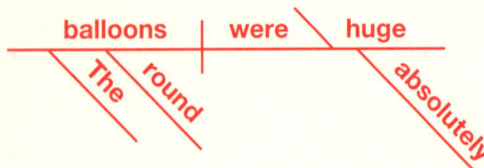

10. We will eat pepperoni pizza tomorrow.

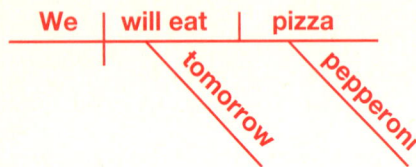

11. The artisans made beautiful shell necklaces.

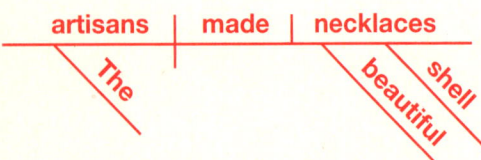

12. Tailors designed warm, snug clothing.

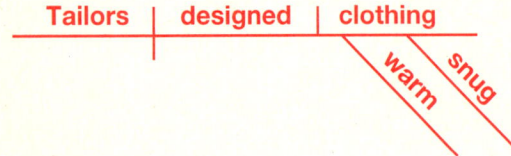

13. The injured boy moved quite gingerly.

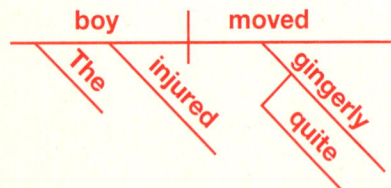

14. The new seeds provided abundant cotton.

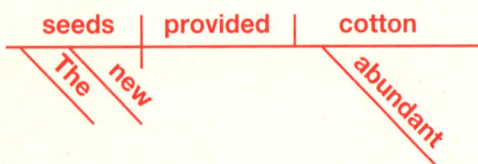

15. Competitive sports greatly influence our clothes.

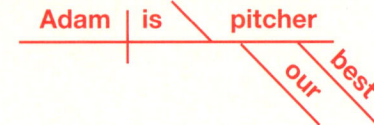

16. Adam is our best pitcher.

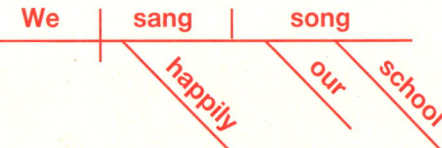

17. We happily sang our school song.

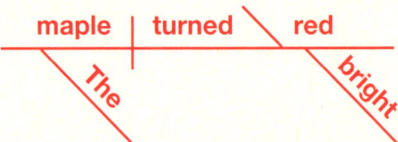

18. The maple turned bright red.

19. The spring air smells delightful.

20. The squirrel playfully chased a monarch butterfly.

Lesson 61
Diagraming Prepositional Phrases

Connect a prepositional phrase to the noun or verb that it modifies. Place the preposition on a slanted line and the object of the preposition on a horizontal line.

Manufacturers make modern automobiles for special needs.

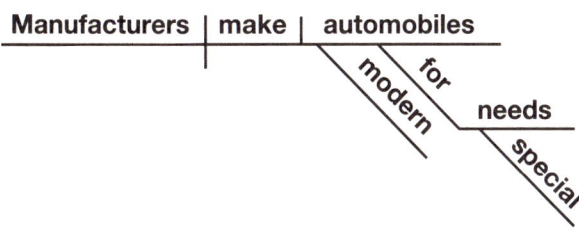

The boat anchored off the beach.

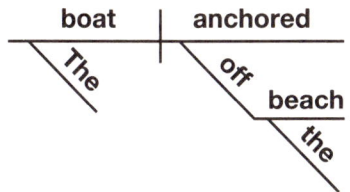

The movie across the street is showing cartoons before noon.

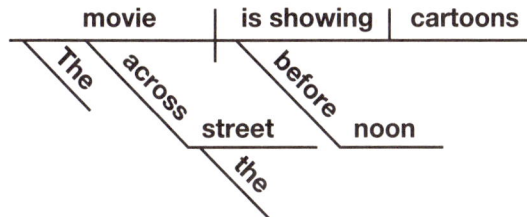

▶ **Exercise 1** Diagram each sentence.

1. We are waiting for the announcement.

2. She achieved success through hard work.

Unit 10, Diagraming Sentences **207**

3. The salesclerk offered a refund for the merchandise.

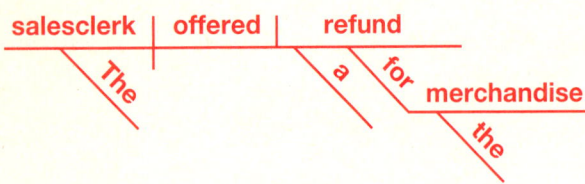

4. Some friends of mine threw me a party for my birthday.

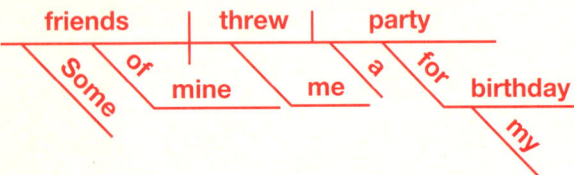

5. Bart reached the store on Shady Lane.

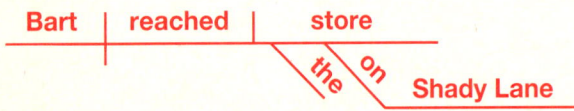

6. Many people opposed the legislation for cultural reasons.

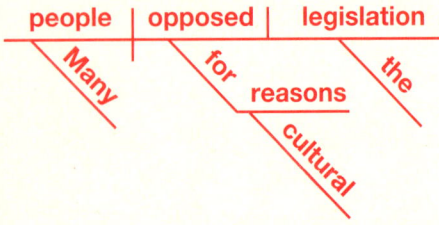

7. The store at the mall is having a sale.

8. The charisma of Hollywood stars also influences modern fashion.

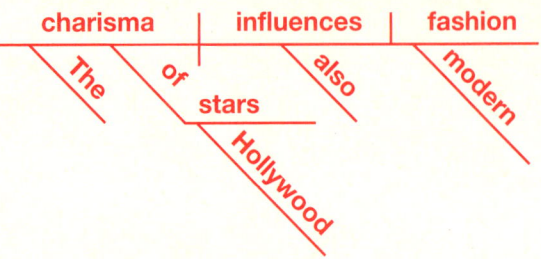

9. The need for affordable childcare grows steadily.

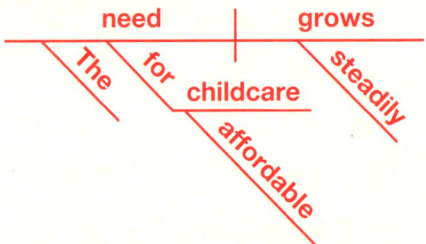

10. His slippers are in the den under the couch.

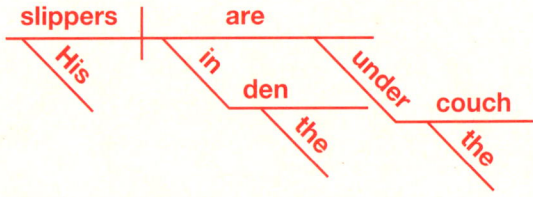

11. In spite of the bad weather, we will visit Grandma.

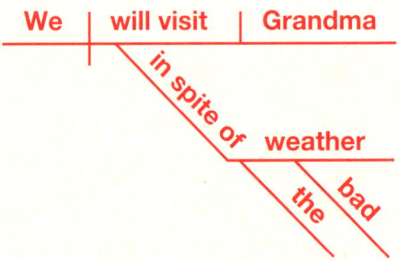

12. Power losses occurred after the storm.

Lesson 62
Diagraming Compound Sentence Parts

Coordinating conjunctions such as *and, but,* and *or* are used to join words, phrases, or sentences. Diagram these compound parts of a sentence by placing the second part of the compound below the first. Write the coordinating conjunction on a dotted line connecting the two parts.

Ships and boats carry goods and many passengers.

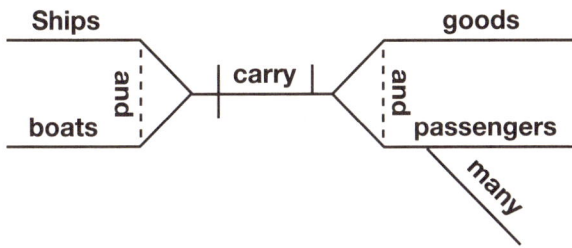

The bus stopped and avoided a collision.   We cut and ate the grapefruit.

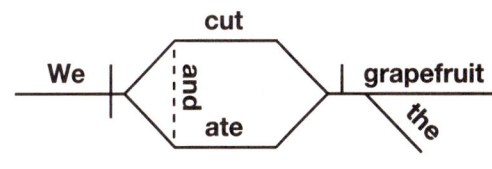

▶ Exercise 1 Diagram each sentence.

1. The research team experimented and tested.

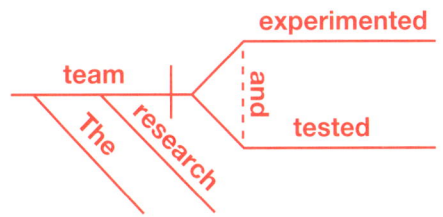

2. New designs and models appeared.

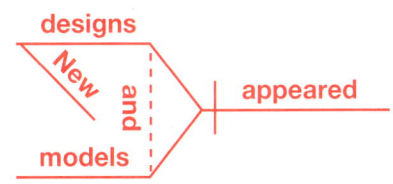

3. The soccer team and the baseball team were winners.

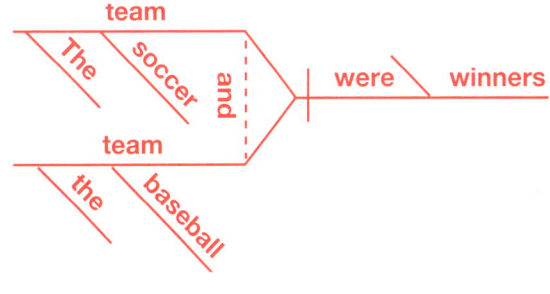

Unit 10, Diagraming Sentences **209**

Name _____ Class _____ Date _____

4. Pioneers and explorers made canoes and kayaks.

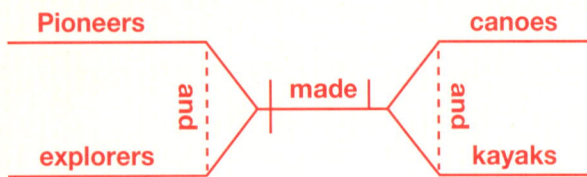

5. Pig skins or cow hides are cured and fashioned.

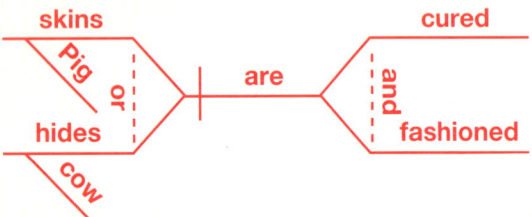

6. Asian farmers grow rice or bamboo.

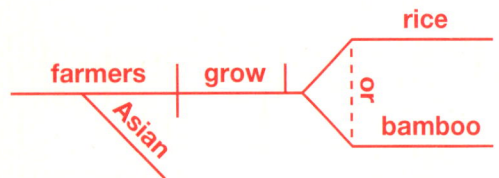

7. The editor read and corrected the manuscript.

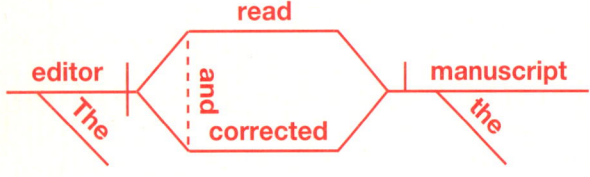

8. Orville and Wilbur Wright designed and built many airplanes.

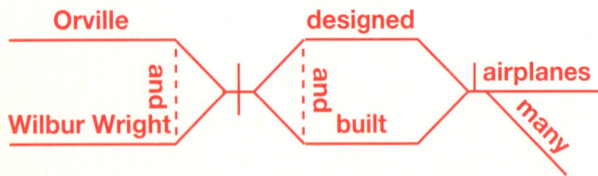

9. The train transported grain and coal.

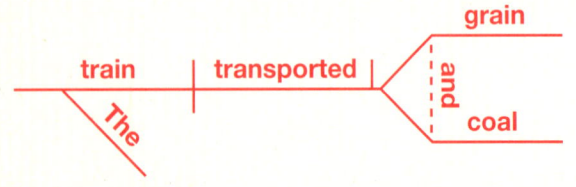

10. I feel very comfortable and quite happy.

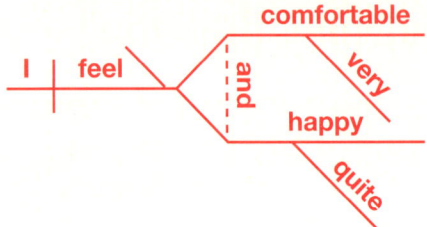

11. African explorers made coastal voyages and river trips.

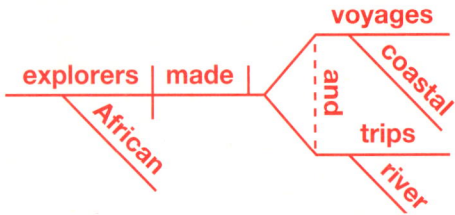

12. Wealth and splendor came to ancient Egypt.

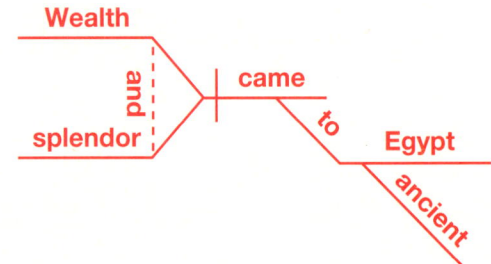

13. The band or orchestra moved the props and scenery.

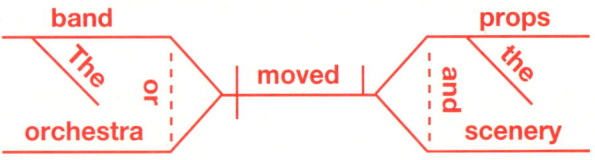

14. The lumber companies possessed and harvested great forests.

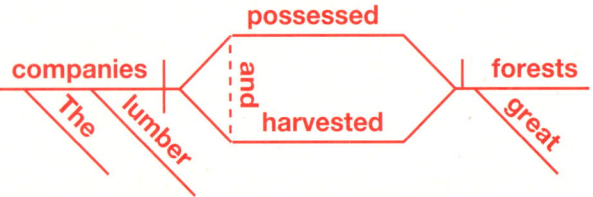

15. He saw a quail and a wild turkey.

Name _____ Class _____ Date _____

Lesson 63
Diagraming Compound Sentences

Diagram each clause of a compound sentence separately. Use a vertical dotted line to connect the verbs of each clause if the main clauses are joined by a semicolon.

Sparrows flitted among the trees; the cicadas buzzed.

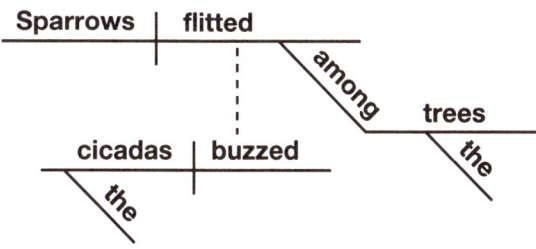

If the main clauses are joined by a conjunction, place the conjunction on a solid horizontal line. Then connect the conjunction to the verb of each clause by vertical dotted lines.

The tractor moved the wagon, and they unloaded the hay.

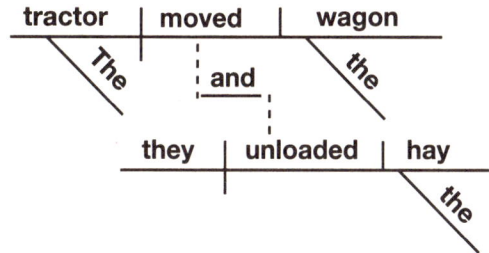

▶ **Exercise 1** Diagram each sentence.

1. Carla investigated the problem, and she told me the result.

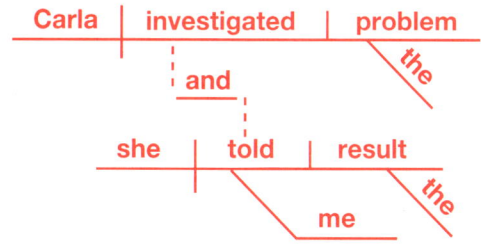

2. Rachel put the canvas on the sled, but she forgot the necessary rope.

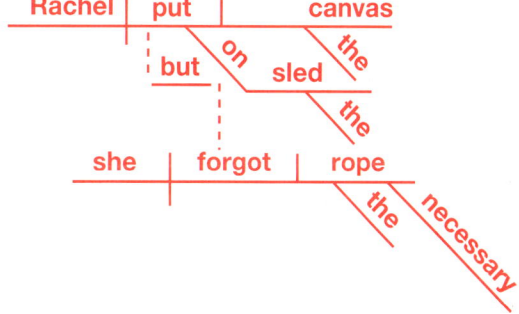

Unit 10, Diagraming Sentences **211**

Name _____ Class _____ Date _____

3. Jane was acquainted with Teri, but she did not know Tiffany.

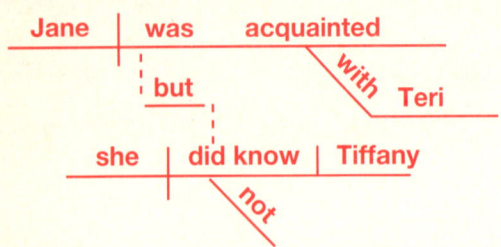

4. I like the black dress, but it is still too long.

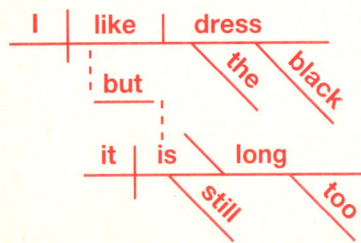

5. Juan obtained the tickets, and he kept them until the game.

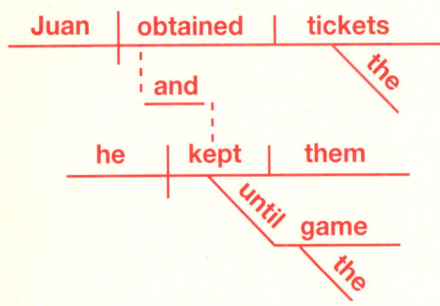

6. Jenny will tell the story; Dudley will play the music.

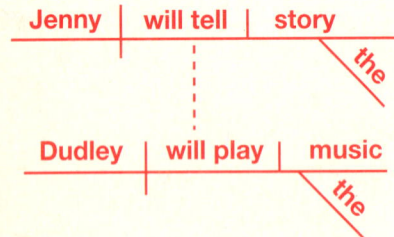

7. The sheep grazed the field, but the grass was very short.

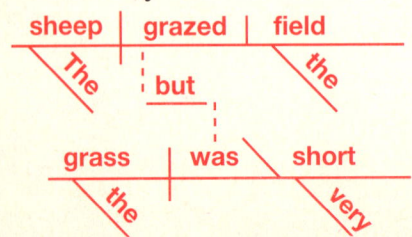

8. The trees give shade on the street, and their leaves renew the air.

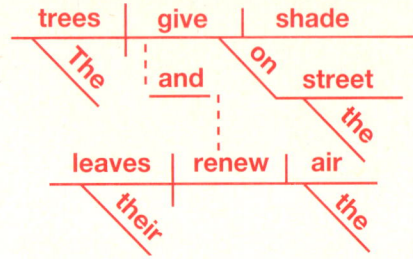

9. This frame costs more, but it is the perfect gift.

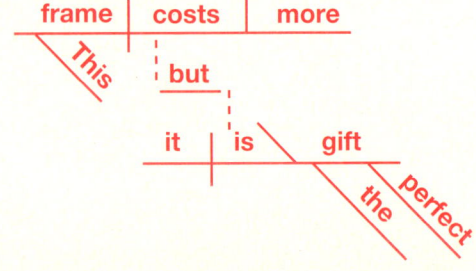

10. Isabel planned it, but her friends did it.

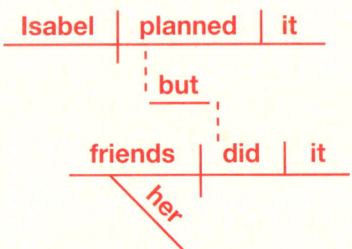

11. Ann will referee the game, and Barry will keep score.

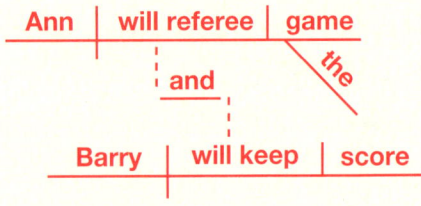

12. Gum is prohibited here, but it is permitted outside.

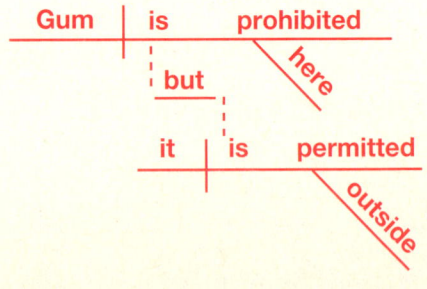

212 *Writer's Choice Grammar Workbook 8*, Unit 10

Lesson 64
Diagraming Complex Sentences with Adjective or Adverb Clauses

To diagram an adjective clause, draw a dotted line between the relative pronoun that introduces the clause and the noun or pronoun it modifies. Relative pronouns are *who, whom, whose, whoever, whomever, which,* or *that.* Diagram the relative pronoun according to its function in its own clause.

Scientists who study dinosaurs are paleontologists.

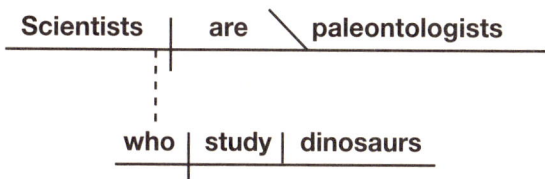

To diagram an adverb clause, draw a dotted line between the verb in the adverb clause and the verb, adjective, or adverb it modifies. Write the subordinating conjunction on the line connecting the verb and the word it modifies.

After he consulted a specialist, he decided against surgery.

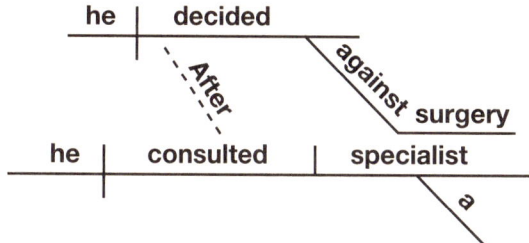

▶ **Exercise 1** Diagram each sentence.

1. The pen that writes best has blue ink.

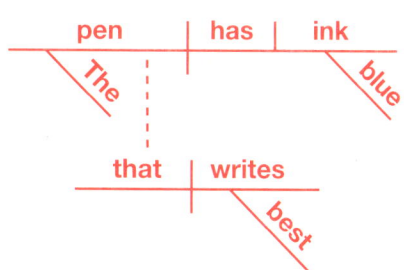

2. It was Dr. Robert Koch who first identified the cause of tuberculosis.

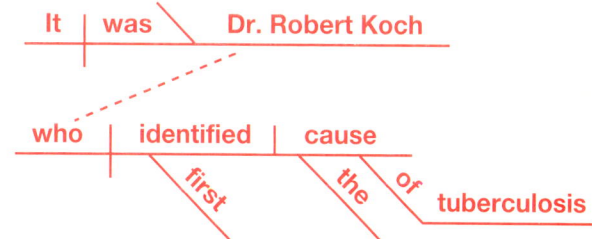

Unit 10, Diagraming Sentences **213**

3. The teacher whom you have for English is excellent.

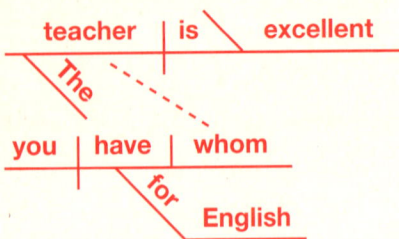

4. I will wait here until you return from the mall.

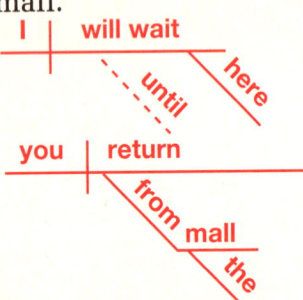

5. We ate a delicious dinner before the band played.

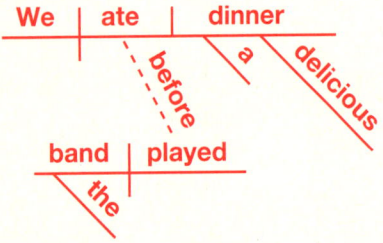

6. Amelia Earhart was the first American woman who flew solo across the Atlantic.

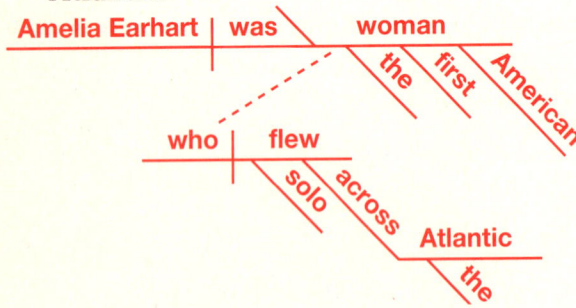

7. Willow trees grew where the water was sufficient.

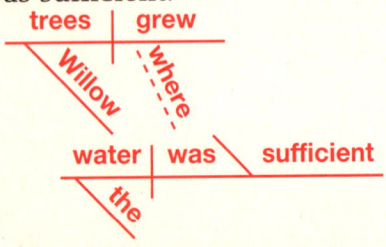

8. Until trees with leaves appeared, giant ferns and conifers were common.

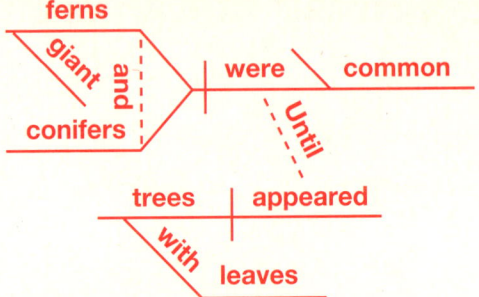

9. While a giraffe eats leaves, hyenas devour a wildebeest.

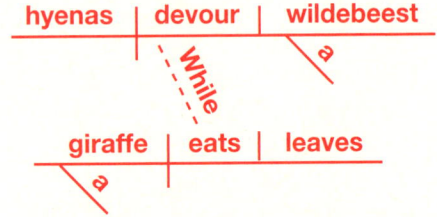

10. Because the tiger may become extinct, the government enforces strict protection laws.

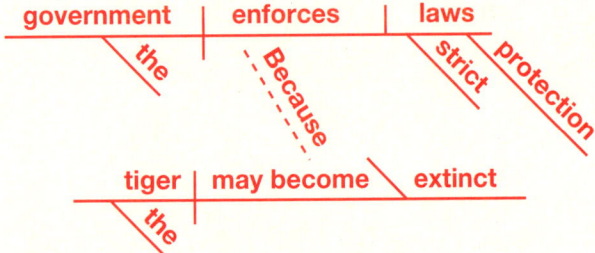

11. After the cold weather arrived, the tomato plants wilted.

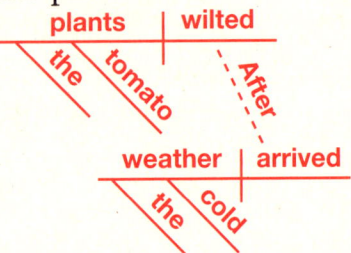

12. It is Chinese food that they prefer for dinner.

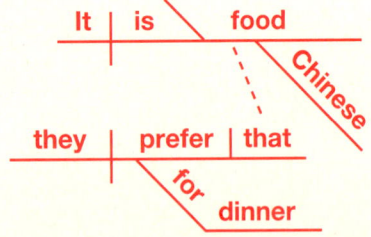

Lesson 65
Diagraming Noun Clauses

Noun clauses can be subjects, direct objects, objects of prepositions, or predicate nouns. Diagram a noun clause by placing it on a "stilt" above the main clause.

Diagram the word introducing a noun clause according to its function in the clause. Occasionally the word that introduces the noun clause, such as *that*, is not truly part of either the noun clause or the main clause. Write such a word on its own line above the clause and connect it with a dotted line.

Whatever happens will delight you.

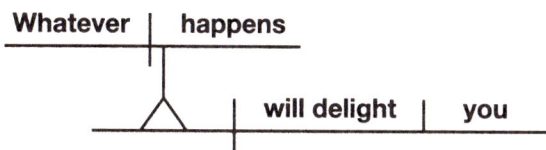

I heard that you won the game.

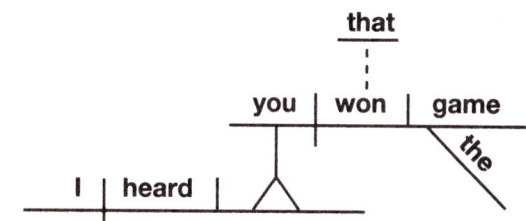

They respect what I achieved.

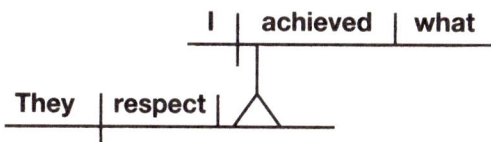

▶ **Exercise 1** Diagram each sentence.

1. Mr. Crosby explained what I am doing wrong.

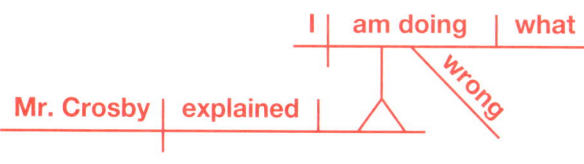

2. Sheila knows who drew that picture.

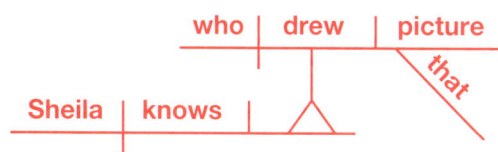

3. Whoever takes a boat ride should wear a life jacket.

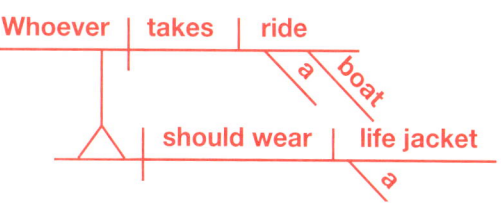

4. We understand how you lost the book.

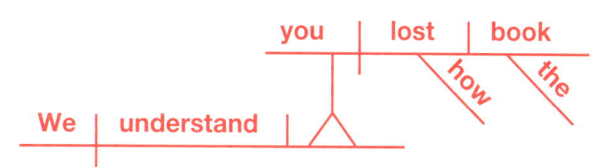

Unit 10, Diagraming Sentences **215**

5. The apple blossoms show that good weather has finally arrived.

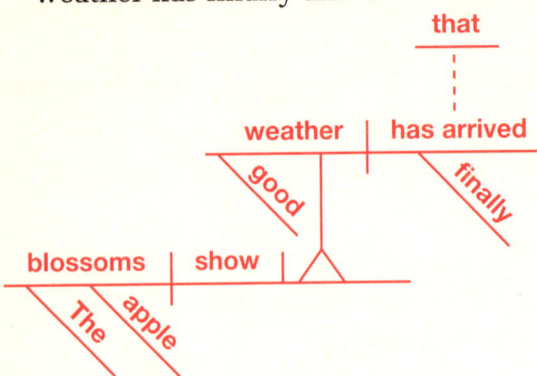

6. I know that Winona is right.

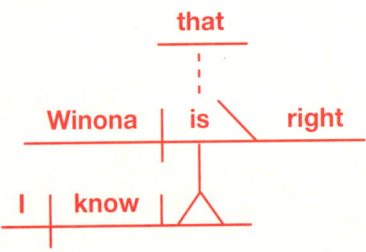

7. The skiers awaited whatever the cold dark clouds brought.

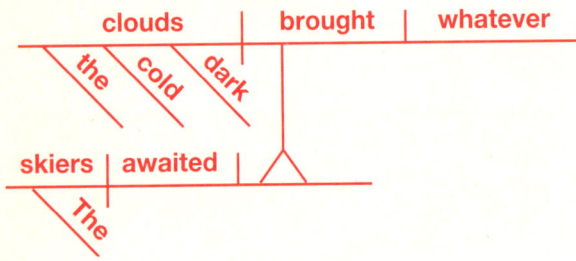

8. Charles thought that he was quite clever.

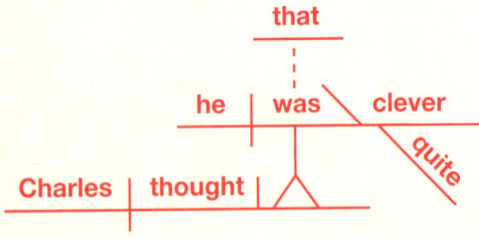

9. I do not understand whatever it is.

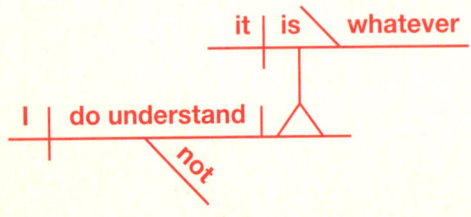

10. Amy wishes that we would stay longer.

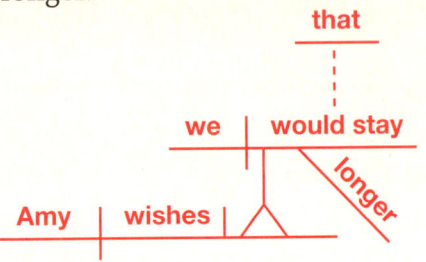

11. The travelers patiently observed what the weatherman wrote.

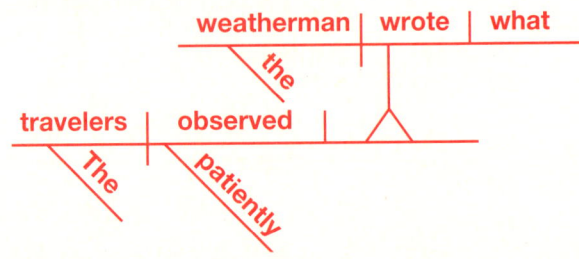

12. Francis feared that I might lose his CD.

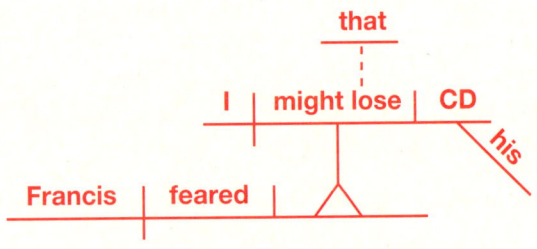

13. What we could win seems unbelievable.

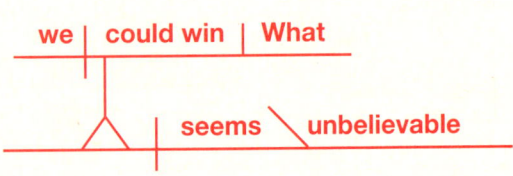

14. Her worry is that she will not finish the test.

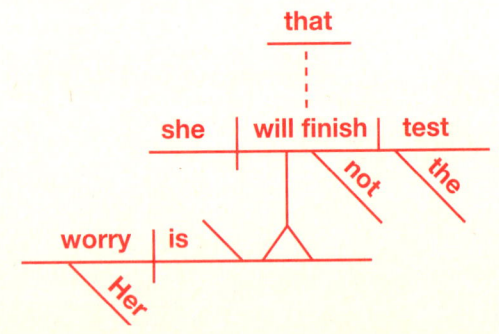

216 *Writer's Choice Grammar Workbook 8*, Unit 10

Name _____ Class _____ Date _____

Lesson 66
Diagraming Verbals

Place a participle or participial phrase beneath the word it modifies. Write the participle on a curve.

The dog, **barking furiously,** woke my family.

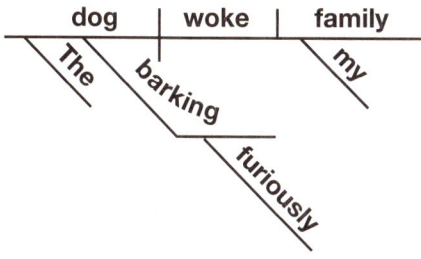

Place a gerund or gerund phrase on a "step" with the gerund written on a curve. Set the step on a "stilt" positioned according to the gerund's role in the sentence. A gerund can be a subject, an object of a verb or preposition, or an appositive.

Cave exploring is an adventure.   Surviving an Alaskan winter takes special precautions.

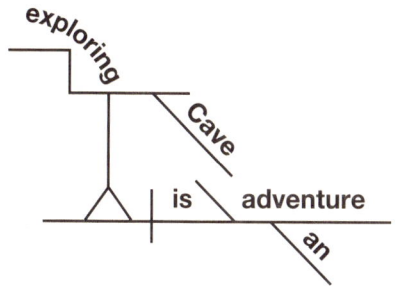 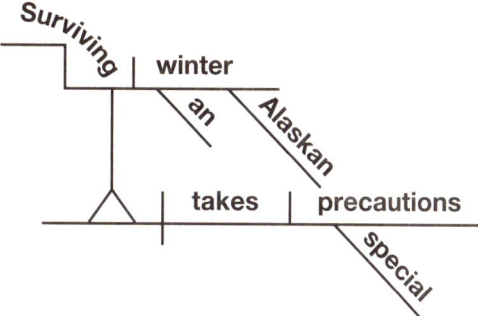

▶ **Exercise 1** Diagram each sentence.

1. Hunting can be a means of food production.

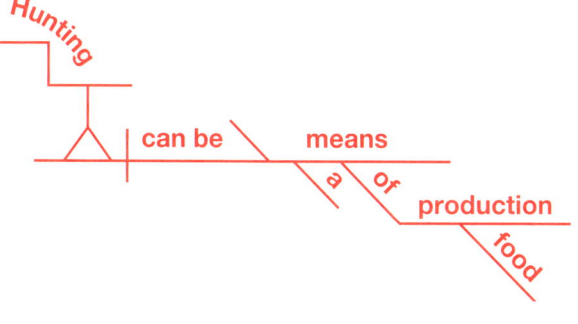

2. Traveling over rugged terrain, many early settlers envisioned a better future.

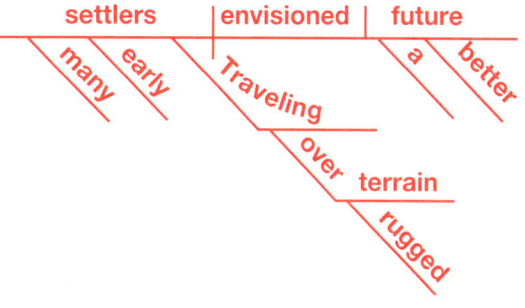

Unit 10, Diagraming Sentences **217**

3. The growing plant became too large for the pot.

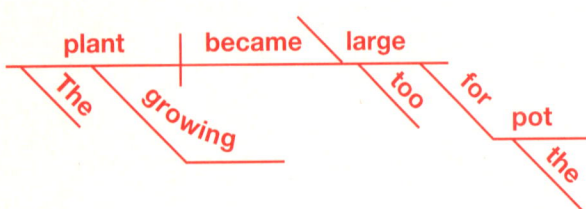

4. Fishing provides hours of enjoyment for Frank.

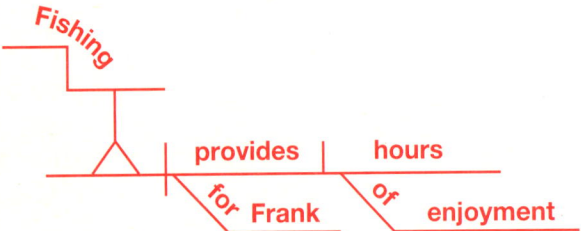

5. Dwelling near a mountain, the family feared a flash flood.

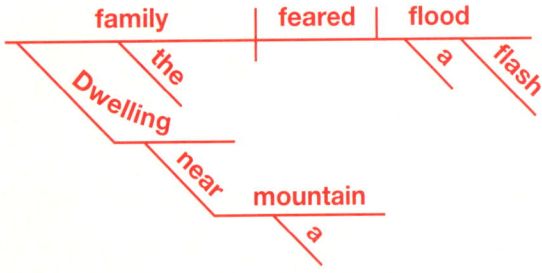

6. Charles was good at building.

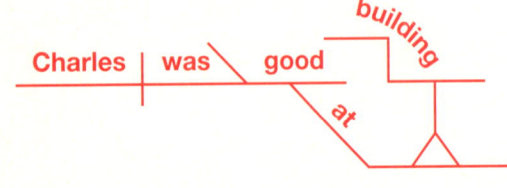

7. Cats enjoy sitting on laps.

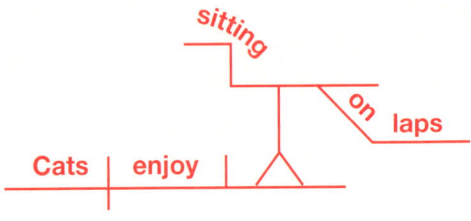

8. The talented potter made a charming jar from clay.

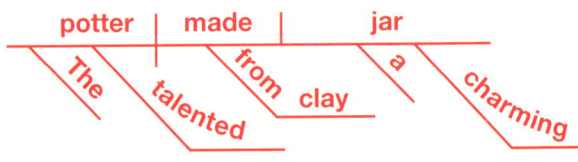

9. Approaching the car, a skunk gave an unmistakable scent.

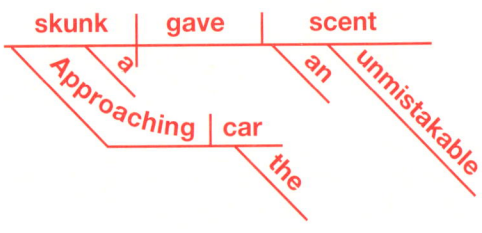

10. Enduring nature's harshness together, the campers felt kinship with the animals.

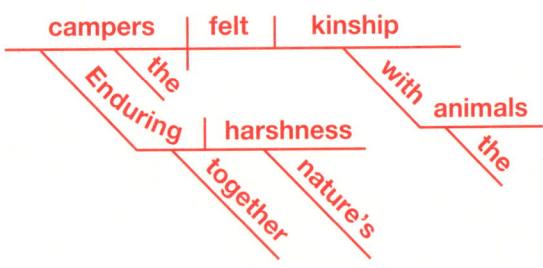

Lesson 67
Diagraming Infinitives

Place an infinitive or infinitive phrase that is used as a noun on a "stilt" positioned according to its role in the sentence. Then, diagram it as you would a prepositional phrase except that its slanted line should extend below the baseline.

The task of a student is **to study hard**.

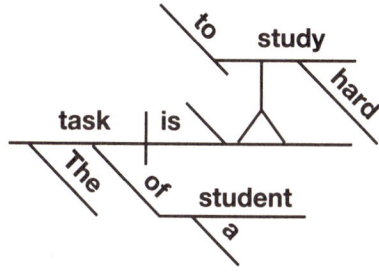

Diagram an infinitive or infinitive phrase that is used as either an adjective or an adverb as you would a prepositional phrase, below the word it modifies, with its slanted line extending below the baseline.

A book **to read** is *The Call of the Wild*.

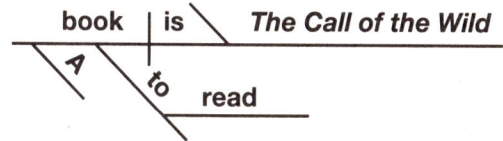

▶ **Exercise 1** Diagram each sentence.

1. I need to wash my dog.

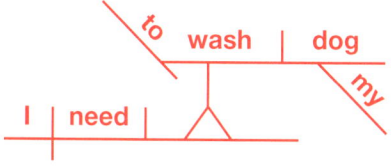

2. Would you like to include Cal?

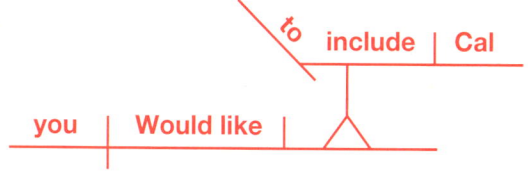

3. Henry is ready to launch his project.

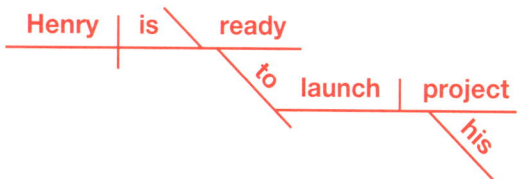

4. It is a job to lift those sacks.

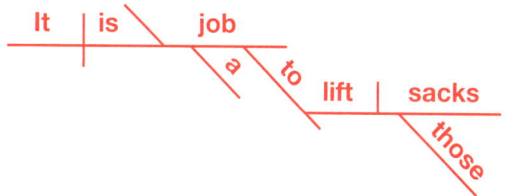

Unit 10, Diagraming Sentences **219**

5. When do you want to arrive?

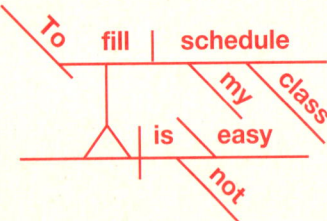

6. To fill my class schedule is not easy.

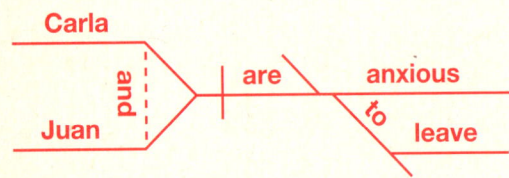

7. Carla and Juan are anxious to leave.

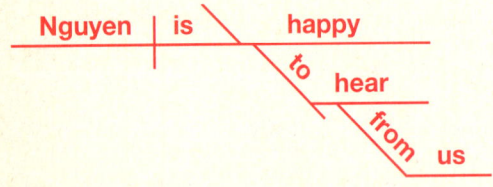

8. Nguyen is happy to hear from us.

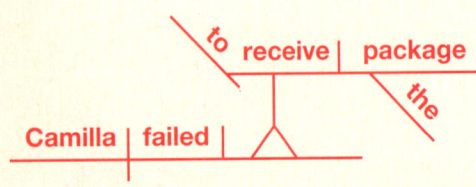

9. Camilla failed to receive the package.

10. Do you want to relate to us your version of the story?

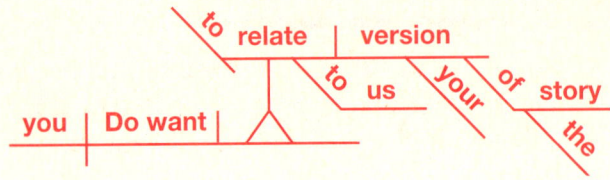

11. My parakeets love to scold each other.

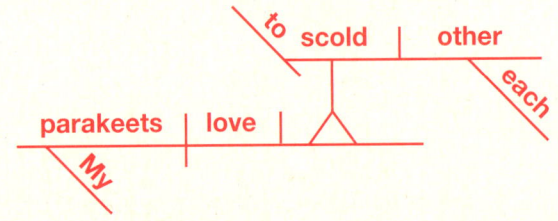

12. Look at the tag to find its price.

13. It is your turn to wipe the dishes.

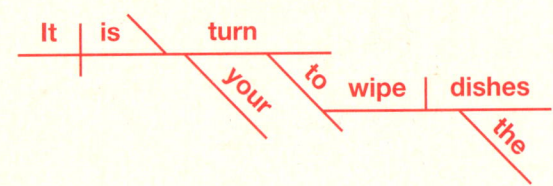

14. I love to feel the spring breezes in the morning.

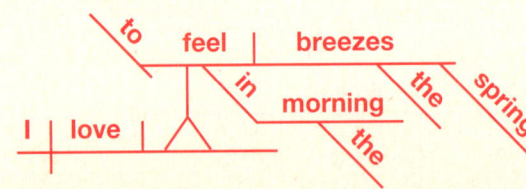

Unit 10 Review

▶ **Exercise 1** Diagram each sentence.

1. Teri won the race.

2. Erica told Theresa the story.

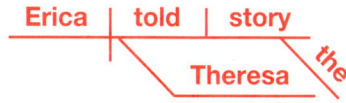

3. My dog is an Irish wolfhound.

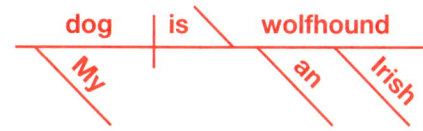

4. After the embarrassing defeat, Chris ran into the darkened locker room.

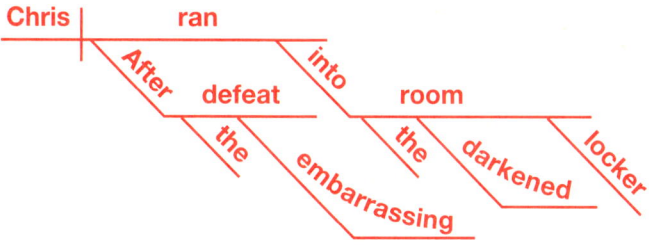

5. The horses paced in the paddock, and the mules brayed and stamped.

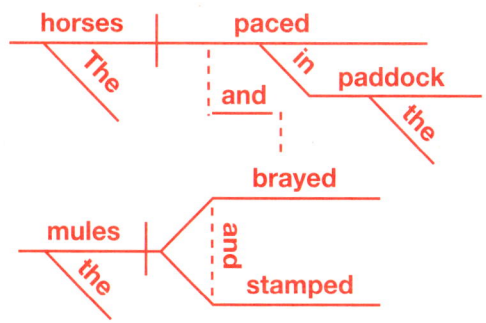

6. People who are tired cannot study well.

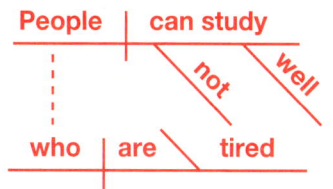

7. I heard the sound of the sea when I walked onto the balcony.

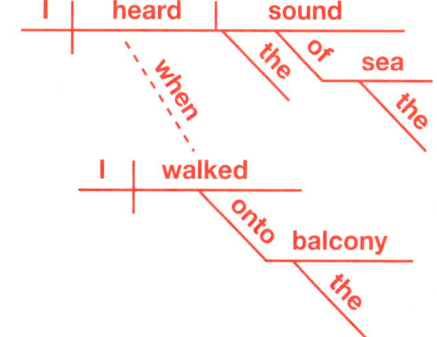

8. Amos remembers how the book ends.

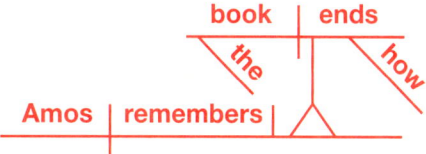

9. Writing is a hobby for Howard.

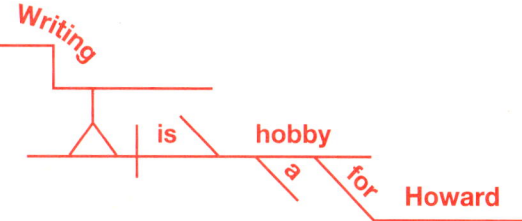

10. Mario wants to learn about jazz.

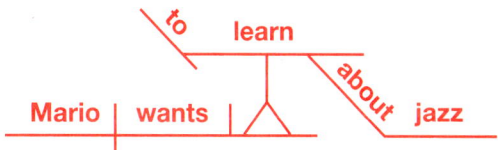

Unit 10, Diagraming Sentences **221**

Cumulative Review: Units 1–10

▶ **Exercise 1** Write above each pronoun *poss.* (possessive), *ind.* (indefinite), *inter.* (interrogative), or *dem.* (demonstrative).

        dem.   **poss.**
    Should this be addressed to her home?

inter.   **poss.**
1. What happened to your coat?

poss.   **poss.**
2. His brother borrowed her calculator.

   ind.   **dem.**
3. If anybody knows about this, inform the store manager.

       ind.   **dem.**
4. Only Gilbert would do something like that.

poss.   **ind.**
5. Their efforts to skate on the ice amused everybody.

      dem. **poss.**
6. Please take these to her desk.

poss.   **ind.**
7. Our plans failed to anticipate everything.

  inter.
8. To whom will Lloyd go for tutoring?

poss.   **poss.**   **poss.**
9. My van had a hole in its muffler, but yours didn't.

                poss.
10. Melanie's story differs from mine.

dem.   **poss.**
11. That can wait until your assignment is finished.

ind.
12. Nobody plays soccer like Sarah.

inter. **poss.**
13. What is her last name?

dem.   **dem.**
14. Those will have to do until these are ready.

ind.   **dem.**
15. Anyone without a ticket will be denied permission to do this.

▶ **Exercise 2** Label each simple subject *SS* and each simple predicate *SP*. Write the type of sentence in the blank: *simple*, *compound*, or *complex*.

                 SS **SP**
__simple__   Ira lives in Arizona near the Grand Canyon.

                 SS   **SP**
__simple__ 1. Brad lost the school election to his friend Janet.

                SS   **SP**   **SS**   **SP**
__complex__ 2. Evelyn finished early because Shirley helped her.

                SS   **SP**   **SS**   **SP**
__compound__ 3. Patricia left yesterday, but she plans to return by Friday.

                SS   **SP**   **SS**   **SP**
__complex__ 4. Victor must decide when he will show the film.

Name _____ Class _____ Date _____

__simple__ 5. James plans to join Mr. Plant in Kentucky next month. [SS SP]

__complex__ 6. If Virginia does not arrive soon, they will leave without her. [SS SP SP SS SP]

__compound__ 7. The change in scenery concerned Rosa, but she kept her feelings to herself. [SS SP SS SP]

__complex__ 8. Lucius moved toward the microphone as the audience applauded his accomplishment. [SS SP SS SP]

__simple__ 9. With the assistance of his math teacher, Terence solved the problem. [SS SP]

__compound__ 10. You can cross the Rio Grande at Brownsville, or you can cross it at Hidalgo. [SS SP SS SP]

__complex__ 11. Gregory asked us how far we would be going. [SS SP SS SP]

__compound__ 12. Many French immigrants journeyed to New Orleans; others sailed to Montreal. [SS SP SS SP]

__simple__ 13. Early on Tuesday Gordon drove to the airport. [SS SP]

__complex__ 14. Sheila believed that our goals were achieved. [SS SP SS SP]

__simple__ 15. Just before sunset the climbers approached the summit of Mt. Rainier. [SS SP]

▶ **Exercise 3** Underline each participle, gerund, or infinitive phrase. In the blank, identify the kind of phrase: *part.* (participial phrase), *ger.* (gerund phrase), or *inf.* (infinitive phrase).

__part.__ <u>Humming softly</u>, Jody put the baby to sleep.

__inf.__ 1. Amy hoped <u>to see a well-known actress</u>.

__ger.__ 2. As he walked through the woods, Dr. Bosch heard <u>chirping</u> overhead.

__inf.__ 3. Harold asked <u>to receive a receipt for his order</u>.

__part.__ 4. <u>Pausing for a few seconds</u>, Yun continued with her recitation.

__ger.__ 5. <u>Making beds</u> occupies much of a housekeeper's time.

__part.__ 6. <u>Pinned helplessly against the ropes</u>, the boxer tried to regain his balance.

__part.__ 7. The money <u>deposited in the bank</u> was for Ina's future education.

__ger.__ 8. Eduardo mastered <u>fencing at school with his coach</u>. *or* <u>fencing at school with his coach</u>.

Unit 10, Diagraming Sentences **223**

Name _____ Class _____ Date _____

__inf.___ 9. Dawn plans <u>to write her representative about the controversy</u>.

__inf.___ 10. Seth stooped <u>to lift the heavy television</u>.

__ger.___ 11. <u>Jogging to the fairgrounds</u> takes only ten minutes.

__part.__ 12. <u>Briefly stopping for breakfast</u>, Jerald reviewed his notes for the test.

__ger.___ 13. <u>Practicing basketball</u> dominates Laurie's spare time.

__inf.___ 14. Rachel's father hurried <u>to catch an early bus</u>.

__ger.___ 15. <u>Raymond's nervous whistling</u> made everyone uncomfortable.

Usage Glossary

Name _____ Class _____ Date _____

Unit 11: Usage Glossary

Lesson 68
Usage: *accept* to *a lot*

Words that are similar can easily be misused.

accept, **except** *Accept* means "to receive" or "to agree to." *Except* means "other than."

I **accept** your help on this project.   Everyone **except** Dena likes to hike.

all ready, **already** *All ready* means "completely prepared." *Already* means "before" or "by this time."

They are **all ready** for lunch.   The team had **already** warmed up.

all together, **altogether** *All together* means "in a group." *Altogether* means "completely."

All together we have a total of ten dollars.
We were **altogether** surprised by their actions.

a lot *A lot* is two words meaning "very much." Never write *a lot* as one word. When possible, avoid using this term by replacing it with a specific number.

A lot of cookies were sold at the bake sale.
Fifty dozen cookies were sold at the bake sale. (more specific)

▶ **Exercise 1** Write *C* for correct or *I* for incorrect to indicate whether the word or words in italics are used correctly.

__I__   Our class has *all ready* studied about South America.

__C__ 1. Dana was a member of every club *except* the Chess Club.

__C__ 2. Our teacher was glad to see us *all together* at the pep rally.

__I__ 3. I had *all ready* been there once before.

__C__ 4. Sheila gracefully *accepted* the second-place award.

__C__ 5. We were *altogether* amazed by the news.

__I__ 6. Everyone boarded the bus *accept* David.

__I__ 7. My solo was *already* for the concert.

__C__ 8. The apartment was *altogether* too small for the four of us.

Unit 11, Usage Glossary   227

Name _____ Class _____ Date _____

___C___ 9. I like everything on my pizza *except* anchovies.

___I___ 10. *Altogether* the coins totaled one dollar.

___C___ 11. I was allergic to the flowers, so I could not *accept* them.

___I___ 12. Jonah looked happy to *except* the new bike.

___C___ 13. The fire was *already* out by the time the firefighters arrived.

___C___ 14. Our costumes were *all ready* for the play.

___C___ 15. I gathered my friends *all together* to tell them the news.

▶ **Exercise 2** Underline the word in parentheses that best completes each sentence.

I really can't eat anything (accept, <u>except</u>) soup.

1. We were (<u>altogether</u>, all together) unprepared for the test.
2. I was (already, <u>all ready</u>) for the dance.
3. Vanessa could not (<u>accept</u>, except) the expensive gift.
4. James bought (a lot, <u>thirty</u>) of the videos.
5. The last time we were (altogether, <u>all together</u>) was two years ago.
6. The baseball card I bought has (<u>already</u>, all ready) increased in value.
7. Everyone (accept, <u>except</u>) Roy went to the soccer game.
8. (A lot, <u>Hundreds</u>) of people watched the parade.
9. Our plans for the trip were (<u>altogether</u>, all together) ruined by the weather.
10. The piano was delivered and is (already, <u>all ready</u>) to be played.

▶ **Writing Link** Write four sentences about what you do in the morning before school. Include the words *accept, except, all ready, already,* and *altogether.*

_____
_____
_____
_____
_____
_____

Name _____ Class _____ Date _____

Lesson 69
Usage: *beside* to *less*

beside, besides *Beside* means "next to." *Besides* means "in addition to."

The hammer was lying **beside** the toolbox.
Besides carrots, the baby likes peas.

between, among Use *between* for two people or things. Use *among* when talking about groups of three or more.

Echo Avenue is **between** Dancer and Foothill.   It was flying **among** the stars.

bring, take *Bring* means "to carry from a distant place to a closer one." *Take* means "to carry from a nearby place to a distant one."

Bring dessert to the family dinner.   **Take** this letter to the post office.

can, may *Can* indicates ability. *May* expresses permission or possibility.

We **can** finish this Monday.   You **may** work on this inside.   It **may** rain.

choose, chose *Choose* means "to select." *Chose* is the past tense of *choose* and means "selected."

Choose your friends wisely.   Yana **chose** to participate in the debate.

fewer, less Use *fewer* with nouns that can be counted. Use *less* with nouns that cannot be counted.

There were **fewer** hot days this summer.   Traffic is **less** congested tonight.

▶ **Exercise 1** Write *C* for correct or *I* for incorrect to indicate whether the word in italics is used correctly.

__C__   Migration *can* be an interesting topic.

__C__ 1. You probably know that birds are *among* the many animals that migrate.

__C__ 2. Some fish migrate *between* fresh and salt water during their lives.

__C__ 3. Salmon *choose* to live at sea but migrate to fresh water for breeding.

__I__ 4. The European eel lives in fresh water but *brings* to the sea to breed, spawn, and hatch.

__C__ 5. Humpback whales spend summers in polar oceans and in winter *may* move to tropical waters.

__C__ 6. Some land mammals *may* also migrate.

Unit 11, Usage Glossary   229

Name _____ Class _____ Date _____

__I__ 7. The caribou of Alaska move *among* the tundra and the boreal forest.

__C__ 8. Food is available in the tundra during summer, but when the winter *brings* deep snow, the caribou move south.

__C__ 9. Some insects also move long distances in search of *less* snow.

__C__ 10. In the fall, the North American monarch butterfly *chooses* groves in California, Florida, or Mexico.

__I__ 11. A migrating animal *may* expend much energy if the weather is bad.

__I__ 12. Migrating birds cannot *bring* their young to the new habitat when they go unless the young birds are strong fliers.

__C__ 13. *Among* some species the sun, the moon, and the stars are used for navigation.

__C__ 14. Others rely on landscape features, such as rivers or mountain ranges, to *take* them to their distant destinations.

__I__ 15. *Beside* these travel aids, some animals are guided by changes in temperature, moisture, and wind direction.

▶ **Exercise 2** Underline the word in parentheses that best completes each sentence.

There are other interesting behaviors of animals (beside, <u>besides</u>) migration.

1. (<u>Among</u>, Between) these special behaviors is hibernation.
2. You (can, <u>may</u>) study hibernation for your project if you like.
3. Animals do not (<u>choose</u>, chose) to reach this inactive, sleeplike state on their own.
4. (Beside, <u>Besides</u>) the animal's body temperature being lower than normal, its heartbeat and breathing slow down.
5. Because an animal in this state needs (fewer, <u>less</u>) energy to stay alive, it can live off fat stored in its body.
6. A hibernating animal (<u>can</u>, may) more easily survive a harsh winter when food is scarce.
7. (<u>Among</u>, Between) warm-blooded hibernators are such birds as nighthawks and swifts.
8. (Beside, <u>Besides</u>) these birds, we find such mammals as bats, chipmunks, hedgehogs, and marmots (<u>among</u>, between) those creatures that hibernate.

230 Writer's Choice Grammar Workbook 8, Unit 11

Name _____ Class _____ Date _____

Lesson 70
Usage: *formally* to *teach*

formally, formerly *Formally* is the adverb form of formal and means "according to certain form." *Formerly* means "in times past."

They **formally** signed a contract.
Formerly, the school had been named after the town.

in, into *In* means "inside." *Into* indicates movement from outside to a point within.

The play will be held **in** the old auditorium.   Pour the milk **into** the bowl.

its, it's *Its* is the possessive form of the personal pronoun *it*. *It's* is the contraction of *it is*.

Its fur is standing straight up!   **It's** a fantastic place to visit.

lay, lie *Lay* means "to put" or "to place." *Lie* means "to recline" or "to be positioned."

Lay your brush down and come here.   Myra needed to **lie** down.

learn, teach *Learn* means "to receive knowledge." *Teach* means "to give knowledge."

Students **learn** to drive in driver education classes.
Who will **teach** the class?

▶ **Exercise 1** Underline the word in parentheses that best completes each sentence.

Not everyone wanted to go (in, <u>into</u>) the quilt shop.

1. (<u>It's</u>, Its) not unusual to see zebras at the zoo.

2. I asked the school nurse if I could (lay, <u>lie</u>) down for a few minutes.

3. The clerk put the groceries (in, <u>into</u>) the bag.

4. The puppet shook (it's, <u>its</u>) head as if to say "no."

5. Mrs. Sanders, the teacher of the year, loves to (learn, <u>teach</u>) children.

6. My mother was (formally, <u>formerly</u>) a teacher, but now she works at home.

7. (<u>It's</u>, Its) chocolate candy that I prefer.

8. I poured the solution (in, <u>into</u>) the beaker.

Name _____ Class _____ Date _____

9. Some children (<u>learn</u>, teach) by example.

10. The man argued that the animal should be in (it's, <u>its</u>) natural habitat.

11. (<u>Lay</u>, Lie) the baked goods on the table in the corner.

12. The class is (<u>in</u>, into) room three, across from the biology lab.

13. (<u>It's</u>, Its) unlikely that Peter will decide to go.

14. Barb was happy to (learn, <u>teach</u>) the children to tie their shoes.

15. (<u>In</u>, Into) the living room is a picture of the entire family.

16. The dog's favorite thing to do was to (lay, <u>lie</u>) on the floor and have its stomach scratched.

17. Tomorrow we will (<u>learn</u>, teach) who won the contest.

18. As I walked (in, <u>into</u>) the room, I saw many of my friends.

19. We will wait patiently until (<u>it's</u>, its) time for the dance.

20. My aunt asked me to (<u>lay</u>, lie) white sheets over the furniture in the empty house.

21. The doctor came (in, <u>into</u>) the office.

22. (<u>It's</u>, Its) time for our exercise class.

23. We will (<u>learn</u>, teach) how to jump hurdles in gym class.

24. The room down the hall was (formally, <u>formerly</u>) mine.

25. We were there to (<u>learn</u>, teach) how to use the library.

26. The dog wagged (it's, <u>its</u>) tail when we returned from vacation.

27. Doug tried to (lay, <u>lie</u>) on the hammock, but he fell off.

28. We were (<u>in</u>, into) our places for the choir show.

29. The bird flapped (it's, <u>its</u>) wings and flew away.

30. Joey couldn't wait to (<u>learn</u>, teach) how to drive.

31. The car moved quickly (in, <u>into</u>) the intersection.

32. The path to our camp (lays, <u>lies</u>) ahead of us.

33. Dad told me not to (lay, <u>lie</u>) in the sun without sunscreen.

34. Will Meagan (learn, <u>teach</u>) her sister to swim?

35. My brother and his date were dressed (<u>formally</u>, formerly) for the prom.

Name _____ Class _____ Date _____

Lesson 71
Usage: *leave* to *sit*

---

leave, **let** *Leave* means "to go away." *Let* means "to allow."

Please don't **leave** yet.   Karen **lets** her brother read her stories.

loose, **lose** *Loose* means "not tightly attached." *Lose* means "to misplace" or "to fail to win."

The bike chain seems **loose**.   Did that tire **lose** air again?

many, **much** Use *many* with nouns that can be counted. Use *much* with nouns that cannot be counted.

Many of the players are ill.   **Much** of our time was spent planning.

precede, **proceed** *Precede* means "to go or come before." *Proceed* means "to continue."

Refreshments will **precede** the recital.   Please **proceed** with the agenda.

quiet, **quite** *Quiet* means "calm" or "motionless." *Quite* means "completely" or "entirely."

All was **quiet** after the storm.   Alex was not **quite** finished with his chores.

raise, **rise** *Raise* means "to cause to move upward." *Rise* means "to move upward."

Please **raise** the window shade.   The balloons gracefully **rise** into the air.

set, **sit** *Set* means "to place" or "to put." *Sit* means "to place oneself in a seated position."

We will **set** out the tulip bulbs.   We can **sit** in the front row.

▶ **Exercise 1** Underline the word in parentheses that best completes each sentence.

My parents never (<u>let</u>, leave) the dog come into the house.

1. When it was time to (<u>leave</u>, let), we said good-bye.

2. (<u>Many</u>, Much) of Terri's friends visited her in the hospital.

3. If the rope is too (<u>loose</u>, lose), the swing will fall.

4. We were told to (precede, <u>proceed</u>) as if nothing had happened.

5. I (leave, <u>let</u>) my brother borrow my skateboard.

Unit 11, Usage Glossary   **233**

Name _____ Class _____ Date _____

6. The library was very (**quiet**, quite).

7. Jeff found a place for us to (set, **sit**) on the grass.

8. Sarah was careful not to (loose, **lose**) the locket her aunt had given her.

9. (**Much**, Many) of the human body is made up of water.

10. On Saturday my mother will (**leave**, let) on a business trip.

11. I (**set**, sit) the suitcases in the guest room.

12. When I opened the gate, the dog got (**loose**, lose).

13. The teacher will (leave, **let**) us use our books during the test.

14. The soldiers will (**raise**, rise) the flag at noon.

15. Where did you (**set**, sit) my keys?

16. The flowers were (quiet, **quite**) beautiful in the spring.

17. My cousin and I (raise, **rise**) at six o'clock in the morning.

18. The band show will (**precede**, proceed) the vocal groups.

19. Katrina was (quiet, **quite**) sure that her answer was correct.

20. Trees that (loose, **lose**) their leaves in the fall are called deciduous.

21. We had seen that movie (**many**, much) times before.

22. Be sure to (**leave**, let) the door unlocked when you go.

23. Uncle Tom always (sets, **sits**) in the recliner.

24. The choir will (raise, **rise**) together at the end of the show.

25. Because we lacked some chemicals, we could not (precede, **proceed**) with the experiment.

26. The old house was (**quiet**, quite) except for the ticking of a clock.

27. (Much, **Many**) of Janet's toys were lost during the move.

28. Sheryl will (**leave**, let) for Europe at the end of the year.

29. There wasn't (many, **much**) gas left in the car.

30. It was impossible to (**let**, leave) everyone off work early.

31. Our dance troupe (**preceded**, proceeded) a float in this year's parade.

32. Isaac was quiet (many, **much**) of the time.

Name _____ Class _____ Date _____

Lesson 72
Usage: *than* to *you're*

than, then *Than* introduces the second part of a comparison. *Then* means "at that time."

Stew is usually thicker **than** soup.
We skated first and **then** roasted marshmallows.

their, they're *Their* is the possessive form of the personal pronoun *they*. *They're* is the contraction of *they are*.

We attended **their** wedding.   **They're** snorkeling near a coral reef.

theirs, there's *Theirs* means "that or those belonging to them." *There's* is the contraction of *there is*.

Those batons are **theirs**.   **There's** time to play another game.

to, too, two *To* means "in the direction of." *Too* means "also" or "excessively." *Two* is the number after one.

Take Blitz **to** the veterinarian.   That was **too** exciting!   Rafi wants **two** CDs.

where at Do not use *at* after *where*.

Where are my music books? (not *Where* are my music books *at?*)

who's, whose *Who's* is the contraction of *who is*. *Whose* is the possessive form of the pronoun *who*.

Who's going on the class trip?   **Whose** assignments are the longest?

your, you're *Your* is the possessive form of the personal pronoun *you*. *You're* is the contraction of *you are*.

This looks like **your** writing.   **You're** just the person I wanted to see.

▶ **Exercise 1** Write *C* for correct or *I* for incorrect to indicate whether the word in italics is used correctly.

___I___   Famous composers have enhanced our lives with *they're* music.

___C___ 1. Born in 1756, Wolfgang Amadeus Mozart was a musician *whose* compositions live on today.

___I___ 2. Mozart, *who's* career was filled with ups and downs, began as a child prodigy.

___C___ 3. Mozart was composing minuets by age five and *then* symphonies by age nine.

Unit 11, Usage Glossary **235**

Name _____ Class _____ Date _____

__C__ 4. *Theirs* was a musical family as Mozart's father was also a composer.

__I__ 5. Maria Anna, Mozart's older sister, was a child prodigy, *two*.

__I__ 6. The Mozarts showed *they're* talents on tours in several countries.

__C__ 7. Wolfgang became accomplished on the piano and the violin, *too*.

__C__ 8. Wolfgang, *whose* friends included Bach, published his first works in 1764.

__I__ 9. *Than*, in 1768, he composed the first of many operas he would write.

__I__ 10. After extensive touring, he returned *too* his native Austria.

__C__ 11. He *then* became a court organist and wrote many religious works.

__C__ 12. *They're* among his most beautiful compositions.

__I__ 13. *Theirs* one great work that is called the "Coronation" mass.

__C__ 14. He *then* wrote music for the Court Opera in Vienna.

__I__ 15. Mozart met Joseph Haydn in 1781 and dedicated some of his works to *they're* friendship.

▶ **Exercise 2** Underline the word in parentheses that best completes each sentence.

Musicians like Mozart often find (their, <u>they're</u>) gifted in almost every kind of musical composition.

1. Wolfgang Amadeus Mozart is known for writing twenty-two operas, (to, <u>too</u>).

2. If (your, <u>you're</u>) an opera fan, you may already have known this fact.

3. Music can sometimes express emotions better (then, <u>than</u>) the spoken word.

4. Singers, accompanied by an orchestra, use (<u>their</u>, they're) talent to bring a dramatic situation to life.

5. (Theirs, <u>There's</u>) usually an emotional story behind every successful opera.

6. Opera companies attempt to balance (<u>their</u>, they're) season with both comic and tragic operas.

7. (<u>Then</u>, Than), there are musical comedies and operettas that are performed in an opera house.

8. Most musical comedies and operettas have more spoken dialogue (then, <u>than</u>) do operas.

236 Writer's Choice Grammar Workbook 8, Unit 11

Name _____ Class _____ Date _____

Unit 11 Review

▶ **Exercise 1** Write in the blank the word or words from the Usage Glossary that are described in parentheses.

__**Between**__ the two houses was a large pear tree. (used for two people or things)

1. We will __**proceed**__ with the tour when the others arrive. (to continue)
2. I like reading better __**than**__ watching television. (used in comparisons)
3. There are __**more *or* fewer**__ mosquitoes this year than last year. (used with nouns you can count)
4. Please do not __**lay**__ your wet jacket on the couch. (to place)
5. We were __**all together**__ for the group picture. (in a group)
6. Tony will __**accept**__ the responsibility for cleaning up after the party. (to receive)
7. I'm not sure that my parents will __**let**__ me go. (to allow)
8. The hammock hung __**between**__ two trees. (used for two people or things)
9. Is that __**your**__ notebook? (possessive form of *you*)
10. Peter __**raises**__ his hand often. (to cause to move upward)
11. After dinner we watched television __**in**__ the family room. (inside)
12. Debra announced that she was able to __**learn**__ sign language. (to receive knowledge)
13. My culture is __**quite *or* altogether**__ different from yours. (completely)
14. The little girl __**set**__ down her juice and hugged her doll. (to place or to put)
15. __**There's**__ something bothering him. (contraction for *there is*)
16. It seems this elevator __**rises**__ very, very slowly. (to move upward)
17. Deidre is the girl __**whose**__ kitten is missing. (possessive form of *who*)
18. __**May**__ I be excused from the table? (expresses permission)
19. __**Take**__ some leftovers home with you. (to carry from nearby to farther away)
20. Derek will __**choose**__ the music for his birthday party. (to select)

Unit 11, Usage Glossary   **237**

Name _____ Class _____ Date _____

Cumulative Review: Units 1–11

▶ **Exercise 1** Draw one line under the subject. Draw two lines under the verb in parentheses that agrees with the subject in number.

Both <u>German shepherds</u> and <u>golden retrievers</u> (<u><u>make</u></u>, makes) excellent guide dogs.

1. The <u>captain</u> and <u>leader</u> of our team (<u><u>is</u></u>, are) Jamison.
2. <u>Water</u> (evaporate, <u><u>evaporates</u></u>) more quickly when exposed to hot, dry conditions.
3. <u>Pam</u> and <u>Zina</u> (<u><u>chase</u></u>, chases) down any new leads for the school newspaper.
4. <u>Everyone</u> here (join, <u><u>joins</u></u>) a fitness club.
5. <u>Many</u> (<u><u>expand</u></u>, expands) their knowledge through reading.
6. This <u>machine</u> (transmit, <u><u>transmits</u></u>) the written word over the telephone line.
7. Mr. Thompsen's shop <u>students</u> (<u><u>construct</u></u>, constructs) a storage shed every year.
8. <u>Workers</u> in each factory (<u><u>assemble</u></u>, assembles) a variety of electronic products.
9. On the pond (<u><u>float</u></u>, floats) many beautiful <u>lily pads</u>.
10. (<u><u>Do</u></u>, Does) many <u>states</u> irrigate land to increase productivity?
11. <u>Language arts</u> (<u><u>is</u></u>, are) my favorite class this year.
12. <u>Nobody</u> (remodel, <u><u>remodels</u></u>) a house overnight!
13. This <u>type</u> of pricing (eliminate, <u><u>eliminates</u></u>) any questions by the consumer.
14. Ten <u>years</u> (<u><u>is</u></u>, are) a long time to go without seeing your brother.
15. Out in the gulf, the <u>crew</u> (drill, <u><u>drills</u></u>) for oil.
16. Every fall the <u>owners</u> of the orchard (<u><u>harvest</u></u>, harvests) a delicious crop of apples.
17. When migrating, many <u>wildebeests</u> (<u><u>cover</u></u>, covers) the African countryside.
18. The <u>eight cents</u> (<u><u>was</u></u>, were) burning a hole in the little boy's pocket.
19. The <u>team</u> of five experts (engineer, <u><u>engineers</u></u>) each new project for the company.
20. The <u>principal</u> or the <u>teachers</u> (<u><u>phone</u></u>, phones) each new family.

Name _____ Class _____ Date _____

▶ **Exercise 2** Underline each prepositional phrase. Draw an arrow from the phrase to the word it modifies.

The whirlwind raised a cloud of dust.

1. Maurey parked his car on the narrow street.
2. Angelique recounted the story about Carlene's frightening experience.
3. The hickory grove near the pond was a favorite quiet place.
4. Their costumes were authentic beyond belief.
5. Each person contributed without fanfare.
6. Raji could not burn refuse inside the city limits.
7. The money was divided evenly among the four girls.
8. Antonio dozed off three times during the speech.
9. Walking toward the crowd, Kevin wondered what was happening.
10. He found his keys under the cushion.
11. Without hesitation, the charity accepted the donation.
12. The road crew worked throughout the night.
13. Raoul hoisted his small daughter onto his back.
14. The below-zero temperatures arrived before our camping trip.
15. The door to the attic was locked.
16. The woman searched frantically for the precious missing earring.
17. The birthday present for the surprise party was hidden.
18. Marjorie lived near the furniture factory.
19. Rowing against the current proved difficult.
20. Fossils have been unearthed in unlikely places.

▶ **Exercise 3** Underline the word in parentheses that best completes each sentence.

No one (<u>accepted</u>, excepted) responsibility for the secret act of kindness.

1. (Alot of, <u>Many</u>) athletes say lack of sleep hinders their performance.
2. Will you (<u>bring</u>, take) the clothes in from the clothesline?
3. John made the touchdown with (<u>fewer</u>, less) than two time-outs left in the game.
4. The puppy put (<u>its</u>, it's) paw into the water to play with his reflection.
5. Please (precede, <u>proceed</u>) with your flight preparations.
6. (<u>Who's</u>, Whose) taking Shelly to band practice?
7. When Marci arrived, the swimming lessons had (<u>already</u>, all ready) begun.
8. The mayor was (<u>among</u>, between) the guests at the wedding.
9. If at all possible, you should (lay, <u>lie</u>) down for a few minutes.
10. The latch on this suitcase seems (<u>loose</u>, lose).
11. (Theirs, <u>There's</u>) no point in arguing if you have already made a decision.
12. I like chocolate ice cream better (<u>than</u>, then) vanilla.
13. Shannon had no choice (accept, <u>except</u>) to go on with her plans to try out for the Olympics.
14. Cathy will (<u>bring</u>, take) the photos over to our house.
15. Jamie (<u>can</u>, may) make dinner if I bring home the groceries.
16. All of Lynne's clothes were (<u>in</u>, into) one suitcase.
17. (<u>Many</u>, Much) of the parents attended the parent-teacher conferences.
18. (<u>Their</u>, They're) main goal was to win the race.
19. There were (to, <u>too</u>) many people and not enough seats.
20. We'll go to the movie first and (than, <u>then</u>) to the museum.

Mechanics

Name _____ Class _____ Date _____

Unit 12: Capitalization

Lesson 73
Capitalization of Sentences, Quotations, and Salutations

Capitalize the first word of every sentence and the first word of a direct quotation that is a complete sentence.

The poet who won the prize teaches at a nearby college.
Alicia said, "**M**y cat likes to sleep on my desk while I'm studying."

When a quoted sentence is interrupted by explanatory words such as *she said*, do not begin the second part of the quotation with a capital letter.

"I like apples," he said, "**b**ut a good orange can't be beat!"

When the second part of a quotation is a new sentence, put a period after the interrupting expression and begin the second part with a capital letter.

"I think you're right," Warren said. "**T**hat man is a local newscaster."

Do not capitalize an indirect quotation. An **indirect quotation** does not repeat a person's exact words and does not appear in quotations. It is often preceded by the word *that*.

The disc jockey on the radio said **that** this is the number-one song.

Capitalize the first word in the salutation and closing of a letter, the title and name of the person addressed, and a title used in place of a name.

Dear **M**s. **G**arcia: **D**ear **S**ir: **T**o whom it may concern: **S**incerely yours,

▶ **Exercise 1** Draw three lines under each letter that should be capitalized. Draw a slash (/) through each letter that should be lowercase. Write *C* in the blank if the sentence is correct.

_____   "would you like to go to a presentation about ~~B~~ats?" my brother asked.

_____ 1. "the speaker is a famous expert on bats," Jon explained.

_____ 2. "don't you think bats are a little unpleasant?" I asked Jon.

__C__ 3. "Not at all," Jon replied. "They're one of the most helpful animal species around."

Name _____ Class _____ Date _____

_____ 4. "They're not too helpful," my friend quipped, "When they swoop down at me."

__C__ 5. "Ha-ha-ha," laughed Jon. "You two need a lesson about bats."

_____ 6. He said that If we knew more about bats, we'd understand that they're not horrible little creatures.

_____ 7. Jon claims They help people in all sorts of ways.

__C__ 8. "Let's go," he said smiling. "I'm taking you both to the lecture."

_____ 9. The auditorium was almost full, So we had to sit near the back.

_____ 10. "I prefer to sit here," Jill whispered. "this way we're farther from the bats."

__C__ 11. She pointed to a row of small cages on a table on the stage.

_____ 12. "guess what we'd probably find in those!" she said with a smile.

_____ 13. Jon shook his head and told us We were being silly.

__C__ 14. "My brother, the bat man!" I whispered to Jill.

_____ 15. "shh," said Jon as a man walked on stage.

_____ 16. "Welcome, bat lovers," said the man, "And all others, too!"

_____ 17. Jon whispered to me, "you and Jill are the others, right?"

__C__ 18. "Tonight," he continued, "I hope I can tell you some things that might help you change your mind about *chiroptera,* the Latin name for the bat."

_____ 19. "Let's ask ourselves," the speaker said, "What we know about bats."

_____ 20. "They're blind," Shouted out one member of the audience. "that's why we say 'blind as a bat.'"

_____ 21. The man on the stage smiled and asked, "how many of you have heard this saying and thought that bats must be blind?"

_____ 22. almost everyone in the audience raised a hand.

_____ 23. "Well," said the professor, "That's one mistake."

_____ 24. "Bats can't see as well as you or I," he told us, "but they're certainly not blind. what else do you think you know about bats?"

_____ 25. "Now," he concluded, "If you have time, you may want to see what I have in these cages."

244 Writer's Choice Grammar Workbook 8, Unit 12

Name _____ Class _____ Date _____

Lesson 74
Capitalization of Names and Titles of Persons

A **proper noun** names a particular person, place, or thing and is capitalized. Capitalize the names of people and the initials that stand for their names.

Indira **G**andhi   **F. S**cott **F**itzgerald   **B**arbara **W**alters

Capitalize a title or an abbreviation of a title when it comes before a person's name or when it is a substitute for a person's name. Do not capitalize a title in other situations.

I listened to **G**overnor McCormick. "I'm awaiting your orders, **C**aptain." Thomas Worthington was the first **g**overnor of Ohio.

Capitalize the names and abbreviations of academic degrees that follow a person's name. Capitalize *Jr.* and *Sr.*

Elaine Hideyoshi, **Ph.D.**   George Johnson, **M.D.**   Randolph Sears **Jr.**

Capitalize words that show family relationships when used as titles or as substitutes for a person's name. Do not capitalize words that show family relationships when they follow an article or a possessive noun or pronoun.

We sent a letter to **U**ncle Phil.   **G**randma and **G**randpa were married in 1946.
Martha's **a**unt is a dentist.   My **f**ather served in the air force.

Always capitalize the pronoun *I*.

Tricia said, "**I** bought my first home!"

▶ **Exercise 1** Underline the choice in parentheses that best completes each sentence.

We visited my (Grandmother, <u>grandmother</u>) in the hospital.

1. We watched as (<u>General</u>, general) Powell told the nation about the war.

2. The sign on the door read Alvaro de Leon, (<u>M.D.</u>, m.d.)

3. Let's ask (<u>Aunt</u>, aunt) Mary to tell us the story again.

4. The woman driving the tank was (<u>Captain</u>, captain) Jenny Monroe.

5. My sister has decided to go to medical school to become a (Doctor, <u>doctor</u>).

6. I'm reading a biography of (<u>Franklin D. Roosevelt</u>, Franklin d. Roosevelt).

7. Please welcome Dr. Leonard Adams, (<u>Ph.D.</u>, Ph.d.)

8. He is really no relation, but he seems like an (Uncle, <u>uncle</u>) to us.

Name _____ Class _____ Date _____

9. The man in the video about airplanes is (Professor, professor) Ludwig Hinze, an expert on aviation.

10. I'd like to introduce my (Cousin, cousin), Jason Palmer, from Detroit.

11. I suggest writing to (Senator, senator) O'Leary about this issue.

12. "What do you think, (Grandpa, grandpa), about the 49ers?" asked Rob.

13. The city vehicle had the (Mayor's, mayor's) name on the door.

14. My (Brother, brother) is a guard on the high school basketball team.

15. We visited the home of Dr. Martin Luther King (Jr., jr.).

▶ **Exercise 2** Draw three lines under each letter that should be capitalized. Draw a slash (/) through each letter that should be lowercase. Write *C* in the blank if the sentence is correct.

_____ W.S. donaldson is Mayor of a small town in Illinois.

_____ 1. The candidate from Topeka lost his race for Governor.

__C__ 2. The president of the company is Sandra Morris.

_____ 3. Mom said cousin Jane will be staying with us over the holidays.

_____ 4. Sean will have to ask his Mom before he can go to the movie with us.

_____ 5. James k. Polk was president during the Mexican War in the 1840s.

_____ 6. Francie Moyer, M.s.w., is the new school guidance Counselor.

__C__ 7. I love this old picture of my great-grandmother standing by her car.

_____ 8. The child cried, "I want to go home, Grandpa, and see uncle Bob."

_____ 9. "Will all students be required to attend the assembly?" Derek asked principal Brower.

_____ 10. The new Minister at our church is Ronald Roberts, D.D.

_____ 11. I could suggest to coach Randolph that i try that play.

_____ 12. David's mother had to go to Austin to talk to one of the Senators.

_____ 13. We have to see dr. Wentworth because my Brother, j.c., is sick.

_____ 14. Emily's Uncle is now known as Matthew Brock, M.D.

_____ 15. James Mueller Jr. is the Captain of our debate team.

Lesson 75
Capitalization of Names of Places

Capitalize the names of cities, counties, states, countries, and continents.

Minneapolis   **M**onroe **C**ounty   **A**labama   **F**rance   **A**frica

Capitalize the names of bodies of water and geographical features.

Lake **H**uron   **B**ay of **B**engal   **S**ierra **M**adre **M**ountains   **E**nglish **C**hannel

Capitalize the names of sections of the country.

the **N**ortheast   the **D**eep **S**outh   the **G**reat **P**lains   **N**ew **E**ngland

Do not capitalize compass points that indicate direction. Do not capitalize adjectives formed from words indicating direction.

east of Toledo   **n**ortherly wind   **s**outhern Illinois   **e**astern Oregon

Capitalize the names of streets and highways, buildings, bridges, and monuments.

Lakeshore **D**rive   **W**ashington **M**onument   **S**ilver **B**ridge   **W**rigley **B**uilding

---

▶ **Exercise 1** Draw three lines under each letter that should be capitalized. Draw a slash (/) through each letter that should be lowercase.

Driving up __f__ifth __a__venue, we suddenly saw the /Silvery /Top of the __c__hrysler __b__uilding.

1. Two hundred years ago, all of the country's largest cities were located in the __n__ortheast and along the Atlantic __o__cean.

2. These cities, including __b__oston, New __y__ork, Philadelphia, and __b__altimore, are still large and important places.

3. Our nation's /Capital is part of this string of /Eastern cities.

4. However, as Americans moved /West, they built other large cities.

5. Once settlers crossed the __a__ppalachian __m__ountains, cities began to grow.

6. Towns such as Buffalo, Pittsburgh, Cincinnati, and __c__leveland were founded on important /Bodies of /Water.

7. The Great __l__akes, the Ohio __r__iver, and the Mississippi __r__iver were natural places for cities.

Unit 12, Capitalization   **247**

Name _____ Class _____ Date _____

8. New states like illinois, missouri, and minnesota had joined the union, and their cities soon became new Centers of power.

9. For example, St. Louis, near the junction of the missouri river and the mississippi river, quickly became a vital center of transportation.

10. One of the most important American ports was new orleans.

11. However, even these great cities of the Central United States were surpassed by others in the 1900s.

12. Large numbers of people moved West and South seeking a good climate and a better life.

13. Because of this explosive growth, the area known as the sun belt is now the fastest-growing part of the United States.

14. Cities such as los Angeles, San francisco, and Phoenix have grown into important business and cultural centers.

15. As such cities as Phoenix rise in population, others, such as detroit, fall.

▶ **Exercise 2** Draw three lines under each letter that should be capitalized. Draw a slash (/) through each letter that should be lowercase. Write *C* in the blank if the sentence is correct.

_____ My mother works in the Eastern part of our city near euclid.

_____ 1. She travels between the Atlantic ocean and the Pacific ocean.

_____ 2. Her company's main office is in Yonkers, North of New York city.

__C__ 3. She spends much of her time visiting companies in the Midwest.

_____ 4. That's convenient because we live in Cleveland, ohio, near the Shores of lake erie.

__C__ 5. Mom can get to the airport by driving west on Lake Shore Drive.

_____ 6. Once she brought me a model of the Sears tower in Chicago.

_____ 7. Another time she brought me a pennant from the silverdome in pontiac, michigan, the home of the detroit Lions.

_____ 8. She has also been to Pittsburgh, in Western Pennsylvania.

248 *Writer's Choice Grammar Workbook 8,* Unit 12

Name _____ Class _____ Date _____

Lesson 76
Capitalization of Other Proper Nouns and Adjectives

Capitalize the names of clubs, organizations, institutions, and political parties.

National **E**ducation **A**ssociation   **R**epublican party   **K**nox **C**ollege

Capitalize brand names but not the nouns following them.

Achilles athletic shoes   **S**uper cola   **B**eanie jeans

Capitalize the names of historical events, periods of time, and documents.

World **W**ar II   the **E**nlightenment   the **D**eclaration of **I**ndependence

Capitalize the names of the days of the week, months of the year, and holidays. Do not capitalize the names of the seasons.

Thursday   **A**ugust   **L**abor **D**ay   summer

Capitalize the first word, the last word, and all important words in the title of a book, play, short story, poem, essay, article, film, television series, song, magazine, newspaper, and chapter of a book.

Newsweek   *The Scarlet Letter*   "Ode to a Nightingale"   *Schindler's List*

Capitalize the names of ethnic groups, nationalities, and languages.

Thai   **H**aitian   **W**elsh   **J**ordanian   **P**akistani   **S**panish

Capitalize proper adjectives that are formed from proper nouns.

Italian restaurant   **K**orean flag   **G**erman shepherd

Mechanics

▶ **Exercise 1** Rewrite each phrase using correct capitalization.

Scottish Folk Music ___Scottish folk music___

1. japanese restaurant ___Japanese restaurant___
2. *The Turn Of The Screw* ___*The Turn of the Screw*___
3. sunday evening ___Sunday evening___
4. Parent-teacher association ___Parent-Teacher Association___
5. the middle ages ___the Middle Ages___
6. Flashtron Video Game System ___Flashtron video game system___
7. *Detroit Free press* ___*Detroit Free Press*___

Unit 12, Capitalization   **249**

Name _____ Class _____ Date _____

8. native american groups **Native American groups**
9. the end of august **the end of August**
10. *Popular mechanics* ***Popular Mechanics***
11. jamaican music **Jamaican music**
12. mayflower compact **Mayflower Compact**
13. french-canadian culture **French-Canadian culture**
14. *Around The World In 80 Days* ***Around the World in 80 Days***
15. Independence day **Independence Day**
16. swifty athletic gear **Swifty athletic gear**
17. *Death Of A Salesman* ***Death of a Salesman***
18. late Spring snowfall **late spring snowfall**
19. American medical association **American Medical Association**
20. The American civil war **the American Civil War**

▶ **Exercise 2** Draw three lines under each letter that should be capitalized. Draw a slash (/) through each letter that should be lowercase.

The film about T̶he renaissance was held at jefferson college.

1. During the reformation, protestants broke away from the catholic church.
2. T. J. was reading a book called *How to attract bats to your backyard.*
3. We are flying on United airlines flight 289 to los Angeles.
4. In Ohio the S̶ummer S̶eason runs from june through september.
5. At the ethiopian restaurant, we had the most delicious pumpkin dish.
6. Sarah's mom supports the republican P̶arty, but her dad supports the democrats.
7. The exhibit of laotian embroidery was a real eye-opener!
8. Have you ever read the poem "Stopping B̶y Woods O̶n A̶ Snowy Evening"?
9. Our cousins will be staying with us the week before new year's day.
10. The D̶iplomats were primarily Kenyan and tanzanian.
11. The seminar is sponsored by a united nations organization.
12. Our toughest opponent this season will be hastings middle school.

Mechanics

250   Writer's Choice Grammar Workbook 8, Unit 12

Name _____ Class _____ Date _____

 Unit 12 Review

▶ **Exercise 1** Draw three lines under each letter that should be capitalized. Draw a slash (/) through each letter that should be lowercase. Write *C* in the blank if the sentence is correct.

_____ World war I began in the C/ity of sarajevo, bosnia.

_____ 1. Hawaii, with its beaches, rain forests, and beautiful C/ity of Honolulu, is in the Pacific ocean more than 2,000 miles W/est of Los Angeles.

_____ 2. would any of you like to work on the chess club banquet committee?

__C__ 3. Who was president of the United States during the Spanish-American War?

_____ 4. "The detroit lions have neat uniforms," Jason stated. "their colors are silver and blue."

_____ 5. We served mom breakfast in bed on Mothers' Day.

_____ 6. Alaska, our largest state, lies on the N/orthwest corner of North America.

_____ 7. I asked aunt Maria to show me her new Z-Tron L/aptop C/omputer.

__C__ 8. "Don't put your finger into that rabbit's cage," the boy at the fair warned, "unless you want a nasty bite."

_____ 9. The man said, "I am sorry, senator Montgomery, but i think you misunderstood the question."

_____ 10. Our S/chool is presenting *The Man Who Came T/o Dinner*.

_____ 11. By the time March arrives, I'm more than a little tired of W/inter.

_____ 12. Most of alaska's large cities are located along the gulf of alaska.

_____ 13. Begin the letter "Dear Mr. Benson" and end it "Sincerely Y/ours."

_____ 14. You can see grant's tomb from the Henry Hudson parkway on the W/est side of Manhattan in New York city.

__C__ 15. My aunt said, "Our trip from Juneau to Ketchikan was very exciting."

_____ 16. I'm anxious to eat at the new mexican restaurant at bayshore mall.

Unit 12, Capitalization   **251**

Cumulative Review: Units 1–12

▶ **Exercise 1** Underline each adjective, adverb, or noun clause. In the blank, identify the kind of clause by writing *adj.*, *adv.*, or *N*. Circle the word or words that the adjective or adverb clause modifies.

adj.   The (package) that Joanne received came by UPS yesterday.

adv. 1. When the time came, the astronauts (climbed) into the shuttle.

adj. 2. The (field) where they played ball was three miles away.

N 3. Whoever arrives home first will put the soup on to heat.

N 4. Everyone knew why she chose engineering as a career.

adv. 5. Whenever the bike trail is completed, we (will) certainly (use) it.

adj. 6. The (elephants) that live in Kenya are protected.

adv. 7. When the sun rises, beautiful colors (appear) above the horizon.

N 8. The couple looked at whichever houses were in their price range.

N 9. Where we go on vacation will be determined by a family vote.

adv. 10. The ballplayers (went) to the swimming pool after they finished their hot summer practice.

adv. 11. Though the concert was long, it (was enjoyed) by all.

adj. 12. Aimee purchased a type of (racquet) that is used by the pros.

N 13. How Stonehenge was constructed remains a mystery.

adj. 14. (Vocalists) who are serious about their singing careers protect their voices.

N 15. Where the tournament will be held is yet to be determined.

adj. 16. (People) who drive a great deal are concerned about rising gasoline prices.

N 17. Sitting around a campfire is what we find very relaxing.

adj. 18. The (gift) that Jack bought was a surprise for his dad.

adv. 19. They (slept) through the night although there had been a storm.

N 20. The clerk will wait on whoever comes into the store.

252 Writer's Choice Grammar Workbook 8, Unit 12

Name _____ Class _____ Date _____

▶ **Exercise 2** Identify each word in italics. Above the word write *S* (subject), *V* (verb), *DO* (direct object), *IO* (indirect object), *conj.* (conjunction), or *int.* (interjection).

    conj.   **S**   **V**   **DO**
Although Jacob ate everything on his plate, *he* still *devoured* a big *dessert*.

      S   **V**   **IO**   **DO**
1. The *president* of the school board *handed* the *graduates* their *diplomas*.

  int.   **S**   **V**   **IO**   **DO**
2. *Alas!* The *runner* finally *brought* the *king* the long-awaited *message*.

    S   **V** **V**   **conj.**   **conj.**
3. The *menu will include* pie, cake, *or* cookies, *but* not all three.

  conj.   **S** **conj.**   **S**   **V**
4. *Neither* the art *teacher nor* the museum *director claimed* to be experts on the Ming dynasty.

        S   **V**   **IO**   **conj.**   **DO**
5. The *Boston Pops Orchestra gave* the *audience* a delightful *and* entertaining *performance*.

  conj. **DO** **conj.** **DO**
6. I will eat *either spaghetti or meatloaf* for dinner.

  S **V**   **IO**   **DO**
7. *Katie gave* the *hospital* all her extra *time*.

    S   **V**   **conj.**
8. The *partners were* happy with the deal *after* they discussed it.

  int. conj.   **S**   **conj.**   **S**
9. *Hey, both television and basketball* interfered with his school work.

    S   **V**   **IO**   **DO** **conj.** **DO**
10. *Janice saved* her *friends* some *tomatoes and peppers* from her garden.

  S   **V**   **DO** **conj.**
11. *Half* of the class *visited* the *Capitol while* the other half was busy at the White House.

  S   **V**   **conj.**   **conj.**   **conj.**
12. *Birds* of prey *include* eagles, falcons, *and* hawks, *whereas* finches, sparrows, *and* pigeons feed mainly on seeds.

  int.   **S**   **V**   **conj.**
13. *Whew! We celebrated* after the game *because* it was our first victory.

  conj.   **S**   **conj.**   **conj.**
14. *Not only* are *they* staying at the beach next summer, *but* they are *also* traveling to Australia in January.

     S   **V**   **IO**   **DO** **conj.**
15. The camp *leaders taught* the *campers* many survival *skills, for* these skills were necessary.

    S   **V**   **conj.**
16. The *divers refused* to give up the search *because* they knew they would soon find the
    DO
sunken *treasure*.

Unit 12, Capitalization   253

Exercise 3 Draw three lines under each letter that should be capitalized. Make a slash (/) through each letter that should be lowercase. Write *C* in the blank if the sentence is correct.

_____   Our A̶unt and U̶ncle plan to visit southern f̲lorida.

_____ 1. The a̲rctic includes the N̶orthern parts of Europe, Asia, and n̲orth America.

___C___ 2. The *Los Angeles Times* was full of reports of earthquake tremors along our country's western coast.

_____ 3. The world's smallest C̶ontinent, Australia, lies between the Indian o̲cean and the South Pacific o̲cean.

_____ 4. We were hungry for both Mexican and Italian F̶ood.

_____ 5. Jessie's grandma came with a̲unt Katie on Labor Day W̶eekend.

_____ 6. Sign the letter "Sincerely Y̶ours," and mail it to 135 Coconut a̲venue, Honolulu, Hawaii.

_____ 7. The L̶ieutenant spoke to Captain Davis about his wish to visit the U.S. Air Force a̲cademy in Colorado s̲prings, Colorado.

_____ 8. "We can choose our friends," said p̲rofessor Evans, "B̶ut we cannot choose our relatives."

_____ 9. The newest breakfast treat at the w̲ilsons' house was Pop Crunch C̶ereal.

_____ 10. My U̶ncle enjoys listening to s̲enator Edwards because this S̶enator is both intelligent and interesting.

_____ 11. On f̲riday, d̲ecember 1, we will attend a W̶inter science fair sponsored by the e̲nvironmental p̲rotection a̲gency.

_____ 12. "I hope c̲ousin Leroy can come," I said. "h̲e always takes us on a F̶erry B̶oat to Staten i̲sland."

Name _____ Class _____ Date _____

Unit 13: Punctuation

Lesson 77
Using the Period and Other End Marks

Different end marks are used with the different types of sentences.

Use a **period** at the end of a declarative sentence. A declarative sentence makes a statement. Also use a period at the end of an imperative sentence. An imperative sentence gives a command or makes a request.

Oak trees can grow very tall. (statement)
Start the motor. (command)   Please identify this tree. (request)

Use a **question mark** at the end of an interrogative sentence. An interrogative sentence asks a question.

Can you show me a black oak?   Is that a chinkapin oak?

Use an **exclamation point** at the end of an exclamatory sentence. An exclamatory sentence expresses strong feeling. Also use an exclamation point at the end of an interjection. An interjection is a word or group of words that expresses strong emotion.

What a tall tree! It would take five people to reach around it!
Wow!   Hey!   Oh, my gosh!   Hooray!   Oops!   Phew!

▶ **Exercise 1** Complete each sentence by adding the correct end mark. In the blank, identify the kind of sentence by writing *dec.* (declarative), *imp.* (imperative), *int.* (interrogative), or *exc.* (exclamatory).

int.   How tall is that oak tree**?**

dec.   1. Many people consider oak trees the monarchs of the forest**.**

dec.   2. Different kinds of oaks are found in most areas of this country**.**

int.   3. How many species of oaks can you name**?**

imp.   4. Make a list of the types you can recognize**.**

dec.   5. If you live in the eastern United States, you probably see white oaks every day**.**

dec.   6. They can grow to a height of 100 feet or more**.**

exc. *or* **dec.**   7. That's longer than four school buses**!** *or* **.**

Unit 13, Punctuation   **255**

exc., exc. 8. Wow! What an enormous height that is!

int. 9. Did you know that another name for the white oak is *stave oak*?

dec. 10. How this name was given to this tree is an interesting story.

imp. 11. Guess how this name came about.

dec. 12. *Stave* is the name for a wooden slat in a barrel.

dec. 13. In past times, barrels were important for storing liquids.

int. 14. Which tree provided the best wood for making barrel staves?

exc. or dec. 15. You guessed it—the white, or stave, oak! or .

dec. 16. Today, some liquids are still stored in white oak barrels.

dec. 17. Even though we have many high-tech plastics and other materials, some products must still be kept in old-fashioned wooden barrels.

exc. or dec. 18. That's almost unbelievable! or .

int. 19. Have you ever seen a model of an 1800s sailing ship?

dec. 20. Their sails hung from gigantic masts fifty or sixty feet tall.

int. 21. Where do you think shipbuilders found the wood for these great ships?

dec. 22. In the forests of the eastern United States, they found magnificent stands of white oak.

dec. 23. In this intriguing way, the monarchs of the forest helped clipper ships become rulers of the high seas; after they were cut down, the mighty oaks reigned over the oceans.

dec. 24. It's not difficult to recognize a white oak in a forest or city.

imp. 25. Look first for its acorns.

dec. 26. Acorns are actually the fruit of an oak tree.

imp. 27. Crack one open and find the seeds inside.

dec. 28. White oak acorns are egg-shaped and about an inch long.

imp. 29. Next, check the leaves.

exc. or dec. 30. White oak leaves can be as long as nine inches—much bigger than your hand! or .

imp. 31. Don't overlook the easiest way to identify a white oak.

exc. or dec. 32. Chances are, it's the biggest tree around! or .

Name _____ Class _____ Date _____

Lesson 78
Using Commas to Signal Pause or Separation

Commas signal a pause or separation between parts of a sentence. Use commas to separate three or more items in a series.

The top sellers were Chou, Eve, and Mike.

Use a comma to show a pause after an introductory word, two or more introductory prepositional phrases, or an introductory participle or participial phrase.

Yes, I helped with the class play.
For love of the sport, he sponsored several youth soccer teams.
Crawling through the tunnel, the rescuers reached the trapped men.

Use a comma after conjunctive adverbs such as *however, moreover, furthermore, nevertheless,* and *therefore.*

Our school enrollment has increased; therefore, we need a new building.

Use commas to set off words that interrupt the flow of thought in a sentence and appositives that are not essential to the meaning of the sentence.

My brother, gulping his food, raced through his meal.
The Koreans, comparative newcomers, produce many electronic products.

Use commas to set off names used in direct address.

Marla, you have the highest score on the test.

▶ **Exercise 1** Complete each sentence by adding commas where necessary. If the sentence is correct as written, write *C* in the blank.

_____ For thousands of years, people have enjoyed making music.

__C__ 1. Modern instruments are made to meet specific standards.

_____ 2. Strings, woodwinds, brass, and percussion are the four families of instruments.

_____ 3. Each family, by the way, is named for the method it uses to produce sound.

_____ 4. Stringed instruments produce tones when a string is bowed, struck, or plucked.

_____ 5. Yes, the vibrating string makes the sound.

_____ 6. Members of the string family include the violin, viola, cello, and bass.

Unit 13, Punctuation **257**

Name _____ Class _____ Date _____

____C____ 7. Pitch is changed by pressing the appropriate spot on the string.

_____ 8. The harp, an ancient instrument, is often used in an orchestra.

____C____ 9. A piano's sound is produced by striking strings with small felt hammers.

_____ 10. Woodwinds, the next family, produce sound from a vibrating reed.

_____ 11. Clarinets and saxophones are played with a single reed; however, oboes and bassoons are played with two reeds fastened together.

_____ 12. Nina, why is the flute called a woodwind?

_____ 13. Lacking a reed, flutes were originally made of wood.

_____ 14. Of all the instruments in an orchestra, the brass ones are the most powerful.

____C____ 15. The player produces sound on a brass instrument by vibrating his or her lips in a cup-shaped mouthpiece.

_____ 16. Trumpets and cornets, their cousins, are the highest pitched brass instruments.

_____ 17. Covering the middle range, French horns and trombones add color and depth.

_____ 18. The sousaphone, named for the March King, is a marching band version of the tuba.

_____ 19. Percussion instruments are struck, pounded, or beaten; therefore, it isn't wrong to think of the piano as a percussion instrument.

_____ 20. Drums, an ancient type of music maker, come in many shapes and sizes.

_____ 21. Keyboard-style percussion instruments include xylophones, vibraphones, marimbas, and bells.

_____ 22. Symphony orchestras use members from all four families; however, marching bands use only woodwinds, brass, and percussion.

▶ **Writing Link** Write a paragraph on a concert you have attended or a recording you enjoy. Be sure to use commas as separators.

_____
_____
_____
_____
_____
_____

Name _____ Class _____ Date _____

Lesson 79
Using Commas with Clauses

Use a **comma** before *and, or,* or *but* when it joins main clauses.

She is now known as a director**,** but she also acted on television shows.

Use a comma after an introductory adverb clause. Do not use a comma with an adverb clause that comes at the end of a sentence. Adverb clauses begin with subordinating conjunctions such as *after, although, as, because, before, considering (that), if, in order that, since, so that, though, unless, until, when, whenever, where, wherever, whether,* or *while.*

Unless she gives her approval, we can't proceed. (introductory adverb clause)
She enjoys herself whenever she is dancing. (adverb clause at the end of a sentence)

Use a comma or a pair of commas to set off an adjective clause that is nonessential and merely gives additional information. Do not use commas to set off an essential adjective clause. Essential clauses are those necessary to the meaning of the sentence. Adjective clauses often begin with the relative pronouns *who, whom, whose, which,* and *that.*

The boy over there, whom I think you have met, is fourteen. (nonessential adjective clause)

The sculptor who carved that statue has a delicate touch with a chisel! (essential adjective clause)

▶ **Exercise 1** Complete each sentence by adding commas where necessary. Use the delete symbol (⌥) to eliminate commas used incorrectly. If the sentence is correct as written, write *C* in the blank.

_____ While you're visiting San Francisco**,** be sure to ride on a cable car.

_____ 1. Make sure you're not late⌥ so that we can get started on time.

_____ 2. Jeremy enjoys camping and hiking**,** and his best friend does, too.

__C__ 3. Because she wanted to be considered for the job, Ellen filled out an application form.

_____ 4. Her older brother**,** whom I've never met**,** goes to Georgetown University.

_____ 5. Where the snow covers the ground all winter**,** animals have difficulty finding food.

Unit 13, Punctuation **259**

Name _____ Class _____ Date _____

__C__ 6. People need to help conserve precious natural resources, or we may run short of important materials in the future.

_____ 7. We went out for pizza, after the volleyball game ended.

_____ 8. They thought they had arrived too early, but I explained that they hadn't.

__C__ 9. Although Iceland is a northerly country, the climate is relatively mild.

_____ 10. Doris Lessing, who is a well-known novelist, grew up in South Africa.

_____ 11. I'll go along, if you want my company.

_____ 12. The woman, who was wearing the exotic hat, turned out to be the spy.

_____ 13. Any team, that makes the playoffs, has to be good!

_____ 14. My brother studies hard, but he knows when to take a break.

_____ 15. Before she started on the test, Maya took several deep breaths to relax.

__C__ 16. Jenny, whose mother works part-time, often helps out at home.

_____ 17. The praying mantis, which is an interesting insect, can be very helpful to people.

_____ 18. The man, who will be speaking at the meeting, has lived in Thailand.

__C__ 19. My best friend, whose mother has remarried, was a member of the wedding party.

_____ 20. Mr. N'Funo called on him, because he raised his hand.

__C__ 21. The woman whom you contacted about the recreation proposal seemed very nice.

_____ 22. Indonesia, which is a large country in Asia, includes many islands.

_____ 23. They can sign up for the audition, but they'll have to prepare a short speech from a play.

_____ 24. When the announcer called my name, I was so embarrassed, that my face turned as red as an apple!

__C__ 25. My little sister rides the bus to school, and my older sister rides her bike.

Lesson 80
Using Commas with Titles, Addresses, and Dates

Use **commas** before and after the year when it is used with both the month and the day. Do not use a comma if only the month and year are given.

My great-uncle was born February 3, 1922, in Russia.
Great-Aunt Laura and he were married in June 1946.

Use commas before and after the name of a state or a country when it is used with the name of a city. Do not use a comma after the state if it is used with a ZIP code.

They moved to a farm near Mount Vernon, Ohio, after their marriage.
Their address was 19833 Township Road 44, Howard, OH 43028.

Use a comma or a pair of commas to set off an abbreviated title or degree following a person's name.

Janet Adams, R.N., was a nurse at the local hospital.
Benjamin Paoletti, Ph.D., taught history at a nearby college.

▶ **Exercise 1** Place a check (✔) beside the sentence in each pair that is correct.

_____ Walt Whitman lived in Brooklyn New York.

✔ Walt Whitman lived in Brooklyn, New York.

1. _____ Lateesha's birthday is January 12 1982.

   ✔ Lateesha's birthday is January 12, 1982.

2. ✔ Samantha Slegeski, D.D.S., is our new family dentist.

   _____ Samantha Slegeski D.D.S. is our new family dentist.

3. _____ Contest entries should be sent to 8340 South Roberts Avenue, Chicago IL, 60617.

   ✔ Contest entries should be sent to 8340 South Roberts Avenue, Chicago, IL 60617.

4. ✔ When she was in the army, my mother was stationed in Frankfurt, Germany, and Biloxi, Mississippi.

   _____ When she was in the army, my mother was stationed in Frankfurt Germany and Biloxi Mississippi.

5. _____ The first speaker will be Ricardo Flores Ph.D.

   ✔ The first speaker will be Ricardo Flores, Ph.D.

Unit 13, Punctuation **261**

6. __✓__ The first performance of the show was on October 13, 1899.

_____ The first performance of the show was on, October 13 1899.

7. _____ Did you know that Cairo, Illinois is named after the city of Cairo, Egypt?

__✓__ Did you know that Cairo, Illinois, is named after the city of Cairo, Egypt?

8. _____ The names on the book's title page were Emily Dahlquist Ph.D. and James A. Morris M.A.

__✓__ The names on the book's title page were Emily Dahlquist, Ph.D., and James A. Morris, M.A.

9. __✓__ The headquarters of the organization are at 190 20th Avenue, Seattle, WA 98122.

_____ The headquarters of the organization are at 190 20th Avenue, Seattle, WA, 98122.

10. _____ The new model started production in September, 1995.

__✓__ The new model started production in September 1995.

▶ **Exercise 2** Complete each sentence by adding commas where necessary. If the sentence is correct as written, write *C* in the blank.

_____ The date on the old letter was June 26**,** 1902.

_____ 1. You can get copies of the brochure by writing to 517 S.W. 11th Street**,** Topeka**,** KS 66612.

_____ 2. The deadline is December 3**,** 1996.

_____ 3. Robert Nikolai**,** M.S.W.**,** is the director of the regional office.

_____ 4. Gerald's mom was transferred to Sacramento**,** California**,** in August 1991.

__C__ 5. The university is in Evanston, Illinois, a suburb of Chicago.

_____ 6. The nurses in charge of the mobile care unit were Shelley Ford**,** R.N.**,** and Allan Cohen**,** L.P.N.

__C__ 7. Who can forget the Bay Area earthquake of October 1990 that interrupted baseball's World Series?

_____ 8. The sign on the door read Gerald R. Kelly**,** M.D.

_____ 9. It looks as if the team will move to Baltimore**,** Maryland**,** or St. Louis**,** Missouri.

__C__ 10. The First World War, called the Great War, erupted in Europe in August 1914.

Name _____ Class _____ Date _____

Lesson 81
Using Commas with Direct Quotes, in Letters, and for Clarity

Use a **comma** or commas to set off a direct quotation.

The farmer wiped his forehead and said, "I hope it rains soon."
"I wish," answered the weather forecaster, "I could give you some good news."

Use a comma after the salutation of a friendly letter and after the closing of both a friendly and a business letter.

Dear Dad,   Sincerely,   Your friend,   Cordially,

Use a comma to prevent misreading.

In order to improve the wool, farmers select sheep carefully.

▶ **Exercise 1** Complete each item by adding commas where necessary. If the item is correct as written, write *C* in the blank.

_____   Sincerely ,Wendy Peterson

__C__   1. The woman at the window said, "I can help you with that."

_____ 2. Dear Aunt Jenny ,

_____ 3. "They really ought to do something about their roof", said the inspector.

__C__   4. "Some people prefer cats," stated the woman on the talk show, "while others favor dogs."

__C__   5. "I've never seen anything like it," she cried, "never in my life!"

_____ 6. If they get too large ,dogs should live outside.

__C__   7. Jillian asked, "Who is going to the carnival with you?"

__C__   8. Yours truly, Denise

_____ 9. "There is little doubt", explained the professor ,"that we will have to deal with the problem sooner or later."

_____ 10. When damaged ,trees sometimes have to be taken down.

__C__ 11. "I want my daddy," the little girl sobbed with tears in her eyes.

_____ 12. Dear Patrick ,

Unit 13, Punctuation   **263**

Name _____ Class _____ Date _____

___C___ 13. The instructor pointed and said, "Don't touch that piece of metal."

___C___ 14. Before the movie, stars talked about working with the famous director.

_____ 15. I will need to leave soon," he said, "but feel free to stay if you want."

___C___ 16. Most cordially, Mr. David Marx

_____ 17. "We shouldn't let a little rain stop us," Ms. Montgomery added.

_____ 18. After Christmas, shoppers can often find bargains.

___C___ 19. "Step back, please," the major said to the man who got too close to the edge.

_____ 20. Dear Serena,

▶ **Exercise 2** Complete each item by adding commas where necessary. Use the delete symbol (✂) to eliminate the commas used incorrectly. If the item is correct as written, write *C* in the blank.

_____ "Don't forget your keys," said Mom.

_____ 1. In place of her, Julia will attend the conference.

_____ 2. "Put the disk ~~,~~ in after you have formatted it," the teacher suggested.

___C___ 3. Felipe asked, "What is the population of Puerto Rico?"

_____ 4. Dear Uncle Mark,

___C___ 5. In case of an emergency, contact the Department of Safety.

_____ 6. "Do you agree with the plan," Corazon asked, "or do you think ~~,~~ we should try something else?"

_____ 7. Dad just smiled ~~,~~ and whispered, "Let's let Mom find out for herself."

_____ 8. Even though it seems difficult, choices must be made.

___C___ 9. "I've never worked on a Fourth-of-July parade float," the new girl explained.

_____ 10. Sincerely yours, Kevin Conyers

_____ 11. "Raptors—eagles, hawks, falcons, and the like—can be found in every state," the narrator explained.

_____ 12. In place of that, one ought to consider this alternative.

_____ 13. "Don't count your chickens," the wise man said, "before they're hatched."

_____ 14. When opening ~~,~~ the can, be sure not to shake it up.

_____ 15. Nora almost dropped the cake ~~,~~ when she saw the cat on the table.

264 *Writer's Choice Grammar Workbook 8,* Unit 13

Name _____ Class _____ Date _____

Lesson 82
Using Semicolons and Colons

Use a **semicolon** to join the parts of a compound sentence when a coordinating conjunction such as *and, or, nor,* or *but* is not used.

You can use water-based or oil-based paint; both have their advantages.

Use a semicolon to join the parts of a compound sentence when the main clauses are long and subdivided by commas, even if these clauses are already joined by a coordinating conjunction.

Among the most important scientific advances of the twentieth century are telecommunications, computer technology, and space travel; but in no area, including these three, have we achieved all that we might achieve.

Use a semicolon to separate main clauses joined by a conjunctive adverb such as *consequently, furthermore, however, moreover, nevertheless,* or *therefore.*

It was snowing heavily; nevertheless, they left for the holidays.

Use a **colon** to introduce a list of items that ends a sentence. Use a phrase such as *these, the following,* or *as follows* before the list. Do not use a colon immediately after a verb or a preposition.

These students should report to the office: Christy Schantz, Tony Ramirez, Emily Chou, and Toderick Evans.

Please bring pencils, paper, and an eraser.

▶ **Exercise 1** Add semicolons or colons where necessary. Use the delete symbol (⌒) to eliminate semicolons and colons used incorrectly. If the sentence is correct as written, write *C* in the blank.

_____ Glass is a useful material**;** it is made from inexpensive raw materials.

_____ 1. Glass can take these forms**:** fine like a spider web, heavy like a telescope lens, stronger than steel, or more fragile than paper.

__C__ 2. The first human-made glass was used as a glaze on ceramic vessels; but it is not known when, where, or how people first learned the glass-making process.

_____ 3. Explained very simply, to make glass, use a mixture of sand, soda, and lime**;** cook and cool.

_____ 4. The result is⌒a solid with the properties of a liquid that can be blown, molded, spun, or drawn into endless shapes.

Unit 13, Punctuation **265**

Name _____ Class _____ Date _____

_____ 5. Early glassmaking was slow and costly for these reasons :furnaces were small, the heat produced was not enough to melt the materials, and glass blowing and pressing were unknown.

__C__ 6. Merchants soon had a need for glass containers when they discovered that oils, honey, and other liquids could be preserved better in glass.

_____ 7. There are many kinds of glass ;each possesses a special quality.

_____ 8. Flat glass is used when very clear, precise vision is required ;it comes in the following classifications :sheet, plate, and float.

__C__ 9. The strong materials of glass-ceramics can withstand extreme temperatures, strong chemicals, and sudden temperature changes; therefore, this kind of glass is used in cookware, turbine engines, and electronic equipment.

_____ 10. Flat glass, optical glass, and decorative glass were used prior to this century ; however, many special types of glass have been invented since 1900.

__C__ 11. The following are some of these types: laminated safety glass, tempered safety glass, colored structural glass, foam glass, and laser glass.

_____ 12. The properties of ordinary glass that make it useful for electrical purposes are: transparency, heat resistance, resistance to the flow of electricity, and its ability to seal tightly to metal as in light bulbs.

__C__ 13. Fiberglass, which is made of tiny but solid rods of glass, has many uses.

_____ 14. The fiberglass industry fills the following needs :heat insulation, yarn and cloth, electrical insulation, firefighters' suits, and automobile bodies.

_____ 15. Raw materials used in making optical glass must be pure in order to make flawless lenses for eyeglasses, cameras, and telescopes ;therefore, the production of optical glass is expensive.

_____ 16. The shaping of glass can be accomplished by these four methods :blowing, pressing, drawing, and casting.

_____ 17. In glass blowing, a worker uses a hollow iron blowpipe with one end dipped in molten glass ;she or he blows gently into the pipe until the molten glass bulges out and forms a hollow tube.

__C__ 18. This glass "bubble" can be formed into the desired shape by squeezing, twirling, or stretching it.

_____ 19. In the pressing method of shaping glass, a hot gob of glass is; dropped in a mold and then pressed with a plunger to fill the mold.

_____ 20. Both blowing and pressing can be done by hand or by machine ;moreover, there is a press-and-blow machine, which uses a combination of these methods to form an object.

Lesson 83
Using Quotation Marks and Italics

Use **quotation marks** before and after a direct quotation and with a divided quotation. Use a comma or commas to separate a phrase such as *she said* from the quotation itself. Place a comma or a period *inside* the quotation marks.

"The key," she replied with a laugh, "is having a good instructor."

Place a question mark or exclamation point *inside* the quotation marks when it is part of the quotation. Place a question mark or exclamation point *outside* the quotation marks when it is part of the entire sentence.

Ms. Arnold asked, "Can anyone answer Shawn's question?" (part of the quotation)

Did Shawn say, "The tamarack is a kind of larch"? (part of the entire sentence)

Use quotation marks for the title of a short story, essay, poem, song, magazine or newspaper article, or book chapter.

"To Build a Fire" (short story)   "Directive" (poem)   "Amie" (song)

Use **italics** to identify the title of a book, play, film, television series, magazine, newspaper, or musical work. In handwritten materials, underlining takes the place of italics.

Animal Farm (book)   *Romeo and Juliet* (play)   *Dayton Daily News* (newspaper)

▶ **Exercise 1** Add quotation marks where needed. Draw a line under the items that should be in italics.

<u>Moby-Dick</u> (book)   "The Road Not Taken" (poem)

1. <u>Model Railroader</u> (magazine)
2. "The Wound-Dresser" (poem)
3. <u>Twice-Told Tales</u> (book)
4. "Incumbents Lose" (newspaper article)
5. <u>All's Well That Ends Well</u> (play)
6. <u>The Muppet Movie</u> (film)
7. "The Minister's Black Veil" (short story)
8. <u>New York Times</u> (newspaper)
9. "It Isn't Easy Being Green" (song)
10. "Dr. Heidegger's Experiment" (short story)
11. <u>Home Alone</u> (film)
12. <u>A Winter's Tale</u> (play)
13. "Schedules" (essay)
14. <u>Leaves of Grass</u> (book)
15. "Nantucket" (book chapter)
16. "Wimoweh" (song)

Name _____ Class _____ Date _____

17. "Players Vote to Strike" (magazine article)
18. "Beat! Beat! Drums!" (poem)
19. <u>M☆A☆S☆H☆</u> (television series)
20. <u>USA Today</u> (newspaper)

▶ **Exercise 2** Complete each sentence by adding quotation marks and italics (underlining) where necessary.

"Emily Dickinson is my favorite poet," he told his listeners, "and <u>Moby-Dick</u> is my favorite novel."

1. Did she say, "Robert Frost is the greatest poet of our century"?

2. Randall had a look of shock on his face as the mayor said, "There is a boy here today without whom none of this would have been possible!"

3. "Do I have to explain again that playing with the deer is not allowed?" the park ranger asked.

4. "<u>Martin Chuzzlewit</u>," the lecturer explained, "is probably Dickens's most underrated novel."

5. The <u>Washington Post</u> featured an article entitled "Ways to Increase Your Energy."

6. "Where is Apartment B?" the woman asked.

7. "Go, Panthers!" the fans yelled. "Beat Tech!"

8. Wasn't it David Copperfield who asked for gruel by saying, "Please, sir, I want some more"?

9. "No," Daniel explained, "it was Oliver Twist who asked for more at the orphanage."

10. When Mr. Harrison said we didn't need to read those pages, Dawn and Cindy said, "Whew!"

11. How could she say, "No, I don't believe we've met before"?

12. I almost fainted when the announcer said, "Our winner is Stacy Langham!"

13. Felice asked the police officer, "Have you seen a little white dog dragging a blue leash?"

14. "Look out below!" Sandy cried as she pushed the hay bale over the edge.

15. "What I can't understand," Rudy added, "is why no one told us the time of the meeting."

Name _____ Class _____ Date _____

Lesson 84
Using the Apostrophe

Use an **apostrophe** and an *s ('s)* to form the possessive of a singular noun or a plural noun that does not end in s.

box + **'s** = box**'s**   James + **'s** = James**'s**
children + **'s** = children**'s**   men + **'s** = men**'s**

Use an apostrophe alone to form the possessive of a plural noun that ends in *s*.

Holmans + **'** = Holman**s'**   wolves + **'** = wolve**s'**   boys + **'** = boy**s'**

Use an apostrophe and an *s ('s)* to form the possessive of an indefinite pronoun.

someone + **'s** = someone**'s**   anybody + **'s** = anybody**'s**

Do not use an apostrophe in a possessive pronoun.

The gloves on the floor are **his**.   Those cookies were **ours**.

Use an apostrophe and an *s ('s)* to form the plurals of letters, figures, and words when they refer to themselves.

Dot your *i*'**s** and cross your *t*'**s**.   No *if*'**s**, *and*'**s**, or *but*'**s**   four *2*'**s**

Use an apostrophe to replace letters that have been omitted in a contraction. A **contraction** is a word that is made by combining two words into one by leaving out one or more letters.

do + not = don't   it + is = it's   you + are = you're   there + is = there's

Use an apostrophe to show missing numbers in a date.

the class of '97   the election of '92

▶ **Exercise 1** Write the possessive form of each word. Add a suitable noun. **Suitable nouns will vary.**

jogging shoes **jogging shoes' laces**

1. fox **fox's tail**
2. women **women's rights**
3. anyone **anyone's chair**
4. princesses **princesses' attendants**
5. Jacksons **Jacksons' house**
6. taxes **taxes' revenues**
7. vacation **vacation's length**
8. children **children's toys**
9. members **members' questions**
10. lion **lion's paw**

Unit 13, Punctuation **269**

Name _____ Class _____ Date _____

11. princess **princess's friend**
12. Ms. Davis **Ms. Davis's briefcase**
13. nobody **nobody's fault**
14. mice **mice's nests**
15. player **player's record**
16. bus **bus's tires**
17. somebody **somebody's pencil**
18. oxen **oxen's stalls**
19. classes **classes' assigned seats**
20. computer **computer's power cord**

▶ **Exercise 2** Add apostrophes where necessary. Use the delete symbol (⌿) to eliminate apostrophes used incorrectly.

Society's needs have led to many inventions throughout its⌿ history.

1. People's need to eat gave rise to the very first machines.
2. Archaeologists' discoveries⌿ of the past include tools that are one million years old.
3. Prehistoric people used crudely chipped stones to form their⌿ axes and spearheads.
4. The inclined plane's discovery became the first principle of technology for cutting tools.
5. About 3500 B.C. in the Middle East, the plow's invention enabled farmer⌿s to increase crop yields.
6. It's one of humankind's oldest inventions.
7. There's a device that's found in everyone's home that makes use of the principle of the inclined plane.
8. This device is Linus Yale's invention in 1848 of the cylinder lock and key.
9. An electronic trimmer's blades act as a pair of wedges⌿ to cut hair or stems⌿ like scissors' blades.
10. The zipper's slide uses wedges⌿ so one can easily open and close this type of fastener.
11. In the 1800s the tin can's invention was useful for preserving and safely transporting canned foods.
12. The consumer's problem, however, was how to easily and safely open these⌿ cans.
13. The can opener, with it⌿s sharp-edged cutting blade or wheel, was not invented until the twentieth century.
14. These and other inventions have made people's lives⌿ easier.

270 Writer's Choice Grammar Workbook 8, Unit 13

Name _____ Class _____ Date _____

Lesson 85
Using the Hyphen, Dash, and Parentheses

Use a **hyphen** to show the division of a word at the end of a line. Always divide the word between its syllables.

Robert is eagerly looking forward to the day when he can buy a computer.

Use a hyphen in compound numbers and in certain compound nouns.

sixty-four birds   twenty-one points   sister-in-law   great-grandmother

Use a hyphen in a fraction that is used as a modifier. Do not use a hyphen in a fraction used as a noun.

The gymnasium was only **one-half** full for the first game. (modifier)
Almost **one third** of all cars in the parking lot were red. (noun)

Hyphenate a compound modifier only when it precedes the word it modifies.

That's a **well-done** hamburger!   Melanie likes her hamburgers **well done**.

Use a hyphen after the prefixes *all-*, *ex-*, and *self-*. Use a hyphen to separate any prefix from a word that begins with a capital letter.

all-district   ex-governor   self-conscious   mid-Atlantic

Use a **dash** or dashes to show a sudden break or change in thought or speech.

Martin's dog Waldo—he's normally very well behaved—jumped on the table.

Use **parentheses** to set off material that is not part of the main statement but is, nevertheless, important to include.

The container held one liter (1.0567 quarts) of juice.

▶ **Exercise 1** Add hyphens where necessary. If the word or phrase is correct as written, write *C* in the blank.

_____   great-grandfather

_____ 1. eighty-eight   __C__ 5. dog is poorly behaved

_____ 2. three-fifths majority   _____ 6. ex-teacher

__C__ 3. noncritical issue   __C__ 7. one half of the students

_____ 4. self-cleaning oven   _____ 8. fifty-four

Unit 13, Punctuation **271**

Mechanics

_____ 9. all-American city
__C__ 10. a well-played game
_____ 11. preDepression cabin
__C__ 12. postwar
_____ 13. all-wood construction
__C__ 14. seventeen
_____ 15. self-confidence
__C__ 16. paper is well written
_____ 17. two-thirds empty
_____ 18. post-Renaissance period
__C__ 19. ex-astronaut
_____ 20. mid-Pacific island

▶ **Exercise 2** Complete each sentence by adding hyphens, dashes, or parentheses where necessary. Use the delete symbol (⌒) to eliminate those used incorrectly. If the sentence is correct as written, write *C* in the blank.

_____ Since pre-Colonial times, the black walnut tree has been prized.

_____ 1. Many people have tasted the delicious nut (actually a seed) that comes from this important forest tree.

_____ 2. The husk's peppery aroma (caused by oils in the husk) is quite strong.

__C__ 3. The husk is, of course, removed—who would want to eat such an odd-tasting thing?—before the nut is shelled and eaten.

_____ 4. You have to be quick if you want to gather walnuts to eat; many animals (squirrels, chipmunks, and other wildlife) love walnuts!

_____ 5. It is work to gather, husk, and shell walnuts—that's why most people buy them already shelled or at least husked at the grocery store.

__C__ 6. Some other plants (tomato plants and apple trees, for example) will not grow near a black walnut.

_____ 7. The tree gives off a poison (not harmful to people) that kills the roots of certain plants.

_____ 8. In pre-Revolutionary days, Americans had many different uses for the black walnut.

_____ 9. They made a blackish-green dye from the husks.

_____ 10. A pioneer's most important possession may very well have been his musket, and the most prized wood for the gun stock was black walnut.

Lesson 86
Using Abbreviations

Abbreviate a person's title and a professional or academic degree that follows a name.

Dr. Francisco Montoya   Ellen Chang, **D.D.S.**   George Rubashov, **Ph.D.**

Use all capital letters and no periods for abbreviations that are pronounced letter by letter or as words. Exceptions are U.S. and Washington, D.C., which do use periods.

NFL (National Football League)   FBI (Federal Bureau of Investigation)
NASA (National Aeronautics and Space Administration)

Use the abbreviations A.M. (*ante meridiem*, "before noon") and P.M. (*post meridiem*, "after noon") for exact times. For dates use B.C. (before Christ) and, sometimes, A.D. (*anno Domini*, "in the year of the Lord," after Christ).

6:30 A.M.   9:15 P.M.   415 B.C.   A.D. 119

Abbreviate calendar items only in charts and lists.

Oct.   **Jan.**   **Dec.**   **Sat.**   **Wed.**   **Fri.**

Abbreviate units of measure only in scientific writing.

feet **ft.**   inch(es) **in.**   pound(s) **lb.**   kilometer(s) **km**

On envelopes only, abbreviate street names and use the two-letter Postal Service abbreviations for the names of states.

Road **Rd.**   Street **St.**   Avenue **Ave.**   Pennsylvania **PA**   Utah **UT**

▶ **Exercise 1** Underline the word or abbreviation in parentheses that best completes each sentence.

The man in the *dashiki* works for (U.N.I.C.E.F., <u>UNICEF</u>).

1. The bonsai tree grew to be only eight (in., <u>inches</u>) tall.
2. The (N.A.A.C.P., <u>NAACP</u>) is one of the oldest civil rights organizations.
3. Elaine Howard, (<u>M.D.</u>, MD), is the new director of the medical center.
4. Pottery chips from around 2000 (<u>B.C.</u>, BC) have been discovered.
5. Suzanne said that Beaumont was about two hundred (km, <u>kilometers</u>) from here.

Unit 13, Punctuation **273**

Name _____ Class _____ Date _____

6. The office building located at 2208 Riverside (Dr., Drive) houses three companies.

7. I'm taking a gymnastics class at the (Y.W.C.A., YWCA) next summer.

8. Rhoda Silber, (Ph.D., PHD), is my mother.

9. A birthday party that began at 6:00 (a.m., A.M.) would be unusual.

10. His ideal weight was between 142 and 158 (lb., pounds) according to the doctor.

11. In (1066 A.D., A.D. 1066) the course of history was changed.

12. Our trip to Houston included a tour of the (N.A.S.A., NASA) headquarters.

13. Joe's family will move into a new apartment on Kingston (Ave., Avenue) tomorrow.

14. The area to be enclosed for the garden was four hundred square (ft., feet).

15. The (IRS, I.R.S.) just sent my mom's company some good news.

16. If you ask me, 10:00 (P.M., PM) is a little late to start your homework.

17. Most of Tim's favorite television shows are on (N.B.C., NBC) this season.

18. The building at 1090 Maryland (Street, St.) is being torn down.

19. The piece of material he bought was only two (yards, yd.) long.

20. Dan and he would love to see an (NFL, N.F.L) game in person.

▶ **Exercise 2** Rewrite each phrase using the appropriate abbreviation.

Salt Lake City, Utah __Salt Lake City, UT__

1. 2100 Michigan Avenue __2100 Michigan Ave.__

2. Mister Alexander Adams __Mr. Alexander Adams__

3. 7 feet, 2 inches __7 ft., 2 in.__

4. 5:15 *ante meridiem* __5:15 A.M.__

5. Doctor Elizabeth Santos __Dr. Elizabeth Santos__

6. 147 pounds __147 lb.__

7. Hazelton, Pennsylvania __Hazelton, PA__

8. Arthur Beecham, Doctor of Dental Science __Arthur Beecham, D.D.S.__

9. Wednesday, December 7 __Wed., Dec. 7__

10. Frederick La Fontaine Junior __Frederick La Fontaine Jr.__

Name _____ Class _____ Date _____

Lesson 87
Writing Numbers

Use **numerals** in charts and tables. In sentences, spell numbers that can be written in one or two words, and use numerals for those requiring more than two words.

The man appeared to be at least seventy-five years old.
More than 650 people attended the education meeting.

Spell out any number that begins a sentence, or reword the sentence so that it does not begin with a number.

Sixty-five thousand four hundred people were at the last game.

Write very large numbers as a numeral followed by the word *million* or *billion*.

The U.S. population is approximately 250 million.

In a sentence, if one number is in numerals, related numbers must be in numerals.

Of the 125 tickets sold, 45 were sold to sophomores.

Spell out ordinal numbers (*first, second,* and so forth).

This is the eighth time I've seen that movie.

Use words for decades, for amounts of money that can be written in one or two words, and for the approximate time of day or when A.M. or P.M. is not used.

the seventies   fifty cents   half past five   six o'clock

Use numerals for dates; for decimals; for house, apartment, and room numbers; for street or avenue numbers; for telephone numbers; for page numbers; for percentages; for sums of money involving both dollars and cents; and to emphasize the exact time of day or when A.M. or P.M. is used.

April 1, 1996   16 percent $207.89   2:51 P.M.

▶ **Exercise 1** Place a check (✔) in the blank next to each sentence that uses numbers or numerals correctly.

__✔__ LaToya is the third alternate on the drill team.

_____ 1. The U.S. Senate has 100 members, thirty-four of whom will be elected this year.

__✔__ 2. My mom attended her fifteenth high school reunion.

_____ 3. I read that India's population may soon be as high as 1,000,000,000!

__✔__ 4. Six people were waiting in line when I arrived.

Unit 13, Punctuation **275**

Name _____ Class _____ Date _____

_____ 5. I thought the movie began shortly after 8 o'clock.

✔ 6. The mayor stated that she believed 75 percent of the voters supported her position.

_____ 7. You can find the regional director in room forty-two.

_____ 8. Of the 320 people who work for the company, only twelve have been there more than ten years.

_____ 9. For information, call four-eight-two-nine-nine-five-zero.

_____ 10. 19 girls were asked back for the second round of tryouts.

✔ 11. I think the answer you are looking for is on page 324.

✔ 12. The airplane was due to arrive from Phoenix at 6:27 P.M.

_____ 13. She's not the 1st nor will she be the last to fall for that joke.

_____ 14. The new library has 7 rooms.

_____ 15. In the late 1980s, the U.S. national debt passed $1,000,000,000,000!

✔ 16. Carmen's house is at 1345 Wexford Road.

_____ 17. Less than two percent of the parts were faulty.

✔ 18. Taking care of twelve hamsters is a lot easier than taking care of twelve cats!

✔ 19. Sixty-five years had passed since they had met.

✔ 20. The zoo has eleven baboons, three orangutans, and twenty-one chimpanzees.

_____ 21. My brother was born on November third, 1979.

✔ 22. They asked us to be there around seven o'clock.

_____ 23. Ricky was very pleased with his 2nd-place finish in the backstroke.

✔ 24. Please take this form to room 68-A.

✔ 25. Rex's new in-line skates cost seventy dollars.

✔ 26. The new research facility was built at a cost of $65 million.

_____ 27. It takes at least 50% of the votes to pass the motion, doesn't it?

_____ 28. "11 warriors, brave and bold," goes the verse of the famous football fight song.

_____ 29. The office is located at seven Columbus Avenue.

✔ 30. Janine has to be home around four o'clock.

276 Writer's Choice Grammar Workbook 8, Unit 13

Name _____ Class _____ Date _____

 Unit 13 Review

▶ **Exercise 1** Place a check (✔) next to each sentence that is punctuated correctly.

__✔__ No, I haven't had a chance to see that movie yet.

__✔__ 1. "That's the strangest looking dog I've ever seen!" Amanda shrieked.

_____ 2. At the end of last month, I thought we would be able to succeed; however now I have begun to doubt whether we can.

_____ 3. Angela, did you remember to feed the gerbils.

__✔__ 4. Sweep out the cabin, unplug the refrigerator, and be sure to lock the doors and windows.

_____ 5. Paul moved here from Portland, Oregon, and Steven moved here from Portland, Maine, they've become best friends over this year.

_____ 6. The CDs on the shelf are their's, and the CD player is her's.

_____ 7. The land of Oz would, I suppose, be a good theme for the dance; after all, its such a great movie.

_____ 8. The positions on a basketball team are: center, forward, and guard.

__✔__ 9. The deadline for applying has been extended to Thursday, May 25, 1996.

_____ 10. Yes, I understand that babysitter's have a lot of responsibility, but we shouldn't have to take children to their doctors appointments, should we?

__✔__ 11. The luscious fruit salad contained bananas, strawberries, oranges, peaches, and I don't know what else.

_____ 12. In some parts of the prairie dogs run wild.

_____ 13. Was it Romeo who said, "To be or not to be?"

_____ 14. The skateboard leaning against the wall is either the girls' or James'.

_____ 15. I'm afraid its going to rain this afternoon before 3 o'clock.

__✔__ 16. Unless you want to end up in the water, you shouldn't play on the diving board.

_____ 17. Send your comments to 345 American Avenue, Room 421, Albuquerque, NM, 87105, or call (505) 555-9872.

__✔__ 18. Ms. Ameche said she had received twenty-seven well-written essays and a few that were not so carefully prepared.

Unit 13, Punctuation **277**

Name _____ Class _____ Date _____

Cumulative Review: Units 1–13

▶ **Exercise 1** Write in the blank the correct form (comparative or superlative) of the adjective or adverb in parentheses.

Georgia is considered the __most (or least) thoughtful__ person in our class. (thoughtful)

1. Craig is a __faster__ runner than Joe. (fast)
2. Florence seemed to be the __most (or least) beautiful__ city we visited during our tour of Italy. (beautiful)
3. Pamela and Christine paddled their canoe __more (or less) quickly__ than Jim and Ryan paddled theirs. (quickly)
4. Of all the maintenance people, Sylvia worked __most (or least) feverishly__. (feverishly)
5. This is the __best__ pasta I have ever tasted. (good)
6. That plant is the __least (or most) likely__ to survive a cold night. (likely)
7. The second television program appeared __worse__ than the first. (bad)
8. Katie's choir rehearsed the __easiest__ song last. (easy)
9. The __farthest__ Miki's family plans to drive is Albuquerque. (far)
10. Sue's essay __more (or less) closely__ resembled the example than Will's essay did. (closely)

▶ **Exercise 2** Underline the word in parentheses that best completes each sentence.

Cameron is (<u>altogether</u>, all together) certain the plane will arrive on time.

1. Marta wants to (<u>learn</u>, teach) how her grandmother bakes bread.
2. Give (you're, <u>your</u>) schedule to Ms. Maroukis.
3. The orchestra will now (precede, <u>proceed</u>) to play a new composition.
4. Everyone (accept, <u>except</u>) Joshua volunteered to stay late.
5. Dr. Sorenson found it difficult to choose (between, <u>among</u>) so many worthy applicants for the scholarship.
6. The company checked (it's, <u>its</u>) advertising budget before buying more newspaper ads.
7. (<u>Leave</u>, Let) the lavender material on the counter.

Name _____ Class _____ Date _____

8. Does the committee (choose, chose) the winner of the essay contest?
9. Ms. Cochran (formally, formerly) played professional tennis; now she is our tennis coach.
10. (Set, Sit) the vase of roses in the center of the table.
11. Dennis knows when (theirs, there's) going to be a sale at the electronics store.
12. An-Li says the movie has (all ready, already) begun.
13. The book Janice is looking for is (beside, besides) the encyclopedia.
14. My dog likes to (lay, lie) in front of the television.
15. (Many, Much) of the tickets were sold before Caitlin arrived.
16. Does anyone know (who's, whose) bringing the pizza?
17. Doreen used (fewer, less) ingredients in her sweet and sour chicken than Sid used in his.
18. The skating competition will be held (in, into) Parker Arena.
19. The shopping mall was (quiet, quite) crowded Friday night.
20. Dr. Wyatt explained the procedure and (than, then) began the examination.

▶ **Exercise 3** Add correct end marks. Delete (⌒) each unnecessary comma, semicolon, or colon.

Kylee, have you seen ⌒ my purple sweater?

1. Anita enjoys writing poetry, but Jean prefers writing stories
2. Carlo's orchard contains orange trees, lemon trees, and cherry trees
3. Take the film to the camera shop ⌒ before you stop at the grocery store
4. Have you seen Meg this afternoon?
5. Some of the guests were drinking tea on the veranda; others were practicing archery on the lawn
6. Wow! Look at all those colorful balloons coming down!
7. Can you see snow ⌒ on top of that mountain?
8. What an extraordinary coincidence that was!
9. In the room above the garage, you will find a secret compartment

Unit 13, Punctuation **279**

Name _____ Class _____ Date _____

10. The gentleman with the black umbrella, who is an ambassador to the United Nations, said hello to us as we were entering the hotel.

11. Fling the boomerang as far as you can, and see where it lands.

12. Though she is proud of all her paintings, Valeria considers this one her masterpiece.

13. The directions to the restaurant are as follows: drive north on Lake Shore Drive, turn left at Huron Street, and turn right at Michigan Avenue.

14. Did Mr. Hamilton buy a mahogany desk, or an oak table at the antique store?

15. That is, an enormous bouquet of flowers!

16. The debate team from Garfield Middle School is arguing that the law should be changed; however, the Brookside team believes the law should remain as it is.

17. I am taking ceramics, and Judi is studying Japanese.

18. Watch out for that snowball, Kelly!

19. Where, would the instruction manual be?

20. Did Susan, or Roberto, bring the CDs?

▶ **Exercise 4** Write the part of speech above each word in italics: *N* (noun), *V* (verb), *pro.* (pronoun), *adj.* (adjective), *adv.* (adverb), *prep.* (preposition), or *conj.* (conjunction).

      N   V   prep.
    Sally waited for Claire *by* the swimming pool.

        conj.   conj.   V
1. Dexter *and* Nina attended the elegant dance, *but* Alex and Nora *stayed* home.

   pro.   N   adj.
2. *They* hid their *ambition* until the *proper* moment arrived.

       V   adv.   N
3. Cedric *paced impatiently* while his sister stabled her *horse*.

  pro.   prep.   adj.
4. *That* completes our tour *of* the *furniture* factory.

  V   adj.   N
5. *Place* the *silver* tray next to the fine *china*.

  pro.   N prep.
6. *She* was introduced to many interesting *people at* the park.

      V   pro. conj.
7. Celeste *wants* to plan the party *herself or* at least plan the menu.

  N   N   N
8. *Brandon* believes his *sister-in-law* has left *town*.

    conj.   adj.   prep.
9. Gina *and* Todd will be attending the *special* gathering *at* Aunt Edna's house.

     pro.   V   adv.
10. The person *who* sent the flowers *wishes* to speak to you *soon*.

Vocabulary and Spelling

Name _____ Class _____ Date _____

Unit 14: Vocabulary and Spelling

Lesson 88
Building Vocabulary: Learning from Context

Clues to the meaning of a new word can be found in the **context**, the words and sentences surrounding it.

TYPE OF CONTEXT CLUE	CLUE WORDS	EXAMPLE
Comparison The thing or idea named by the unfamiliar word is compared with something more familiar.	also same likewise similar, similarly identical, identically	His writing is barely *legible*. It is **similar** to chicken scratchings in a barnyard.
Contrast The thing or idea named by the unfamiliar word is contrasted with something more familiar.	but on the other hand on the contrary unlike however	What I'm saying is no *conjecture*. **On the contrary,** I happen to know that it is absolutely true.
Cause and effect The unfamiliar word is explained as a part of a cause-and-effect relationship.	because since therefore as a result consequently	The judge seems *partial* to the debate team from Smathers Middle School **because** she always nods when they give their speeches.

▶ **Exercise 1** Use context clues to determine the meaning of the word in italics. Choose the correct meaning from the list and write its letter in the appropriate blank.

A. a sudden, unexpected desire
B. unimportant
C. untidy
D. avoid doing
E. unconcerned
F. out of style
G. tall and slender
H. bill

I. special vocabulary of a particular group
J. a job that requires little work
K. having to do with veins
L. prove wrong
M. motivation for doing something
N. talk about past experiences
O. gradual increase
P. unsuspicious

__P__ Steven is very *credulous;* he'll believe almost anything.

Unit 14, Vocabulary and Spelling **283**

Name _____ Class _____ Date _____

__H__ 1. After we received the shipment of computer paper, the company sent us an *invoice* asking us to pay the amount within thirty days.

__B__ 2. That *trifling* problem is just not worth worrying about for one second.

__N__ 3. It was fun to listen to the two brothers *reminisce* about their childhood on the farm.

__I__ 4. I couldn't understand a word of those computer scientists' technical *jargon*.

__J__ 5. Being treasurer of the Spanish Club is definitely not a *sinecure;* on the contrary, it requires a lot of time and effort.

__G__ 6. Most of the players on the basketball team are *rangy,* while the members of the football team tend to be husky.

__L__ 7. Because they had left a few holes in their argument, we were able to *refute* it.

__D__ 8. Tell the captain he can be confident that I will never *shirk* my duty.

__M__ 9. A chance to play in the city-wide championship game should be plenty of *incentive* for the volleyball team to work hard.

__O__ 10. In response to the *crescendo* of applause, the candidate returned to the stage and waved to her supporters.

__K__ 11. Eating too much fatty food can harm the *vascular* system and restrict the flow of blood throughout the body.

__E__ 12. When the team went ahead by eighteen points, they grew *complacent* and stopped scoring.

__C__ 13. You can tell by looking at his messy room that he is a *slovenly* person.

__F__ 14. Don't bring your tapes of that band to the party; their music is so *outmoded* it sounds as if it's from the 1970s.

__A__ 15. We hadn't planned to go; we went to the movie purely on a *whim*.

▶ **Writing Link** Choose three vocabulary words from the lesson and use them in your own sentences.

_____

_____

_____

_____

284 Writer's Choice Grammar Workbook 8, Unit 14

Name _____ Class _____ Date _____

Lesson 89
Building Vocabulary: Word Roots

The **root** of a word is the part that carries the main meaning. Some roots can stand alone. Others make little or no sense without other word parts added to them. Knowing the meanings of roots can help you figure out the meanings of unfamiliar words.

ROOT	WORD	MEANING
audi means "hear"	audible	able to be heard
	audition	tryout where a person's talents are displayed
bio means "life"	biology	study of living things
	biography	story of a person's life
ben means "good"	beneficial	good or positive
	benefit	do something good
meter means "measure"	speedometer	instrument for measuring speed
	chronometer	instrument for measuring time
port means "carry"	portable	able to be carried
	export	goods sold, or carried, outside the country

▶ **Exercise 1** In the blank, write a short definition of the italicized root. Use a dictionary if necessary.

*bio*sphere life

1. *vid*eo see
2. at*tract* pull *or* draw
3. *phon*ograph sound
4. in*cred*ible believe
5. geo*logy* science
6. *milli*pede thousand
7. *dent*ist tooth
8. *son*ic sound
9. tele*vis*ion see
10. *phot*ograph light
11. *flex*ible bend
12. im*mort*al death
13. *astro*nomy star
14. *cent*ury hundred
15. con*ven*tion come
16. *lect*ure speech
17. *dec*ade ten
18. *chron*icle time
19. *man*ual hand
20. *tele*phone distant

Vocabulary and Spelling

Unit 14, Vocabulary and Spelling **285**

Name _____ Class _____ Date _____

▶ **Exercise 2** Complete each sentence by filling in a word that uses the root in parentheses.

The farmer used his ___**tractor**___ to pull our car out of the ditch. (tract)

1. Because Brian is a good ___**photographer**___, he was asked to take pictures for the school newspaper. (photo)

2. The members of the political party came together at their ___**convention**___ in Houston to nominate their candidates. (ven)

3. If you want to know what the temperature is outside, just look at the ___**thermometer**___. (meter)

4. When we watch ___**television**___, we see pictures from far away in our own homes. (tele)

5. I'm reading a book about the life of Mother Teresa; it's called ___**Biography**___ of a Saint. (bio)

6. Take another look at your essay and ___**revise**___ it if you think it's necessary. (vis)

7. Our town is holding a ___**centennial**___ to celebrate its founding one hundred years ago. (cent)

8. When the jet plane flew over our neighborhood, it created an unbelievably loud ___**sonic**___ boom. (son)

9. For Spanish class we had to write a ___**dialogue**___ between two people; they could talk about anything we wanted. (log)

10. Since the automatic starter on Mom's lawn mower doesn't work, she has to pull the rope to start it ___**manually**___. (man)

11. Even though we could see the movie, we couldn't hear it because the ___**audio**___ track was faulty. (audi)

12. I have mostly cassette tapes, but I also like to listen to old records on my dad's ___**phonograph**___. (phon)

13. The box says the pet carrier is ___**portable**___, but when our cat, who weighs 22 pounds, is inside it, I can barely lift it! (port)

14. The ___**chronological**___ table of American presidents lists them in the order they served. (chron)

15. The store tried to ___**attract**___ more customers by offering a special two-for-one sale. (tract)

Name _____ Class _____ Date _____

Lesson 90
Building Vocabulary: Prefixes and Suffixes

Prefixes and suffixes are word parts that can be added to roots. A **prefix** is added to the beginning of the root. A **suffix** is added at the end.

un (prefix) + kind (root) = unkind ("not kind")
kind (root) + ness (suffix) = kindness (noun form of the adjective *kind*)

Prefixes and suffixes can change, even reverse, the meanings of roots. Suffixes, unlike prefixes, can also change the part of speech of the root word. For example, adding *-ness* to *kind* (an adjective) makes it into *kindness* (a noun). Adding *-ly* makes it into *kindly* (an adverb).
Learning prefixes and suffixes can help you figure out the meaning of unfamiliar words.

PREFIXES	MEANING
co-	with
il-, im-, in-, ir-, dis-, non-, and *un-*	not, the opposite of
post-	after
pre-	before
sub-	below or beneath

SUFFIXES	MEANING
-al, -ly, and *-y*	in the manner of, having to do with
-ee, -eer, -er, -ian, -ist, -or	one who does (something)
-ful, -ous	full of

▶ **Exercise 1** Add a prefix or suffix to each italicized root word. Write the new word in the blank and underline the suffix or prefix.

__logic<u>ally</u>__ in the manner of being *logical*

__protest<u>er</u>__ 1. one who *protests*

__<u>ir</u>regular__ 2. not *regular*

__grim<u>y</u>__ 3. having to do with *grime*

__angr<u>ily</u>__ 4. in the manner of being *angry*

__<u>in</u>adequate__ 5. the opposite of *adequate*

__driv<u>er</u>__ 6. one who *drives* a car

__<u>co</u>sign__ 7. to *sign* together

Name _____ Class _____ Date _____

tactful 8. full of *tact*
contentedly 9. in the manner of being *contented*
unattractive 10. the opposite of *attractive*
sunny 11. having to do with *sun*
investor 12. one who *invests* money
spiteful 13. full of *spite*
postelection 14. after the *election*
subfreezing 15. below *freezing*
excitedly 16. in the manner of being *excited*
impolite 17. the opposite of *polite*
player 18. one who *plays*
reversal 19. having to do with the action of *reversing* something
prearranged 20. *arranged* ahead of time
courageous 21. full of *courage*
musical 22. having to do with *music*
illiterate 23. the opposite of *literate*
sloppily 24. in the manner of being *sloppy*

▶ **Exercise 2** Underline the prefix or suffix in each word. Write the meaning of the word. Use a dictionary if necessary.

immobile — **not capable of being moved**

1. unpopular — **not popular**
2. postpone — **to put off for a later time**
3. bravely — **in the manner of being brave**
4. coauthor — **author with another person**
5. comical — **having to do with comedy**
6. harpist — **one who plays a harp**
7. painter — **one who paints**

288 Writer's Choice Grammar Workbook 8, Unit 14

Lesson 91
Building Vocabulary: Synonyms and Antonyms

Synonyms are words that have the same, or nearly the same, meaning. For example, *end* and *finish* are synonyms, as are *big* and *large*. When searching for just the right word to use, the best place to find synonyms is in a thesaurus. A dictionary also has information on synonyms and their usage.

Antonyms are words that have the opposite, or nearly opposite, meaning. *Begin* and *finish* are antonyms, as are *big* and *small*. The easiest way to form antonyms is by adding a prefix meaning *not*. *Un-, il-, dis-, in-, im-, ir-,* and *non-* are all prefixes that reverse the meaning of a root. They form antonyms such as **un**fair, **il**legal, **dis**interested, **in**efficient, **im**perfect, **ir**regular, and **non**fat. Sometimes an antonym can be made by changing the suffix. *Joy**ful*** and *joy**less*** are antonyms.

▶ **Exercise 1** Write a synonym in the blank to replace the word or words in italics. Use your dictionary or thesaurus as needed. **Answers may vary.**

__difficult__   Solving this week's crossword puzzle was *hard*.

__zest__   1. Mei's *enthusiasm* for competition was second to none.

__beneficial__   2. Eating healthy foods is definitely *good* for the body.

__tranquil__   3. This beautiful lake is so *calm* at sunrise.

__perplexity__   4. Their response to the question was one of total *confusion*.

__parched__   5. My throat is so *dry* I could drink a gallon of water.

__courtyard__   6. The hotel where Christine stayed in New Mexico had a lovely little *patio*.

__durable__   7. My grandfather always talks about how *long-lasting* his first lawn mower was.

__scampered__   8. The scorpion *moved* under a rock when we approached it.

__severe__   9. Ray has a *very bad* cold; he ought to be in bed instead of at school.

__herbivore__   10. Diplodocus, one of the largest dinosaurs, was a *plant-eater*.

__automobiles__   11. The freeway heading into Los Angeles was absolutely choked with *cars*.

__reflected__   12. Martin *thought* about why the character in the novel would have behaved the way she did.

Unit 14, Vocabulary and Spelling

Name _____ Class _____ Date _____

__moist__ 13. I knew we had a problem when I noticed that the wall behind the refrigerator was *wet*.

__friendliest__ 14. When Roger first moved to his new school, Jose was the *nicest* person he met.

__excellently__ 15. Serafina sang her solo last night *very well*.

__begin__ 16. Will you *start* dancing when everyone else does?

__sharp__ 17. The *acute* pain in my stomach didn't go away, so my mom called the doctor.

__abandon__ 18. I hope you won't *desert* me when I need you.

▶ **Exercise 2** Write an antonym in the blank to replace the word in italics. Use your dictionary or thesaurus as needed. Answers will vary.

__happy__ Mr. Nakajima seemed *glum* when I visited him in the hospital.

__arrive__ 1. Rachel's flight was scheduled to *depart* at 4:45 A.M.

__unavailable__ 2. The candidate will be *available* for questions this afternoon.

__shorter__ 3. The movie was actually *lengthier* than it seemed.

__opening__ 4. The *closing* time of the shop was posted in the window.

__impossible__ 5. What you are suggesting seems *possible*.

__depressed__ 6. Philip's mood seemed *buoyant* after what he had been through.

__disbelieve__ 7. They *believe* the political candidate's remarks.

__insensitive__ 8. Lisa is one of the most *sensitive* people I know.

__insincere__ 9. Gina told me that Jim's apology was *heartfelt*.

__hot__ 10. I couldn't think of going outside on such a *frigid* day!

__inadvisable__ 11. Many of the company's activities were *advisable*.

__unpolite__ 12. I was surprised by how *polite* the visitor was.

__inexpensive__ 13. The bracelet he gave her for her birthday was very *costly*.

__faraway__ 14. The goalie on our soccer team moved to a *nearby* town.

__unclearly__ 15. We all felt that Herb expressed his ideas *clearly*.

Name _____ Class _____ Date _____

Lesson 92
Building Vocabulary: Homographs and Homophones

Homographs are words that are spelled alike but have different meanings and sometimes different pronunciations. The root *homo* means "same," and *graph* means "write." *Beat* and *beat* are homographs. You can **beat** an opponent in a game, and you can appreciate a song's **beat**.

Homophones are words that sound alike but are spelled differently and have different meanings. *Male* and *mail* are homophones.

▶ **Exercise 1** Write the italicized homograph's part of speech. Write *N* for noun, *V* for verb, or *adj.* for adjective.

__N__ Sarah carefully opened the fragile *box.*

__V__ I will *box* in the tournament.

__adj.__ 1. Her dress for the dance was a *pale* shade of purple.

__N__ The farmer had to repair a *pale* in the wooden fence.

__N__ 2. Many postal workers sorted the *mail* over the holidays.

__V__ Will you please *mail* this letter for me?

__V__ 3. My brother could *yak* on the phone all night.

__N__ The *yak* is a large, shaggy-haired wild ox of Tibet.

__N__ 4. A large *bull* charged the toreador as the crowd shouted, "Olé."

__N__ The Pope sent out an official *bull* to all his priests.

__V__ 5. Will that sweater *fray* at the seams?

__N__ A *fray* started after the football game between the cross-town rivals.

__adj.__ 6. Walking on the *piled* carpeting was like walking on cushions.

__V__ Our neighbor *piled* the firewood along the chain-link fence.

__V__ 7. All passengers will *abandon* the sinking ship.

__N__ Following final exams, the students left the school with reckless *abandon.*

__N__ 8. The *slug* slowly crept across the pavement.

__V__ Sometimes the boxers *slug* each other during a match.

Unit 14, Vocabulary and Spelling **291**

Name _____ Class _____ Date _____

__N__   9. The little girl refused to sit on Santa's *lap*.

__V__   The waves *lap* quietly against the sides of the boat.

__V__   10. My best friend, Julie, *won* the writing contest at school.

__N__   While sightseeing in South Korea, we had to exchange dollars for *won*.

▶ **Exercise 2** The words in parentheses are homophones. Underline the word that best completes each sentence.

The harder the wind (<u>blew</u>, blue), the colder it felt on the mountain.

1. The explorers finally discovered the (sight, <u>site</u>) of the ancient temple.
2. Chickens, ducks, and turkeys are all types of (foul, <u>fowl</u>).
3. By the time our friends arrived, they were several (<u>hours</u>, ours) late.
4. Phil was taking his favorite (you, <u>ewe</u>) to the state fair sheep contest.
5. If you don't (need, <u>knead</u>) bread long enough, it won't bake properly.
6. If you can, (<u>would</u>, wood) you please come a few minutes early to help me set up the chairs?
7. I'll never forget my first glimpse of the (<u>sea</u>, see) as we drove over the hill.
8. Finishing a marathon race is a (reel, <u>real</u>) accomplishment, no matter what your time.
9. Don't stand out there freezing—come on (<u>in</u>, inn).
10. Brittany likes to (reed, <u>read</u>) mysteries.
11. Helen should have received that package by now, since we (scent, <u>sent</u>) it last week.
12. Have you ever wanted to (sore, <u>soar</u>) in the sky like an eagle?
13. Sailing around the world alone in a tiny sailboat is an incredible (feet, <u>feat</u>).
14. We watched as the robin hopped down the sidewalk and ate a (<u>whole</u>, hole) fat worm.
15. Jordi is allergic to (<u>bee</u>, be) stings, so she always has to carry a special sting kit.
16. My sister gets up at half past (fore, <u>four</u>) in the morning to deliver newspapers.
17. I'm glad that people can now be (find, <u>fined</u>) for littering the beach.
18. This juice is (<u>made</u>, maid) from Florida oranges, isn't it?

Name _____ Class _____ Date _____

Lesson 93
Basic Spelling Rules I

SPELLING *IE* AND *EI*

The *i* comes before the *e*, except when both letters follow *c* or when both letters are pronounced together as an *ā* sound. However, many exceptions to this rule exist.

bel**ie**ve (*i* before *e*)   rec**ei**ve (*ei* after *c*)   **ei**ght (*ā* sound)   h**ei**ght (exception)

SPELLING UNSTRESSED VOWELS

An unstressed vowel is a vowel sound that is not emphasized when the word is pronounced. For example, in *com-bi-na-tion* the second syllable, *bi*, is unstressed. To determine how an unstressed vowel is spelled, think of a related word in which that syllable is stressed. To determine the spelling of the second syllable in *combination*, think of the word *combine*.

▶ **Exercise 1** Write each word adding the missing vowel or vowels.

ach—ve **achieve**

1. retr—ve **retrieve**
2. v—l **veil**
3. penc-l **pencil**
4. fant-sy **fantasy**
5. attend-nt **attendant**
6. w—rd **weird**
7. c—ling **ceiling**
8. perc—ve **perceive**

9. rel—ve **relieve**
10. influ-nce **influence**
11. neg-tive **negative**
12. dram-tist **dramatist**
13. mel-dy **melody**
14. conc—ve **conceive**
15. n—ghbor **neighbor**
16. gr—ve **grieve**

ADDING PREFIXES

When adding a prefix to a word, simply keep the spelling of the word and attach the prefix. If the prefix ends in the same letter as the first letter of the word, keep both letters.

un + happy = **un**happy   co + operate = **co**operate

Unit 14, Vocabulary and Spelling   **293**

Name _____ Class _____ Date _____

SUFFIXES AND FINAL *Y*

When a word ends in a consonant + *y*, change the *y* to *i* before adding a suffix. When the word ends in a vowel + *y*, keep the *y*. If the suffix begins with an *i*, keep the *y*.

fly + es = fl**ies**   key + s = key**s**   fly + ing = fl**ying**   play + ing = play**ing**

SUFFIXES AND SILENT *E*

When adding a suffix that begins with a consonant to a word that ends in silent *e*, keep the *e*.

achieve + ment = achiev**ement**

When adding a suffix that begins with a vowel or *y* to a word that ends in a silent *e*, drop the *e*.

give + ing = gi**ving**

When adding -*ly* to a word that ends in *l* plus silent *e*, drop the *le*.

possible + ly = possib**ly**

When adding a suffix that begins with *a* or *o* to a word that ends in *ce* or *ge*, keep the *e*.

change + able = chang**eable**

When adding a suffix that begins with a vowel to a word that ends in *ee* or *oe*, keep the *e*.

canoe + ing = cano**eing**

▶ **Exercise 2** Use the spelling rules in this lesson to spell the words indicated.

state + -ment __statement__

1. *pre-* + wash __prewash__
2. like + -able __likable__
3. reply + -es __replies__
4. hoe + -ing __hoeing__
5. *co-* + write __cowrite__
6. compete + -ing __competing__
7. live + -ly __lively__
8. manage + -able __manageable__
9. debate + -able __debatable__
10. *post-* + election __postelection__
11. amaze + -ment __amazement__
12. try + -ing __trying__
13. *semi-* + formal __semiformal__
14. noise + -y __noisy__
15. *dis-* + service __disservice__
16. agree + -able __agreeable__
17. possible + -ly __possibly__
18. quote + -ing __quoting__

Lesson 94
Basic Spelling Rules II

DOUBLING THE FINAL CONSONANT

Double the final consonant when a word ends in a single consonant following one vowel if the word is one syllable. The same rule applies if the word has an accent on the last syllable and the accent remains there after the suffix is added.

mop + -ing = mo**pp**ing   mad + -er = ma**dd**er
compel + -ing = compe**ll**ing   admit + -ed = admi**tt**ed

Do not double the final consonant when the suffix begins with a consonant.

color + -ful = color**ful**   kind + -ness = kind**ness**   bad + -ly = bad**ly**

Special case: When a word ends in *ll* and the suffix *-ly* is added, drop one *l*.

full + -ly = fu**lly**   dull + -ly = du**lly**

FORMING COMPOUND WORDS

When forming compound words, the spelling rule is very simple. Just put the two words together, even if it means having two consonants together.

book + keeper = boo**kk**eeper   back + pack = bac**kp**ack

▶ **Exercise 1** Write in the blank the new word formed by combining the two words or word and suffix indicated.

jog + -ing **jogging**

1. retreat + -ing **retreating**
2. count + -ed **counted**
3. jack + knife **jackknife**
4. unforget + -able **unforgettable**
5. ship + -ed **shipped**
6. war + -ed **warred**
7. shrill + -ly **shrilly**
8. regret + -able **regrettable**
9. bold + -ness **boldness**
10. win + -er **winner**
11. occur + -ence **occurrence**
12. light + house **lighthouse**
13. leader + -ship **leadership**
14. zoo + keeper **zookeeper**
15. remember + -ing **remembering**
16. wrap + -er **wrapper**
17. busy + body **busybody**
18. refer + -ence **reference**

Unit 14, Vocabulary and Spelling **295**

Name _____ Class _____ Date _____

GENERAL RULES FOR FORMING PLURALS

Most nouns form their plurals by adding -s. However, nouns that end in *ch, s, sh, x,* or *z* form their plurals by adding -es. If the noun ends in a consonant + *y*, change *y* to *i* and add -es. If the noun ends in *lf*, change the *f* to a *v* and add -es. If the noun ends in *fe*, change the *f* to a *v* and add -s.

desk**s**   fox**es**   histor**ies**   sel**ves**   kni**ves**

SPECIAL RULES FOR FORMING PLURALS

To form the plural of proper names and one-word compound nouns, follow the general rules for plurals. To form the plural of hyphenated compound nouns or compound nouns of more than one word, make the most important word plural.

Anderson**s**   Montez**es**   doormat**s**   blueberr**ies**
sister**s**-in-law   secretar**ies** of defense

Some nouns have irregular plural forms.

geese   mice   teeth   children   oxen

Some nouns have the same singular and plural forms.

deer   sheep   fish   antelope

▶ **Exercise 2** Write in the blank the plural form of each word.

brother-in-law **brothers-in-law**

1. notch **notches**
2. buzz **buzzes**
3. box **boxes**
4. baby **babies**
5. studio **studios**
6. shelf **shelves**
7. giraffe **giraffes**
8. belief **beliefs**
9. video **videos**
10. life **lives**
11. self **selves**
12. Morris **Morrises**
13. passer-by **passers-by**
14. goose **geese**
15. antelope **antelope**
16. head of state **heads of state**
17. sheep **sheep**
18. strawberry **strawberries**

Name _____ Class _____ Date _____

 # Unit 14 Review: Building Vocabulary

▶ **Exercise 1** Underline the word or words in parentheses that correctly complete the sentence. Use a dictionary if necessary.

Cara's favorite class is (<u>biology</u>, biography).

1. (<u>Post</u>, pre) *meridiem* means "after noon."
2. The United States (<u>exports</u>, imports) grain to Russia.
3. A metronome, ticking rhythmically, helped the piano student keep the music's (<u>beat</u>, beet) consistent.
4. Lynn, a law student, carries class notes in a leather (scolex, <u>portfolio</u>).
5. The postal worker delivers our (male, <u>mail</u>) in the afternoons.
6. Dixie's shovel and (<u>pail</u>, pale) lay abandoned in the hot sand.
7. Did you test the car's (breaks, <u>brakes</u>)?
8. Because they cosigned the bank papers for a loan, (one, <u>both</u>) of them will have to pay it back.

▶ **Exercise 2** Write a synonym and an antonym for each word. Use your dictionary or thesaurus as needed. Answers, especially synonyms, may vary.

WORD	SYNONYM	ANTONYM
remember	recall	forget
1. few	sparse	many
2. choose	select	reject
3. delight	gladden	disappoint
4. dirty	grimy	clean
5. disorder	chaos	order
6. labor	toil	rest
7. assist	help	hinder
8. foolish	silly	wise

Unit 14, Vocabulary and Spelling **297**

Name _____ Class _____ Date _____

#	Word	Synonym	Antonym
9.	true	actual	false
10.	common	ordinary	rare
11.	boring	dull	interesting
12.	useless	futile	useful
13.	merry	happy	morose
14.	inspire	motivate	discourage
15.	avoid	shun	confront
16.	courage	bravery	cowardice
17.	steady	firm	unsteady
18.	bold	daring	timid
19.	joy	gladness	despair
20.	clumsy	awkward	graceful
21.	morning	daybreak	evening
22.	stand	rise	sit
23.	last	final	first
24.	float	bob	sink

▶ **Exercise 3** Add a prefix or suffix to the root of each italicized word. Write the new word in the blank.

unmoved	not *moved*
dancer	1. one who *dances*
meekly	2. in the manner of *meekness*
antimatter	3. the opposite of *matter*
beautiful	4. full of *beauty*
subsoil	5. below the *soil*
musician	6. one who makes *music*
joyous *or* joyful	7. full of *joy*
boldly	8. in the manner of *boldness*

Vocabulary and Spelling

298 Writer's Choice Grammar Workbook 8, Unit 14

Name _____ Class _____ Date _____

 Unit 14 Review: Basic Spelling Rules

▶ **Exercise 1** Underline the word or phrase that is spelled correctly.

Our school (principle, <u>principal</u>) has many progressive ideas.

1. We will meet our (freinds, <u>friends</u>) at the movie tomorrow night.
2. Owning a dog is a large (responsability, <u>responsibility</u>).
3. The blizzard (<u>delayed</u>, delaid) my dad's flight.
4. Tamara and Vivian are going (shoping, <u>shopping</u>) for bathing suits.
5. The (<u>chiefs of staff</u>, chieves of staff) gathered in the conference room.
6. Pedro's (sister-in-laws, <u>sisters-in-law</u>) organized a surprise party for him.
7. We laughed when Grandpa's (fishook, <u>fishhook</u>) got caught on his pants.
8. Julius was (<u>totally</u>, totaly) stunned to see his cat run up the oak tree.
9. The song says that Wyatt Earp was (couragous, <u>courageous</u>) and bold.
10. Visiting the Grand Canyon was an (<u>unforgettable</u>, unforgetable) experience.
11. I am sure Gracie will (recieve, <u>receive</u>) many compliments on her new purple sweater.
12. The twins plan to attend (seperate, <u>separate</u>) summer camps.
13. Carbohydrates, proteins, minerals, and vitamins are important (nutriants, <u>nutrients</u>) for the body.
14. Is your little brother as (nosei, <u>nosy</u>) as mine is?
15. The (monkies, <u>monkeys</u>) at the zoo entertained our class all afternoon.
16. Fireflies are (becomming, <u>becoming</u>) very active in the evenings now.
17. Please cut the pizza into two (<u>halves</u>, halfs).
18. Juanita (<u>led</u>, lead) our field hockey team to victory.
19. My parents took many (photoes, <u>photos</u>) when we vacationed at Gettysburg.
20. Look at all the (<u>deer</u>, deers) scrambling out of the wood.
21. The weather has been extremely (changable, <u>changeable</u>) lately.
22. Dr. Berkowitz gave Amad (medecine, <u>medicine</u>) to help reduce the swelling of his sprained ankle.

Unit 14, Vocabulary and Spelling   **299**

Name _____ Class _____ Date _____

▶ **Exercise 2** Write in the blank the word formed by combining two words or by combining the word with the prefix or suffix indicated.

skate + -ing **skating**

1. remarkable + -ly **remarkably**
2. incredible + -ly **incredibly**
3. broken + -ness **brokenness**
4. mis- + spelling **misspelling**
5. peace + -able **peaceable**
6. benefit + -ed **benefitted**
7. back + pack **backpack**
8. use + -able **usable**
9. fancy + -ful **fanciful**
10. employ + -ment **employment**
11. refer + -ed **referred**
12. co- + operate **cooperate**
13. dis- + service **disservice**
14. imply + -ed **implied**
15. fly + -ing **flying**
16. occur + -ence **occurrence**
17. grand + child **grandchild**
18. busy + -est **busiest**
19. un- + necessary **unnecessary**
20. sad + -er **sadder**

▶ **Exercise 3** Write in the blank the plural form of each word.

music box **music boxes**

1. atlas **atlases**
2. key **keys**
3. echo **echoes**
4. wife **wives**
5. fox **foxes**
6. branch **branches**
7. audience **audiences**
8. blueberry **blueberries**
9. sheep **sheep**
10. Jones **Joneses**
11. foot **feet**
12. piano **pianos**
13. Monday **Mondays**
14. son-in-law **sons-in-law**
15. roomful **roomfuls**
16. giraffe **giraffes**

300   Writer's Choice Grammar Workbook 8, Unit 14

Composition

Name _____ Class _____ Date _____

Unit 15: Composition

Lesson 95
The Writing Process: Prewriting

The **prewriting** stage of the writing process is an idea stage. Before you write, gather ideas and make choices about three things: your topic, your purpose, and your audience. Together, these three things make up the prewriting stage.

There are several ways that you can find a **topic**, or subject to write about. *Freewriting*, writing whatever comes to mind, can lead you to a general topic. You might also *make lists* that relate to one key word or idea or *ask general questions* about a subject that interests you.

Along with choosing a topic, you need to determine the **purpose**, or reason, for writing. Your purpose might be to describe, to amuse, to inform, to narrate, or to persuade.

Finally, you need to choose an **audience**, or who will read your written piece. Ask yourself "Whom am I trying to persuade?" or "Whom am I trying to inform?" The style, the words, and the information you include will depend on who your readers will be.

▶ **Exercise 1** Spend ten minutes freewriting about a recent event that happened in your school.

Answers will vary.

Unit 15, Composition   **303**

Name _____ Class _____ Date _____

▶ **Exercise 2** From your freewriting in Exercise 1, choose a specific topic that you could write about.

Answers will vary but should be related to the writing from Exercise 1.

▶ **Exercise 3** Choose at least two purposes for the topic you chose in Exercise 2. Determine an audience for each purpose.

Answers will vary; check that the chosen purpose and audience are appropriate for the topic.

▶ **Exercise 4** Write one or two questions that you might research before writing about each topic below.

Topic: Your community's activities for teen-agers
What kind of activities do teenagers in our community enjoy?
Does the community provide those activities?

1. **Topic:** Your school's music programs

2. **Topic:** Air pollution

3. **Topic:** Organizations in your community that need young volunteer workers

Name _____ Class _____ Date _____

4. **Topic:** Popular hairstyles

_____
_____
_____

5. **Topic:** Preparing healthful meals

_____
_____
_____

▶ **Exercise 5** Identify two possible purposes for each topic below.

Topic: How an eighth-grader can earn money during the summer
Purpose 1: to inform an eighth-grade reader of ways to earn money
Purpose 2: to persuade eighth-graders to earn their own money

1. **Topic:** An abandoned house in your neighborhood
   Purpose 1: to narrate how scary the house seemed when you were younger
   Purpose 2: to inform readers about the dangers of going into the house

2. **Topic:** Your school's student council elections
   Purpose 1: to persuade readers to vote for certain candidates
   Purpose 2: to inform readers about the candidates' opinions and goals

3. **Topic:** Resolving fights with friends
   Purpose 1: to inform readers of non-violent methods of resolving conflict
   Purpose 2: to describe the silly things friends sometimes fight about

4. **Topic:** Your household chores
   Purpose 1: to describe how your room looks before and after you clean it
   Purpose 2: to persuade the reader to volunteer for household tasks

5. **Topic:** Fixing something that is broken
   Purpose 1: to inform the reader of how to fix something
   Purpose 2: to narrate the difficulty you had fixing something

Unit 15, Composition

▶ **Exercise 6** Identify one audience and one purpose for each topic.

Topic: An increase in allowance

Purpose: To persuade your parents to raise your allowance

Audience: Your parents

1. **Topic:** A movie you saw last weekend

   Purpose: To persuade your friends to see the movie

   Audience: Your friends

2. **Topic:** Your commitment to physical fitness

   Purpose: To inform those who are bored with their workouts about what you do to stay in shape

   Audience: People who work out

3. **Topic:** An embarrassing moment from elementary school

   Purpose: To narrate

   Audience: Current elementary school students

4. **Topic:** Explaining the steps to your favorite dance

   Purpose: To describe

   Audience: Other dance enthusiasts

Name _____ Class _____ Date _____

Lesson 96
The Writing Process: Drafting

After the prewriting stage, begin **drafting**, or writing, your piece in paragraph form. From the topic and purpose, you can create the **theme**, the point the piece will try to make. State the theme in a **thesis statement** in the first paragraph. Each paragraph usually has a *topic sentence*, or a statement of the main idea, and several supporting sentences that relate details about the topic. While writing, consider your chosen audience. The audience, as well as the theme and purpose, determines the style or voice of your writing. The **style** or **voice** gives your writing its "feel."

▶ **Exercise 1** Create five thesis statements. For each thesis, use one topic and one purpose from the list below. You may repeat a topic to use with a different purpose.

PURPOSES	TOPICS		
to describe	horseback riding	the Navy	painting
to inform	oil	cats	comic books
to narrate	U.S. population	television	the moon
to persuade	*Star Trek*	fairy tales	cars
to instruct	the Civil War	baseball	poetry
to create a mood	coffee	popular music	watches
to entertain	swimming	Michigan	newspaper

Purpose: to describe   **Topic:** moon

To the naked eye, the moon looks like a large wedge of blue cheese.

1. _____

2. _____

3. _____

4. _____

5. _____

Name _____ Class _____ Date _____

▶ **Exercise 2** Write a topic sentence and two supporting sentences for three of the following topics and purposes.

Topic: computers **Purpose:** to instruct

Computers are machines that process and store information.

They consist of a monitor, a keyboard, and the computer itself, which does the processing.

A computer disc stores the information for running the computer and operating programs.

1. **Topic:** your state **Purpose:** to persuade

2. **Topic:** popular music **Purpose:** to inform

3. **Topic:** cars **Purpose:** to describe

308 *Writer's Choice Grammar Workbook 8,* Unit 15

Name _____ Class _____ Date _____

4. Topic: the night sky **Purpose:** to descibe

_____
_____
_____
_____
_____
_____

5. Topic: fads **Purpose:** to amuse

_____
_____
_____
_____
_____
_____

6. Topic: a friend **Purpose:** to narrate

_____
_____
_____
_____
_____
_____

7. Topic: etiquette **Purpose:** to inform

_____
_____
_____
_____
_____
_____

Name _____ Class _____ Date _____

▶ **Exercise 3** Describe a voice or style that would be appropriate for the following audiences.

Type of writing and audience: letter to U.S. senator

Voice or style: formal and respectful

1. Type of writing and audience: a note to a friend

   Voice or style: informal and fun

2. Type of writing and audience: a paper for the American Science Foundation

   Voice or style: formal and persuasive

3. Type of writing and audience: editorial

   Voice or style: persuasive and serious

4. Type of writing and audience: an article for a school newspaper on the gymnastics finals

   Voice or style: factual and informative

5. Type of writing and audience: an apology to a teacher

   Voice or style: sincere and respectful

▶ **Exercise 4** Write a paragraph about a specific change you would like to see in your community. Your audience is made up of political leaders from your community.

Students should focus on a specific area of concern. Paragraphs should be informative, somewhat persuasive, and written in a formal style.

Name _____ Class _____ Date _____

Lesson 97
The Writing Process: Revising

After you complete a first draft, you will want to revise, or improve, your writing. Revising allows you to improve the quality of your sentences and paragraphs. As you revise, check for three things. First, make sure that your paragraphs support your theme. Second, make sure that your organization is logical and that your details support your topic sentences. Third, check for clarity. Your sentences should be clear and logically linked.

▶ **Exercise 1** Rewrite each paragraph, leaving in only the details that support the topic sentence.

1. One of my favorite authors is Toni Morrison, an African American writer who was born in Ohio. Many famous writers were born in Ohio. My favorite book by Morrison is *The Bluest Eye*. It is about a girl who thinks that her horrible life will be better if she can change the color of her eyes. Another one of my favorite writers is Richard Wright. I just finished reading *Song of Solomon*, another of Morrison's award-winning novels.

   One of my favorite authors is Toni Morrison, an African American writer who was born in Ohio. My favorite book by Morrison is *The Bluest Eye*. It is about a girl who thinks that her horrible life will be better if she can change the color of her eyes. I just finished reading *Song of Solomon*, another of Morrison's award-winning novels.

2. Charles stood on the pitcher's mound, staring down at the batter. He fiddled with the ball in his glove, not sure what pitch to throw. The shortstop backed up to the outfield grass, anticipating the play. Charles knew that the outcome of the game could be decided by this one pitch. He couldn't believe that two of his teachers had given tests on the day of the big game. He wound up and fired toward home plate, pouring every ounce of energy into his right arm.

Unit 15, Composition **311**

Name _____ Class _____ Date _____

Charles stood on the pitcher's mound, staring down at the batter. He fiddled with the ball in his glove, not sure what pitch to throw. Charles knew that the outcome of the game could be decided by this one pitch. He wound up and fired toward home plate, pouring every ounce of energy into his right arm.

_____
_____
_____
_____
_____
_____
_____

3. Benjamin's backpack was full of practical camping gear. We got to our campsite and decided the first thing we had to do was build a fire. Sarah went to gather wood, while Benjamin pulled some old newspapers from his backpack and began tearing them into strips. Alicia and Ted cleared a spot on the ground and went searching for rocks to place around the fire. Colorado is known for its abundance of granite rocks. Sarah's mom joked that she had forgotten the matches, but she had just left them in the car. The last time we went camping, we didn't have a fire.

We got to our campsite and decided the first thing we had to do was build a fire. Sarah went to gather wood, while Benjamin pulled some old newspapers from his backpack and began tearing them into strips. Alicia and Ted cleared a spot on the ground and went searching for rocks to place around the fire. Sarah's mom joked that she had forgotten the matches, but she had just left them in the car.

_____
_____
_____
_____
_____
_____
_____

Name _____ Class _____ Date _____

▶ **Exercise 2** Revise the paragraphs so that each sentence is linked logically to the sentence before it. You may have to change the order of the sentences.

1. Those two have known each other since the summer before first grade. Anila and Katie do almost everything together. Katie's family moved to another town when Katie was in the third grade. Six months later they moved back—right next door to Anila. In second grade, the girls made a pact that they would room together in college. They are closer than any other eighth-graders I know.

   Anila and Katie do almost everything together. They are closer than any other eighth-graders I know.

   Those two have known each other since the summer before first grade. In second grade, the girls made a pact that they would room together in college. Katie's family moved to another town when Katie was in the third grade. Six months later they moved back—right next door to Anila.

2. At seven o'clock I eat breakfast with my brother Chuck. I have a routine that I try to follow every morning. I arrive at the bus stop by 7:25, even though the bus doesn't get there until 7:35. I get up at 6:45 and make my bed before I get in the shower. That way, I'm not tempted to crawl back in for five more minutes of sleep. Chuck and I need those ten minutes at the bus stop to talk.

   I have a routine that I try to follow every morning. I get up at 6:45 and make my bed before I get in the shower. That way, I'm not tempted to crawl back in for five more minutes of sleep. At seven o'clock I eat breakfast with my brother, Chuck. I arrive at the bus stop by 7:25, even though the bus doesn't get there until 7:35. Chuck and I need those ten minutes at the bus stop to talk.

Name _____ Class _____ Date _____

3. An example of the proper way to use *lie* is "I need to lie down because I'm not feeling well." I always need to look in a dictionary to see which word to use. An example of the proper way to use *lay* is "Do you want me to lay the clothes on top of the dryer?" I have trouble using the words *lie* and *lay*.

I have trouble using the words *lie* and *lay*. I always need to look in a dictionary to see which word to

use. An example of the proper way to use lie is "I need to *lie* down because I'm not feeling well." An

example of the proper way to use *lay* is "Do you want me to lay the clothes on top of the dryer?"

▶ **Exercise 3** Revise the paragraph below for order and clarity.

Many animals can perform amazing leaps. Only one is the champion jumper of the animal world. If you guessed the kangaroo, you're wrong. It's not even the frog, or grasshopper either. A special elastic material in its rear legs lets the flea make vertical leaps. The distances are astounding. This elastic material is like a tiny spring. It stores energy. Then it is suddenly released when the flea jumps. This gives the flea its stupendous jumping ability. If humans could jump 130 times their own height, they could jump over the Eiffel Tower! The tiny flea, which can jump 130 times its own height, takes the prize.

Many animals can perform amazing leaps, but only one is the champion jumper of the animal world.

That animal is not the kangaroo, frog, or grasshopper. The tiny flea, which can jump 130 times its

own height, takes the prize. Thanks to a special elastic material in its rear legs, the flea makes

vertical leaps of astounding distances. Like a tiny spring, this elastic material stores energy, which is

suddenly released when the flea jumps. This mechanism gives the flea its stupendous jumping

ability. If humans could jump 130 times their own height, they could jump over the Eiffel Tower!

Composition

314 *Writer's Choice Grammar Workbook 8,* Unit 15

Name _____ Class _____ Date _____

Lesson 98
The Writing Process: Editing

After revising your writing to make it clear, you need to edit your work. When you **edit**, you correct errors in grammar, usage, spelling, capitalization, and punctuation. Use the following proofreading marks.

TO:	USE THIS MARK:	EXAMPLES
insert	^ (caret)	cor^rect
delete	ℯ (dele)	theℯ
insert a space	#	all#right
close up a space	⌒	tele‿phone
capitalize	≡	g̲e̲orgia
lower case	/	Ⱬlock
check spelling	⟨ sp ⟩	⟨nucleer⟩ sp
switch order	∽	the store local
indicate new paragraph	¶	...at the end.¶ The winter...

▶ **Exercise 1** Edit each sentence for spelling, punctuation, and capitalization errors.

We won't be abel to make it to philadephia by five o^clock.

1. mike asked Mary to go to a fourth of July picnick.

2. I looked around for her, but she w^as not their.

3. The can⌒oe capsized, making Cecil ⟨angri⟩ sp.

4. In the event of an ⟨emergincy⟩ sp, please exit the b^ilding?.

5. In 1976, he attend⌒ed the university of california.

6. I use A special racket when I^m in a ⟨tournamint⟩ sp.

7. He#made a small down payment with the Ⱬoney he earned mowing mr. kahn's yard.

Unit 15, Composition   315

Name _____ Class _____ Date _____

8. My grandfather owns a store hardware in idaho.

9. Making speeches is the best way to refine your communication skills.

10. I answered the phone, but no one was there.

11. She gave me a note, which I didn't understand.

12. I remember when he came to our school.

13. this Summer I read the book *The Gathering* By Virginia Hamilton.

14. Sante fe, New mexico, is a beautiful spot.

15. Proofread your sentences closely for spelling errors.

16. Raphael's closet was filled with clothes that didn't fit.

17. Alisha's house is on Forest avenue.

18. Can you lend me some money to buy Katherine a valentine's day present?

19. The subway was fourty minutes late on wendesday.

20. I need new glasses.

▶ **Exercise 2** Edit each sentence for spelling, punctuation, capitalization, and grammar.

The fakt that Julia can do this amazes me.

1. He passed the ball in the nick of time.

2. after a while, the thief came back through the window.

3. Symphonic music filled the concert hall.

4. Willie spent thirteen dollors on his Girlfriend.

5. The Smiths bring plenty of of matches when they goes camping.

6. Josie and me are coming down this wekend.

7. i wonder why he didn't bring his sister.

316 *Writer's Choice Grammar Workbook 8*, Unit 15

Name _____ Class _____ Date _____

8. John f. kennedy was a popular president.

9. Did mary called from the university of austin observatory?

10. The secret passage led them too a hiddne room.

11. First pre heat the oven, than bake, for twenty minutes.

12. The countrys landfills are all most full.

13. We had grate time watching the Houston astros.

14. MS. ruiz and I has the same middle name.

15. Maria's Uncle an Aunt live near Mt. Rushmore.

16. There aren't no apples in the refrigerater.

17. After the Midnight movie, they took there time going home.

18. Kalyn and Luisa runs three miles everday.

19. Mr. franklin delivered the letter from mymom on tuesday.

20. Latoya and me explaind the accident to officer Kelton.

▶ **Exercise 3** Edit each paragraph.

1.   One of the most exciting times to watch of these butter flies is in late Winter and early spring. They emerge from hibernation, and you can see them flew about, long before the leafs and flowers blooms. It is interesting to see them feed on the sap from recently cut trees and ranches. Later in spring, the caterpillars begin to hatch.

2.   Lamont arrived and I arrived in Baltimore on March 8. Aunt Glenda and uncle Leon were waiting fore us at the the airprot. They had tickets for a base ball game, so went strait their and then we all three went out to eat at an Jamaican restaurant called Mickey's. Its a day we'll never forget.

Unit 15, Composition 317

Name _____ Class _____ Date _____

3. My friend Kyle and ~~me has~~ I've decided to start a recycling program in our nieghborhood. We've called a meeting on thursday and have invited allof the neighbors. Were going to ask themto save there aluminum, plastic, and glass containers. Every Saturady morning we'll go door-to-door andcollect them. Then, with my stepFather's help, we'll load them into his van. ~~and then~~ after we have a full load, we'll thake them to the recycling bins at madisons grocery.

Name _____ Class _____ Date _____

Lesson 99
The Writing Process: Presenting

After you have completed your writing, it's time to **present** it to your audience. Whether it is a teacher, a family member, or a judge, your audience is something you've been thinking about since the prewriting stage. Your audience has helped determine the style or voice of your writing.

You might present some pieces of writing by handing them to your teacher. You might present other pieces more publicly. For example, you could send a letter you've written to a local newspaper or to your governor, prepare a movie review for the school newspaper, or give a speech to the members of a club. Writers have many ways or places in which to present their work—including newsletters, newspapers, magazines, radio, television, and even the stage and concert hall!

▶ **Exercise 1** Suggest a place in which to present each type of writing described below.

review of an art show at your school __school newspaper or local art magazine__

1. letter complaining about a product that was faulty __company that manufactured product, consumer magazine, or local newspaper editorial page__

2. poem about children __poetry magazine or school newspaper__

3. request for information about water pollution in your community __city water department or local environmental group__

4. humorous song about people who play football __local radio station or a printed football program distributed at local games__

5. research report on the effects of loud music on listeners __science or music magazine__

6. family recipe for holiday cookies __family holiday cards or cooking section of newspaper__

7. public service announcement describing a car wash sponsored by your class __radio, television station, or an announcement placed in local businesses__

8. article describing teen-agers' opinions of a law that raises the driving age __enclosed with a letter to a law-making body or a letter to the editor__

9. biography of someone famous who lives in your city __local newspaper or magazine__

10. review of a children's movie __children's or parents' magazine or newsletter__

Unit 15, Composition **319**

Name _____ Class _____ Date _____

11. campaign speech for student council __students in your class or written version for school__
    __newspaper__

12. request for donations to save a local endangered animal __local clubs or an announcement__
    __placed in local businesses__

13. travel log and slides of your recent trip to Japan __family and friends or travel club or travel__
    __magazine__

▶ **Exercise 2** Choose a form of writing in Exercise 1 that interests you. Write a piece that fits into that category. Then describe your audience and list possible places in which to present your work.

_____
_____
_____
_____
_____
_____
_____
_____
_____
_____
_____
_____
_____

Audience: _____
_____

Places to Present: _____
_____

Name _____ Class _____ Date _____

Lesson 100
The Writing Process: Outlining

Outlining is a way to organize prewriting information before you begin your first draft. The information in an outline is ordered from general to specific. To write an outline, indicate your main topics with roman numerals. Indicate supporting details with capital letters. If you subdivide your supporting details, use regular numbers. If a main topic has subtopics, there must be at least two subtopics. If you divide a subtopic, there must be at least two divisions. An outline of an essay about how to plan a party might begin like this:

I. Things to do before the party
   A. Send invitations
   B. Buy food
      1. Pizza for ten
      2. Plenty of soft drinks
II. Things to do after the party
   A. Take friends home
   B. Clean up

▶ **Exercise 1** Reorganize the topics in the outline so that they are in the proper order.

I. I want to develop better student/adult relations
   A. Why I am running for student council
      1. Redecorate cafeteria
      2. Student/teacher mentor program
   B. Put more student artwork in halls
      1. I want to make school more cheerful
      2. Student suggestion box in office

I. Why I am running for student council

   A. I want to make school more cheerful

      1. Redecorate cafeteria

      2. Put more student artwork in halls

   B. I want to develop better student/adult relations

      1. Student suggestion box in office

      2. Student/teacher mentor program

Name _____ Class _____ Date _____

▶ **Exercise 2** Organize the following topics and details into an outline about Antarctica.

Rarely above 32° F (0° C)
World's lowest temperature recorded here in 1983
Size
Larger than either Europe or Australia
Plants and animals
Large enough to be considered a continent
Coastal waters have large numbers of penguins, seals, and whales
Temperature
Interior has only a few small plants and insects

I. Size

    A. Large enough to be considered a continent

    B. Larger than either Europe or Australia

II. Temperature

    A. Rarely above 32° F (0° C)

    B. World's lowest temperature recorded here in 1983

III. Plants and animals

    A. Interior has only a few small plants and insects

    B. Coastal waters have large numbers of penguins, seals, and whales

▶ **Exercise 3** Prewrite for 10 minutes about a place you have visited. Then construct an organized outline from your notes.

_____
_____
_____
_____
_____
_____
_____
_____
_____
_____
_____

Name _____ Class _____ Date _____

Lesson 101
Writing Effective Sentences

To capture and keep your reader's attention, you need to use a variety of sentence types in your writing. Vary the length of your sentences by making some long and some short. This helps to create a sound and a rhythm in your writing that will hold your reader's interest. Too many short sentences make your writing sound choppy. Too many long sentences make your writing harder to follow. Also, vary the order of words and phrases in sentences. Instead of always starting with the subject and verb, try starting with a phrase. You can also create variety by combining two sentences that express the same idea into one sentence.

Most of your sentences will be in the **active voice** with the subject performing the action. For example, **"Hal baked the cake"** is in the active voice. Sentences written in the **passive voice** have less direct action: **"The cake was baked by Hal."** Both examples give the same information, but the sentence written in the active voice is more direct and more interesting than the one written in the passive voice. Generally, use passive voice only when you do not know or do not want to state who or what is performing the action.

▶ **Exercise 1** Rewrite each sentence. Add details and use active voice to make each sentence more interesting. **Answers will vary.**

The present was given to me by my aunt. **Aunt Carlotta gave me a copy of my favorite book, autographed by the author.**

1. Matt and his dad go on vacation together.
   _____
   _____

2. Principal Hoffman had been tricked.
   _____
   _____

3. The bulletin board fell down from the wall.
   _____
   _____

Name _____ Class _____ Date _____

4. Alton works on computers.

5. The Beatles were a band that had many hit songs.

6. Janet is employed at a coffee house.

7. The house lights were turned on by Lucinda.

8. The new year was celebrated by all of us.

9. Gabriel plays guitar.

10. The pilot amused the passengers.

▶ **Exercise 2** In each sentence determine whether the verb is in the active voice or in the passive voice. Rewrite the sentence to be in the opposite voice.

Sixteen candles decorated the cake. **active; The cake was decorated with sixteen candles.**

1. The letter was written by Yori. **passive; Yori wrote the letter.**
2. The painting was stolen by the thief. **passive; The thief stole the painting.**
3. The car was driven by Frederick. **passive; Frederick drove the car.**
4. Anthony was hit by a car. **passive; The car hit Anthony.**

Name _____ Class _____ Date _____

5. Jeanine worked on her paper. **active; The paper was worked on by Jeanine.**
6. The glasses were broken by the server. **passive; The server broke the glasses.**
7. He put the clothes there last week. **active; The clothes were put there by him last week.**
8. Mr. Hall teaches history. **active; History is taught by Mr. Hall.**
9. The gift was accepted by Tricia. **passive; Tricia accepted the gift.**
10. Mike figured out the strategy. **active; The strategy was figured out by Mike.**
11. The soldiers attacked the fort. **active; The fort was attacked by the soldiers.**
12. Alvin broke the compass. **active; The compass was broken by Alvin.**
13. Aretha paddled the canoe down the river. **active; The canoe was paddled down the river by Aretha.**
14. The radio was turned on by Veronica. **passive; Veronica turned on the radio.**
15. The kiln was fired by Mrs. Pei. **passive; Mrs. Pei fired the kiln.**

▶ **Exercise 3** Combine each set of three sentences to make one sentence that is more effective. **Sentences will vary.**

    a. All living things are made of cells.
    b. Protozoans are single-celled animals.
    c. Humans have millions of cells.

Living things can be single-celled, like protozoans, or they can have many millions of cells like humans.

1. a. Looking for fossils is fun.
   b. Fossils can be thousands of years old.
   c. Fossils are the remains of ancient animals and plants.

It is fun to look for fossils when you realize that they are the remains of animals and plants that lived thousands of years ago.

2. a. Newspapers are filled with information.
   b. Most newspapers cost less than a dollar.
   c. I like reading newspapers.

I like reading newspapers, because they are filled with information and usually cost less than a dollar.

3. a. Cars are a convenient form of transportation.
   b. Cars emit exhaust.
   c. Exhaust from cars causes air pollution.

   Although cars are a convenient form of transportation, their exhaust causes air pollution.

4. a. Twelve people volunteered.
   b. Six said they could work part time.
   c. Six said they could work full time.

   Of the twelve volunteers, six said they could work part time and six said they could work full time.

5. a. I turn on the radio every day.
   b. There are many radio stations.
   c. I like to listen to rock music.

   There are many radio stations, but when I turn on the radio I like to listen to rock music.

6. a. I want to buy a yearbook.
   b. The yearbooks are ten dollars this year.
   c. I've been saving money.

   I'm saving ten dollars so that I can buy a yearbook.

7. a. My friend's name is Roscoe.
   b. We're going to the concert.
   c. We were able to get front-row seats.

   My friend Roscoe and I have front-row seats for the concert.

8. a. On Saturday, I have to baby-sit for my brother.
   b. She invited me to the dance Saturday.
   c. How can I tell her?

   How can I tell her I can't go to the dance with her on Saturday because I have to baby-sit for my brother?

9. a. My dog's name is Big Ben.
   b. He loves to swim.
   c. Big Ben is a golden retriever.

   My golden retriever, Big Ben, loves to swim.

10. a. Many people suffer from stress.
    b. Stress causes heart disease.
    c. High blood pressure can be a sign of stress.

    Many people suffer from stress, which causes heart disease and high blood pressure.

Name _____ Class _____ Date _____

Lesson 102
Building Paragraphs

Sentences in a paragraph can be arranged in different ways. **Chronological order** places events in the order in which they happened. **Spatial order** is the way that objects appear and relate to each other, as in a room or on a street. **Compare/contrast order** shows similarities and differences between objects or ideas.

The following paragraphs use the same idea, but the first uses compare/contrast order, the second uses spatial order, and the third uses chronological order.

    I had trouble deciding between the two shirts. I liked the first shirt because it was my favorite color and fit nicely. However, it was just too expensive. The second shirt was five dollars cheaper and almost as nice as the first, so I bought it instead.

    The pullover shirt I bought has swirls of white and blue on a red background. It has a blue knitted collar and short sleeves with blue knitted cuffs. At the neckline are three white buttons.

    Before I buy a new shirt, I follow a special routine. First, I look for at least three shirts I want to try on. Then I go back to the dressing room and put each one on in front of the mirror. After I've done that, I ask my friend to give me his opinion.

▶ **Exercise 1** Identify the type of order used in each sentence. Write *CC* for compare/contrast order, *S* for spatial order, or *CH* for chronological order.

CH   Sew the shoulder seams before the side seams.

CC   1. Sports cars are better than luxury cars when it comes to performance.

S   2. While Mel's place was just next door, the only way to get there from here was down the stairs and around the fence.

S   3. The lake was covered with so many geese that we had trouble seeing the tiny rowboat.

CH   4. On Tuesday, the council voted on the referendum, but it was not until Friday that they received the court order.

S   5. In the entrance to the museum sat a large marble statue surrounded by gilded paintings.

CC   6. The offices of both Findlay and Brown are run like well-oiled machines.

CH   7. He was born in 1922, which was before the Great Depression.

CC   8. Evergreen trees stay green all year, but deciduous trees lose their leaves in winter.

| CH | 9. First, postal workers sort the letters by zip code according to state, and then they file them in the appropriate mail slots. |

| S | 10. Gale's upstairs apartment overlooked the park, and as you walk in, you get a breathtaking view through her picture window. |

▶ **Exercise 2** Number the following sentences in chronological order.

__5__ Explain to her that you want the seats my brother reserved for us.

__1__ Follow these steps when you call to order our concert tickets.

__4__ When she comes to the phone, tell her that I told you to call.

__6__ Call and let me know when we can pick them up.

__3__ Ask to speak to Rachel.

__2__ Call the first of the three numbers listed in the phone book.

▶ **Exercise 3** Use compare/contrast order to write a paragraph about one of the following topics: your favorite relative, your last year in school compared to this year in school; the effect of pollution on the area where you live.

328 *Writer's Choice Grammar Workbook 8,* Unit 15

Name _____ Class _____ Date _____

▶ **Exercise 4** Write three short paragraphs about your favorite store or restaurant. Use spatial order in your first paragraph, chronological order in your second paragraph, and compare/contrast order in your third paragraph.

Name _____ Class _____ Date _____

▶ **Exercise 5** **Arrange these sentencers in chronological order.**

__4__ These chemicals stimulate the nerves, which, in turn, send messages to the brain.

__1__ Your tongue is covered with tiny bumps, small ones toward the front, larger ones toward the back.

__3__ When you eat something, chemicals in the food touch the tips of the nerve endings in the taste buds.

__5__ The experience of flavor is created by the combination of taste and the smell of the food.

__2__ Inside these approximately 9000 bumps are tiny bundles of nerves called taste buds.

Name _____ Class _____ Date _____

Lesson 103
Paragraph Ordering

Revising a first draft includes checking the unity, or **coherence**, of paragraphs. Open each paragraph with a topic sentence that states the main idea. Follow it with supporting sentences that back up that idea. Connect the sentences in a clear and logical way. Use words and phrases called **transitions** to link the sentences so they flow naturally. The following are some common transition words: *and, also, but, however, next, after, then, finally, since, therefore*. Sometimes you can organize multiple points using words like *first, second*, or *on the other hand*. Paragraphs in a paper should be coherent in the same way sentences in a paragraph should be coherent. Use transitions to link paragraphs.

▶ **Exercise 1** Underline the sentence in each paragraph that should be the topic sentence.

1. First, ask your neighbors if they have any odd jobs you can do. You might be able to help a neighbor with a garden, baby-sit, or take care of someone's pet while he or she is on vacation. Another way to earn money is to have a yard sale. <u>If you are short on cash during your summer vacation, here are some ways to earn money.</u> You and your friends can gather old clothes or household items that are no longer needed and share the profits from the sale.

2. The first stage is infancy. The infancy stage is the first year of a child's life. In the second stage, the child is called a toddler. The toddler stage is from ages one to three. Between the ages of three and five, a child is called a preschooler. <u>There are three stages of early childhood.</u>

3. I have to decide whether to join the volleyball team or the basketball team. I can't play on both teams because the teams practice on the same days. I played on the volleyball team last year, so it might be fun to do something different this year. <u>Before the end of the day, I have to make a tough decision.</u> On the other hand, I know more people on the volleyball team.

Unit 15, Composition **331**

Name _____ Class _____ Date _____

Exercise 2 Write three cohesive and unified paragraphs, using the given facts. Add details to make each paragraph more interesting.

1. Jerome does volunteer work.
   He volunteers at the local children's hospital.
   He helps to plan play-time activities for the young children.
   Donnella is his favorite patient.

   _____
   _____
   _____
   _____
   _____
   _____
   _____

2. Teresa and I are planning a surprise party.
   Kira will be twelve this Saturday.
   Teresa is going to take her somewhere.
   We're going to decorate the house while she's gone.
   She'll be surprised when she walks through the door.
   Everyone will be hiding inside the house.

   _____
   _____
   _____
   _____
   _____
   _____
   _____
   _____
   _____

3. To find out what's happening in the world, I can read the newspaper or watch the news on television.
I can't decide whether I get more information from the newspaper or television.
On television, I can see what things look like.
News stories are shorter on television because the time is limited.
Newspapers give me more information because they don't have to worry about time.
I can read newspapers whenever I want to during the day.

▶ **Exercise 3** Each sentence below represents the topic sentence of a paragraph about Martin's Lake. Check the sentence that best continues the story started in paragraph one.

Paragraph One: Nothing cools me off better on a hot summer day than bobbing around in Martin's Lake. Let the sun burn off my pale shell, as long as there's cool refreshing pond water to rinse away the heat!

_____ In the winter, dozens of ice skaters glide across the lake or hover around the fire barrel.

_____ Citizens of Martinsville enjoy night fishing at the lake.

✔ My summer romance with Martin's Lake began when I was twelve.

_____ A gaggle of geese honk out their warnings to lake visitors.

Unit 15, Composition 333

Name _____ Class _____ Date _____

▶ **Exercise 4** Write a two-paragraph announcement about an upcoming event at your school. Make sure details are presented in proper chronological order and that paragraphs one and two are clearly linked.

Lesson 104
Personal Letters: Formal

A **personal letter** is often a letter to a friend or relative, an invitation, or a thank-you note. Different situations call for different kinds of personal letters. A letter to an adult relative or an adult acquaintance will probably have a different tone and style of writing than a letter to a friend or someone your own age. A letter to an adult is usually more formal. Avoid slang when writing formal letters, and show respect for your reader. However, a formal letter does not have to be uninteresting. Use descriptive language in a formal letter, and include some personal information. If you are writing a thank-you note, include a detailed description of the gift and what you intend to do with it.

Dear Uncle Otis,

    Thank you for your wonderful birthday present. The portable stereo you gave me is something I have been hoping for. I plan on taking it to my aerobics class to replace the old radio my instructor uses. I can also take it outside while I practice basketball.
    I hope that you and Aunt Florence are doing well, and I hope that you can come see me play when the basketball season begins. I look forward to seeing you at Thanksgiving.
    Again, thank you for the thoughtful present.

Love,
Rhonda

▶ **Exercise 1** Revise the following letter to make its style more formal.

Hey Grandma,

    How's it going? Thanks for throwing me that awesome birthday party. It was a real blow-out! My friends thought you guys were really cool, even though you're older.
    Man, that cake you made was so great, and even though I thought the games you and Mom made up were going to be really goofy, my friends were into them!
    Thanks again, you're the greatest.

See ya,
Chris

Name _____ Class _____ Date _____

Dear Grandma,

 Thank you for having that great birthday party for me. My friends and I had a wonderful time. All of my friends thought Mom and you were great.

 The cake you baked was delicious, and the games you and Mom made up were fun. In fact, my friends and I are going to play those same games the next time we all get together.

 Thanks again for making it such a good birthday.

Love,

 Chris

▶ **Exercise 2** Write either a formal letter to a relative, inviting him or her to a school activity, or a formal letter to a teacher, counselor, or coach expressing thanks for something special she or he did.

Name _____ Class _____ Date _____

Lesson 105
Personal Letters: Informal

Informal letters are a good way to keep in touch with friends and relatives close to your own age. You might send an informal letter to a pen pal or write an informal letter on a postcard. In an informal letter, you can use slang and language that is more conversational in tone.

▶ **Exercise 1** Write a letter to a friend who has moved to another city or town. Explain what you have been doing while your friend has been away.

_____
_____
_____
_____
_____
_____
_____
_____
_____
_____
_____
_____
_____
_____
_____
_____
_____
_____
_____
_____

Unit 15, Composition

Name _____ Class _____ Date _____

▶ **Exercise 2** Write a postcard to a relative who is close to your age. Imagine that you are on vacation in the town, city, or area where you live. Describe what it looks like and what there is to do.

_____
_____
_____
_____
_____
_____
_____
_____
_____
_____

▶ **Exercise 3** Write a postcard to a friend describing a place you have been to that your friend has not visited.

_____
_____
_____
_____
_____
_____
_____
_____
_____
_____

Name _____ Class _____ Date _____

Lesson 106
Business Letters: Letters of Request or of Complaint

A **letter of request** is a letter asking for information or service. It is written in a formal style. When writing a letter of request, it is important to be clear and courteous. Explain what you need and why you need it. Be sure to provide the reader with enough information to answer your request.

▶ **Exercise 1** Revise the following letter of request.

Ms. Eckhart:
I need more information about that program of yours, the Youth Recycling Initiative. I'm real good with recycling stuff, I know alot about it. I'd like to do some work for you because maybe someday I'll get into recycling as a career. So please send me some information, and I hope we can work together.
Thanks,
Emmett Turner

Dear Ms. Eckhart:

I am interested in joining your Youth Recycling Initiative and would like more information on your program. I have studied our community's recycling efforts, and I think I could contribute something useful to the program. I am thinking about a career in a field that is related to recycling, and this program would be a good opportunity to learn more about it. Please send me more information on your program. My address is 2211 Stratford Street, Charleston, South Carolina 12345. I can also be reached by telephone at 555-4321.

Sincerely,

Emmett Turner

Unit 15, Composition **339**

Name _____ Class _____ Date _____

A **letter of complaint** is a letter informing someone of a problem or a concern. It is sometimes a request for action. Even though you may be upset when writing such a letter, you do not want to offend your reader. The letter should be reasonable, clear, and concise. Explain the problem and how you wish the reader to respond to it.

▶ **Exercise 2** Revise the following letter of complaint.

Restaurant Manager
Torito's
531 Smith Rd.
Lexington, KY 40516

April 3, 1996
Restaurant Manager,
What's up with your price changes? Are you trying to keep kids out? We've been giving you all this business after school for two years, and this is the thanks we get? Boy, am I mad!
I tell you, you better lower your prices again! We're all going to go somewhere else if you don't, and then you'll be sorry when you go out of business and you're poor and broke.
With anger,
Jill and Billy

Dear Restaurant Manager:

As loyal customers for the last two years, we are upset with your decision to raise all of your menu prices. My friends and I enjoy coming to your restaurant after school, and now we are not sure we can afford to do that.

Perhaps you could increase the size of your portions, or create a "value meal" section on your menu.

We want to continue coming to your restaurant because you have always treated students well. We hope you will take our limited budgets into consideration and adjust your prices.

Sincerely,

Jill McDougal and Bill Lee

340 *Writer's Choice Grammar Workbook 8*, Unit 15

Name _____ Class _____ Date _____

Lesson 107
Business Letters: Stating Your Opinion

An **opinion letter** states your view of a subject. Audiences for an opinion letter might include a newspaper's editors and readers, government officials, leaders of organizations, or business people. When writing an opinion letter, your tone should be formal. A good opinion letter also contains plenty of facts to support your opinion.

The following is an example of a brief, but effective, opinion letter:

Sports Editor
Daily Chronicle
1574 Clarence Dr.
Ion, WA 43125

July 16, 1996

Dear Editor:
Not only is Clarence Williams a football hero, but he is a hero in community service as well. One of your writers recently made the mistake of assuming that Clarence is not involved in making this community a better place. Just because Clarence won't blow his own horn, it doesn't mean he's not involved with the community.
Clarence established the Big Red Fund, which challenges 3,000 students in 7 junior high schools to stay in school and study hard. Clarence has visited the schools and donated money for computers and science laboratory equipment. Also, Clarence worked with a local food bank to deliver meals to 100 needy families at Christmas.
Although he receives no media attention for his deeds, Clarence Williams is indeed making a contribution to our community.

Sincerely,
Judy O'Rourke

▶ **Exercise 1** Revise the following opinion letter. Add details if necessary.

Dear Congressman Riley,
I can't believe you voted against more funding for community parks! How ridiculous! We need more money here in your hometown for our local park. Maybe if you were here more often you would know that. Maybe you can still do something about it. Lots of people and especially kids are counting on you.
Local businesses won't donate money. They say there are more important things to spend

money on in this town. And they won't listen to kids anyway, and the adults here aren't doing anything!

Help!

Aminah Wilson

The Honorable David Riley

The State House

15 North High Street

Atlanta, Georgia 62110

September 28, 1996

Dear Congressman Riley:

Every day I ride my bicycle past shabby, littered Town Park. Our once-beautiful park is filled with weeds, broken playground equipment, and graffiti. I am disappointed in you for voting against additional funding for community parks. I believe that elected officials should consider the needs of voters in their community before voting on a bill. I do not think that you did that. You could have asked adults and children to find out how much the parks mean to them before casting a vote on the bill. Local business leaders did donate some money toward renovating the park, but it simply was not enough.

In the future, I hope you will consider the needs of the citizens you represent when you cast your vote.

Sincerely,

Aminah Wilson

▶ **Exercise 2** Imagine that your school has suggested fining parents if their children skip school. Develop an opinion on this issue, weighing the good points and bad points. Then write an opinion letter to the principal of the school.

Index

Index

A

A, an (usage), 8, 123
A, an, the (articles), 8, 123
    diagraming, 205
Abbreviations, correct use of, 18–19, 273
Abstract nouns, defined, 4, 63
Accept, except, 12, 227
Action verbs, defined, 4, 75
Active voice, explained, 6, 97
    in writing, 323
Adjective clauses, 9, 159
    diagraming, 213
    essential, 161
    nonessential, 40, 161
Adjective phrases
    as infinitive phrases, 179
    as participial phrases, 10, 171
    as prepositional phrases, 145
Adjectives, defined, 7–8, 121, 123, 125, 127, 133
    articles as, 8, 123
    avoiding errors in, 36–37, 133
    comparative forms, 7–8, 36–37, 125
    demonstrative, 127
    diagraming, 205
    hyphen in compound, 271
    as participles, 10, 121, 171
    predicate, 82, 121
    proper, 8, 124
    superlative forms, 7–8, 36–37, 125
Adverb clauses, 9, 40, 163
    diagraming, 213
Adverb phrases
    as infinitive phrases, 179
    as prepositional phrases, 145
Adverbs, defined, 8, 129
    avoiding errors in, 8, 133, 135
    comparative forms, 8, 131
    conjunctive, 9, 149
    diagraming, 205
    intensifiers, 129
    negative words as, 8, 135
    superlative forms, 8, 131
Agreement
    pronoun-antecedent, 7, 34, 109
    subject-verb, 11, 28–31, 187, 189, 191, 193, 195
        and collective nouns, 191
        and compound subjects, 11, 30–31, 195
        and indefinite pronouns, 11, 29, 193
        and intervening prepositional phrases, 11, 28, 189
        in inverted sentences, 11, 28–29, 189
        and special subjects, 11, 191
        with titles, 11, 191
All ready, already, 12, 227
All together, altogether, 12, 227
A lot, not *alot,* 12, 227
Already, all ready, 12, 227
Altogether, all together, 12, 227
Among, between, 12, 229
Antecedents, defined, 7, 109
    agreement of pronouns with, 7, 34, 109
    clear pronoun reference, 7, 111
Antonyms, 289
Apostrophes, rules for using, 17–18, 41–43, 69, 269
    in contractions, 18, 69, 269
    in possessive nouns and pronouns, 17, 41–43, 65, 69, 269
    in plurals, 17, 42, 69, 269
Appositive phrases, 10, 39, 71
Appositives, defined, 10, 71
Articles, 8, 123
Audience, in writing, 20, 303
Auxiliary verbs, defined, 4, 89

B

Bad, badly, 133
Bad, worse, worst, 36, 125
Beside, besides, 12, 229
Between, among, 12, 229
Bring, take, 12, 229
Business letters, 21–22, 339–341
    letters of complaint, 340
    letters of request, 22, 339
    opinion letters, 22, 341
But
    preposition, 8
    coordinating conjunction, 9, 147

C

Can, may, 12, 229
Capitalization, rules for, 14–15, 44, 243, 245, 247, 249, 273
    of abbreviations, 15, 245, 273
    in direct quotations, 14, 44, 243
    in family names and titles of persons, 15, 245
    of first words of sentences, 14, 47, 243
    of names of places, 15, 247
    of proper adjectives, 15, 44, 249
    of proper nouns, 3, 15, 44, 245, 247, 249
    of salutations and closings of letters, 14, 243
Case of pronouns, 6, 107
Choose, chose, 12, 229
Chronological order, 20, 327
Clauses, defined, 9–10, 155, 157, 159, 161, 163, 165
    See also Adjective clauses, Adverb clauses, Dependent clauses, Independent clauses, Main clauses, Noun clauses, Subordinate clauses
Clue words, 19, 283
Coherence, of paragraphs, 331
Collective nouns, defined, 4, 67, 191
    agreement of verb with, 67, 191
Colons, rules, 17, 265
Commas, rules, 16, 38–40, 257, 259, 261, 263
    with addresses and dates, 16, 261
    and adjective clauses, 16, 40, 259
    and adverb clauses, 16, 40, 259
    with appositives, 16, 39, 71, 257
    and compound sentences, 16, 57, 259
    after conjunctive adverbs, 9, 16, 149, 257
    in direct address, 16, 257
    in direct quotations, 17, 38–39, 263
    and introductory phrases, 16, 257
    with nonessential elements, 16, 39–40, 71, 161, 257, 259
    after salutations and closes in letters, 16, 263
    in a series, 16, 38, 257
    with titles, 18, 261
Common nouns, defined, 3, 61

Comparative form, modifiers, 7–8, 36–37, 125, 131
Compare/contrast order, 20, 327
Comparison
　of adjectives, 7–8, 125
　of adverbs, 8, 131
　irregular, 8, 36, 125, 131
Complements
　direct objects, 6, 77, 175, 179
　indirect objects, 4, 79
　subject, 82
Complete predicates, defined, 3, 53
Complete subjects, defined, 3, 53
Complex sentences, defined, 10, 157
　diagraming, 213, 215
Compound elements
　nouns, 20, 65
　numbers, hyphens in, 271
　predicates, 3, 55
　　diagraming, 209
　prepositions, 141
　sentences, 10, 57, 155
　　diagraming, 211
　subjects, 3, 55, 147, 195
　　diagraming, 209
Concrete nouns, defined, 4, 63
Conjunctions, defined, 9,
　conjunctive adverbs, 9, 149
　coordinating, 9, 27, 147, 195
　　diagraming, 209, 211
　correlative, 9, 147, 195
　list, 9
　subordinating, 9, 163
Conjunctive adverbs, 9, 149
Context clues, 19, 283
Contractions, 18, 43, 69, 135, 269
Conversations, punctuating, 267
Coordinating conjunctions, 9, 27, 147, 195
Correlative conjunctions, 9, 147, 195

D

Dashes, 18, 271
Dates, punctuating, 261
Declarative sentences, defined, 10, 47, 255
　diagraming, 201
Degrees of form (comparison), 7–8, 125, 131
Demonstrative adjectives, 127
Demonstrative pronouns, 6, 117, 127
Dependent (subordinate) clauses, 9–10, 157, 159, 161, 163, 165
　punctuating, 259

Diagraming Sentences
　adjective clauses, 213
　adjectives, 205
　adverb clauses, 213
　adverbs, 205
　compound sentence parts, 209
　compound sentences, 211
　declarative, 201
　direct objects, 203
　exclamatory, 201
　gerunds, gerund phrases, 217
　imperative, 201
　indirect objects, 203
　infinitives, infinitive phrases, 219
　interrogative, 201
　noun clauses, 215
　participles, participial phrases, 217
　predicate nouns and adjectives, 203
　predicates, 201, 209
　prepositional phrases, 207
　complex sentences, 213, 215
　　adjective clauses, 213
　　adverb clauses, 213
　　noun clauses, 215
　subjects, 201, 209
　verbals, 217, 219
Direct objects, defined, 4, 6, 77
　diagraming, 203
　gerunds as, 175
　infinitives as, 179
Double negatives, avoiding, 8, 135
Drafting, 20, 307
　chronological order, 20, 327
　compare/contract order, 20, 327
　practice, 307–310
　spatial order, 20, 327
　style, voice, 307
　theme, 307
　thesis statement, 307
　topic sentence and related sentences, 307

E

Each, agreement with, 193
Editing, 21, 315
　proofreading marks, 315
Either, agreement with, 195
Emphatic verbs, defined, 6
Except, accept, 12, 227
Exclamation points, 16, 49, 255
　quotation marks and, 17, 267
Exclamatory sentences, defined, 10, 49, 255

　diagraming, 201

F

Fewer, less, 12, 229
Formally, formerly, 13, 231
Fragments, sentence, 24–25, 51
Freewriting, 20, 303

G

Gerund phrases, defined, 11, 175
Gerunds, defined, 11, 175
Good, better, best, 36, 125
Good, well, 125, 133

H

Helping verbs, 4, 89
Homographs, 291
Homophones, 291
Hyphens, rules, 18, 271

I

Imperative sentences, defined, 10, 49, 255
　diagraming, 201
In, into, 13, 231
Indefinite pronouns, defined, 6, 29, 113, 193
　list, 11, 113, 193
Independent (main) clauses, 9–10, 155, 157
Indirect objects, defined, 4, 79
　diagraming, 203
Indirect quotations, 243
Infinitive phrases, defined, 11, 179
　diagraming, 219
Infinitives, defined, 11, 179
　diagraming, 219
　as nouns, 11, 179
Inquiry, letters of, 339
Inside addresses in letters, 21–22
Intensifiers, 129
Intensive pronouns, 6, 115
Interjections, defined, 9, 150, 255
　list, 150
Interrogative pronouns, defined, 6, 117
Interrogative sentences, defined, 10, 47, 255
　diagraming, 201
Into, in, 13, 231
Intransitive verbs, defined, 4, 77
Inverted order in sentences, 3, 11, 28–29
Irregular verbs, 5, 32–33, 99, 101
Italics, 17, 267
Its, it's, 13, 43, 231

Index **345**

L

Lay, lie, 13, 231
Learn, teach, 13, 231
Leave, let, 13, 233
Less, fewer, 12, 229
Let, leave, 13, 233
Letter writing, 21–22, 335, 337, 339, 341
    business, 21–22, 339–341
        letters of complaint, 340
        letters of request, 22, 339
        opinion letters, 22, 341
    personal, 21–22, 335, 337
        formal, 335
        informal, 337
    See also Business letters, Personal letters
Lie, lay, 13, 231
Linking verbs, 4, 81–82
Loose, lose, 13, 233

M

Main (independent) clauses, 9–10, 155, 157
Many, much, 13, 233
May, can, 12, 229
Modifiers
    adjective clauses, 9, 159, 161
    adjectives, 7–8, 121, 123, 125, 127, 133
    adverb clauses, 9, 163
    adverbs, 8, 129, 131, 133, 135
    comparisons, degrees, 7–8, 125, 131
    comparisons, double and incomplete, 8
    comparisons, irregular, 8, 36, 125, 131
Much, many, 13, 233

N

Negatives, double, avoiding, 8, 135
Negative words as adverbs, 8, 135
Neither, agreement with, 30–31, 147, 195
Nominative case, pronouns in the, 6
Nor, in compound sentences, 30–31, 147, 195
Noun clauses, 9, 165
    diagraming, 215
Nouns, defined, 3–4, 61, 63, 65, 67, 191
    abstract, 4, 63
    as appositives, 71
    collective, 4, 67, 191
    common, 3, 61
    compound, 20, 65
    concrete, 4, 63
    contractions, 69
    as gerunds, 175
    as indirect objects, 79
    as infinitives, 179
    as objects of prepositions, 142
    plurals, 3, 20, 65, 69
    possessive, 4, 41–43, 65, 69
    predicate, 82
    proper, 3, 61, 245, 247, 249
    singular, 3
    as subjects, simple and complete, 3, 53
Numbers and numerals, 18–19, 275
    and hyphens, 271

O

Objective case, pronouns, 6, 107, 111, 143
Objects
    direct, 4, 6, 77, 175, 179, 203
    indirect, 4, 79, 203
    of prepositions, 10, 142–143
Outlines, writing, 21, 321
    sentence outlines, 21
    topic outlines, 21, 321

P

Paragraphs, building, 20, 327, 331
    chronological order, 20, 327
    compare/contrast order, 20, 327
    spatial order, 20, 327
    transitions in, 331
Paragraphs, ordering, 20, 331
    coherence, 331
    transitions, 331
    unity, 331
Parentheses, 18, 271
    punctuation with, 18
Participial phrases, defined, 10, 173
    comma after, 257
    diagraming, 217
    practice, 173–174
Participles, defined, 10, 33, 171
    as adjectives, 10, 121, 171
    diagraming, 217
    as verbs, 171
Passive voice, 6, 97, 323
Periods, rules, 15, 47, 49, 255
Personal letters, 21–22, 335, 337
    formal, 335
    informal, 337
Personal pronouns, defined, 6, 34, 107
    cases, 6, 107
    first person, 6
    intensive, 6, 115
    list, 6, 107
    as objects, 6, 35, 107, 111
    possessive, 6, 42–43, 113
    reflexive, 6, 115
    second person, 6
    as subjects, 6, 34–35, 107, 111
    third person, 6
Phrases, defined, 10-11
    See also Appositive phrases, Gerund phrases, Infinitive phrases, Participial phrases, Prepositional phrases, Verbal phrases
Plural nouns, 3, 20, 65, 69
Plurals, spelling of, 20, 65, 296
Possessive apostrophes, 17, 41–43, 65, 269
Possessive nouns, 4, 17, 41–43, 65, 69
Possessive pronouns, 6, 42–43, 113
Precede, proceed, 13, 233
Predicate adjective, defined, 81–82, 121
    diagraming, 203
Predicate noun, defined, 81–82
    diagraming, 203
Predicates
    complete, 3, 51, 53
    compound, 3, 55
    diagraming, 201, 209
    simple, 3, 53
Prefixes, 19, 287, 293
Prepositional phrases, defined, 10, 142
    diagraming, 207
    as adjectives, 145
    as adverbs, 145
    object of the preposition, 10, 142–143
Prepositions, defined, 8, 141
    compound, 8, 141
    list, 8, 141
Presentation, of writing, 21, 319
Prewriting, 20, 303
    choose a topic, 20, 303
    determine the audience, 20, 303
    determine the purpose, 20, 303
    freewriting, 20, 303
    practice, 303–306
Principal parts of verbs, 4–5, 89, 99, 101
Proceed, precede, 13, 233
Progressive verbs, 6, 91, 95
Pronouns, defined, 6, 107

antecedents of, 7, 34, 109
agreement with, 11, 29, 113, 193
as objects of prepositions, 111, 143
cases of, 6, 107
declension of, 6–7, 107
demonstrative, 6, 117, 127
first person, 6
in incomplete comparisons, 111
indefinite, 6, 11, 29, 113, 193
intensive, 6, 115
interrogative, 6, 117
number of, 6, 107
as objects, 6, 107, 111, 143
personal, 6, 34, 107
possessive, 6, 42–43, 113
reflexive, 6, 115
relative, 6, 159
second person, 6
as subjects, 6, 34–35, 107, 111,
third person, 6
who, whom, 7, 143
Proofreading, 21, 315
marks, 315
Proper adjectives, 8, 15, 124, 249
Proper nouns, defined, 3, 61, 245
Punctuation rules. *See specific types.*
Purpose, in writing, 20, 303

Q

Question marks, 15, 47, 255
and quotation marks, 17, 267
Quiet, quite, 13, 233
Quotation marks, 17, 267–268
with colons or semicolons, 17
with commas or periods, 17, 267
in direct quotations, 17, 38–39, 267–268
with question marks or exclamation points, 17, 267
within a quotation, 17
with titles of short works, 17, 267
Quotations, capitalizing, 14, 44, 243

R

Raise, rise, 13, 233
Reflexive pronouns, 6, 115
Regular verbs, 4–6, 89, 91, 93, 95, 97
Relative pronouns, 6, 159
Revising, 20, 311
coherence, 331
Rise, raise, 13, 233
Roots of words, 19, 285
Run-on sentences, 26–27, 57

S

Semicolons, 16, 155, 265
Sentence, defined, 47, 49
Sentence fragments, 24–25, 51
Sentence outlines, 21
Sentence structure
complex, 10, 157
compound, 10, 57, 155
simple, 10, 57, 155
Sentences, effective, 323
active voice, 6, 97, 323
varied length, 323
varied structure, 323
Sentences, kinds of
declarative, 10, 47, 201, 255
exclamatory, 10, 49, 201, 255
imperative, 10, 49, 201, 255
interrogative, 10, 47, 201, 255
Sentences, run-on, 26–27, 57
Series
commas in, 16, 38, 257
colon before, 17, 265
Set, sit, 14, 233
Simple predicates, defined, 3, 53
diagraming, 201
Simple sentences, defined, 10, 57, 155
Simple subjects, defined, 3, 53
diagraming, 201
Singular nouns, 3
Sit, set, 14, 233
Spatial order, 20, 327
Spelling
adding *-ly* and *-ness,* 20, 295
doubling the final consonant, 19, 295
forming compound words, 20, 295
of plural nouns, 20, 296
of prefixes, 19, 293
of suffixes, 19, 294–295
of *ie* and *ei,* 19, 293
of unstressed vowels, 19, 293
Subject complements, 82
Subject-verb agreement, 11, 28–31, 187, 189, 191, 193, 195
and collective nouns, 191
and compound subjects, 11, 30–31, 195
and indefinite pronouns, 11, 29, 193
and intervening prepositional phrases, 11, 28, 189–190, 193
in inverted sentences, 11, 28, 189
and special subjects, 11, 191
with titles, 11, 191

Subjects
agreement of verb with, 11, 28–31, 187, 189, 191, 193, 195
complete, 3, 51, 53
compound, 3, 55, 147, 195
diagraming, 209
gerunds as, 11, 175
diagraming, 217
infinitives as, 11, 179
diagraming, 219
simple, 3, 53
diagraming, 201
Subordinate (dependent) clauses, 9–10, 157, 159, 161, 163, 165
punctuating, 259
Subordinating conjunctions, 9, 163
Suffixes, 19–20, 287, 294
Superlative form, modifiers, 7–8, 37, 125, 131
Synonyms, 289

T

Take, bring, 12, 229
Teach, learn, 13, 231
Tenses, defined, 5, 85
future, 5, 95
future perfect, 5, 95
past, 5, 33, 85
past perfect, 5, 93
present, 5, 85, 95
present perfect, 5, 93
Than, then, 14, 235
Their, they're, 14, 235
Theirs, there's, 14, 235
Theme, in writing, 307
Then, than, 14, 235
There's, theirs, 14, 235
Thesis statement, 307
They're, their, 14, 235
To, too, two, 14, 235
Topic, choosing, 20, 303
Topic outlines, 21
Topic sentences, 307
Transitions, 331
Transitive verbs, defined, 4, 77
Two, to, too, 14, 235

U

Understood subject, 201
Usage glossary, 12–14, 225–240

V

Verb phrases, defined, 4, 89
Verbal phrases, 10–11, 171, 173, 175, 179
Verbals, defined, 10–11

Index **347**

See also Gerunds, Infinitives, Participles
Verbs, defined, 4, 53, 75
   action verbs, 4, 53, 75
      intransitive, 4, 77
      transitive, 4, 77
   agreement with subjects, rules, 11, 28–31, 187, 189, 191, 193, 195
   emphatic, 6
   helping (auxiliary), 4, 89
   intransitive, 4, 77
   irregular, 5, 32–33, 99, 101
   linking, 4, 81–82
   list, of irregular, 5, 99, 101
   main, 4, 89
   principal parts of regular, 4, 89
   progressive forms, 6, 91, 95
   tenses of, 5, 32–33, 85, 93, 95
      See Tenses
   transitive, 4, 77
   voice of, active and passive, 6, 97, 323
Vocabulary, building, 19, 283, 285
   from context, 19, 283
   homographs and homophones, 291
   prefixes and suffixes, 19, 287
   synonyms and antonyms, 289
   word roots, 19, 285
Voice of verbs, defined, 6
   active, 6, 97, 323
   effective use of, 323
   passive, 6, 97, 323

W

Well, good, 133
Where at, avoiding, 14, 235
Who, whom, 7, 143
Who's, whose, 14, 235
Writing process. *See* specific steps.
Writing letters, 21–22, 335, 337, 339, 341
Writing paragraphs, 20–21, 327, 331
Writing sentences, 323
   See also Sentences, effective

Y

You, as understood subject, 201
Your, you're, 14, 235

Name _____ Class _____ Date _____

Unit 1 Test: Subjects, Predicates, and Sentences

▶ **Subtest 1** Add punctuation marks where they are needed. Identify the kind of sentence in the blank: *dec.* (declarative), *int.* (interrogative), *exc.* (exclamatory), or *imp.* (imperative).

_____ 1. Why are you making that noise

_____ 2. Many animals hibernate during the winter

_____ 3. Please watch carefully

_____ 4. Aren't you interested in finding out the answer

_____ 5. What a wonderful present this is

_____ 6. Paul doesn't know why he forgot to pack

_____ 7. The man fell from a window eleven stories high and lived

_____ 8. How does a ballpoint pen work

_____ 9. Stop that, please

_____ 10. She isn't sure whether she can come to the party

▶ **Subtest 2** Write *S* in the blank if the item is a sentence. Write *frag.* if the item is a sentence fragment. Then write whether the *subject*, *predicate*, or *both* are missing.

_____ 1. Sometimes birds crash into picture windows.

_____ 2. Every student in the school.

_____ 3. Landed on the moon in July 1969.

_____ 4. Take your raincoat with you.

_____ 5. Can you call me back later?

_____ 6. Painted our house.

_____ 7. We called the fire department.

_____ 8. Doug, Jon, and Elizabeth, my family members.

_____ 9. In the late afternoon.

_____ 10. Were listening to the new tape.

Name _____ Class _____ Date _____

▶ **Subtest 3 Draw one line under each complete subject. Draw two lines under each complete predicate.**

1. Most people enjoy movies.
2. Railroad travel can be a lot of fun.
3. Jessica's parents are Vietnamese immigrants.
4. The bald eagle is our national bird.
5. Did Mozart die in his mid-thirties?
6. The film *Amadeus* depicts Mozart's life.
7. Cross-country skiing is easy and enjoyable.
8. You don't need mountains for cross-country skiing!
9. The Smothers Brothers had a television show in the 1960s.
10. Abraham Lincoln and Stephen Douglas debated in 1858.

▶ **Subtest 4 Write *S* before each simple sentence, *C* before each compound sentence, and *R* before each run-on sentence.**

_____ 1. Viola is a character in Shakespeare's play *Twelfth Night*.

_____ 2. Philip rides horses, he's really good at it.

_____ 3. Rick's cat is orange, but Emily's is black and white.

_____ 4. Walt Whitman and Emily Dickinson were outstanding American poets.

_____ 5. Don't ever touch a downed power wire, it's very dangerous.

_____ 6. Herman Melville is the author of *Moby-Dick,* and *The Scarlet Letter* was written by Nathaniel Hawthorne.

_____ 7. Parents have to be patient with their children and forgive their mistakes.

_____ 8. First, we'll go to the music store, and then you can show me the jeans you want to buy at the Jeans Corral.

_____ 9. In the darkness gleamed a pair of eyes, boy, was it creepy!

_____ 10. Helen ran past the door, she stopped and turned around and went in.

Name _____ Class _____ Date _____

Unit 2 Test: Nouns

▶ **Subtest 1** Write *prop.* in the blank if the noun is proper or *com.* if it is common.

_____ 1. holiday

_____ 2. woman

_____ 3. American Revolution

_____ 4. Whitney Houston

_____ 5. monarch

_____ 6. the Amazon River

_____ 7. state

_____ 8. Larry Bird

_____ 9. planet

_____ 10. Miami

▶ **Subtest 2** Write *con.* in the blank if the noun is concrete or *abst.* if it is abstract.

_____ 1. rabbit

_____ 2. generosity

_____ 3. love

_____ 4. heat

_____ 5. beauty

_____ 6. airliner

_____ 7. courage

_____ 8. music

_____ 9. sand

_____ 10. democracy

▶ **Subtest 3** Circle each collective noun. Underline each compound noun.

1. Jennifer's sister-in-law teaches basketmaking.

2. My great-aunt has a music box that plays "America the Beautiful."

3. The group of children loved it when I read a storybook to them.

4. The team ran down the field.

5. The players smashed through a sign taped between the goalposts.

6. Our family went to pick out a new sofa for our family room.

7. The crowd had become rowdy waiting for the candidate to appear.

8. The runners-up looked a little disappointed.

9. The audience clapped enthusiastically when the band finished playing.

10. We ran from the swarm of bees, but even so Shelley was stung.

Name _____ Class _____ Date _____

▶ **Subtest 4** Write the form of the word indicated.

_____ 1. baby (plural)

_____ 2. Alexander (possessive)

_____ 3. baby is (contraction)

_____ 4. fox (plural)

_____ 5. Sharon is (contraction)

_____ 6. secretary of state (plural)

_____ 7. my dad (possessive)

_____ 8. King James (possessive)

_____ 9. Joe Montana is (contraction)

_____ 10. our neighbors (possessive)

_____ 11. baseball bat (plural)

_____ 12. maid of honor (plural)

_____ 13. volleyball (plural)

_____ 14. giraffes (possessive)

_____ 15. Indiana is (contraction)

_____ 16. freedom (possessive)

_____ 17. bookmark (plural)

_____ 18. Stevens (plural)

_____ 19. Teri (possessive)

_____ 20. bike helmet (plural)

▶ **Subtest 5** Underline each appositive or appositive phrase. Draw an arrow from the appositive or appositive phrase to the word or words it identifies.

1. The sign read "Welcome to Madison, the capital of Wisconsin."

2. Denali, a mountain in Alaska, is also known as Mt. McKinley.

3. Mr. Carty, the husband of our French teacher, is the soccer coach.

4. Elaine's sister Shannon is in the fifth grade.

5. The painter Henri Matisse was admired for his use of color.

6. My cat Ginger caught three mice last week.

7. William Wilder, a famous movie director, wrote this book.

8. This is Michael's brother Graham.

9. Missouri, the Show-Me state, borders Illinois.

10. Ronald Reagan's wife Nancy also appeared in films.

11. Nathan's cousin goes to Stanford, a university in California.

12. *Huckleberry Finn*, a novel by Mark Twain, depicts life in nineteenth-century America.

Name _____ Class _____ Date _____

Unit 3 Test: Verbs

▶ **Subtest 1** Draw two lines under each action verb. Write *T* in the blank if the verb is transitive or *I* if it is intransitive.

_____ 1. The deer zipped across the open field.

_____ 2. Everyone knew the answer to that question.

_____ 3. He watched for the shooting star.

_____ 4. Today the Dolphins battle the Cowboys in Miami.

_____ 5. Leaves covered the front lawn.

_____ 6. Natalie plays gin rummy.

_____ 7. Remember your hiking boots this time.

_____ 8. We listened carefully to the question.

_____ 9. The fans cheered loudly.

_____ 10. My little brother has the chicken pox.

▶ **Subtest 2** Underline each direct object. Circle each indirect object.

1. The accountant gave his clients financial advice.

2. The doctor wrote the patient a prescription.

3. I saw two boys from my class at the shopping center.

4. Receiving gifts gives my grandparents pleasure.

5. Deborah sold a local businessman her painting.

6. Birthdays offer people a chance to celebrate.

7. Charles Kettering invented the self-starter for a car.

8. Don't send Brian the book yet.

9. Rita designed the posters for the recycling drive.

10. My friends and I sent our English teacher a get-well card.

Name _____ Class _____ Date _____

▶ **Subtest 3** Write *PN* above each predicate noun and *PA* above each predicate adjective.

1. Doesn't that coffee cake smell delicious?
2. Ben turned green with envy.
3. Toni and Brett were our class representatives.
4. My dog, Mitzi, is growing fatter every day.
5. The screeching tires sounded awful.
6. They aren't very good soccer players, are they?
7. My dad's moustache looks great.
8. Lyndon Johnson became president in 1963.
9. Brad feels ill in front of an audience.
10. The punishment seems a little bit harsh.

▶ **Subtest 4** Draw two lines under each verb or verb phrase. Write the tense of the verb in the blank: *present, past,* or *future.*

_____ 1. My dad and I went to the history museum.
_____ 2. Will you send me the catalog in a few weeks?
_____ 3. I always take the first street on the left.
_____ 4. We ate at a Thai restaurant.
_____ 5. Carlos and Tina will give their report next.
_____ 6. He feels better after his nap.
_____ 7. Shall I include you on the list?
_____ 8. Nina and I talked for an hour and a half.
_____ 9. We will be at the mall from 1:30 to 2:30.
_____ 10. The baby wanted her rattle.
_____ 11. Hillary will call you either tomorrow or Thursday.
_____ 12. Roger plays saxophone in the school band.

Name _____ Class _____ Date _____

▶ **Subtest 5** Write the tense or form of the verb in the blank: *pres. prog.* (present progressive), *past prog.* (past progressive), *pres. perf.* (present perfect), *past perf.* (past perfect) or *fut. perf.* (future perfect).

_____ 1. Gwen had admired the sand castle.

_____ 2. By next September we will have lived in our apartment three years.

_____ 3. They were winning the game with two minutes left.

_____ 4. Are you going to Jennifer's slumber party?

_____ 5. By Tuesday our dog will probably have had her puppies.

_____ 6. Have you heard the news about Ms. Walsh?

_____ 7. Ashley is running for class president this year.

_____ 8. The beavers were building a large dam across the stream.

_____ 9. Before the game the coach had spoken to each player.

_____ 10. An owl has hooted outside the window three nights in a row.

_____ 11. My cat, Mimi, is always sleeping on my pillow.

_____ 12. We have decided on our vacation plans.

_____ 13. By the ninth inning Marty will have batted five times.

_____ 14. Until 1992 we had never lived in the same town for more than one year.

_____ 15. I was hoping for a phone call.

▶ **Subtest 6** Write *A* in the blank if the verb is active or *P* if the verb is passive.

_____ 1. The quarterback threw the ball downfield.

_____ 2. The lineman leaped over another player.

_____ 3. The ball was caught by the speedy wide receiver.

_____ 4. Some dogs eat table scraps often.

_____ 5. They are fed from the table by their masters.

_____ 6. That play was presented by our local theater.

_____ 7. Audiences loved it!

_____ 8. A fine dinner is enjoyed by most people.

Name _____ Class _____ Date _____

_____ 9. Our family likes the Chinese restaurant on Michigan Avenue.

_____ 10. We were served the most delicious shrimp dish last week.

▶ **Subtest 7** Write in the blank the past or past participle of the irregular verb in parentheses.

1. There _____ a hole in the screen where mosquitoes came in. (be)
2. We have _____ in that lake every summer that I can remember. (swim)
3. I'm sure no one has _____ of that solution yet. (think)
4. For a week, my mother _____ nervous about starting her new job. (feel)
5. We have _____ our best. (do)
6. The newspaper carrier _____ the paper on the porch step. (lay)
7. The wagon train _____ Missouri and headed west on the Oregon Trail. (leave)
8. Angelique _____ in both the 400-meter race and the 800-meter race. (run)
9. Our cousins from Minnesota _____ to visit for a week. (come)
10. He _____ lunch with several other teachers. (eat)
11. My sister and I _____ that movie last week. (see)
12. The pilot _____ me look at the instrument panel of the jet. (let)
13. The candidate _____ her word that she would work for a tax cut. (give)
14. My aunt has _____ three-bean salad to Thanksgiving dinner five years in a row. (bring)
15. Milton High won the coin toss and _____ to kick off. (choose)
16. Curt _____ our door key on the way home from school. (lose)
17. Jennifer has _____ ballet lessons for five years. (take)
18. We had _____ that vase once before. (break)
19. Only two people _____ the answer to the riddle. (know)
20. Tamara had _____ postcards to all of her friends during her vacation in New Mexico. (write)

356 *Writer's Choice Grammar Workbook 8,* Unit 3

Name _____ Class _____ Date _____

Unit 4 Test: Pronouns

▶ **Subtest 1** Draw an arrow from the personal pronoun in the second sentence to its antecedent in the first sentence.

1. The Great Lakes lie in the middle of the country. They are important resources.

2. Darnay and Robert asked Mr. Gonzalez about the photo. The teacher explained it to the students.

3. A telemarketer called Mr. Grover on the phone last night. Mr. Grover couldn't talk to her.

4. Sarah saw the bird on the ground. It had a broken wing.

5. Wilbur and Orville Wright flew the first airplane. The world honors them as the fathers of flight.

6. Our team worked very hard to win the championship trophy. When the commissioner handed the trophy to us, the crowd cheered.

7. My brother asked for the sugar. Dad handed it to Tony.

8. Do these students want to be part of the best class ever at Fairmount High? Just ask them!

9. Lisa knew the answer to the question. The teacher called on her.

10. Janelle saw Mike and Dave on Third Street. They were walking to the ice cream shop.

▶ **Subtest 2** Underline the word or words in parentheses that best complete each sentence.

1. One of the best chess players in our class is (she, her).

2. Ms. Simon asked (we, us) students to help with the clean-up.

3. Darrell and (I, me) both enjoy computer games.

4. Rex and (he, him) became friends at summer camp.

5. (David and he, David and him) are nominated for the award.

Name _____ Class _____ Date _____

6. (Juanita and I, Me and Juanita) decided to leave the dance early and go to her house.

7. He did just as good a job as (she, her).

8. Give the tape to (he, him) after you finish with it.

9. My sister is one-half inch taller than (I, me).

10. (My brother and I, I and my brother) are interested in radio-controlled cars.

▶ **Subtest 3** Label each pronoun *per.* (personal), *poss.* (possessive), or *ind.* (indefinite).

1. My dog is not a purebred dog; he is just a mutt.

2. Someone took her backpack by mistake.

3. Each should pick up a schedule form.

4. You should talk to both of them about it.

5. His puppy got its leg caught in the chair.

6. I guess everything for the party is ready.

7. Ours is very similar to theirs.

8. "Nobody Knows the Trouble I've Seen" is a lovely spiritual.

9. She shouldn't let others do her work for her.

10. I am afraid there is nothing we can do about it now.

▶ **Subtest 4** Label each pronoun *ref.* (reflexive), *int.* (intensive), or *inter.* (interrogative).

1. Ali and Doug found themselves in a new part of town.

2. Whom did Tracey ask about the computer?

3. Lamont himself has already read these newspapers.

4. "Bake scrumptious cookies yourself!" the cover of the cookbook read.

5. Which has Emily decided to take?

6. Whom did you see at the mall?

7. Who thinks that film is really great entertainment?

8. Mother Teresa herself walked the streets of Calcutta helping the sick.

9. Who returned the books to the library?

10. The man standing in the door was Uncle Doug himself.

Name _____ Class _____ Date _____

Unit 5 Test: Adjectives and Adverbs

▶ **Subtest 1** Underline each adjective. Circle each adverb.

1. I do not think the lions in the zoo are tame.
2. The volcano erupted with a gigantic explosion.
3. The Peruvian belt was exceedingly colorful.
4. He seemed unhappy about the grade, but I thought that score was very good.
5. Victorian novels by authors such as Dickens, Thackeray, and the Brontës are among the most popular of all.
6. In English class we saw a movie about a Canadian mountie.
7. That ear-splitting sound you hear is a saw.
8. The family lives in a modern house.
9. The dinner at the Vietnamese restaurant was a huge success.
10. She always wears the most fashionable clothes.

▶ **Subtest 2** Draw an arrow from each adverb to the word it modifies.

1. Roger absentmindedly walked to the window and looked out.
2. Riding that roller coaster is an extremely scary experience!
3. The toboggan slid down the hill very fast.
4. Do not throw the ball hard.
5. They usually shared the food equally.
6. She was truly sorry for the accident.
7. Dani is almost finished with the book.
8. The thief reluctantly gave the ring to its rightful owner.
9. "Give me the jewel box," the detective said calmly.
10. We have never visited New York City.

Name _____ Class _____ Date _____

▶ **Subtest 3** Write the correct form of the adjective or adverb indicated.

1. This car seems to be the _____ of all the cars in the test group. (quick)
2. Lemon is probably the _____ fruit of all. (bitter)
3. The trombones are supposed to play the _____ of all the instruments here. (loud)
4. I thought *Julie of the Wolves* was _____ than *Little Women*. (interesting)
5. Yesterday I saw the _____ daffodil I have ever seen. (yellow)
6. Melanie completed the exam _____ of all the applicants for the scholarship. (easily)
7. The giant size isn't _____ than the jumbo size, is it? (large)
8. They go to the cafeteria to study _____ than they go to the learning center. (often)
9. Omar behaved _____ on the camping trip than Steven did. (bravely)
10. Eduardo played the _____ of all the chess team members in the last match. (well)

▶ **Subtest 4** Underline the word or words in parentheses that best complete each sentence.

1. His first attempt at making a pie was not (bad, badly).
2. Can't (anybody, nobody) give us a hand with this trunk?
3. We had to cancel play practice because the director wasn't feeling (good, well).
4. I couldn't get (anyone, no one) to pick up the phone.
5. Rembrandt painted (most beautiful, most beautifully) of all the painters I've studied.
6. Can't we do (nothing, anything) to help the injured bird?
7. The new car model performed (bad, badly) during the magazine's tests.
8. In fact, it got the (most poorly, poorest) marks in its class.
9. We (will, won't) ever improve unless we practice harder.
10. My sister Erin hopes to do (good, well) on her driver's test.

360 Writer's Choice Grammar Workbook 8, Unit 5

Name _____ Class _____ Date _____

Unit 6 Test: Prepositions, Conjunctions, and Interjections

▶ **Subtest 1** Underline each preposition. Circle the object of each preposition.

1. The radio station will play Beatles songs throughout the night.
2. In spite of the tough loss the team was still in first place.
3. Do you know the song "Over the River and Through the Woods"?
4. Last night's game was against Marshall Middle School.
5. Rob was elected class president instead of Eric.
6. The kitten sniffed inside the paper bag and then jumped into it.
7. The town you are discussing is beyond Shelbyville, near the new dam.
8. Josh's friend Sam is from Michigan.
9. The submarine cruised silently below the surface of the ocean.
10. Put the vase of flowers in front of the bowl.
11. According to the author, the poet led a quiet life.
12. The bird didn't see the cat lurking behind the bush.
13. Walk toward the maple tree if you want a nice surprise.
14. The barking dog couldn't get outside the fence.
15. The hero jumped from the rock onto the speeding stagecoach.
16. Some rude people kept jabbering during the movie.
17. The concert was canceled on account of the ice storm.
18. The bees buzzed loudly around the hive.
19. We had to hurry because of his lateness.
20. We decided to meet at the theater at eight.
21. The fruit salad requires two cans of pineapple and one can of oranges.
22. Marla couldn't choose between the pink dress and the yellow one.
23. The ball rolled down the stairs.
24. Dad drove around the city for two hours.

Name _____ Class _____ Date _____

▶ **Subtest 2** Underline the word in parentheses that best completes each sentence.

1. Keena and I went to the movies with (she, her).
2. From (who, whom) did you get that information?
3. Aside from Thomas, Christopher, and (her, she), nobody has passed the test.
4. Did you see the boy sitting across from (I, me) at lunch?
5. You will be attending the conference in place of (he, him).
6. I'll give the book to (them, they) after history class.
7. To (who, whom) did you give the petition?
8. Winning the award was very important to Dale and (I, me).
9. She is standing in front of (them, they).
10. The singer of (who, whom) I spoke is coming to town to perform.

▶ **Subtest 3** Underline each prepositional phrase. Write *adj.* in the blank if it is an adjective phrase. Write *adv.* if it is an adverb phrase.

_____ 1. We traveled by bus and airplane.

_____ 2. Our softball team finished second in its league.

_____ 3. She is a woman with a great reputation.

_____ 4. Jonathan is quite tall for his age.

_____ 5. Please hand me the can on the top shelf.

_____ 6. Our guests arrived in late afternoon.

_____ 7. In my opinion that is a very exciting story.

_____ 8. Has your family ever been to Florida?

_____ 9. Theirs is the house across from the school.

_____ 10. That quotation would be perfect for my poster.

_____ 11. Phil ordered a chicken salad sandwich without tomatoes.

_____ 12. Mr. Konrad nearly fell asleep during the concert.

_____ 13. The book seemed long in spite of its interesting plot.

_____ 14. The bicycle next to the tree is mine.

_____ 15. Her attitude toward the situation has improved tremendously.

Name _____ Class _____ Date _____

▶ **Subtest 4** Draw one line under each conjunction. Draw two lines under the word in parentheses that best completes each sentence.

1. Both his brother and his sister (enjoy, enjoys) playing backgammon.
2. You or they (are, is) going to be asked the questions.
3. Not only the Belgians but also the Swiss (speak, speaks) French.
4. The women and the man (expect, expects) to wait at the airport.
5. Neither your parents nor your grandfather (come, comes) to the meeting.
6. Either algebra or history (are, is) the most difficult class for Ramona.
7. Tulips and daffodils (are, is) certainly signs of spring.
8. Dogs make good pets, but fish (are, is) less trouble.
9. Neither Chris nor the Davidson twins (do, does) well under pressure.
10. (Are, Is) Chicago or Detroit the better team?

▶ **Subtest 5** Underline each conjunctive adverb. Circle each interjection.

1. He arrived late for the play; therefore, he had to wait until the end of the first scene to take his seat.
2. Maya decided not to go the mall; besides, she had plenty of homework to do.
3. Well, I'm glad that's over; nevertheless, I'm glad I tried it.
4. Collecting sports cards is a popular hobby; likewise, building model airplanes is an enjoyable pastime.
5. I will not seek the nomination; furthermore, I will not accept it.
6. Sabrina practices the piano every day; moreover, she plans to take extra lessons.
7. Phew, that was close!
8. Only eight tickets to the dance have been sold; consequently, it is canceled.
9. Whoops, that ice is slippery; however, we have to get to the car.
10. I did all right on the English quiz; still, I wish I had done a little better.

Name _____ Class _____ Date _____

▶ **Subtest 6** **Write in the blank the part of speech of the word or words in italics: prep.
(preposition), conj. (conjunction), or int. (interjection).**

_____ 1. He was standing *beside* the queen of England.

_____ 2. *Hey!* That's my bike!

_____ 3. His excuse for leaving seemed reasonable, *but* he still tried to help with the cleanup.

_____ 4. *Both* Indira Gandhi *and* Margaret Thatcher headed large democracies.

_____ 5. Afghanistan is located *between* Pakistan and Iran.

_____ 6. Tina arrived early, *but* Franny was late.

_____ 7. Look out *for* the spilled milk!

_____ 8. *Well,* Sandy's application was received on time; thus, she will be allowed to play.

_____ 9. *Along with* Mary Chapin-Carpenter, Kathy Mattea is a rising country music star.

_____ 10. *Whew!* It's hot out!

_____ 11. *Wow!* Reggie is a smart fellow!

_____ 12. The drugstore is right *around* the corner.

_____ 13. They decided to go ahead with the plan *in spite of* the chairperson's opposition.

_____ 14. *Not only* are gerbils fascinating creatures, *but* they *also* make interesting pets.

_____ 15. The cottage is located *beside* a lovely stream.

_____ 16. The students at our school like football *and* basketball best.

_____ 17. *Neither* one *nor* the other is a very appealing choice.

_____ 18. You can have hot dogs *or* tacos.

_____ 19. *Oh, no!* He missed the shot!

_____ 20. By such a foolish act he endangered his own reputation *and* put others at risk.

364 Writer's Choice Grammar Workbook 8, Unit 6

Name _____ Class _____ Date _____

Unit 7 Test: Clauses and Complex Sentences

▶ **Subtest 1** Write *S* in the blank before each simple sentence, *C* before each compound sentence, and *Cx.* before each complex sentence.

_____ 1. The children were playing at the beach when they heard the news.

_____ 2. The Beatles are no longer a musical group, but many people still love their music.

_____ 3. Raising beef cattle is hard work; crop farming can also be very time-consuming.

_____ 4. Dutch and Flemish are similar and related languages.

_____ 5. The last apple dangled on the bare apple tree until Dorothy picked it.

_____ 6. Tom plans to study journalism, and someday he will be an anchorperson.

_____ 7. The answer to the second question is *B*.

_____ 8. Each student will receive a diploma, and everyone is invited to the reception afterwards.

_____ 9. Although he was tired, Dante waited up for his sister to return.

_____ 10. Do you like pears?

_____ 11. My dog flunked obedience school; however, her dog passed.

_____ 12. Lynn will be able to come, but Robin is busy.

_____ 13. Maples lose their leaves in the fall, but pines keep their needles.

_____ 14. Houseplants can make a room look cheerier, though some are hard to maintain.

_____ 15. If you scream at the sound of the gong, you'll frighten the person next to you.

_____ 16. Everyone was eager for the show to begin.

_____ 17. Because Julia had practiced hard, she won the first round of the competition.

_____ 18. Geoff has become an avid gardener since he helped Grandmother with her garden last spring.

_____ 19. Bonnie brought the apple pie, and Jim made the chocolate chip cookies.

_____ 20. When Krista came to visit, we had a great time.

Name _____ Class _____ Date _____

_____ 21. Someone forgot to turn out the lights.

_____ 22. Before the meeting began, each member of the group was given a copy of the agenda.

▶ **Subtest 2** Draw one line under each main clause. Draw two lines under each subordinate clause.

1. During the Super Bowl, many people are glued to their televisions.
2. I don't remember her name, but her face is familiar.
3. The mail carrier will stop at the post office after she finishes her route.
4. Elena took the last cupcake, which we were saving for David.
5. He resigned from the club and joined another one.
6. I won't be going to the party since I have to study.
7. She plays both the violin and the viola very well.
8. Did you get the license number of the car that splashed mud on your coat?
9. When he's in this mood, it's better to leave him alone.
10. My cousin wants to be a doctor, and she is majoring in biology in college.
11. We knew that it wouldn't be easy to finish the float on time.
12. Don't come to the meeting unless you're prepared to work hard.
13. Jeannie cut her finger, and we had to rush her to the hospital.
14. I get nervous whenever I think about it.
15. Although he is good at baseball, his favorite sport is definitely soccer.

▶ **Subtest 3** Underline each adjective clause. Draw an arrow from the adjective clause to the word it modifies.

1. *Mork and Mindy* was the TV show that made Robin Williams famous.
2. She is my friend who enjoys eating in Chinese restaurants.
3. The woman whose purse I found was grateful when I returned it.
4. He's the man whom we all admire.

Name _____ Class _____ Date _____

5. The princess said the secret word that opened the locked door.

6. The part of the woods where it is very dark is easy to get lost in.

7. I sent the comment to the woman who edits the newsletter.

8. That movie, which was so expensive to make, is a flop.

9. She's a singer whom I enjoy hearing.

10. Ask Lisa, who knows everything about computers.

11. Do you remember the time when we got caught in the rain and were soaked?

12. Is this the present that you really want for your birthday?

13. Give her the book that Dana recommended so highly.

14. Justin drove past the corner where the terrible accident happened.

15. My dad bought a new car that is very comfortable.

▶ **Subtest 4** Place a check [✔] beside each sentence that contains an essential clause.

_____ **1.** He's the driver who finished third in the Grand Prix race last month.

_____ **2.** In the opera, Mimi dies of tuberculosis, which was a very common disease in the 1800s.

_____ **3.** The team that wins this game will be number one in the state!

_____ **4.** "Hard Times," which was written by Stephen Foster, is a beautiful song.

_____ **5.** Anyone who fails to obey traffic signals is very irresponsible.

_____ **6.** Agda, whose mother was born in Poland, showed some slides of her trip.

_____ **7.** This is the part where the monkey comes out from behind the rock.

_____ **8.** This apartment is the first one in which Eileen has felt comfortable.

_____ **9.** That girl who just transferred here from North Carolina has a southern accent.

_____ **10.** This is one book that I really want to read!

_____ **11.** The Gonzalez's house, which is next to the grocery store, has a big porch on the front.

Name _____ Class _____ Date _____

_____ 12. The finches sit on a little perch that is attached to the feeder.

_____ 13. Dr. Martin Luther King Jr., whom I admire very much, was killed in 1968.

_____ 14. Why don't you ask Rita, who is a very good surfer?

_____ 15. Choosing to play the oboe, which is one of the most difficult instruments, is typical for Shawn.

_____ 16. Dad sent a fruit basket to his sister, who lives in Tampa.

_____ 17. Do you remember the time when we all went to the beach?

_____ 18. The player whose autograph I want will be at the game.

_____ 19. The oldest runner who ran in the marathon race was eighty-one.

_____ 20. Rosemary Sutcliff, whose books I love, writes about the England of the past.

▶ **Subtest 5** Underline each subordinate clause. Write *adj.*, *adv.*, or *N* in the blank to tell how each clause is used in its sentence.

_____ 1. That's the auditorium where the play will be presented.

_____ 2. Sarah was early because her dad dropped her off.

_____ 3. His sister, who is sixteen, just got her driver's license.

_____ 4. Whoever has the lowest score wins in golf.

_____ 5. The explorer did not know how to get out of the trap.

_____ 6. Although the temperature is very high in Arizona, it doesn't feel terribly uncomfortable.

_____ 7. Do you recall when they are arriving?

_____ 8. When people burn trash, the air can become polluted.

_____ 9. Children should realize that playing in the street is dangerous.

_____ 10. The parachute, which was first designed by Leonardo da Vinci, is an intriguing device.

_____ 11. What really annoys me is her constant whistling.

_____ 12. Nick won't finish his report unless he works on it tonight.

_____ 13. The tent that I want is big enough for three people.

_____ 14. They will award the blue ribbon to whoever is most deserving.

Name _____ Class _____ Date _____

Unit 8 Test: Verbals

▶ **Subtest 1** Underline each participial phrase. If the participial phrase requires commas, add them to the sentence.

1. Marissa wearing the red sweatshirt is sitting next to her mother in the second row.
2. Summoning up his courage Miguel approached the podium to give his speech.
3. Stuffing the clothes in I packed my suitcase hastily.
4. The referee standing in the end zone is the former coach of our soccer team.
5. The scouts exhausted from their five-mile hike lay down under the trees and instantly fell asleep.
6. Nodding over his open book Jerrold could not stay awake.
7. Waiting for a ride home Cynthia counted the number of red cars that drove by.
8. Mr. Manley found the missing papers rolled up inside a bottle.
9. Watching closely the audience still could not figure out how the magician performed the trick.
10. Surprised by the darkness Margaret was even more shocked when she turned on the lights and discovered the party.

▶ **Subtest 2** Write *V* in the blank if the word in italics is a verb in a verb phrase. Write *part.* if the word is a participle used as an adjective. Write *ger.* if the word is a gerund.

_____ 1. The folksinger ended her concert by *leading* the audience in a song.

_____ 2. We used the big stone slab as a *resting* place.

_____ 3. After she graduates from high school, Yvonne is *planning* to attend the state university.

_____ 4. The first step in *playing* the guitar is to learn how to hold it.

_____ 5. You can convert a decimal number to a percentage by *multiplying* the number by one hundred.

_____ 6. We were *listening* to the sound of the rain on the metal roof when we heard a pitiful meow from outside the door.

_____ 7. "Don't bother talking if this guy is *walking*" was the last line of the song.

Name _____ Class _____ Date _____

_____ 8. *Swimming* is Tanya's favorite sport.

_____ 9. The committee will be *making* its decision next week.

_____ 10. Don and Tony signed up for a *cooking* class at the cultural arts center.

_____ 11. All the other vehicles had *stopped* to allow the motorcade to pass.

_____ 12. *Wilted* from the heat, the flowers lost their beauty.

_____ 13. *Making* up silly stories is Clarissa's favorite pastime.

_____ 14. He found Delia *wandering* through the park.

_____ 15. *Decorating* a cake is harder than it looks.

▶ **Subtest 3** Write *inf.* in the blank if the group of words in italics is an infinitive phrase. Write *prep.* if the group of words is a prepositional phrase.

_____ 1. I'm ready *to go anywhere*.

_____ 2. On the way *to the relay race* Reba realized that she had forgotten her lucky socks.

_____ 3. The first person in my family *to graduate from high school* was my older brother.

_____ 4. *To Shaun's surprise* the ball hit the crossbar of the goalpost and bounced back onto the field.

_____ 5. The catcher signaled the pitcher *to throw a fast ball*.

_____ 6. In March our earth science class is taking a trip *to Mammoth Cave*.

_____ 7. My plan is *to read all of Gary Paulsen's books*.

_____ 8. Before reading the last chapter of the book, we tried *to predict the ending*.

_____ 9. Our art class made several colorful kites *to fly in the park*.

_____ 10. These books must be returned *to the public library* by Friday.

_____ 11. Tamara is hoping *to learn Spanish*.

_____ 12. *To float across a pool of cold water* is one of the joys of summer.

_____ 13. The road *to the old castle* was long and treacherous.

_____ 14. Yesterday Peter received an invitation *to the dance*.

_____ 15. Sabrina wants us *to see the town*.

Name _____ Class _____ Date _____

Unit 9 Test: Subject-Verb Agreement

▶ **Subtest 1** Draw one line under the simple subject. Draw two lines under the correct verb form in parentheses.

1. This book of poems (is, are) my favorite.
2. The dogs (sniffs, sniff) the food in the kitchen.
3. A herbivorous animal (eats, eat) only plants.
4. (Doesn't, Don't) you want to see the show?
5. A good chess player (has, have) to be able to concentrate.
6. The baking sweet rolls (smells, smell) fantastic!
7. His portable tape player (goes, go) everywhere with him.
8. The nature show about weasels (was, were) one of the best.
9. The clerks in this store (wraps, wrap) hundreds of packages a day during the holidays.
10. Merlyn's parents (sells, sell) computer software.
11. (Is, Are) there seats in that row?
12. Three dollars (is, are) lying on the sidewalk.
13. Her sunglasses (was, were) beside the pool.
14. The news (is, are) on Channel 5 now.
15. Mathematics (was, were) Julian's best subject.
16. The herd of goats (grazes, graze) in the pasture.
17. Twenty liters of soda (was, were) consumed at the picnic.
18. There (is, are) three cookies on the plate.
19. Ten dollars (is, are) the price of a ticket.
20. My mother (work, works) in that office building.
21. Sheep (enjoys, enjoy) munching on an apple every now and then.
22. *The Women of Avignon* (is, are) one of Picasso's early cubist paintings.

Name _____ Class _____ Date _____

▶ **Subtest 2** Draw two lines under the correct form of the verb in parentheses.

1. The captain and best player of the volleyball team (is, are) Tiffany.
2. All of the food on the table (looks, look) delicious.
3. Neither the winner nor the losers (needs, need) to feel unhappy.
4. Many (hopes, hope) the situation will improve by itself.
5. Looking at the cupcakes, she said, "Another (sounds, sound) good to me."
6. Both types of cars (is, are) manufactured in the United States.
7. (Does, Do) any student want to be on the planning committee for the dance?
8. Almost everything (takes, take) time if you want to do it right.
9. Maine, New Hampshire, and Vermont (takes, take) pride in their Yankee heritage.
10. If anyone (arrives, arrive) late, ask him or her to wait.
11. Either the goats or the llama (is, are) hungry.
12. Serious athletes (doesn't, don't) smoke cigarettes.
13. The president and the treasurer of the Spanish club (is, are) Hillary and Robert.
14. Much of our budget (is, are) spent on refreshments for the meetings.
15. Because others (was, were) interested in the concert, I gave up my seat.
16. Everybody in the sweepstakes (has, have) an equal chance to win.
17. David and his two dogs (comes, come) to the park every day after school.
18. Several of the houses (is, are) painted yellow.
19. Anyone who (tries, try) out for the team has to be in good health.
20. Many in the class (was, were) happy with their grades.
21. There (is, are) nothing we can do about it now.
22. A few of the deer (was, were) in the field near the stream.
23. Chocolate or vanilla (is, are) the favorite flavor.
24. Some of the pie (was, were) eaten.

Name _____ Class _____ Date _____

Unit 10 Test: Diagraming Sentences

▶ **Subtest 1** Diagram the simple subject and simple predicate of each sentence.

1. Cats make good pets.

2. Mail this package.

3. Tina wore a beautiful coat.

4. We can talk about it later.

5. Alex flew a kite in the contest.

▶ **Subtest 2** Diagram the simple subject, simple predicate, direct object, and indirect object of each sentence.

1. Jason collects baseball cards.

2. Please give me the magazine.

3. The hawk caught the fish.

4. Hiroko sent her parents a letter.

5. We saw iguanas at the zoo.

Name _____ Class _____ Date _____

▶ **Subtest 3** Diagram each sentence completely.

1. Everybody at the beach saw the playful dolphin.

2. The elderly man carefully crossed the busy street.

3. Few people are good at archery.

4. Chess demands concentration and discipline.

5. The race car crashed and burned.

6. English and history are Carmen's favorite subjects.

7. My mother likes small, sporty cars, but my father wants a minivan.

8. Ernest Hemingway was a great American author, and he tried to lead and exciting life.

9. The boy who received the player's autograph looked extremely happy.

10. Fernando smiled when he won first prize.

11. Dad and I love cheering for our favorite team.

12. The best book to read is definitely *David Copperfield*.

Unit 11 Test: Usage

▶ **Subtest 1** Underline the word in parentheses that best completes each sentence.

1. Please (accept, except) this gift as a token of my appreciation.
2. Max was (all ready, already) for the debate.
3. My whole family found seats (altogether, all together) in the back of the auditorium.
4. Troy unpacked the printer and set it up (beside, besides) the computer.
5. This will be a secret (between, among) you and me.
6. Would you (bring, take) a dessert when you come to our house for the picnic?
7. (Can, May) I see the menu, please?
8. If you add (less, fewer) water, the mixture will not hold together well.
9. Danielle (choose, chose) the red sweatshirt instead of the blue one.
10. I sampled all of the foods at the international dinner (accept, except) the creamed herring.
11. Scattered (between, among) the poppies in the field were a few daisies.
12. Please (take, bring) the dog with you when you go for a walk.
13. This winter we have seen (less, fewer) cardinals at the bird feeder than we saw last winter.
14. I'm not (all together, altogether) pleased with the results.
15. I had (already, all ready) opened the letter when I saw that it was addressed to our neighbor.
16. Will you (let, leave) me help you make the pie?
17. We (can, may) always count on Arnette to see the humorous side of any situation.
18. Is anyone (besides, beside) Erin interested in going to the art museum?
19. We'll (leave, let) now so you can get back to your project.
20. Today our class will (chose, choose) a site for a new tree on the school grounds.

Name _____ Class _____ Date _____

▶ **Subtest 2** Write *C* in the blank if the word in italics is used correctly or *I* if it is used incorrectly.

_____ 1. The downy woodpecker is black and white and has a red patch on the back of *it's* neck.

_____ 2. We ran *into* the house when we saw the first flash of lightning.

_____ 3. Meeka *formally* lived in New Jersey, but now she resides in Pennsylvania.

_____ 4. You can *lay* the books on the counter while I search for my library card.

_____ 5. Ernesto wants to *learn* me how to ride a horse.

_____ 6. If we *loose* the basketball game tonight, our team will be third in the league instead of second.

_____ 7. *Much* of the trees in this forest have been damaged by gypsy moths.

_____ 8. In the parade our school marching band will *precede* the first float.

_____ 9. The ending of this story is *quite* mysterious.

_____ 10. The sun began to *raise* above the ridge just as the rooster crowed.

_____ 11. Did you *set* the terrarium on a sunny windowsill?

_____ 12. Dwayne is a better volleyball player *then* I am.

_____ 13. We are going to the matinee, but *they're* going to the late show.

_____ 14. This looks like the Millers' car, but I'm not sure if it's *theirs*.

_____ 15. There are *to* many cats in this house!

_____ 16. *Who's* notebook has a red cover?

_____ 17. Is *you're* aunt a volunteer at the school?

_____ 18. After you finish reading the instructions, *proceed* with the experiment.

_____ 19. We decided to *set* for a while on the stone bench at the end of the pond.

_____ 20. The *two* girls at the copy machine were speaking in French.

Name _____ Class _____ Date _____

Unit 12 Test: Capitalization

▶ **Subtest 1** Underline the choice in parentheses that best completes the sentence.

1. (Uncle, uncle) Burt has a white beard and wears gold-rimmed glasses.

2. The author of this book is Arthur Schlesinger (Jr., jr.)

3. Reading stories to young children is something (I, i) like to do.

4. William Henry Harrison was (President, president) for only about a month before he died.

5. The college catalog listed Elena Diaz, (Ph.D., Ph.d.), as a member of the history department.

6. I learned that (John F. Kennedy, John f. Kennedy) had two brothers and a father who were also active in politics.

7. My appointment card listed the dentist's name, Kuniko Webber, (D.D.S., d.d.s.)

8. I'd like to show you a picture of (Aunt, aunt) Edith ice skating when she was only four.

9. My other (Aunt, aunt), whose name is Elizabeth, is my mother's twin sister.

10. The reporters asked (Senator, senator) Riley numerous questions at the press conference.

11. In 1942 (Grandfather, grandfather) enlisted as a soldier in World War II.

12. "This book," said Colin, "(Contains, contains) many photographs of President Abraham Lincoln."

13. We would like to invite (Professor, professor) Brinker, an expert on city planning, to speak to our class.

14. My (Grandmother, grandmother) has enjoyed backpacking ever since she was a teenager.

15. Arnold Ackerson (Sr., sr.) is a respected member of the city council.

16. "Could you give me some help with this math problem, (Dad, dad)?"

17. "(Our, our) family doctor is Eve Pfeil, M.D.," Mom told the nurse.

18. The (Mayor, mayor) announced that several streets will be repaved this summer.

19. The man shaking hands with the cadets is (General, general) William Hartsook.

20. "Well, Cliff," said Crystal, "(What, what) should we do after the picnic?"

▶ **Subtest 2** Draw three lines under each letter that should be capitalized.

1. On my thirteenth birthday we are going to a chinese restaurant.
2. The first chapter of the book was titled "trouble."
3. In the magazine section of the library, I read articles in *omni* and *personal computing*.
4. Some of the basketball players prefer swift brand athletic shoes.
5. This fall, in either october or november, our class will go on a hayride at a farm in the country.
6. One of the loveliest poems by John Keats is "ode to autumn."
7. In switzerland some people speak italian, others speak german, and still others speak french.
8. The news reporter quoted the president of the american medical association.
9. On july 16 a well-known russian violinist will give a recital at carnegie hall.
10. The middle ages lasted roughly from A.D. 500 to 1500.
11. This computer software is produced by the hypercom company.
12. Our plan is to drive north along the east coast from boston to new york.
13. Hans read aloud "concord hymn," a poem about the impact of the battle of Concord, which helped spark the american revolution.
14. Did you know that thanksgiving day always falls on the fourth thursday in november?
15. The newspaper stand offered the *cleveland plain dealer* and the *akron beacon journal*.
16. One of Paul McCartney's most widely recorded songs is "yesterday."
17. Last saturday we heard a group of chilean musicians at the wagnalls music and arts center.
18. The declaration of independence was written in 1776 and the constitution in 1787.
19. My favorite novel about world war I is *all quiet on the western front.*
20. In washington, D.C., we visited the smithsonian institution and the national gallery of art.

Name _____ Class _____ Date _____

Unit 13 Test: Punctuation

▶ **Subtest 1** Add punctuation (or underline for italics) where necessary. Use the delete symbol (⌒) to eliminate punctuation used incorrectly. If the sentence is correct as written, write *C* in the blank.

_____ 1. Go up the stairs walk down the hall and open the second door on the left.

_____ 2. Jessica had the following items in her book bag a copy of Huckleberry Finn, the latest issue of Sports Illustrated and her book report on the short story A Curtain of Green by Eudora Welty.

_____ 3. Aunt Judy, my dad's sister, is running for city council.

_____ 4. A plant, that can be grown successfully indoors, is the philodendron.

_____ 5. Ms. Robertson our club adviser moved here from Fort Wayne Indiana in June 1996.

_____ 6. You have to be prepared for anything the first-aid instructor cautioned us because you never know when your help might be needed

_____ 7. Gavin wondered how they would ever make up the lost time.

_____ 8. Evelyn Sanchez M.D. has been our family doctor, as long as I can remember.

_____ 9. Was it Huckleberry Finn who said of Mark Twain, "He told the truth, mainly

_____ 10. The dog running across the field is here every day after school.

▶ **Subtest 2** Add apostrophes to each sentence where necessary. If the sentence is correct as written, write *C* in the blank.

_____ 1. The girls volleyball team had an undefeated season.

_____ 2. Theirs is the first house on the left after the corner.

_____ 3. Mr. Steinforth handed back Wills geometry test.

_____ 4. I think youre the only person interested.

_____ 5. James's sister works at the convenience store on Main Street.

_____ 6. There isnt much we can do about it now.

_____ 7. I guess if you look at it that way, its rather funny.

_____ 8. Heath took someones place in the play.

Name _____ Class _____ Date _____

_____ 9. My rabbit twitches its ears when I come into the room.

_____ 10. Does your name have two *r*s in it?

_____ 11. Mr. Collins cant remember why he wanted to speak to Elizabeth.

_____ 12. Brian's baseball mitt reached third base, but the ball didn't.

▶ **Subtest 3** Write *C* in the blank if the sentence is correct. Write *I* if the sentence is incorrect.

_____ 1. Sixty five people applied for only ten openings in the program.

_____ 2. I have always thought that Corey's dog was well-behaved.

_____ 3. Our great-grandfather came to this country from Latvia.

_____ 4. The president of the club made a short predinner speech.

_____ 5. The Ohio River—it has always been one of this country's most important transportation links—begins in Pennsylvania.

_____ 6. Two-thirds of all the plants died in the ice storm.

_____ 7. A pound cake calls for one pound (0.454 kilogram) of flour.

_____ 8. Now that is what I call a well-done steak!

_____ 9. The sailor was planning a transAtlantic voyage.

_____ 10. The woman at the hardware store said this was a quick drying paint.

▶ **Subtest 4** Underline the choice in parentheses that best completes the sentence.

1. Martin's uncle is a retired (FBI, F.B.I.) agent.

2. The vase dates from 500 (B.C., bc) or earlier.

3. People showed up for our garage sale at (six thirty, 6:30) A.M.!

4. The final price tag for the new museum was (90 million, 90,000,000) dollars.

5. Most historians accept (A.D., ad) 476 as the date of the fall of the Roman Empire.

6. Of the 120 graduates in the work-study program, more than (eighty-five, 85) found jobs.

7. (Sixty thousand five hundred, 60,500) people attended the football game.

8. Karla was very pleased with finishing (third, 3rd) in the race.

9. The show begins at (nine o'clock, 9 o'clock).

10. Scoring above 92 (percent, %) earned Neil an *A* in the class.

380 Writer's Choice Grammar Workbook 8, Unit 13

Name _____ Class _____ Date _____

Unit 14 Test: Vocabulary and Spelling

▶ **Subtest 1** Circle the letter of the correct word or words, using your knowledge of context clues, word roots, prefixes and suffixes, synonyms and antonyms, and homographs and homophones.

1. As the supply of drinking water began to dwindle, the survivors knew they would soon be very thirsty. (Choose a synonym for *dwindle*.)
   a. shrink   b. grow   c. overheat   d. cool

2. The difference between the first- and second-place finishers was minuscule; we felt they both deserved to win. (Choose an antonym for *minuscule*.)
   a. tiny   b. noticeable   c. gigantic   d. unfair

3. My brother is a Chicago Bulls fanatic; in fact, he wears only clothes that are red and black! (Choose a word or phrase that means the same thing as *fanatic*.)
   a. player   b. devoted fan   c. expert   d. follower

4. Whenever she climbed to the top of the lighthouse, she suffered from vertigo. (Choose a phrase that means about the same as *vertigo*.)
   a. nausea
   b. laughter
   c. fear
   d. dizziness

5. The settlers built makeshift huts to live in until they could build cabins. (Choose a word that is not a synonym of *makeshift*.)
   a. temporary   b. crude   c. ugly   d. substitute

6. Children between the ages of nine and twelve often suffer from preadolescent problems. (Choose a meaning for the prefix *pre-*.)
   a. below   b. before   c. first   d. after

7. Unfortunately, because the measurements were imprecise, the parts of the bird feeder didn't fit together very well. (Choose an antonym for *imprecise*.)
   a. exact   b. inaccurate   c. metric   d. confusing

8. The astronomer used techniques of photometry to study the sun and stars. (Choose the meaning of the root *photo*.)
   a. sound   b. closed   c. distant   d. light

9. Sandra knew she had chosen most of the right answers on the test. (Choose a homophone for *right*.)
   a. correct   b. wrong   c. write   d. right

10. After the raiders savagely destroyed the village, the angry survivors promised retribution. (Choose a synonym for *retribution*.)
    a. rebuilding   b. renewal   c. reawakening   d. revenge

Name _____ Class _____ Date _____

▶ **Subtest 2** Underline the word in parentheses that is spelled correctly.

1. I'll (probably, probablely) see you tomorrow.
2. My little sister's finger painting was (tapped, taped) to the refrigerator.
3. That new building downtown is going to be sixty (storys, stories) high!
4. In his dream Shawn was riding a (beautyful, beautiful) black horse across a field.
5. To (achieve, acheive) all your goals will require much work and determination.
6. Those who (committed, commited) the pranks will suffer the consequences.
7. We asked our (nieghbors, neighbors) to feed our cat while we were away.
8. We rearranged the furniture in my room; the new arrangement is more (practical, practicil) than the old one.
9. He was only (stateing, stating) the obvious when he said we had a big problem.
10. The ex-football player now competes in (rodeoes, rodeos).
11. When my brother Felipe gets married, I'll have three (sister-in-laws, sisters-in-law).
12. Mandy was (extremely, extremly) happy when her dog had eight puppies.
13. Both passenger and (frieght, freight) trains use these tracks.
14. I had three (roomates, roommates) at band camp.
15. By late November all the (leafs, leaves) have fallen from the trees.
16. Rick won't be able to go (canoing, canoeing) with us.
17. Losing all your notes for a class is very (upseting, upsetting).
18. The (backpack, backkpack) I'm taking on the hiking trip was made in Norway.
19. The fox (slipped, sliped) out of its lair as darkness fell.
20. In some states it's (ilegal, illegal) to ride in a car without fastening the seat belt.
21. When he was asked about the defeat, the losing coach (replyed, replied), "That's football."
22. I have a hard time (remembering, rememberring) to set my alarm.
23. The (hieght, height) of the tower is 110 feet.
24. I could tell that the cat was only (toyying, toying) with the mouse.

Name _____ Class _____ Date _____

Unit 15 Test: Composition

▶ **Subtest 1** Edit the following paragraphs and rewrite them based on your editing marks.

Our' school have a great gymnastics team. They was started by Mr. Murphy, who was once an Olympic gymnast. every year he invites the best tumblers, to join the team. Last spring i was hoping to be invited; and this week I finally got my chance.

I was reelly nervous my 1st day of practice. Watching the other team members perform difficult routines. I wondered how I would ever keep up with them. Then coach murphy organized a tumbling race. I come in 2nd, ahead of all but one of the veteran team members. Mr. Murphy was impressed and I, was no longer nervous. by the end of practise, I was looking forward too the first meat.

Name _____ Class _____ Date _____

▶ **Subtest 2 Rewrite each topic sentence to capture a reader's attention in a more interesting way. Be sure to use the correct verb voice and to add supporting detail.**

1. We tried a new restaurant yesterday. _____

2. Spring is now Cheryl's favorite season. _____

3. Bob met his next-door neighbor in an odd way. _____

4. The golf tournament was not what I expected. _____

5. Some ideas are better left untried. _____

6. The lights went out. _____

7. They reached a fork in the road. _____

8. It began when Aunt Agnes gave me a coat. _____

9. The movie was boring. _____

10. Carlo stared at the painting he had produced. _____

▶ **Subtest 3** Edit the following paragraphs for unity, clarity, and organization. Then rewrite the paragraphs based on your changes.

A place has opened on Main Street. An interesting place has opened. It is called Sentimental Scoops, And it is designed like an old-fashioned ice cream shop. The counter is an antique as well. It was saved from an old ice cream shop that closed several years ago. Antique tables and chairs add character to what used to be an empty storeroom. Homemade ice cream is served in glass bowls. Homemade ice cream is served on your favorite kind of cone. Made from traditional recipes are sodas, sundaes, and other treats with real whipped cream and lots of toppings.

It is also the best place to go for special occasions. Like birthdays, Not only is Sentimental Scoops a great ice cream shop. On your birthday a free ice cream cone can be received by you. Or you can order an Ice Cream Extravaganza for your entire group. A huge bowl filled with several different kinds of ice cream and toppings—all your choice—is the Extravaganza. I heartily recommend Sentimental Scoops to everyone.

Name _____ Class _____ Date _____

▶ **Subtest 4** Make an outline for an opinion letter you would write about the salaries paid to professional athletes. Write the appropriate information under each heading.

Opinion:
_____
_____
_____
_____

Audience:
_____
_____
_____
_____

Attitude of audience:
_____
_____
_____
_____

What audience needs to know:
_____
_____
_____
_____

Supporting evidence:
_____
_____
_____
_____

Answer Key to Testing Program

UNIT 1 TEST: SUBJECTS, PREDICATES, AND SENTENCES

Subtest 1
1. int.; ?
2. dec.; .
3. imp.; .
4. int.; ?
5. exc.; !
6. dec.; .
7. exc.; !
8. int.; ?
9. imp. *or* exc. ; . *or* !
10. dec.; .

Subtest 2
1. S
2. frag.; predicate
3. frag.; subject
4. S
5. S
6. frag.; subject
7. S
8. frag.; predicate
9. frag.; both
10. frag.; subject

Subtest 3 (complete subject | complete predicate)
1. Most people | enjoy movies.
2. Railroad travel | can be a lot of fun.
3. Jessica's parents | are Vietnamese immigrants.
4. The bald eagle | is our national bird.
5. Mozart | Did die in his mid-thirties?
6. The film *Amadeus* | depicts Mozart's life.
7. Cross-country skiing | is easy and enjoyable.
8. You | don't need mountains for cross-country skiing!
9. The Smothers Brothers | had a television show in the 1960s.
10. Abraham Lincoln and Stephen Douglas | debated in 1858.

Subtest 4
1. S
2. R
3. C
4. S
5. R
6. C
7. S
8. C
9. R
10. R

UNIT 2 TEST: NOUNS

Subtest 1
1. com.
2. com.
3. prop.
4. prop.
5. com.
6. prop.
7. com.
8. prop.
9. com.
10. prop.

Subtest 2
1. con.
2. abst.
3. abst.
4. con.
5. abst.
6. con.
7. abst.
8. con.
9. con.
10. abst.

Subtest 3 (collective noun; *compound noun*)
1. sister-in-law; *basketmaking*
2. great-aunt; *music box*
3. group; *storybook*
4. team
5. *goalposts*
6. family; *family room*
7. crowd
8. *runners-up*
9. audience; band
10. swarm

Subtest 4
1. babies
2. Alexander's
3. baby's
4. foxes
5. Sharon's
6. secretaries of state
7. my dad's
8. King James's
9. Joe Montana's
10. our neighbors'
11. baseball bats
12. maids of honor
13. volleyballs
14. giraffes'
15. Indiana's
16. freedom's
17. bookmarks
18. Stevenses
19. Teri's
20. bike helmets

Subtest 5 (appositive or appositive phrase; word or words identified)
1. the capital of Wisconsin; Madison
2. a mountain in Alaska; Denali
3. the husband of our French teacher; Mr. Carty
4. Shannon; sister
5. Henri Matisse; painter
6. Ginger; cat
7. a famous movie director; William Wilder
8. Graham; brother
9. the Show-Me state; Missouri
10. Nancy; wife
11. a university in California; Stanford
12. a novel by Mark Twain; *Huckleberry Finn.*

UNIT 3 TEST: VERBS

Subtest 1
1. zipped; I
2. knew; T
3. watched; I
4. battle; T
5. covered; T
6. plays; T
7. remember; T
8. listened; I
9. cheered; I
10. has; T

Subtest 2 (direct object; *indirect object*)
1. advice; *clients*
2. prescription; *patient*
3. boys
4. pleasure; *grandparents*
5. painting; *businessman*
6. chance; *people*
7. self-starter
8. book; *Brian*
9. posters
10. card; *teacher*

Subtest 3 (predicate noun; *predicate adjective*)
1. *delicious*
2. *green*
3. representatives
4. *fatter*
5. *awful*
6. players
7. *great*
8. president
9. *ill*
10. *harsh*

Subtest 4
1. went; past
2. Will send; future
3. take; present
4. ate; past
5. will give; future
6. feels; present
7. Shall include; future
8. talked; past
9. will be; future
10. wanted; past
11. will call; future
12. plays; present

Subtest 5
1. past perf.
2. fut. perf.
3. past prog.
4. pres. prog.
5. fut. perf.
6. pres. perf.
7. pres. prog.
8. past prog.
9. past perf.
10. pres. perf.
11. pres. prog.
12. pres. perf.
13. fut. perf.
14. past perf.
15. past prog.

Subtest 6
1. A
2. A
3. P
4. A
5. P
6. P
7. A
8. P
9. A
10. P

Subtest 7

1. was
2. swum
3. thought
4. felt
5. done
6. laid
7. left
8. ran
9. came
10. ate
11. saw
12. let
13. gave
14. brought
15. chose
16. lost
17. taken
18. broken
19. knew
20. written

UNIT 4 TEST: PRONOUNS

Subtest 1 (personal pronoun; antecedent)

1. They; Great Lakes
2. it; photo
3. her; telemarketer
4. It; bird
5. them; Wilbur and Orville Wright
6. us; team
7. it; sugar
8. them; students
9. her; Lisa
10. They; Mike and Dave

Subtest 2

1. she
2. us
3. I
4. he
5. David and he
6. Juanita and I
7. she
8. him
9. I
10. My brother and I

Subtest 3

1. My (poss.); he (per.)
2. Someone (ind.); her (poss.)
3. Each (ind.)
4. You (per.); both (ind.); them (per.); it (per.)
5. His (poss.); its (poss.)
6. I (per.); everything (ind.)
7. Ours (poss.); theirs (poss.)
8. Nobody (ind.); I (per.)
9. She (per.); others (ind.); her (poss.); her (per.)
10. I (per.); nothing (ind.); we (per.); it (per.)

Subtest 4

1. themselves (ref.)
2. Whom (inter.)
3. himself (int.)
4. yourself (ref.)
5. Which (inter.)
6. Whom (inter.)
7. Who (inter.)
8. herself (int.)
9. Who (inter.)
10. himself (int.)

UNIT 5 TEST: ADJECTIVES AND ADVERBS

Subtest 1 (adjective; adverb)

1. not; the; the; tame
2. The; a; gigantic
3. The; Peruvian; *exceedingly*; colorful
4. unhappy; the; that; *very*; good
5. Victorian; the; the; most popular
6. English; a; a; Canadian
7. That; ear-splitting; a
8. The; a; modern
9. The; the; Vietnamese; a; huge
10. *always*; the; most fashionable

Subtest 2 (adverb, *word modified*)

1. absentmindedly, *walked*; out, *looked*
2. extremely, *scary*
3. very, *fast*; fast, *slid*
4. not, *Do throw*; hard, *Do throw*
5. usually, *shared*; equally, *shared*
6. truly, *sorry*
7. almost, *is finished*
8. reluctantly, *gave*
9. calmly, *said*
10. never, *have visited*

Subtest 3

1. quickest
2. most bitter
3. loudest
4. more interesting
5. yellowest
6. most easily
7. larger
8. more often
9. more bravely
10. best

Subtest 4

1. bad
2. anybody
3. well
4. anyone
5. most beautifully
6. anything
7. badly
8. poorest
9. won't
10. well

UNIT 6 TEST: PREPOSITIONS, CONJUNCTIONS, AND INTERJECTIONS

Subtest 1 (preposition, *object of preposition*)

1. throughout, *night*
2. In spite of, *loss*; in, *place*
3. Over, *River*; Through, *Woods*
4. against; *Marshall Middle School*
5. instead of, *Eric*
6. inside, *bag*; into, *it*
7. beyond, *Shelbyville*; near, *dam*
8. from, *Michigan*
9. below, *surface*; of, *ocean*
10. of, *flowers*; in front of, *bowl*
11. According to, *author*
12. behind, *bush*
13. toward, *tree*
14. outside, *fence*
15. from, *rock*; onto, *stagecoach*
16. during, *movie*
17. on account of, *storm*
18. around, *hive*
19. because of, *lateness*
20. at, *theater*; at, *eight*
21. of, *pineapple*; of, *oranges*
22. between, *dress, one*
23. down, *stairs*
24. around, *city*; for, *hours*

Subtest 2

1. her
2. whom
3. her
4. me
5. him
6. them
7. whom
8. me
9. them
10. whom

Subtest 3

1. by bus and airplane; adv.
2. in its league; adv.
3. with a great reputation; adj.
4. for his age; adv.
5. on the top shelf; adj.
6. in late afternoon; adv.
7. In my opinion; adv.
8. to Florida; adv.
9. across from the school; adj.
10. for my poster; adv.
11. without tomatoes; adj.
12. during the concert; adv.
13. in spite of its interesting plot; adv.
14. next to the tree; adj.
15. toward the situation; adj.

Subtest 4 (conjunction; *word in parentheses*)

1. Both, and; *enjoy*
2. or; *are*
3. Not only, but also; *speak*
4. and; *expect*
5. Neither, nor; *comes*
6. Either, or; *is*
7. and, *are*
8. but; *are*
9. Neither, nor; *do*
10. or; *Is*

Subtest 5 (conjunctive adverb; *interjection*)
1. therefore
2. besides
3. *Well,* nevertheless
4. likewise
5. furthermore
6. moreover
7. *Phew*
8. consequently
9. *Whoops;* however
10. still

Subtest 6
1. prep.
2. int.
3. conj.
4. conj.
5. prep.
6. conj.
7. prep.
8. int.
9. prep.
10. int.
11. int.
12. prep.
13. prep.
14. conj.
15. prep.
16. conj.
17. conj.
18. conj.
19. int.
20. conj.

UNIT 7 TEST: CLAUSES AND COMPLEX SENTENCES
Subtest 1
1. Cx.
2. C
3. C
4. S
5. Cx.
6. C
7. S
8. C
9. Cx.
10. S
11. C
12. C
13. C
14. Cx.
15. Cx.
16. S
17. Cx.
18. Cx.
19. C
20. Cx.
21. S
22. Cx.

Subtest 2 (main clause, *subordinate clause*)
1. *During the Super Bowl,* many people are glued to their televisions.
2. I don't remember her name/her face is familiar.
3. The mail carrier will stop at the post office *after she finishes her route.*
4. Elena took the last cupcake, *which we were saving for David.*
5. He resigned from the club and joined another one.
6. I won't be going to the party *since I have to study.*
7. She plays both the violin and the viola very well.
8. Did you get the license number of the car *that splashed mud on your coat?*
9. *When he's in this mood,* it's better to leave him alone.
10. My cousin wants to be a doctor/she is majoring in biology in college.
11. We knew *that it wouldn't be easy to finish the float on time.*
12. Don't come to the meeting *unless you're prepared to work hard.*
13. Jeannie cut her finger/we had to rush her to the hospital.
14. I get nervous *whenever I think about it.*
15. *Although he is good at baseball,* his favorite sport is definitely soccer.

Subtest 3 (adjective clause; *word modified*)
1. that made Robin Williams famous; *show*
2. who enjoys eating in Chinese restaurants; *friend*
3. whose purse I found; *woman*
4. whom we all admire; *man*
5. that opened the locked door; *word*
6. where it is very dark; *part*
7. who edits the newsletter; *woman*
8. which was so expensive to make; *movie*
9. whom I enjoy hearing; *singer*
10. who knows everything about computers; *Lisa*
11. when we got caught in the rain and were soaked; *time*
12. that you really want for your birthday; *present*
13. that Dana recommended so highly; *book*
14. where the terrible accident happened; *corner*
15. that is very comfortable; *car*

Subtest 4
1. yes
2. no
3. yes
4. no
5. yes
6. no
7. yes
8. yes
9. yes
10. yes
11. no
12. yes
13. no
14. no
15. no
16. no
17. yes
18. yes
19. yes
20. no

Subtest 5
1. where the play will be presented; adj.
2. because her dad dropped her off; adv.
3. who is sixteen; adj.
4. Whoever has the lowest score; N
5. how to get out of the trap; N
6. Although the temperature is very high in Arizona; adv.
7. when they are arriving; N
8. When people burn trash; adv.
9. that playing in the street is dangerous; N
10. which was first designed by Leonardo da Vinci; adj.
11. What really annoys me; N
12. unless he works on it tonight; adv.
13. that I want; adj.
14. whoever is most deserving; N

UNIT 8 TEST: VERBALS
Subtest 1
1. , wearing the red sweatshirt,
2. Summoning up his courage,
3. Stuffing the clothes in,
4. standing in the end zone
5. , exhausted from their five-mile hike,
6. Nodding over his open book,
7. Waiting for a ride home,
8. rolled up inside a bottle
9. Watching closely,
10. Surprised by the darkness,

Subtest 2
1. ger.
2. part.
3. V
4. ger.
5. ger.
6. V
7. V
8. ger.
9. V
10. part.
11. V
12. part.
13. ger.
14. part.
15. ger.

Subtest 3
1. inf.
2. prep.
3. inf.
4. prep.
5. inf.
6. prep.
7. inf.
8. inf.
9. inf.
10. prep.
11. inf.
12. inf.
13. prep.
14. prep.
15. inf.

UNIT 9 TEST: SUBJECT-VERB AGREEMENT
Subtest 1 (simple subject; verb form in parentheses)
1. book; is
2. dogs; sniff
3. animal; eats
4. you; Don't
5. player; has
6. rolls; smell
7. player; goes
8. show; was
9. clerks; wrap
10. parents; sell
11. seats; Are
12. dollars; are
13. sunglasses; were
14. news; is
15. Mathematics; was
16. herd; grazes
17. liters; were
18. cookies; are

19. dollars; is
20. mother; works
21. Sheep; enjoy

22. *The Women of Avignon*; is

Subtest 2
1. is
2. looks
3. need
4. hope
5. sounds
6. are
7. Does
8. takes
9. take
10. arrives
11. is
12. don't
13. are
14. is
15. were
16. has
17. come
18. are
19. tries
20. were
21. is
22. were
23. is
24. was

UNIT 10 TEST: DIAGRAMING SENTENCES

Subtest 1

1. Cats | make

2. (you) | Mail

3. Tina | wore

4. We | can talk

5. Alex | flew

Subtest 2

1. Jason | collects | cards

2. (you) | give | magazine / me

3. hawk | caught | fish

4. Hiroko | sent | letter / parents

5. We | saw | iguanas

Subtest 3

1.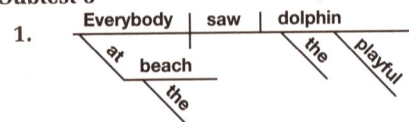

2.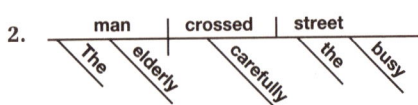

3.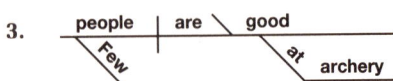

4.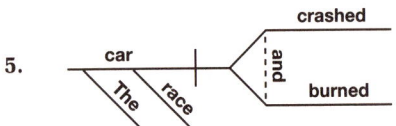

5.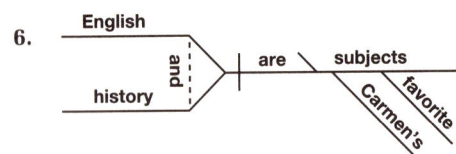

6.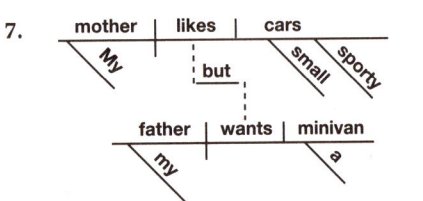

7.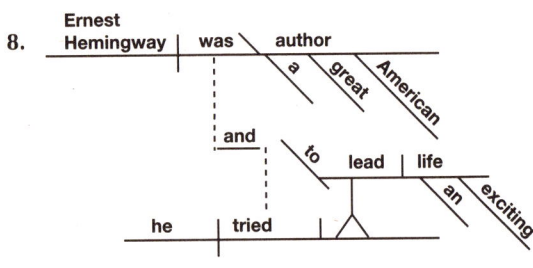

8.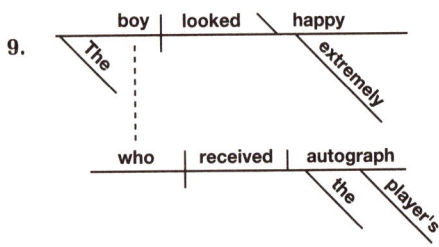

9.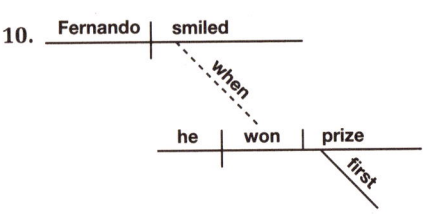

10.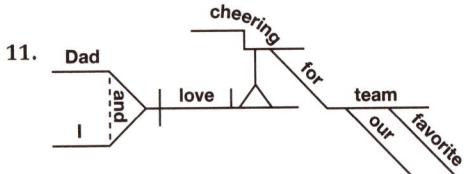

11. Dad / I (and) | love | cheering / for / team / our favorite

12.
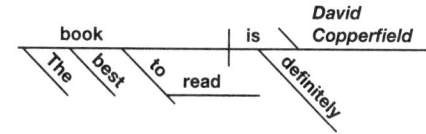

UNIT 11 TEST: USAGE GLOSSARY
Subtest 1
1. accept
2. all ready
3. all together
4. beside
5. between
6. bring
7. May
8. less
9. chose
10. except
11. among
12. take
13. fewer
14. altogether
15. already
16. let
17. can
18. besides
19. leave
20. choose

Subtest 2
1. I
2. C
3. I
4. C
5. I
6. I
7. I
8. C
9. C
10. I
11. C
12. I
13. C
14. C
15. I
16. I
17. I
18. C
19. I
20. C

UNIT 12 TEST: CAPITALIZATION
Subtest 1
1. Uncle
2. Jr.
3. I
4. president
5. Ph.D.
6. John F. Kennedy
7. D.D.S.
8. Aunt
9. aunt
10. Senator
11. Grandfather
12. contains
13. Professor
14. grandmother
15. Sr.
16. Dad
17. Our
18. mayor
19. General
20. what

Subtest 2
1. Chinese
2. Trouble
3. *Omni; Personal Computing*
4. Swift
5. October; November
6. Ode; Autumn
7. Switzerland; Italian; German; French
8. American Medical Association
9. July; Russian; Carnegie Hall
10. Middle Ages
11. Hypercom Company
12. East Coast; Boston; New York
13. Concord Hymn; Battle; American Revolution
14. Thanksgiving Day; Thursday; November
15. *Cleveland Plain Dealer; Akron Beacon Journal*
16. Yesterday
17. Saturday; Chilean; Wagnalls Music and Arts Center
18. Declaration of Independence; Constitution
19. World War; *All Quiet on the Western Front*
20. Washington; Smithsonian Institution; National Gallery of Art

UNIT 13 TEST: PUNCTUATION
Subtest 1
1. Go up the stairs, walk down the hall, and open the second door on the left.
2. Jessica had the following items in her book bag: a copy of *Huckleberry Finn*, the latest issue of *Sports Illustrated*, and her book report on the short story "A Curtain of Green" by Eudora Welty.
3. C
4. A plant that can be grown successfully indoors is the philodendron.
5. Ms. Robertson, our club adviser, moved here from Fort Wayne, Indiana, in June 1996.
6. "You have to be prepared for anything," the first-aid instructor cautioned us, "because you never know when your help might be needed."
7. C
8. Evelyn Sanchez, M.D., has been our family doctor as long as I can remember.
9. Was it Huckleberry Finn who said of Mark Twain, "He told the truth, mainly"?
10. C

Subtest 2
1. girls'
2. C
3. Will's
4. you're
5. C
6. isn't
7. it's
8. someone's
9. C
10. r's
11. can't
12. C

Subtest 3
1. I
2. I
3. C
4. C
5. C
6. I
7. C
8. C
9. I
10. I

Subtest 4
1. FBI
2. B.C.
3. 6:30
4. 90 million
5. A.D.
6. 85
7. Sixty thousand five hundred
8. third
9. nine o'clock
10. percent

UNIT 14 TEST: VOCABULARY AND SPELLING
Subtest 1
1. a
2. c
3. b
4. d
5. c
6. b
7. a
8. d
9. c
10. d

Subtest 2
1. probably
2. taped
3. stories
4. beautiful
5. achieve
6. committed
7. neighbors
8. practical
9. stating
10. rodeos
11. sisters-in-law
12. extremely
13. freight
14. roommates
15. leaves
16. canoeing
17. upsetting
18. backpack
19. slipped
20. illegal
21. replied
22. remembering
23. height
24. toying

UNIT 15 TEST: COMPOSITION

Subtest 1 (Answers will vary.)

Our school has a great gymnastics team. It was started by Mr. Murphy, who was once an Olympic gymnast. Every year he invites the best tumblers to join the team. Last spring I was hoping to be invited, and this week I finally got my chance.

I was really nervous my first day of practice. Watching the other team members perform difficult routines, I wondered how I would ever keep up with them. Then Coach Murphy organized a tumbling race. I came in second, ahead of all but one of the veteran team members. Mr. Murphy was impressed, and I was no longer nervous. By the end of practice, I was looking forward to the first meet.

Subtest 2 (Answers will vary.)

1. We ventured into the new Vietnamese restaurant on Fourth Street yesterday.
2. Spring is Cheryl's favorite season now that she has taken up gardening.
3. Bob met his next-door neighbor the night a tree fell on his house.
4. I had expected hushed voices and silent admiration, but the golf tournament attracted loud fans who often applauded.
5. After ending up with a mountain of torn crepe paper and three broken wheels instead of a parade float, we decided that some ideas are better left untried.
6. The first sign that things weren't quite right at the boathouse occurred when the lights suddenly went out.
7. They had been driving for three hours and were hopelessly lost when they reached a fork in the road.
8. My life as a fashion designer began when Aunt Agnes gave me a stylish coat for my birthday.
9. The much-advertised movie, which we couldn't wait to see, was as exciting as watching ice melt.
10. Carlo stared wide-eyed at the incredibly beautiful painting he had produced.

Subtest 3 (Answers will vary.)

An interesting place has opened on Main Street. It is called Sentimental Scoops, and it is designed like an old-fashioned ice cream shop. Antique tables and chairs add character to what used to be an empty storeroom. The counter is an antique as well—it was saved from an old ice cream shop that closed several years ago. Homemade ice cream is served in glass bowls or on your favorite kind of cone. Sodas, sundaes, and other treats with real whipped cream and lots of toppings are made from traditional recipes.

Not only is Sentimental Scoops a great ice cream shop, it is also the best place to go for special occasions like birthdays. On your birthday you can receive a free ice cream cone, or you can order an Ice Cream Extravaganza for your entire group. The Extravaganza is a huge bowl filled with several different kinds of ice cream and toppings—all your choice. I heartily recommend Sentimental Scoops to everyone.

Subtest 4 (Answers will vary.)
Opinion:
1. Professional athletes are paid too much.
2. Professional athletes deserve the salaries they receive.
3. Athletes and their salaries are of no concern.

Audience: other students; readers and editors of a newspaper to which the letter is being written; owners of professional sports teams

Attitude of audience: Individuals' opinions will vary. Owners might point out the need for great athletes to keep their business alive, the profits they produce, and the enjoyment residents of the community gain from attending games.

What audience needs to know: how much athletes are being paid; the duties they perform; the comparison of athletes' salaries to salaries for other professionals and the average salary of a resident of the community; how the budget for a professional sports team is figured

Supporting evidence: reasons athletes' salaries are appropriate or inappropriate; costs of professional teams versus the benefits they provide

CORRELATION CHART

GOALS	WRITER'S CHOICE GRADE 8	WRITER'S CHOICE GRAMMAR WORKBOOK GRADE 8
I. To provide students further practice with grammar usage		
1. subjects, predicates, and sentences	Unit.Lesson 7.1 Sentence Fragments 8.2 Sentences and Sentence Fragments 8.1 Kinds of Sentences 8.3 Subjects and Predicates 8.4 Identifying Subjects and Predicates 8.5 Compound Subjects and Compound Predicates 7.2 Run-on Sentences 8.6 Simple and Compound Sentences Grammar Review 8 Russell Baker, from *Growing Up* (model)	Unit.Lesson 1.3 Sentence Fragments 1.1 Kinds of Sentences: Declarative and Interrogative 1.2 Kinds of Sentences: Exclamatory and Imperative 1.4 Subjects and Predicates: Simple and Complete 1.5 Subjects and Predicates: Compound 1.6 Simple and Compound Sentences
2. nouns	9.1 Kinds of Nouns 9.5 Collective Nouns 7.8 Incorrect Use of Apostrophes 9.2 Compound Nouns 9.3 Possessive Nouns 9.4 Distinguishing Plurals, Possessives, and Contractions 7.7 Incorrect Use of Commas 9.6 Appositives Grammar Review 9 James Haskins, from *Barbara Jordan* (model)	2.7 Nouns: Proper and Common 2.8 Nouns: Concrete and Abstract 2.9 Nouns: Compounds, Plurals, and Possessives 2.10 Nouns: Collective 2.11 Distinguishing Plurals, Possessives, and Contractions 2.12 Appositives
3. verbs	10.1 Action Verbs 10.2 Transitive and Intransitive Verbs 10.3 Verbs with Indirect Objects 10.4 Linking Verbs and Predicate Words 7.4 Incorrect Verb Tense or Form 10.5 Present and Past Tenses 10.6 Main Verbs and Helping Verbs 10.7 Progressive Forms 10.8 Perfect Tenses 10.9 Expressing Future Time 10.10 Active and Passive Voice 10.11 Irregular Verbs 10.12 More Irregular Verbs Grammar Review 10 Thornton Wilder, from *Our Town* (model)	3.13 Action Verbs 3.14 Verbs: Transitive and Intransitive 3.15 Verbs with Indirect Objects 3.16 Linking Verbs and Predicate Words 3.17 Present and Past Tenses 3.18 Main Verbs and Helping Verbs 3.19 Verb Forms: Present Progressive and Past Progressive 3.20 Perfect Tenses: Present and Past 3.21 Expressing Future Time 3.22 Active and Passive Voices 3.23 Irregular Verbs I 3.24 Irregular Verbs II
4. pronouns	11.1 Personal Pronouns 11.2 Pronouns and Antecedents 7.5 Incorrect Use of Pronouns 11.3 Using Pronouns Correctly 11.4 Possessive Pronouns 11.5 Indefinite Pronouns	4.25 Pronouns: Personal 4.26 Pronouns and Antecedents 4.27 Using Pronouns Correctly 4.28 Pronouns: Possessive and Indefinite

Correlation Chart

GOALS	WRITER'S CHOICE GRADE 8	WRITER'S CHOICE GRAMMAR WORKBOOK GRADE 8
4. pronouns (continued)	Unit.Lesson 11.6 Reflexive and Intensive Pronouns 11.7 Interrogative and Demonstrative Pronouns Grammar Review 11 Bonita E. Thayer, from *Emily Dickinson* (model)	Unit.Lesson 4.29 Pronouns: Reflexive and Intensive 4.30 Pronouns: Interrogative and Demonstrative
5. adjectives and adverbs	12.1 Adjectives 12.2 Articles and Proper Adjectives 7.6 Incorrect Use of Adjectives 12.3 Comparative and Superlative Adjectives 12.4 Demonstratives 12.5 Adverbs 12.6 Comparative and Superlative Adverbs 12.7 Using Adverbs and Adjectives 12.8 Avoiding Double Negatives Grammar Review 12 Elizabeth Borton de Treviño, from *I, Juan de Pareja* (model)	5.31 Adjectives 5.32 Articles and Proper Adjectives 5.33 Comparative and Superlative Adjectives 5.34 Demonstratives 5.35 Adverbs 5.36 Comparative and Superlative Adverbs 5.37 Using Adverbs and Adjectives 5.38 Avoiding Double Negatives
6. prepositions, conjunctions, and interjections	13.1 Prepositions and Prepositional Phrases 13.2 Pronouns as Objects of Prepositions 13.3 Prepositional Phrases as Adjectives and Adverbs 13.4 Conjunctions 13.5 Conjunctive Adverbs 13.6 Interjections Grammar Review 13 Michael Dorris, from *Morning Girl* (model)	6.39 Prepositions and Prepositional Phrases 6.40 Pronouns as Objects of Prepositions 6.41 Prepositional Phrases as Adjectives and Adverbs 6.42 Conjunctions: Coordinating and Correlative 6.43 Conjunctive Adverbs and Interjections
7. clauses	7.1 Sentence Fragments 7.2 Run-on Sentences 14.1 Sentences and Clauses 14.2 Complex Sentences 14.3 Adjective Clauses 14.4 Essential and Nonessential Clauses 14.5 Adverb Clauses 14.6 Noun Clauses Grammar Review 14 Mickey Mantle, from "The Education of a Baseball Player" (model)	7.44 Sentences and Main Clauses 7.45 Complex Sentences and Subordinate Clauses 7.46 Adjective Clauses 7.47 Essential and Nonessential Clauses 7.48 Adverb Clauses 7.49 Noun Clauses
8. verbals	15.1 Participles and Participial Phrases 15.2 Gerunds and Gerund Phrases 15.3 Infinitives and Infinitive Phrases Grammar Review 15 Wilma Rudolph, from "Wilma" (model)	8.50 Participles and Participial Phrases 8.51 Gerunds and Gerund Phrases 8.52 Infinitives and Infinitive Phrases

GOALS	WRITER'S CHOICE GRADE 8	WRITER'S CHOICE GRAMMAR WORKBOOK GRADE 8
9. subject-verb agreement	Unit.Lesson 7.3 Lack of Subject-Verb Agreement 16.1 Making Subjects and Verbs Agree 16.2 Problems with Locating the Subject 16.3 Collective Nouns and Other Special Subjects 16.4 Indefinite Pronouns as Subjects 16.5 Agreement with Compound Subjects Grammar Review 16 Diane Ackerman, from "Bats" (model)	Unit.Lesson 9.53 Making Subjects and Verbs Agree 9.54 Locating the Subject 9.55 Collective Nouns and Other Special Subjects 9.56 Indefinite Pronouns as Subjects 9.57 Agreement with Compound Subjects
10. diagraming sentences	18.1 Diagraming Simple Subjects and Simple Predicates 18.2 Diagraming the Four Kinds of Sentences 18.3 Diagraming Direct and Indirect Objects 18.5 Diagraming Predicate Nouns and Predicate Adjectives 18.4 Diagraming Adjectives, Adverbs, and Prepositional Phrases 18.6 Diagraming Compound Sentence Parts 18.7 Diagraming Compound Sentences 18.8 Diagraming Complex Sentences with Adjective and Adverb Clauses 18.9 Diagraming Noun Clauses 18.10 Diagraming Verbals I 18.11 Diagraming Verbals II	10.58 Diagraming Simple Subjects and Predicates 10.59 Diagraming Direct and Indirect Objects and Predicate Words 10.60 Diagraming Adjectives and Adverbs 10.61 Diagraming Prepositional Phrases 10.62 Diagraming Compound Sentence Parts 10.63 Diagraming Compound Sentences 10.64 Diagraming Complex Sentences with Adjective or Adverb Clauses 10.65 Diagraming Noun Clauses 10.66 Diagraming Verbals 10.67 Diagraming Infinitives

II. To provide students further practice with correct usage

11. special usage problems	17.1 Using Troublesome Words I 17.2 Using Troublesome Words II 17.3 Using Troublesome Words III Grammar Review 17 Judith Herbst, from "Star Fever" (model)	11.68 Usage: *accept* to *a lot* 11.69 Usage: *beside* to *less* 11.70 Usage: *formally* to *teach* 11.71 Usage: *leave* to *sit* 11.72 Usage: *than* to *you're*

III. To develop in students the ability to use proper punctuation and capitalization

12. capitalization	7.9 Incorrect Capitalization 19.1 Capitalizing Sentences, Quotations, and Salutations 19.2 Capitalizing Names and Titles of People 19.3 Capitalizing Names of Places 19.4 Capitalizing Other Proper Nouns and Adjectives Grammar Review 19 Brent Ashabranner, from *Morning Star, Black Sun* (model)	12.73 Capitalization of Sentences, Quotations, and Salutations 12.74 Capitalization of Names and Titles of Persons 12.75 Capitalization of Names of Places 12.76 Capitalization of Other Proper Nouns and Adjectives
13. punctuation, abbreviations, and numbers	20.1 Using the Period and Other End Marks	13.77 Using the Period and Other End Marks

GOALS	WRITER'S CHOICE GRADE 8	WRITER'S CHOICE GRAMMAR WORKBOOK GRADE 8
13. punctuation, abbreviations, and numbers (continued)	Unit.Lesson 7.7 Incorrect Use of Commas 20.2 Using Commas I 20.3 Using Commas II 20.4 Using Commas III 20.5 Using Semicolons and Colons 20.6 Using Quotation Marks and Italics 7.8 Incorrect Use of Apostrophes 20.7 Using Apostrophes 20.8 Using Hyphens, Dashes, and Parentheses 20.9 Using Abbreviations 20.10 Writing Numbers Grammar Review 20 Jamaica Kincaid, from *A Small Place* (model)	Unit.Lesson 13.78 Using Commas to Signal Pause or Separation 13.79 Using Commas with Clauses 13.80 Using Commas with Titles, Addresses, and Dates 13.81 Using Commas with Direct Quotes, in Letters, and for Clarity 13.82 Using Semicolons and Colons 13.83 Using Quotation Marks and Italics 13.84 Using the Apostrophe 13.85 Using the Hyphen, Dash, and Parentheses 13.86 Using Abbreviations 13.87 Writing Numbers

IV. To provide further practice in vocabulary and spelling

14. vocabulary and spelling	23.2 Context Clues 23.3 Prefixes and Suffixes 23.4 Synonyms and Antonyms 23.5 Homographs and Homophones 23.6 Spelling Rules 23.7 Becoming a Better Speller	14.88 Building Vocabulary: Learning from Context 14.89 Building Vocabulary: Word Roots 14.90 Building Vocabulary: Prefixes and Suffixes 14.91 Building Vocabulary: Synonyms and Antonyms Review: Building Vocabulary 14.92 Building Vocabulary: Homographs and Homophones 14.93 Basic Spelling Rules I 14.94 Basic Spelling Rules II Review: Basic Spelling Rules

V. To provide students further practice in the writing process

15. composition Prewriting	2.2 Prewriting: Determining Audience and Purpose 2.3 Prewriting: Investigating a Topic 2.4 Prewriting: Organizing Ideas 24.6 Gathering and Organizing Information 5.7 Reports: Researching a Topic	15.95 The Writing Process: Prewriting 15.100 Outlining
Drafting	2.5 Drafting: Writing It Down 5.9 Reports: Planning and Drafting 3.4 Using Spatial Order 4.2 Using Chronological Order	15.96 The Writing Process: Drafting 15.101 Writing Effective Sentences 15.102 Building Paragraphs 15.103 Paragraph Ordering
Revising	2.6 Revising: Taking a Fresh Look 2.7 Revising: Writing Unified Paragraphs 2.8 Revising: Writing Varied Sentences 5.10 Reports: Revising, Editing, and Presenting	15.97 The Writing Process: Revising